SPAIN UNDER T

VOLU

SPAIN UNDER THE HABSBURGS

Second Edition

JOHN LYNCH

VOLUME ONE

EMPIRE AND ABSOLUTISM

1516–1598

New York University Press
New York
1984

First published 1964
Reprinted 1965
Second edition 1981
First U.S.A. paperbound edition 1984

Library of Congress Cataloging in Publication Data

Lynch, John, 1927–
    Spain under the Habsburgs.

    Includes bibliographies and index.
    Contents: v. 1. Empire and absolution, 1516–
1598—v. 2. Spain and America, 1598–1700.
    1. Spain—History—House of Austria, 1516–1700.
I. Title.
DP171.L92   1981   946'.04   81–11064
ISBN 0–8147–5002–8 (v. 1)   AACR2
ISBN 0–8147–5003–6 (v. 2)
ISBN 0–8147–5004–4 (set)
ISBN 0–8147–5009–5 (v. 1 pbk.)
ISBN 0–8147–5010–9 (v. 2 pbk.)
ISBN 0–8147–5011–7 (set pbk.)

Manufactured in the United States of America

CONTENTS

ILLUSTRATIONS

MAPS

PREFACE TO THE SECOND EDITION

THE present edition differs from the first in a number of ways. Recent research has extended our knowledge and improved our understanding of early modern Spain, and I have sought to incorporate the results in the new text. Sections of both volumes have been re-written in the light of works published between 1965 and 1980, in some cases to add new material, in others to modify an argument or revise an interpretation. Yet I have not wished to alter the essential framework and character of the book, if that were possible, nor have I changed the hypotheses and speculations which were inherent in it and which belong to the unfinished debate on the rise and fall of Habsburg Spain. I have added a bibliography of recent works, describing the trends in the historiography of the subject in the last fifteen years and indicating the most important advances which have been made. Most of the maps have been re-drawn, and there is a new selection of illustrations.

INSTITUTE OF LATIN AMERICAN STUDIES   J.L.
UNIVERSITY OF LONDON

PREFACE TO THE FIRST EDITION

THE present work is the first of a projected two-volume history of Spain from 1516 to 1700. It is written in the belief that recent research, mainly by Spanish and French historians, has yielded new information sufficient to justify a reappraisal of the period, and in the hope that the story of Spain's rise to world power and her subsequent decline can be made intelligible in spite of the persisting gaps in our knowledge. Without neglecting political issues, I have tried to do justice to economic and social forces, on which there is now more material than there was twenty years ago, and also to the fundamental factors of religion and relations between church and state. The history of Spain is often distorted by looking at it solely from the point of view of Castile and in terms of Castilian problems; therefore, while the dominant position of Castile has to be recognised for what it was—superiority in manpower and resources—I have also paid some attention to the equally Spanish but distinctive regions of Catalonia and Aragon. The history of Spanish America, of course, is another story, and I have not attempted to tell it here; but the economy and the policy of Spain would be incomprehensible without reference to her possession of a colonial empire, and it is in this context that I have treated the Spanish Indies, viewing them mainly as instruments of wealth and power. There seemed little point in providing a distilled version of the cultural history of Spain's Golden Age, a subject in which the reader is already well served, but it is hoped that the book provides a historical framework useful to the student of literature.

I should like to record my gratitude to those who have helped me in the writing of this book, to Professor R. A. Humphreys, who kindly read the manuscript and helped me to improve it, to Mr. A. N. Ryan, who scrutinised many of its pages and gave me the benefit of his advice, to Dr. J. S. Cummins, who provided me with bibliographical information and with assistance in points of translation, and to the University of Liverpool, whose generous grants in aid of research enabled me to study Spanish history in Spain itself. Above all, I wish to thank my wife, who has given me not only advice on the book but also the conditions in which it could be written.

UNIVERSITY COLLEGE, LONDON   J.L.
    May, 1963

CHAPTER I

THE HABSBURG INHERITANCE

1. THE UNION OF THE CROWNS

ON 19 October 1469 Isabella, heiress to the throne of Castile, married Ferdinand, son and heir of John II of Aragon. It was hardly a love-match, though the nineteen-year-old bride, plain and not strikingly feminine, grew fond enough of her husband to be jealous of his numerous infidelities. Equally it was not a dynastic arrangement imposed on them from above. Ignoring the opposition of her brother, the reigning monarch Henry IV, and resisting Portuguese, French, and English suitors, Isabella decided by herself alone to marry Ferdinand and won her way only by great determination and political sense and with a national consciousness that was rare among her contemporaries. On the fragile foundations of the marriage Spain's future was to be built. Inheriting distinct and mutually hostile kingdoms, shattered by social and political strife, Ferdinand and Isabella left to their Habsburg successors the makings of a nation state, united, peaceful, and powerful beyond any in Europe.

In 1469 few would have rated their prospects so highly. As they were related by consanguinity and had married without papal approval—though with a dispensation forged in Spain—canonically they were living in sin and soon they were excommunicated. They had to reckon, moreover, with the savage hostility of Henry IV, who resented Aragonese intrigues among his own rebellious subjects and favoured a Castilian alliance with Portugal or France; and there was some support for the succession rights of Henry's daughter, Joanna, whose legitimacy was disputed but whom Henry himself declared his heir. Driven as rebels from Castile, the young couple could hope for little from Aragon. John II, it is true, had encouraged their marriage, in the hope of improving his own position which was threatened by the rebellion of Catalonia and the hostility of France, but his preoccupations in both these directions prevented him from giving them much practical assistance. But even should they survive to claim their inheritance, what was it worth? Civil wars had reduced both kingdoms to conditions of ruinous anarchy. In a ten years' war with its king (1462–72) Catalonia had weakened the crown of Aragon, reinforced its own economic decline, and lost part of its territory to France. In Castile, where civil war lasted even longer (1464–80), a rampant

I

aristocracy not only evaded the crown but controlled it; in the person of the degenerate Henry IV, nicknamed 'the Impotent' (hence the dispute over Joanna's right of succession), and kicked in effigy from the throne by a group of rebel nobles headed by the archbishop of Toledo, royal authority could sink no lower. With only their wits to assist them, Ferdinand and Isabella rode the storms of peninsular politics and survived to secure the legitimisation of their marriage, the throne of Castile on the death of Henry IV in 1474, and the union of the crowns of Castile and Aragon when Ferdinand succeeded his father in 1479. Only Navarre and Granada remained outside the union, the former a satellite of France, the latter an independent Moorish kingdom. Portugal—whose king had married Joanna, upheld her rights, and still aspired to draw Castile away from the eastern kingdoms of the peninsula— was beaten off in the battle of Toro in 1476.

The dominions of the Catholic Monarchs—a title later given to them by their Borgia protégé, Pope Alexander VI—now possessed a joint government under the same dynasty.[1] As Spain lacked a tradition of unity and the institutions to give it expression, the success of this government depended on the willingness of the two sovereigns to co-operate. By the Agreement of Segovia (1475) Isabella assumed the internal government of Castile, with Ferdinand specialising in foreign affairs and both participating in the administration of justice. But formal agreement was less important than the personal understanding which infused their relations. Each intervened actively in the affairs of the other's kingdoms, sometimes together, sometimes separately, but usually in agreement.[2] Isabella disliked being spoken of alone, and the habit of referring to all their decisions and actions as those of 'the King and Queen' led the chronicler, Hernando del Pulgar, to satirise the much-worked formula by heading an imaginary chapter of his history of the reign 'On such and such a day the King and Queen gave birth to a daughter'. But in fact their instinctive political sympathy, together with their willingness to take advice from each other, make it difficult on any given occasion to assign ideas or policy

---

[1] The reign of Ferdinand and Isabella still awaits an adequate history. Traditional Spanish accounts of Isabella are panegyric in form; the best example of these is C. Silió Cortés, *Isabel la Católica. Fundadora de España* (Madrid, 1954). R. B. Merriman, *The Rise of the Spanish Empire in the Old World and the New* (4 vols., New York, 1918–34), vol. ii, is still useful as a political narrative. The rule of Ferdinand has been better served, especially in the authoritative works of J. Vicens Vives, *Política del Rey Católico en Cataluña* (Barcelona, 1940); *Fernando el Católico, príncipe de Aragón, rey de Sicilia 1458–1478* (Madrid, 1952); *Instituciones económicas, sociales y políticos de la época fernandina* (Zaragoza, 1952); see also *Juan II de Aragón (1398–1479)* (Barcelona, 1953). For an indication of the present state of research see *Fernando el Católico Vida y obra*, V Congreso de Historia de la Corona de Aragón (*Estudios, I*, Zaragoza, 1955).

[2] See A. de la Torre, 'Fernando el Católico, Gobernante', *Fernando el Católico. Vida y obra*, pp. 9–19.

to one or the other; the only criterion for action was the search for the best solutions to their mutual problems.

Consequently, the emergence of Castile as the dominant partner in the union was not due to a narrow nationalism, but had the fullest support of Ferdinand—a measure of the king's realism, not of the queen's prejudice. Geographically, Castile had the advantage of a central position, its territory was three times as large as that of Aragon and its component states, Catalonia and Valencia, and with six million out of a total of seven million inhabitants it was clearly superior in manpower. These facts, combined with the poverty of the eastern states, naturally gave Castile the leading rôle in the union and made it the base of the crown's operations, the more so as its laws and institutions did not restrain royal action by the kind of checks which existed in the eastern kingdoms. The king of Aragon, therefore, raised no objection to Castilian supremacy; if anything, he worked for it with a greater sense of urgency than Isabella herself. In the marriage pact he had sworn to reside always in Castile and not to leave without agreement of his wife. His own kingdoms he ruled through viceroys, and from 1494 with the assistance of the Council of Aragon—a new institution which, in spite of being composed exclusively of representatives of Aragon, Catalonia, and Valencia, resided always in Castile, under the direct influence of the crown and the court.

The supremacy of Castile was reflected also in the expansion of her language and the renaissance of her culture. Castilian was already the written language of the Basques. The literary use of Galician virtually ceased from the fifteenth century. Catalan, the most robust of the non-Castilian languages, survived at a popular level and even as an official language, but as a literary medium it retreated rapidly before the language of Castile. In Catalonia and even more in Valencia Castilian became more widely used by men of letters, and it was in Castilian that the literature of Spain's golden age flowered so brilliantly. But the influence of language did not stop there. It was also regarded as an instrument of political expansion, as can be seen in the thought of one of the most distinguished figures of the Spanish renaissance, the humanist and philologist, Antonio de Nebrija. In the eloquent prologue of his Castilian grammar, dedicated to Queen Isabella, Nebrija expressed his conviction that 'language was always the instrument of empire'. With an inspired sense of timing, on the eve of the discovery of America, he reflected the surging patriotism of his contemporaries: 'When your Highness has subjected many barbarous peoples and nations of foreign tongues . . . they will have to accept the laws which the conqueror imposes on the conquered, and with them our language.' But Castilian, he believed, would be learnt—with the help of his grammar—not only by subject peoples but also by 'the

Basques, the Navarrese, the French, the Italians, and all others who have any traffic and communication with Spain'.[3] Within the peninsula, at least, the tendency was already strong, and there the language of Castile was the language of authority and as such an instrument of unification.

In so far as a sense of nationalism existed in Spain at the time, it was Castilian rather than Spanish in inspiration, as is evident in the thought of Nebrija. But even in this limited sense Nebrija was probably precocious. Most of the subjects of the Catholic Monarchs still thought of themselves as Castilians, Aragonese, Catalans, and Basques, rather than as Spaniards. From one point of view they had no alternative. Ferdinand and Isabella gave Spain a common government but not a common administration. The union of the crowns was personal, not institutional; each kingdom preserved its identity and its laws. In spite of their title, 'Kings of Castile, of León, of Aragon, of Sicily', Ferdinand and Isabella were each primarily sovereigns of their own particular kingdoms rather than monarchs of Spain, a fact which was to become only too apparent on the death of Isabella, when Ferdinand had to leave Castile and the two kingdoms briefly returned to a separate existence. Institutional differences were expressed in the different systems of law and in the different cortes, or parliaments, those of Castile and those of Aragon; even within the crown of Aragon there were separate cortes for its component states, for Catalonia and Valencia as well as for Aragon proper. Within the crown of Castile, in addition to the law of Castile there was the law of the Basque provinces, which also had their own customs régime, and, after the annexation of Navarre in 1512, the law of Navarre. These divisions were reinforced by customs barriers between the constituent kingdoms which were just as effective as those between themselves and foreign countries. The union of the crown, therefore, was only the beginning of the unification of Spain. The task of assimilating and integrating the various states remained, and in pursuing it Ferdinand and Isabella were more vacillating and less absolutist than is often supposed. Nevertheless, whatever hope there was for the permanent unity of Spain, as opposed to a temporary dynastic alliance, lay in the constancy with which the monarchs did pursue it. For unity was not a condition natural to the inhabitants of Spain. The lead had to come from above. In support of a common policy, it is true, Ferdinand and Isabella could draw on the joint resources of their various states, especially those of Castile which possessed the most effective instrument of unification—a monarchy potentially absolute, untrammelled by representative institutions, and ready to dispute the power of the nobility. This gave them the means of

[3] A. de Nebrija, *Gramática de la lengua castellana* (1492), ed. I. González-Llubera (Oxford, 1926), pp. 3–9. On the expansion of Castilian see R. Menéndez Pidal, *La lengua de Cristóbal Colón* (Buenos Aires, 1942), pp. 52–71.

forming a national state, and ultimately an empire. But those means had to be organised and their subjects pushed in new and unaccustomed directions. And first they had to impose their authority in Castile.

To rescue the crown from disputing factions and restore the basic conditions of law and order, Ferdinand and Isabella had to take issue with the most powerful of their subjects. By the fifteenth century the Castilian aristocracy, monopolising the fruits of the reconquest of Spain from the Moors—land and office—had grown powerful enough to make itself an independent authority, changing dynasties, possessing itself of royal land, and using the resultant power as an instrument of its own irresponsible ambitions. The monarchs, therefore, sought to increase their own power by reducing that of the aristocracy. Reluctant to innovate, they used the agencies with which their subjects were already familiar. One of them, the *hermandades*, or police forces organised by many towns, had already proved its worth in the lawless times of Henry IV.[4] This they reorganised into the *Santa Hermandad* (Holy Brotherhood), forced everyone to contribute to its expenses including —and this was an innovation—the nobility and the clergy, and brought it under control of the crown by means of a royal council, the *Consejo de la Hermandad* (1476). The *Santa Hermandad* played a vital rôle in the reduction of the nobility and the pursuit of criminals, whatever their status. But more direct action was needed to curb an aristocracy pampered by generations of royal indulgence. Therefore, feudal castles were destroyed, private wars were declared illegal, the *adelantados*, or frontier governors, were displaced, and the great officers of the crown were reduced to precise and limited functions and deprived of all influence in government and the formulation of policy. At the same time, royal land, recklessly alienated in the past, was recovered and extended, and the crown began to compete with its own subjects in wealth and in the power which wealth gave. The Masterships of the Military Orders, which had been one of the principal sources of disorder, were incorporated in the crown and ruled by another royal council, the *Consejo de las Ordenes* (1495). Above all, the administration of justice was gradually reformed by strengthening the royal courts at the expense of feudal ones. The *audiencia*, or high court of justice, frequently presided over by the monarchs themselves, became the supreme judicial body, and with the establishment of minor *audiencias* in local districts royal justice made deeper inroads on the private law of feudal lords. Justice was no longer for sale, as in the corrupt reign of Henry IV, but was impartially and inexorably applied.

Before the reign of the Catholic Monarchs the crown had been unable to escape aristocratic control by allying itself with the towns, for many of the

---

[4] L. Suárez Fernández, 'Evolución histórica de las hermandades castellanas', *Cuadernos de Historia de España*, xvi. (1951), 5–78.

latter were already partisans or subordinates of the aristocracy. By the middle
of the fifteenth century, however, townspeople were weary of feudal anarchy.
Conscious of the practical inconvenience of disorder, civil war, and rupture
of normal communications, they were ready for a lead. The first *hermandades*
were urban movements, and it was municipal anxiety for peace, security,
and resumption of trade which provided one of the most favourable conditions for the success of the royal programme. But Ferdinand and Isabella
had no intention of rescuing the crown from the aristocracy merely to
subordinate it to the towns. Many of the latter still retained the privileges
they had been granted when they were frontier posts in the wars against the
Moors, and, with them, the memory of past independence. This the crown
sought to erase. By use of the *corregidores*, royal officials sent for the first
time in 1480 to all Castilian towns and converted into a permanent institution,
the Catholic Monarchs closely controlled municipal life in Castile.[5] The
office was also imposed on Vizcaya and Guipúzcoa, and with it the central
authority began the policy of inserting royal officials into the semi-autonomous regions of the periphery. Although it could not introduce these powerful agents into Aragon-Catalonia, it was able to reduce the independence of
municipal corporations there by initiating the *régimen insaculatorio*, whereby
office-holders were drawn from lists of suitable candidates, that is from those
well disposed to the crown, which reserved the right to revise elections. The
towns themselves were the more ready to acquiesce in royal policy as they
benefited from the improvement of administration and even more from the
restoring of municipal finances, credit, and trade.[6]

Measures which in Castile were simply designed to strengthen royal
authority looked more like a policy of denationalisation when applied to
the eastern kingdoms. And Ferdinand's policy of improving the position of
the crown in Catalonia was not confined to municipal affairs and local
government. With a sense of unity more pronounced than that of Isabella,
he was anxious to assimilate his kingdoms to those of Castile. He encouraged
the intermarriage of Catalan and Castilian noble families, appointed Castilian
churchmen to important benefices in Catalonia, and on occasion—against
the constitutions—filled Catalan offices with Castilians. He even took the
policy to an institutional level, admitting the Spanish Inquisition to Aragon
and Catalonia. Yet this was the only institution common to both crowns,
and the protests with which it was received in the eastern kingdoms were a
sign of their sensitivity to encroachments on their independence, and a

[5] F. Albi, *El corregidor en el municipio español bajo la monarquía absoluta* (Madrid, 1943);
R. S. Chamberlain, 'The Corregidor in Castile in the Sixteenth Century', *Hispanic
American Historical Review*, xxiii. (1943), 222–57.
[6] See J. Vicens Vives, *Ferran II i la ciutat de Barcelona, 1479–1516* (3 vols., Barcelona,
1936–37).

warning perhaps to Castile not to overstep the mark. Ferdinand himself did not do so. He saw no reason to modify his pluralist conception of the Spanish monarchy, and his intervention in Catalonia brought political and economic reform rather than a general despoliation of its liberties. In view of the poverty of the eastern kingdoms in manpower and resources there was little temptation to attack their institutions or to subject them to a rigid centralisation. From the Catholic Monarchs, therefore, the Habsburgs were to inherit not a monolithic régime but a variegated and decentralised one, a personal union of independent states.

The anarchic condition of Spanish society on the eve of the new order was reflected in the state of the church. Like the crown it had lost prestige and property in the civil wars of the mid-fifteenth century, in which its most powerful members had participated on one side or the other for reasons that had little to do with religion; and like the aristocracy it reacted vehemently to any attack on its privileges, especially its exemption from taxation. The behaviour of many of the higher clergy was indistinguishable from that of the aristocracy, whence they usually came; and a warrior-bishop, like Archbishop Carrillo of Toledo, was not an exceptional figure. The monastic orders with few exceptions—notably the Carthusians and Franciscan Observants—had abandoned their original discipline, and their monasteries were often little more than places of diversion. When the Catholic Monarchs undertook to reform the religious orders, many of their members had to be forcibly expelled from their houses; the Dominicans of Salamanca defended themselves with arms. The condition of the secular clergy was even worse. Products of the existing system, which made virtually no provision for the training of priests, they were often completely unprepared for the performance of their duties; in 1473 the Council of Aranda had to order the clergy to celebrate Mass at least four times a year. In periods of decline, of course, it is usually the vices of the clergy which receive publicity while their virtues are ignored. The Spanish church was not devoid of piety and integrity, and standards were preserved among the middle groups of bishops, abbots and canons. The Catholic Monarchs, therefore, had material on which to work, and with the collaboration of Cardinal Ximénez de Cisneros they were able to begin the long-needed task of reform, an essential feature of which was careful selection of candidates for preferment. For this reason, as well as in the interests of their own sovereignty, they were anxious to reduce the jurisdiction of Rome. In ecclesiastical as in secular affairs they were determined to control as well as to reform, and it was in their reign that the independence of the Spanish church was undermined and its relations with Rome carefully circumscribed. In order to control the Spanish clergy they sought to establish nomination to benefices by the crown and not by the papacy. After a struggle they obtained from Sixtus IV the right to petition in favour of their candidates for all the major ecclesiastical benefices in Spain, with an understanding that the candidates presented by the crown would in fact be the ones appointed by Rome.[7] And even this extensive right was gradually extended to more and more benefices. Yet the concern of the Catholic Monarchs for religion can be exaggerated. They had little appreciation of the wider problems of the church; the papacy earned little prestige from the pontificate of Alexander VI, a Spanish Borgia elected with the active support of Ferdinand and Isabella. Even within Spain reasons of state sometimes took precedence over the needs of the church; Ferdinand, who had to find sinecures for the numerous illegitimate children with whom he littered the country, made one of them, Alonso de Aragón, archbishop of Zaragoza, whose own illegitimate son succeeded him in the see.

The reduction of the three estates—nobility, clergy, and towns—naturally involved the reduction of the institution in which they had been traditionally represented, the cortes.[8] In Castile this was no problem, for its cortes were utterly dependent on the crown, which controlled their composition and even the right of representation, and summoned or ignored them at its will. While they had the right to petition, they had no legislative power. In Castile the power to make laws had always rested exclusively in the crown. New laws did not require the assent of the cortes unless they contradicted an older law; according to an ordinance of 1387 the crown could not revoke a valid law without the consent of the cortes, but its legislative power was otherwise unlimited. The financial power of the cortes was no greater; it was understood that before taking extraordinary revenue the crown should consult the cortes, and this was written into law at the cortes of Valladolid in 1307; but even this limited function was weakened by the exemption of the nobility and the church from taxation and the crown's possession of alternative means of supply, both of which factors isolated the towns and weakened any opposition they cared to make. The cortes of Castile were thus quite unable to make redress of grievances precede supply of money, and thereby lacked any bargaining device vis-à-vis the crown. Yet they could be useful as a means of reaching public opinion, and in the early years of their reign Ferdinand and Isabella sought their collaboration, or that of

[7] T. de Azcona, La elección y reforma del episcopado español en tiempo de los Reyes Católicos (Madrid, 1960).

[8] See R. B. Merriman, 'The Cortes of the Spanish Kingdoms in the Later Middle Ages', American Historical Review, xvi. (1910–11), 476–95; M. Colmeiro, Cortes de los antiguos reinos de León y de Castilla: Introducción (Madrid, 1883); for an indication of recent studies see 'Recent Works and Present Views on the Origins and Development of Representative Assemblies', Relazioni del X Congresso Internazionale di Scienze Storiche, i. (Florence, 1955), 58–63.

the third estate, in their campaign against the nobility. Later, when their assistance was no longer required, they were ignored, infrequently summoned, and their composition was restricted to representatives of the towns, only eighteen of which were granted rights of representation.

In the states of the crown of Aragon the cortes possessed more authentic privileges and greater means of evading government control. Those of Aragon consisted of four estates, nobles, gentry, clergy, and towns, and although their summoning was a royal prerogative, the right to attend was fixed and did not, as in Castile, depend on royal writ. Unlike the Castilian monarch, the king of Aragon could not legislate without the cortes, nor could he impose any new tax without their consent.[9] And even during the intervals between meetings of cortes the crown could not escape their attention, for they left in session a *Diputación del Reyno*, or committee of estates, to supervise the observance of laws by public officials and private persons and to oversee the administration of public revenue. The cortes of Catalonia and Valencia were basically similar to those of Aragon. The Catalan body consisted of three estates, with about twelve towns represented in the third; no legislation could be made without their consent, no new taxes could be imposed without their voting them, and in the concluding session the king was obliged to swear to measures which the cortes had passed before they granted him the subsidy; and after the cortes had risen a committee of estates, the *Diputación General del Reyno*, similar to that of Aragon, performed a watch-dog function. More powerful than those of Castile, the cortes of Catalonia were probably more efficient than those of Aragon. But all the cortes of the eastern kingdoms were potentially instruments of opposition to the crown. Yet, interested as he was in restoring royal authority, Ferdinand did not challenge their privileges. He introduced the device of sending official lists from which the representatives of the towns had to be chosen; otherwise he left them structurally intact.

The immunity of the eastern kingdoms to the absolute power of the crown, especially in taxation and conscription, an immunity which lasted throughout the Habsburg period, is usually explained in purely constitutional terms and attributed to the legal apparatus with which they could defend themselves, unlike the helpless realms of Castile. Certainly the institutions of Aragon and Catalonia were more robust than those of Castile and the power of their monarch less absolute. It is also true that the joint crowns accepted the conditions of their union—that the component parts of the new Spain retain their identity and their laws. In any case, Ferdinand and Isabella had no desire

[9] Much has been made of the fact that absolute unanimity was required before any measures could be passed. But this was largely theoretical; in practice the rule of majority vote prevailed.

to provoke further civil wars by headlong clashes with traditional interests. But institutions do not explain everything. The question still remains—why was the crown content to be less absolute in Aragon than it was in Castile? And why did the protective institutions of the former survive even in new conditions, while those of Castile were rendered yet more impotent? The answer to this must be sought in the economic and social conditions of each kingdom.

Of the two regions Castile was richer in manpower and in taxable wealth; only there could the crown find in sufficient quantity the two basic instruments of power—recruits for its army and money for its treasury. For the social structure of Castile, containing as it did a large peasant population, much of which lived in conditions of disguised unemployment near starvation level, provided a ready surplus for the recruitment of troops; and the wealth of Castile, which was shortly to be primed with the income from America, enabled taxpayers to meet the growing demands of the state. The crown, therefore, had a compelling reason for seeking direct access to both men and money and for removing any obstacles in its path. In Aragon-Catalonia, on the other hand, the resources available were little more than useful additions to what the crown already possessed in Castile. As these kingdoms had little to offer so they had little to protect and the crown had few reasons for breaking the protective barriers. Had the eastern kingdoms been richer in resources, then it is difficult to avoid the conclusion that their institutions would have suffered the same fate as those of Castile. For any absolute monarchy intent on building a state and increasing its power is forced to make direct contract with its subjects, and if the crown of Spain had been deprived of essential power in its periphery kingdoms then it would have been forced to take issue with them. As it was, with power enough in Castile, the risk was not worth taking. Aragon and Catalonia were saved from the more extreme forms of absolute government by their poverty, and their immunity survived with the permission of the crown. The proof of this lies in the fact that when it was necessary the crown had no hesitation in imposing its will, even in the face of resistance. In the Catalan cortes of 1510 the representatives of Barcelona opposed the grant of subsidy on constitutional grounds, because the king had not given satisfaction to their demands; Ferdinand promptly ordered the recall of the Barcelona representatives and this was enough to bring them to heel. Later in the century, faced with opposition in Aragon, Philip II was to test the validity of its liberties even more searchingly. And it was not until the seventeenth century, precisely when Castile had reached the end of its resources, that the central government attempted to break the immunities of the eastern kingdoms in order to tap their manpower and money.

The cortes, then, were not a regular or essential part of government. This rôle was filled by the royal councils, headed by the Council of Castile, whose growing legislative as well as judicial and consultative functions reduced the significance of the cortes still further. The Catholic Monarchs reorganised the Council of Castile into a more efficient agency of administration, and added new councils to specialise in different areas (such as the Council of Aragon) or in different departments of government (such as the Council of Military Orders), staffing them with a core of professional lawyers and centralising the work of government on lines which lasted throughout the period of the Habsburgs. But to impose the authority of the state by means of officials—and its army—cost money; consequently the reorganisation undertaken by the crown presupposed its possession of greater financial power. The recovery of royal lands was not enough; it was also urgent to reorganise taxes, improve their collection and to provide for their administration at the centre. In these matters reform began in 1480 with the creation within the Council of Castile of a department of finance headed by an assiduous Asturian, Alonso de Quintanilla. With more effective direction from above, and collectors posted to all parts of the kingdom, revenue increased spectacularly—from 800,000 maravedis in 1470 to twenty-two millions in 1504. But this was due essentially to better administration under peaceful conditions and not to any reform of taxation itself, which retained its traditional structure. The immunities of nobility and clergy were preserved, with the result that the tax-paying sections of the community were subject to ever-increasing demands. The *alcabala*, a tax on mercantile transactions, was retained, together with the whole range of taxes inherited from the middle ages. The only uniform contribution was the *cruzada*, or crusade subsidy, obtained by the Catholic Monarchs from the pope for the war of Granada and providing a fruitful and permanent income from then onwards. Traditional customs duties were continued, though they also yielded more as trade improved in post-war conditions.

In giving Spain its state apparatus the Catholic Monarchs, operating from Castile and accepting the constitutional limitations of the union they had forged, liquidated the past and provided a basis on which their successors could build a national state. In the administrative sphere their work was creative and decisive, and to Castile, if not to the entire amalgam of their possessions, they left a government which had been centralised and reformed and was increasingly obeyed. By the end of the reign Isabella's ideal of a well-ordered society—'men-at-arms in the field, bishops in their pontificals, robbers on the gallows'—was on its way to being fulfilled. Yet there was a reverse side to their achievements and a price to be paid for them. The increase of taxation, unequally distributed among their subjects, inaugurated a long process of official plunder which had ruinous results for the Castilian economy. Government intervention in so many departments of public life swelled the ranks of bureaucracy, which ended by becoming a parasite on the nation and was always in danger of stagnation unless inspired by royal initiative. The predominance of Castile involved a partial neglect of the eastern kingdoms, for the absence of the monarch inevitably meant that their affairs were dealt with relatively slowly.

But the greatest defect in the policy of the Catholic Monarchs, and one which did irreparable damage to the interests of their country, was the complacency with which they regarded social and economic conditions in Spain. Much had been taken from the Castilian aristocracy, but much still remained to it. The objective of the monarchs was no more than a minimum one—to prevent the more powerful of their subjects from competing for sovereignty and managing the affairs of the country as they willed. Once this had been done they were content to leave the nobility undisturbed; indeed they sought its alliance for the work of administration. It may be true, as is constantly asserted, that they filled the royal councils and other agencies with professional lawyers, and made a practice of giving office and preferment to smaller men, to jurists like Palacios Rubios, ecclesiastics like Ximénez, and soldiers like Gonzalo de Córdoba.[10] Contemporaries were aware of this too. The jurist and chronicler Lorenzo Galíndez de Carvajal (1472–1532) noted that they 'were more inclined to appoint prudent people suitable for their service, even though they were of middle rank, rather than those of noble houses'; and somewhat later the chronicler Diego Hurtado de Mendoza referred to their practice of employing jurists, 'people mid-way between the great and the small, whose profession was to study law'. But the vice-royalties, governorships, and most of the higher military appointments were reserved for the great nobles. And from the lesser nobility the Catholic Monarchs took their provincial officials, the *corregidores*. In any case feudalism was not abolished in Spain the day the crown assumed the masterships of the Military Orders; the seigneurial jurisdiction of the nobility survived, buttressed by a vast landed wealth. Behind the façade of royal authority, indeed with its connivance, the higher nobles continued to enjoy an economic preponderance which made them the most powerful section of Castilian society.

2. ARISTOCRACY AND LAND IN CASTILE

The majority of Spaniards, about 95 per cent., lived in the country and were peasants; few of them owned the land on which they worked, for

[10] On the principles of appointment employed by the Catholic Monarchs see R. Menéndez Pidal, ed. W. Starkie, *The Spaniards in Their History* (London, 1950), pp. 158–64.

land in Spain was virtually monopolised by the aristocracy and the church.[11] Between peasants and nobles there was nothing resembling a middle class, either in the economic or in the social sense. The most that can be said is that there was a small minority of people who were neither peasants nor nobles —merchants and professional men (many of whom were Jews), clerics, and small rural proprietors. These groups comprised less than 4 per cent. of the population. At the top of the social pyramid was the aristocracy, an even smaller minority but possessing power and wealth in inverse proportion to its numbers. Including great magnates and higher ecclesiastics, gentry and urban patriciate, this class formed less than 2 per cent. of the population and owned about 95–97 per cent. of the land. Amassing territory conquered from the Moors, adding to it by depredations on crown land, protecting it by entail, and turning it into sheep-runs for the profitable wool trade, the Castilian aristocracy of the later middle ages had based its political power on unassailable economic foundations. To break this power would have been a formidable task and it could hardly be done in a single generation.

Ferdinand and Isabella were content to wrest political power from its hands and place it where it rightly belonged, in the crown. But to do this they accepted a compromise: they recognised the aristocracy's immunity from taxation and its possession of seigneurial jurisdiction, and sanctioned its monopoly of land. They did not even succeed in making courtiers out of the nobility, as is so often supposed. A powerful noble had two residences —a palace in town and an estate in the country. In the latter he possessed real power and exercised a feudal jurisdiction over his tenants which was still a challenge to the sovereignty of the state. Half a century after the accession of the Catholic Monarchs, the Duke of Infantado, of the formidable Mendoza family, was still lord of 800 villages and 90,000 vassals, and ruled his estates in Guadalajara like a powerful princeling. When royal prestige declined on the death of Isabella and the exclusion of Ferdinand from Castile, the Duke of Medina Sidonia could offer 2,000 cavalry and 50,000 ducats to Ferdinand's rival, Philip of Austria, as well as intervene actively in politics. And even if the Castilian aristocracy was eventually eclipsed as an independent political power, it still retained enormous material power based on its landed property.[12] Far from reducing this, the Catholic Monarchs sanctioned its extension, and thus compensated the nobility for its political losses by preserving

---

[11] On social and economic conditions in this period see S. Sobrequés Vidal, 'La época de los Reyes Católicos', in J. Vicens Vives, ed., *Historia social y económica de España y América* (5 vols., Barcelona, 1957–59), ii. 407–92. See also J. Vicens Vives, *Apuntes del curso de Historia Económica de España* (2 vols., Barcelona, 1956), i. 249–70.

[12] On the origins of the latifundia in Spain see L. Redonet y López-Dóriga, 'El latifundio y su formación en la España medieval', *Estudios de Historia Social de España*, i. (1949), 139–203.

its economic gains. For the rights of property fixed by Ferdinand and Isabella lasted throughout the Habsburg period and beyond. In the cortes of Toledo (1480) they passed measures which forced nobles to disgorge crown lands which they had seized since the reign of Henry IV (1454), but at the same time they gave them absolute security for acquisitions made before that date, which were precisely the greatest and the most important. In addition, they confirmed the right of *mayorazgo*, or entail, which enabled landed proprietors to render their estates immune from alienation and tie them in perpetuity to their family. They approved the practice of aristocratic marriage alliances which could only result in concentrating property still further in the hands of the possessing class. Finally, in Granada they pursued a policy which was unmistakably pro-aristocratic. Granada was a new conquest, but with the exception of lands in the western part of the kingdom which were given to peasants and artisans in Lower Andalucía, its rich territory was granted entirely to nobles in compensation for what they lost in 1480.

Facts like these explain the enormous fortunes possessed by the Castilian nobility from then onwards. At the top were about 300 magnates, styled grandees from the middle of the fifteenth century, many of them related by marriage to each other and some of them to the crown. Extremadura was divided, almost half and half, between the Suárez de Figueroa and the Order of Alcántara.[13] The immense plains of La Mancha were shared among the Orders of Santiago and Calatrava, the archbishop of Toledo, and the marquis of Villena. In Murcia the greatest single landowners were the Fajardos; in Salamanca the Zúñiga (dukes of Béjar), and the Alvarez de Toledo (dukes of Alba); in the Alcarria the Mendoza (dukes of Infantado). The Enríquez (Admirals of Castile) possessed most of the provinces of Valladolid and Valencia, as well as estates in Andalucía, and the Pimentel (counts of Benavente) that of León. But outstripping all the rest were the great magnates of Andalucía, which was divided in vast latifundia among the Gúzman (dukes of Medina Sidonia), the Cerda (dukes of Medinaceli), the Ponce de León (dukes of Arcos), the Fernández de Córdoba (dukes of Sesa), and the Mendoza (counts of Teudilla and of Priego); the rest belonged to the archbishop of Toledo. In general the higher aristocracy owned more than half the land of Castile. Most of the remainder was divided in smaller lots among the lesser aristocracy and the church, whose best benefices were in any case claimed by the younger sons of the nobility. Less than 5 per cent. was owned by the middle sections of society, urban or rural. The peasants owned practically nothing. It can hardly be said, therefore, that the problem of the aristocracy was solved by the Catholic Monarchs.

The easy success of the nobility created in the whole of Castilian society

[13] Sobrequés Vidal, *op. cit.*, p. 420.

a pro-aristocratic mentality and gave it its characteristic imprint for centuries to come. And their ranks, if they could be gained, offered a means of escape from fiscal burdens in an age of rising taxes. The middle sections of society, on the other hand, received few benefits from royal policy. No doubt the restoration of public order and authority and the consequent release of pent-up economic forces stimulated trade and industry and made some difference to their incomes. But it was precisely under the Catholic Monarchs that they lost perhaps the most enterprising of their number. In the interests of religious uniformity the Jews were expelled from the country and the *conversos*, or converts from Judaism, were exposed to a campaign of investigation that undermined their security. In the economic and urban life of Spain the Jews had occupied key positions; as financiers, artisans, and officials they dominated productive enterprises except in agriculture.[14] Granted their number, prosperity, and influence, it is not surprising that they should arouse envy and hatred, especially among the aristocracy and clergy; and their attachment to Judaism, even after nominal conversion, was an affront to the religious susceptibilities of the Catholic Monarchs and many of their subjects. Therefore, the monarchs had no hesitation in damaging the economy of the country to secure their objectives. The issues at stake were clear enough, and were made even clearer to them by the urban reaction to their anti-Jewish policy, especially to the decision to establish the Inquisition. The municipalities of Seville, Toledo, Barcelona, Valencia, and Zaragoza made urgent and reasoned protests about the damage which the establishment of the Inquisition entailed for their towns, causing as it did the flight of the *conversos* and of their capital; and the monarchs invariably replied that they preferred the religious to the material welfare of the country. And this was perfectly true. For the numbers involved were not insignificant; apart from those executed by the Inquisition, thousands of *conversos* left the country. Their liquidation, accompanied by seizure of their property, had a paralysing effect on the economy of the country because it abstracted not only a vital part of the community but also a considerable amount of capital. For this reason, and not on doctrinal grounds, there was much resistance to the establishment of the Inquisition in the eastern kingdoms, whose commercial centres, especially in Catalonia and Valencia, were seriously hit. Not content with this, the crown also decided to expel the Jews themselves; out of an estimated 200,000 at the beginning of the reign, about 150,000 refused baptism and were forced to leave Spain in 1492, taking with them their skill and their wealth. These measures, in conjunction with the pro-aristocratic bias that was already deeply embedded in society, were a powerful deterrent to the growth of a middle class in Spain.

[14] See A. A. Neuman, *The Jews in Spain* (2 vols., Philadelphia, 1948). And see below, pp. 20–22.

If the policy of the Catholic Monarchs offered little to urban society, it offered even less to the rural masses. The only exception was Catalonia, where a peasants' revolt against feudal landowners led to both sides putting the case in the hands of King Ferdinand. His judgement was given in the Sentence of Guadalupe (1486), which abolished feudal services in return for compensation to the lords and gave the Catalan peasants some measure of property rights.[15] In Aragon, on the other hand, where the problem of the peasantry was analogous to that in Catalonia, the crown gave its support to the feudal lords. In Castile, with a complete disregard for the real situation, the crown confirmed the right of tenants to abandon their lord, change their residence and take with them their goods (1481). But in view of the aristocratic monopoly of land the right was largely theoretical and simply a reflection of aristocratic confidence; as the peasant had no place to escape to, it was hardly necessary to fix him to the soil by legislation. In Aragon and most of Castile, therefore, the peasant remained a tenant paying his rent in kind and often in services, and possessing no security of tenure; otherwise he was a landless labourer. Beset by plague, drought, and famine, he was also completely at the mercy of his lord or his employer, against whom he had no legal protection. And he looked in vain for any legislation in favour of the small proprietor.

Yet throughout southern and central Spain there were vast tracts of untilled land. The main reason why it was not given over to farming was that its use was monopolised by the owners of livestock, especially of the flocks of migrant merino sheep in which Spain abounded. Since the thirteenth century the major economic activity of Castile was the raising of merino sheep for their wool, with the result that there arose a serious imbalance between arable and pastoral agriculture. By the time of the Catholic Monarchs the situation called for government leadership, but here too royal policy was conservative and aristocratic in bias. Again Catalonia was an exception. In the eastern kingdom, where Ferdinand provided conditions for a brief economic revival, he refused to sanction the absolute claims of the sheep-breeders to property rights; in 1511 in the cortes of Monzón he prohibited the passage of the herds of sheep through cultivated land. This decision was crucial for the development of agriculture in the Mediterranean regions of Spain. But it was quite the opposite of that taken ten years previously in Castile. What was possible in Catalonia, of course, was not necessarily possible in Castile, where powerful interests had a stake in sheep-breeding and the wool trade. But the crown did not merely sanction the

[15] J. Vicens Vives, *Historia de los remensas en el siglo XV* (Barcelona, 1945); *El Gran Sindicato remensa (1488–1508). La última etapa del pleito agrario catalán durante el reinado de Fernando el Católico* (Madrid, 1954).

status quo: it short-sightedly worsened it. It came out firmly on the side of pastoral interests, embodied in their organisation, the Mesta, which the Catholic Monarchs defended against all opposition and controlled by assigning a royal councillor as its president (1500).[16] No one who enclosed pasture for cultivation had any chance of success against the attacks of cattle-owners, who invariably received royal support. This support culminated in the notorious *Ley de arriendo del suelo* (law of land lease) of 1501, which gave the Mesta the right to use in perpetuity and at fixed rents any land it had once used as pasture; although the Mesta only rented the land, this measure gave it a virtual entail of its pastures—and in any dispute its own officials were judges. Immense tracts of land in Andalucía and Extremadura were thus tied to the Mesta and to the interests of its directors. Agriculture could hardly have been made less attractive

Why was royal policy in Castile so different from that in Catalonia, and why did Ferdinand and Isabella abdicate so utterly to pastoral interests? Partly because it was not entirely a question of abdication. One of the main beneficiaries of their policy was the crown, which received a quick and sure revenue from the taxes on sheep and the sale of wool; therefore instead of promoting agriculture and awaiting its returns, the crown preferred the easy way out of its financial difficulties and one which had proved its worth in the past. Moreover, commercial and industrial interests were involved: the sale of the merino wool abroad was extremely lucrative, and its manufacture at home was the only Castilian industry of any importance. But the aristocracy had the biggest stake of all; many of them had turned their lands almost entirely to pasture, because it gave them a profitable commodity to sell and one which, unlike arable farming in the arid conditions of Castile, needed little investment of money and manpower. This powerful alliance of interests determined the fate of agricultural production. From the beginning of the sixteenth century Spain inevitably began to suffer a serious shortage of grain; in 1506, for the first time, the population had to be fed from large-scale imports of wheat and thereafter became increasingly dependent on foreign supplies.[17] Many parts of Spain were close to famine in 1506, and the danger haunted her for the rest of the century and beyond.

On foundations like these it was impossible to build a balanced economy. The Catholic Monarchs hardly attempted to do so. The traditional theory that they promoted industry in Castile is not sustained by existing evidence, for the industries cited are either those producing luxury goods or those working for a local market. The immense pile of edicts with which they

[16] J. Klein, *The Mesta* (Cambridge, Mass., 1920), pp. 52, 316–26.
[17] E. Ibarra y Rodríguez, *El problema cerealista en España durante el reinado de los Reyes Católicos (1475–1516)* (Madrid, 1941).

regulated manufacturing processes cannot disguise the lack of coherence in their policy and the fact that they had already committed themselves to the aristocratic interest by the protection given to stock-breeding. In fact, their regulations handicapped industry. From about 1480 Ferdinand encouraged the extension of gilds which were then stifled with a surfeit of regulations. In 1511 he issued the Ordinance of Seville, a collection of no less than 120 rules prescribing the lawful process of weaving cloth. Throughout the sixteenth century Spanish industry was shackled by regulations of this kind; at a time when industry in the rest of Europe was beginning to escape from gild control, that of Castile was put into a corporative straight-jacket. The only industries of any stature were the iron industry of the Basque provinces, which could draw on natural resources and shelter under the protection of regional privileges, and the textile industry of Castile, which was given a new impetus by the discovery of America and the opening of new markets there, especially from about 1505. But industry in general was dealt another blow by the flight of the *converso* artisans. It was no coincidence that from the time the Inquisition was established the crown had to publish edicts inviting foreign workers to Spain (1484), and to take the unprecedented step of granting foreign workers who came to Castile exemption from all taxes for ten years.[18]

The expansion of Castilian commerce, on the other hand, coincided with the reign of Ferdinand and Isabella and owed something to their initiative.[19] There was already a tradition of commerce in Castile and this was strengthened by the peaceful conditions which they provided. Export of wool was the chief item of foreign trade, and the crown did its best to promote it, if only to increase its revenue therefrom. During the reign the wool trade was systematically organised. Agents were sent to the principal foreign markets —Bruges, La Rochelle, London, and Florence—to review demand, prices, and competition, and from these centres they sent information to the court. Once this had been assimilated, contacts were established between foreign merchants and the authorities of the Mesta in order to organise export. The Catholic Monarchs also sought to reserve the carrying trade to Spain by means of navigation acts. Nevertheless, the protection given by the Catholic Monarchs to industry and commerce was not part of a considered programme, even of a mercantilist kind; their interest in this direction was small indeed compared to the protection given to aristocratic landowners. In any case, the country lacked capital to invest in productive enterprises.

---

[18] Vicens Vives, *Apuntes del curso de Historia Económica de España*, p. 263.

[19] See M. Mollat, 'Le rôle international des marchands espagnols dans les ports occidentaux à l'époque des Rois Catholiques', V Congreso de Historia de la Corona de Aragón (*Estudios*, I), pp. 35–61.

The discovery of America was still too recent for its mineral wealth to be available for industrial expansion in Spain. Later, when treasure imports began to mount they were quickly dispersed abroad to pay for foreign wars and for foreign goods, including grain. Castile remained essentially an agrarian, pastoral, and feudal country as it had been in the middle ages. And the Catholic Monarchs never even began to undertake the admittedly formidable task of integrating the various regions of Spain into an economic whole.

The economic relations between the constituent kingdoms were not radically altered in the formative years of Spain's national history. In 1479, when Ferdinand and Isabella began to govern their joint possessions, the Catalan merchants believed that a period of *hermandad hispánica*, of Spanish fraternity, had begun. For the impoverished Catalans and their declining trade, the assurance of a market in Castile and Andalucía for their cloths and spices, and a share in the export of wool, would have been inestimable benefits. But their illusions were shattered—not because of Castilian aversion to Catalans but because the powerful Mesta opposed them and because their chief rivals for Mediterranean trade, the Genoese, had more to offer to the crown than the penurious Catalans, whose demands were consequently ignored. Catalans were still regarded as foreigners and were refused admittance to the fairs of Medina del Campo on equal footing with the merchants of Castile. For these reasons the two streams of the medieval Spanish economy, the Mediterranean and the Atlantic, continued their separate courses and maintained a division which bedevilled the economy of Habsburg Spain and remained unchanged until the second half of the eighteenth century. This was a reflection, of course, on the concept of unity held by the Catholic Monarchs, for the unity of a country cannot be complete without its economic integration. And in their reign there was a new opportunity. The empire in America could have been a decisive bond: here, apparently, was a field open to common interests and to a genuinely Spanish enterprise.

The political unity of Spain was virtually complete when Isabella sponsored the expedition of Columbus in 1492, and the state she and her husband had created was sufficiently mature to found an overseas empire and to exploit it. Yet the American trade was closed to the subjects of the crown of Aragon. The reasons advanced to explain such a policy are not always convincing: the political antagonism between Castile and Catalonia, and the fact that legally America was exclusively the patrimony of Castile, were hardly relevant issues. The anxiety of the crown to control the new enterprise and monopolise its fruits, and therefore to exclude foreigners, is more to the point, for these needs could be better served by canalising the enterprise through Castile, which had discovered the Indies. In any case, Catalonia at first held back and showed little interest in America until later in the sixteenth century, when Catalan merchants made formal attempts to participate in the Indies trade. By that time, however, the favourable Atlantic location of Andalucía and Castile had proved decisive and had given them a natural monopoly of communications with America which the crown itself sanctioned in order to exclude foreigners and to reserve trade and bullion to Spain. Whatever the reasons, however, the fact remained that Spain's American empire was primarily a Castilian empire. This gave added weight to the preponderance of Castile in the union of the Spanish kingdoms and sharpened the economic divisions between them. Meanwhile, in yet another direction, Castile had begun to impose its policies on the whole of Spain.

3. THE SPANISH INQUISITION

The medieval Inquisition, a special court for the detection, trial, and punishment of heresy, had existed since 1233 when it was created by the papacy to deal with the Albigensian heresy in Southern France. Although it subsequently extended its operations to other countries, it invariably encountered royal resentment of papal intervention. It entered Aragon— not Castile—but never flourished there. Everywhere it was virtually obsolete by the fifteenth century, not to be revived in Rome until 1542, in the new context of Protestantism. The essential constitutional feature of the medieval Inquisition was papal control, exercised through the General and Provincials of the Dominican Order.

The Spanish Inquisition differed from the papal Inquisition both in its origin and in its organisation.[20] In the first place, there was no serious heresy in fifteenth-century Spain and no one was trying to found a new religion. The Spanish Inquisition was created to deal with convert Jews. During the middle ages, as has been noticed, the Jews had made striking progress in Spain, establishing themselves in key positions in the political and economic life of the country, even as royal counsellors. Their relations with Christians, which had long been amicable, were shattered in the second half of the fourteenth century; in a period of great economic depression, their exceptional success aroused resentment which eventually turned into hatred and erupted at times into violence like the massacres of 1391. To save their lives and their fortunes many Jews, especially in Andalucía, became Christians;

[20] In spite of its age and its bias the work of H. C. Lea, *A History of the Inquisition of Spain* (4 vols., New York and London, 1922, first published 1906–7), is still the most detailed and comprehensive account of the subject that exists. But modern historiography has greatly advanced the subject: see Henry Kamen, *The Spanish Inquisition* (London, 1965); Ricardo García Cárcel, *Orígenes de la Inquisición española. El tribunal de Valencia, 1478–1530* (Barcelona, 1976); and Bartolomé Bennassar, *L'Inquisition espagnole* (*xve–xixe siècles*) (Paris, 1979).

these baptised Jews were known as *conversos*, or New Christians, and numbered over 100,000. Protected by their new religion they made even further progress, for now the church as well as the state was open to them and in both they acquired positions of responsibility. In many cases, as conversion to Christianity had been simulated, it was known, or suspected, that they secretly continued to adhere to the Jewish religion. It was only to be expected that many of the converts were insincere—or Judaisers, as they were called—for the mass conversions of the fourteenth and fifteenth centuries were the result of persecution and terror. And persecution did not cease with conversion: there were frequent and sometimes murderous clashes between Old and New Christians, as in Toledo in 1467 and in Córdoba in 1473. Finally, many of the New Christians became the bitterest enemies of their former brethren. Anxious to protest their own orthodoxy and to protect themselves against the suspicions of the Old Christians, converts denounced not only Jews but also fellow converts, and this spirit of rivalry and jealousy may have aggravated the intolerance of the Inquisition itself; many officials of the early Spanish Inquisition, including Torquemada, were descended from New Christians.[21]

Fear of the apostasy of the Judaisers and the conviction that church and state were being undermined from within were the decisive reasons for the creation of the Inquisition in Spain. The Catholic Monarchs were prepared to use force to ensure unity of religion, and were pressed to do so by powerful groups among the Old Christians, especially the clergy and the aristocracy. The arch-inspirer of the Inquisition in Spain was the prior of the Dominican community in Seville, Alonso de Hojeda, who exercised great influence on the Catholic Monarchs; it was he who denounced the existence of numerous groups of *conversos* allegedly practising Judaism. But the Dominican offensive fed upon the anti-semitism of the masses. Artisans, tradesmen, labourers, many Old Christians of the poorer classes envied the material and social success of the Jews and *conversos*, their position as crown financiers, their talents as scientists and men of the professions, and their marriage alliances with the aristocracy, and they accused them of being pseudo-converts. The first generation of *familiares*, those agents of the Inquisition so active as spies and informers, were recruited among the popular sectors rather than the upper classes, who only later became interested in Inquisition offices. The crown too had motives additional to religion. While the Inquisition was not created with the sole object of robbing the *conversos*,

[21] Américo Castro, *The Structure of Spanish History*, trans. Edmund L. King (Princeton, 1954), pp. 421–30, 532, 540, argues that 'the Inquisition had been in the making since the beginning of the fifteenth century', largely by 'deserters from Israel'. The thesis is not entirely convincing.

acquisitive motives were not absent from official calculations. Royal finances were in a state of crisis at the time, before the reforms of Ferdinand and Isabella had come to fruition; therefore those who advised economic measures against the *conversos*—confiscation of property—were given a hearing. For some time, however, the Catholic Monarchs stayed their hand; they were fully occupied establishing their rule and could only proceed piecemeal. During this period Pope Sixtus IV renewed previous attempts made by the papacy to introduce the papal Inquisition, but without success, for Ferdinand and Isabella were anxious to limit rather than extend opportunities for papal intervention. Moreover, many of the most important posts in their own administration were filled with *conversos*, and there must have been a desperate and discreet struggle on the part of these men to prevent the introduction of a tribunal that could only mean anguish for themselves. However, when their hands were free, the monarchs requested licence from the pope to establish the Inquisition—but not the papal Inquisition. They were seeking a tribunal which would be entirely under their control, excluding intervention from Rome. For this reason Sixtus IV hesitated to grant their request, but he finally capitulated and by bull of 1 November 1478 he authorised the crown to appoint Inquisitors with jurisdiction over heretics. So the Spanish Inquisition came into being.[22] Owing perhaps to further opposition within Spain, two years passed before it began to operate. Then, on 27 September 1480, by virtue of the powers received from the pope, the Catholic Monarchs appointed the first inquisitors for Seville, which was regarded as a hot-bed of Judaisers.

The early actions of the Inquisition in Andalucía were ruthless and violent: the first *auto de fe* was held at Seville on 6 February 1481, and six victims were burned. Other tribunals sprang up elsewhere, and judging by the number and frequency of the death sentences and by the heavy confiscation of property, their measures were harsh and oppressive. This early reign of terror provoked frantic opposition from the *conversos*—appeals to Rome, to regional immunities, to local magistrates, and also to the monarchs, to whom they offered money. When nothing else availed them, they had recourse to violent counter-measures, the most spectacular being the assassination of the Inquisitor of Aragon, Pedro de Arbués, in the cathedral of Zaragoza in 1485. Such resistance only prompted the Inquisition to greater efforts. and in spite of opposition from the other regions it spread beyond Castile into the length and breadth of Spain. It was also deaf to the protests of Rome.

---

[22] On the role of the papacy see B. Llorca, S.J., *Bulario pontificio de la Inquisición española en su período constitucional (1478–1525)* (Rome, 1949).

Perturbed by the violence of the first tribunals, Sixtus IV regretted the extensive powers he had conceded to the Spanish crown and tried to halt the drastic programme of the Spanish Inquisition by restricting its independence and its powers. But in the face of the determination of Ferdinand and Isabella and of the negotiations undertaken on their behalf by Cardinal Rodrigo Borgia—the future Alexander VI—he gave way once again. He authorised the creation of a Supreme Council of the Inquisition and the appointment of an Inquisitor general with full delegated power in the person of Fray Tomás de Torquemada, royal confessor and prior of the Dominican monastery of Santa Cruz in Segovia.

Beyond the fact that he was a pious and sombre man and an implacable enemy of heresy, little is known for certain about Torquemada, and his biography remains to be written. In spite of many assertions to the contrary, he was not the architect of the Spanish Inquisition and there is no evidence that his was the deciding influence in the actual establishment of the new tribunal. But once he had been appointed Inquisitor general in 1483 he was responsible for giving the Inquisition its definitive organisation. Among the powers granted to Torquemada was that of modifying the traditional rules of the Inquisition to meet the requirements of Spain. This made the institution virtually self-governing and gave the Spanish Inquisition a character of its own independent of Rome. Between 1484 and 1489, the year of his death, Torquemada drew up a series of Instructions which defined the constitution of the tribunal and established its procedure. These were extended periodically until 1561 when Inquisitor general Valdés issued a revised constitution which, with a few later modifications, governed the Inquisition for the rest of its history.

The Spanish Inquisition was created in the form of a council of state, the Council of the Supreme and General Inquisition—usually called the Suprema —with jurisdiction in all matters of heresy. Thus the conciliar formula favoured by the Catholic Monarchs for the solution of their administrative problems was applied to religion too. To secure royal control over the new institution and exclude that of the pope, the monarchs then had to ensure that the president of the Suprema had full control of the appointment and dismissal of individual inquisitors, and that they themselves controlled the president. Therefore they created a new office, unknown to the medieval Inquisition, an Inquisitor general, who presided over the meetings of the Suprema and was head of the entire Inquisition. Appointment to the office of Inquisitor general rested exclusively with the crown, as did appointment of subordinate officials, though in practice these were usually appointed by the Inquisitor general and the Suprema. In this way the crown avoided both the possibility of papal intervention and the danger of the Inquisition itself becoming independent. The Suprema, also appointed by the crown, consisted of six members, who included representatives of the Dominican order and the Council of Castile. It heard appeals from the local tribunals, and also controlled the financial administration of the Inquisition, its property and the proceeds of its confiscations, the profits of which went to the royal treasury.

Who were the Inquisitors? Not all were Dominicans. In the beginning, it is true, these took the lead, but they soon lost whatever monopoly they may have exercised. Subsequently the Inquisitors were almost always senior members of the secular clergy, university graduates making their way in a career in church or state. Out of forty-five Inquisitors General between 1481 and 1820, only five were Dominicans. As for the provincial tribunals, they were never controlled by the Dominicans. In Toledo only one friar held the office between 1482 and 1598; here too most of the Inquisitors were university graduates, products of the *colegios mayores*, the nurseries of the Spanish bureaucracy.

Canonically, as the Inquisition was an ecclesiastical tribunal, the pope was its head. In theory this was admitted by the Spanish authorities, but in practice papal jurisdiction was rigidly excluded. Similarly the papacy managed to cling to the principle of its appellate jurisdiction, but was unable to apply it. The practical effect of this was that it became impossible to appeal a case from the Spanish Inquisition to Rome, and in this direction Spain was to set an example even to Protestant countries. In matters of heresy the Inquisition had jurisdiction over all laymen and clergy—but not bishops—to the exclusion of all other courts. From its judgement there was no appeal, not even to the pope, who in three centuries of the Spanish tribunal's existence managed to claim from it only three cases for his judgement. Independent of the papacy, the Spanish Inquisition was a close and subordinate ally of the crown, and on more than one occasion its authority was to be abused for political purposes. Indeed, this dual character of the Spanish Inquisition, deriving from the close alliance of church and state in Spain, was one of its most peculiar features; it combined the spiritual authority of the church with the temporal power of the crown.

Operating under the central council of the Inquisition were permanent local tribunals which represented for the mass of the people the real embodiment of its power. There were some thirteen of these tribunals in Spain, situated in the principal towns; outside Spain tribunals operated in the Canaries, Sicily, and Sardinia, and from the 1570's in the Indies. The introduction of the Inquisition in the states of the crown of Aragon was strongly opposed; there it was seen as an alien institution, an agent of Castilian intervention, and a possible threat to economic interests. In 1484 the cortes of Valencia denounced the new tribunal, which had been operating in the eastern kingdom since 1481, as a violation of its *fueros*. The action of Ferdinand in importing the Inquisition was resented by almost all senior officials, partly because it was regarded as a new power in the land, partly because its initial impact was so severe.

The Inquisition in Valencia claimed almost 1,000 victims in 1488 alone. Up to 1530 this tribunal tried 2,354 people, 1,197 of them men, 1,157 women; the nobility provided few of the accused, the clergy rather more, while the middle sectors, specially the merchant groups, were represented by 44·6 per cent., and the popular classes, especially artisans, by 47 per cent. If it was less severe than Toledo (6,150 up to 1505) and Seville (20,000 up to 1524), the Valencia tribunal was much harsher than 'lenient' tribunals such as Ciudad Real (269 up to 1530). The death penalty was imposed in only a minority of cases, but the proportion was high in the earlier years. In Valencia out of 1,842 victims whose sentences are known 754, or 41 per cent., were executed up to 1530. The Seville tribunal was even harsher; elsewhere burnings were less frequent. Altogether the Spanish Inquisition put to death some 5,000 people in the period up to 1530. In the period 1560–1700, on the other hand, among 50,000 cases there were 500 death sentences, or 1 per cent. The primary purpose of the Inquisition was to extinguish Judaism, and the majority of the early victims, perhaps 80–90 per cent. of all those executed, were alleged Judaisers. The rest were accused of miscellaneous offences, Lutheranism, blasphemy, witchcraft and, in the case of moriscos, adherence to Islamic ways. As the moriscos were also regarded as a security threat, the rôle of the Inquisition here approached that of a police force at the service of the state.

The legal procedure of the Spanish Inquisition was marked by the fact that the tribunals combined two functions, judicial and police. They were not ordinary courts of law, because they also had powers of investigation, and in addition to the punishment of offenders they also wanted their confession and renunciation in order to save their souls. This dual purpose was reflected in the actual procedure they used. The procedure of the medieval Inquisition was by pure *inquisitio*, that is to say the inquisitor acted as both prosecutor and judge. Superficially the Spanish Inquisition proceeded more impartially, by way of *accusatio*, with a public prosecutor as an accuser and the inquisitors acting only as judges. But this was legal fiction and simply meant that the inquisitor had the assistance of a trained lawyer in making the prosecution; it was the inquisitors who gathered evidence, and like their medieval predecessors they were prosecutors as well as judges.

Each locality had to be visited every year by an inquisitor who solemnly published an *Edict of Faith*, which, in the form of a minute questionnaire, imposed on every Christian under pain of major excommunication the obligation to denounce known heretics. When the tribunal itself saw a suspicious situation—which was mainly in the first century of its existence—it would begin by publishing an *Edict of Grace*, which allowed a period of 30–40 days to all who wished to come forward voluntarily to confess faults and errors. Confession usually meant pardon and only light penalties, but there was a condition attached—that the penitent reveal his accomplices. Both edicts were open to serious abuses. In particular, the Edict of Faith, by enjoining denunciations, forced the faithful to co-operate in the work of the Inquisition and made everyone its agent or its spy, offering moreover an irresistible temptation for the relief of private malice. The two edicts usually led to a crop of denunciations—which were also expected to contain the names of witnesses—and it was either these or the investigations of the inquisitors themselves which initiated the legal proceedings.

If the accusations were accepted then the accused was imprisoned in the secret gaols of the Inquisition, usually in humane conditions, but utterly secluded from the outside world and deprived of all contact with his family and friends. The case then proceeded, slowly and in strict secrecy, and based throughout on the assumption that the accused was guilty. But the greatest defect in the legal procedure of the Spanish Inquisition was the fact that the accused was kept uninformed about the identity of his accusers and their witnesses, who were thereby relieved from responsibility, while the accused was left largely helpless in preparing his defence. His only safeguard was that he could draw up a list of his enemies, and if it contained any of the accusers then their evidence would be discounted. Otherwise almost any kind of evidence and any type of witness were accepted for the prosecution, whereas the questions put to the defence witnesses, and whether they were called at all, were entirely at the discretion of the inquisitors. Once the case for the prosecution was ready, the organisation of the defence could begin. The accused was allowed an officially appointed lawyer, but he could refuse him and request another. He was also provided with a counsellor whose function it was to convince him that he should make a sincere confession. The pressure of the counsellor, together with the secrecy of the accusers and witnesses, undoubtedly weakened the position of the defendant which his own lawyer and witnesses could hardly be expected to redress. Indeed, the secrecy of informers and witnesses was an innovation in Spain, alarming to contemporaries, and contrary to the procedure of other courts of law. But the situation of the accused was rendered even more desperate by the power of the Inquisition, like other tribunals of the time, to use torture to procure evidence and confession. Bloodshed and anything likely to cause permanent injury were forbidden, but this still left room for three painful methods of torture, all of which were well known and not peculiar to the

Inquisition: the rack, the hoist, and the water-torture. Even if their use was infrequent and accompanied by medical safeguards, they were horribly inappropriate in matters of conscience.

After evidence had been taken and qualified theologians consulted if necessary—all of which invariably took a long time, sometimes four or five years—sentence was passed. If the accused confessed his guilt in the course of the trial *before* sentence was passed and his confession was accepted, then he was absolved and dismissed with lighter punishment. Otherwise sentence would be acquittal or condemnation. A verdict of guilty did not necessarily mean death. It depended first of all on the gravity of the offence, and the penalties, which were derived from medieval civil and canon law, might involve penance, fine or flogging for minor offences, and the dreaded galleys or crippling confiscation of property for more serious ones. But it also depended on many other factors, such as the circumstances of the time, the character of the accused, and above all on the temperament of the judges, not all of whom were equally relentless. In proportion to the number of cases the death penalty was rare. On the other hand a repentant heretic who relapsed again never escaped the death penalty. Those who persisted in heresy, or in their denial of guilt, were burnt alive. Those who repented at the last minute and *after* sentence, whether sincerely or not, were strangled first, then burnt. The execution itself was not performed by the Inquisition but by the civil authorities. The Spanish *auto de fe* was merely an elaborately staged public exhibition at which the sentence was pronounced and discussed amidst much ceremony. The heretic was then 'relaxed' to the secular arm, which carried out the sentence of burning, often at a different time and place. Beginning as a means of instilling awe and terror in the faithful, the *auto de fe* soon degenerated into a social occasion of perverse excitement and became a kind of religious entertainment to celebrate a royal wedding or a monarch's visit or some other public function. But only major cases were completed with an *auto de fe*. In minor ones the sentences were published privately.

Although the Spanish Inquisition was established primarily to deal with *conversos*, its jurisdiction extended to all matters of heresy, and consequently it also turned its attention to converted Moors, or moriscos, and to native Spanish heretics, Protestant or otherwise. The jurisdiction of the inquisition, however, was confined to Christians and it was not a means of converting unbelievers by force. It punished heresy and apostasy, but not the profession of a different faith, baptism being a pre-condition of heresy. For this reason, Jews, Moslems, and American Indians were excluded from its authority. The inquisition never prosecuted a Jew for being a Jew, or a Moslem for being a Moslem. It pursued converts from each faith who were suspected, rightly or wrongly, to be secret apostates. Those Moors and Jews who refused baptism were expelled from Spain. But the work of the Spanish Inquisition was not confined to heresy: it also had jurisdiction in cases of bigamy, sodomy, and blasphemy, and on occasion, because of its efficiency, it even received administrative functions, such as the enforcement of customs regulations on the frontier. Of all its activities, however, one of the most characteristic and perhaps one of the most pernicious was related to the question of *limpieza de sangre*, or purity of blood.

The New Christians were objects of suspicion and prejudice which took the form of a spirit of exclusiveness among Old Christians and was prevalent even before the establishment of the Spanish Inquisition. Attempts had already been made to deprive them of official positions, in spite of the protests of the papacy, and this prejudice against Jewish blood continued, even among some religious orders. By the end of the sixteenth century various bodies excluded men of 'tainted' descent from admittance; these included the Inquisition itself, the Orders of Santiago, Alcántara, Calatrava, and St. John, all the university colleges, and many cathedral chapters, including that of Toledo, where *estatutos de nobleza*, regulations requiring proofs of nobility and purity of blood before candidates could obtain admission, were first promulgated. Discrimination of this kind was reflected in the policy of the Inquisition, which continued to regard Jewish ancestry as a security risk to church and state, and whose sensitivity to genealogy seemed to increase after its initial campaign had liquidated large numbers of *conversos*.[23] And the Inquisition, of course, was the instrument for testing purity of descent. All the above institutions required the most rigorous investigation to trace the slightest stain in the remotest grade of parentage. And there were two sources of descent which caused impurity of blood—from an ancestor who was Jewish or Moorish, or from one who had been sentenced by the Inquisition. Anyone who desired a tranquil career in church or state, or in many cases even admittance to one, applied to the Inquisition for certificates attesting their purity of blood, and for this purpose they described their genealogy, named witnesses and paid a fee. The whole process encouraged perjury, bribery and collusion, and offered yet another occasion for the gratification of spite. Those families with unimpeachable proof of a long Castilian lineage free of Moorish or Jewish blood seized the opportunity to discredit their rivals for office and social status by denouncing them as *conversos*. In spite of this a large minority of *conversos* managed to survive, and throughout the sixteenth century they were to be found in commercial and professional

---

[23] A. Domínguez Ortiz, 'Los conversos de origen judío después de la expulsión', *Estudios de Historia Social de España*, iii. (1955), 223-431.

occupations. Positions in church and state were not completely closed, though they occupied them in conditions of insecurity. Even during the reign of the Catholic Monarchs they were to be found in high places; men like Luis Santángel, notary-prebend of King Ferdinand, Alfonso de la Cavallería, vice-chancellor of the Council of Aragon, Fray Hernando de Talavera, confessor of the queen and archbishop of Granada, were all of Jewish race, though all at one time or another were objects of suspicion or persecution. In subsequent reigns descendants of *conversos* still managed to make their way in the world, the most distinguished example being Antonio Pérez, secretary of Philip II. But, socially rebuffed by the Old Christians and unwelcome as marriage partners, they remained an enclosed group of virtually second-class citizens. All this left its imprint on the Castilian mentality; the exaggerated sense of honour and hypersensitivity to ancestry and blood were nurtured in these conditions, and what had once been at least in part a religious prejudice became an attempt to limit the number of aspirants to office and social status.

Not content with the persecution of suspect converts, the search for religious unity and the conviction that it was impossible to solve the problem of the *conversos* while their former brethren were still tolerated led the Catholic Monarchs to undertake a much greater purge—the expulsion of the Jews. While the war with Granada lasted the action was not practicable; in any case the Jews contributed large subsidies to the enterprise. But their prolonged and direct contact with the numerous Jews in Lower Andalucía at the time when they were fighting another alien religion, reinforced the monarchs' desire for religious unity. A few months after the fall of Granada an edict was published (30 March 1492) by virtue of which the Jews were given four months to become Christians or leave the kingdom. Out of 200,000 Jews, about 150,000 chose to go. Portugal took many of these, but as a condition of the marriage of their daughter Isabella to Manoel I, the Catholic Monarchs insisted that Portugal too expel them. Others went to France, Africa, and the Ottoman Empire, where they settled in cities like Salonica and Constantinople, preserving their Castilian language and a bitter hatred of Spain. Meanwhile, what of the Moors?

4. RECONQUEST AND EXPANSION

The union of the two major Iberian kingdoms created a formidable block of power, which, once it had been organised within, began to swell beyond its own frontiers. The fusion of religious and political ideals revived the spirit of crusade against Islam which had been dead for over a century. Without Granada the reconquest was incomplete and Spain itself dismembered;

and with the joint forces of Castile and Aragon ready for action the time had come to reduce the last remnants of Islam on Iberian soil. The enterprise was primarily Castile's affair, and was undertaken on her initiative; but Castile could not have brought it to fulfilment without the material collaboration of Aragon, Catalonia, and Valencia, who sent their quotas of troops, ships, money, and supplies as if the cause was their own. Even so the war was long and bitter, and it was ten years before the Moorish kingdom was overcome and Granada itself forced to capitulate.[24] The settlement was deceptively generous: the Moors were allowed to remain in the country with their own religion, laws, and magistrates. On these terms the Catholic Monarchs entered the Alhambra in triumph on 2 January 1492. A new kingdom with 300,000 inhabitants was added to the crown of Castile, and immense prestige and confidence; immense power too, not only from the wealth of the conquered territory and the new security to her southern coastline, but also from the military experience gained and the progress made in infantry techniques. In the mountain warfare of Granada the Spanish infantry was born, and a new general discovered; Europe was soon to be aware of Gonzalo de Córdoba and his troops. But there were liabilities as well as assets. Isabella and her advisers, though not Ferdinand, found it impossible to tolerate Moors, either those in Granada or those who had long lived peacefully in the rest of Spain. For the acquisition of Granada added a new dimension to the problem by increasing the number of Moors in Spain to some 500,000 out of a population of seven million. And there was no perfect solution. From 1502 Isabella initiated in Castile the policy of forced conversion, giving the Moors the alternative of baptism or expulsion. Her successors could do no better.

The logical process of crusade against Islam was to take the war across the narrow sea separating Spain from North Africa; this would also serve Spanish strategic interests by giving additional protection to the southern flank of the peninsula. With her forces freed from the war of Granada Castile was ready to turn reconquest into expansion and challenge Islam in the Mediterranean. But almost before the challenge was made she turned away from North Africa. In 1492 Columbus discovered America; crusading and imperial ideals began to focus on the New World, which was soon recognised as a far more fruitful field of empire. Expansion in Africa and America were not irreconcilable; the search for a way to outflank Islam was one of the impulses behind the early voyages of discovery. But Ferdinand also had interests in Europe, and possessed claims against France as well as

---

[24] A. de la Torre, 'Los Reyes Católicos y Granada', *Hispania*, xv. (1944), 244-307, xvi. (1944) 339-82.

against Islam. Indeed France was the more immediate enemy and pressed Aragon too closely for her comfort. Having exploited the difficulties of Ferdinand's father in Navarre and Catalonia, she took the counties of Roussillon and Cerdagne, the remains of Aragonese possessions in Languedoc, while in Castile Louis XI backed Isabella's enemies. Ferdinand was aware of this pressure and he persuaded Isabella to renounce the traditional Castilian policy of alliance with France and bring her kingdom into line with the anti-French policy of Aragon.

But Ferdinand was no war-monger; he preferred diplomacy. Using the prestige of his position as king of Castile, from as early as 1475 he began to seek allies in key positions surrounding France—in England, the Low Countries, and Germany—developing for the purpose a system of resident ambassadors hitherto unknown outside Italy.[25] Eventually he concerted an active alliance with the emperor Maximilian, sealed by the marriage of his daughter Joanna, with Maximilian's son, the archduke Philip (1496). This was only one of the many marriage alliances in which the Catholic Monarchs ruthlessly traded their children. But it was to prove the most decisive, for it not only gave Spain her future dynasty but began her tragic association with northern and central Europe. This was not apparent in 1496, for although the House of Habsburg brought together the imperial crown of Germany and the duchy of Burgundy in the person of the emperor Maximilian, Joanna was not heir to the kingdoms of the Catholic Monarchs. By 1500, however, death had reduced the ranks of their children, and Joanna was heir apparent. And in the same year her son and heir, Prince Charles, was born, and it was he who was to secure the Habsburg inheritance. Aragonese hostility towards France, therefore, had brought Spain a long way from Granada and the Mediterranean. And Ferdinand was prepared to go even further. To complete the encirclement of France in the north he prepared an alliance with England which resulted in the marriage of his daughter Catherine with the son of Henry VII in 1501. By this time, however, France had begun to break through Ferdinand's diplomatic defences in the south. Having returned the counties of Roussillon and Cerdagne to Aragon, Charles VIII launched his army into Italy to claim the kingdom of Naples in 1494. Again he found himself confronted by Ferdinand. The latter had strengthened his diplomatic representation in Rome and Venice, and now he countered French action by an alliance with Venice, Pope Alexander VI, the Duke of Milan, and the Emperor Maximilian. This he sanctioned with a powerful Spanish army

[25] G. Mattingly, *Renaissance Diplomacy* (London, 1955), pp. 138–52. On the foreign policy of the Catholic Monarchs see also A. de la Torre, *Documentos sobre las relaciones internacionales de los Reyes Católicos* (3 vols., Madrid, 1949–51); J. M. Doussinague, *La política internacional de Fernando el Católico* (Madrid, 1944).

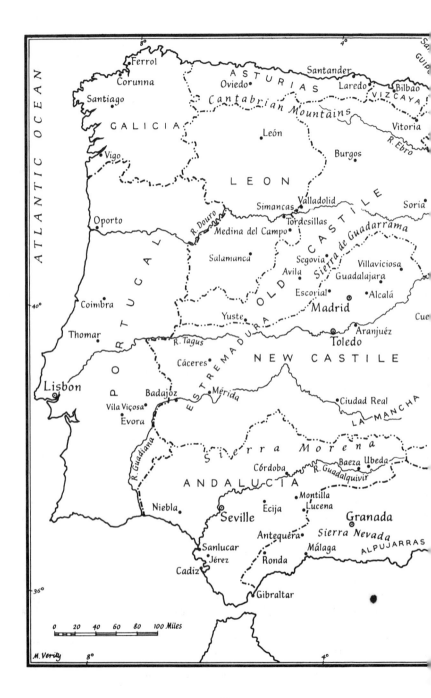

BÉARN

P y r e n e e s

E
plona

RIBAGORZA

ROSELLÓN

Marseilles

Toulon

Urgel

Monzón

CATALONIA

Gerona

Manresa

Zaragoza

Lérida

Cervera

pila

RAGON

Barcelona

Tarragona

Tortosa

VALENCIA

BALEARIC IS.

MINORCA

MALLORCA

Valencia

IBIZA

Alicante

cia

a   Cartagena

SPAIN IN THE SIXTEENTH CENTURY

0   250 Miles

Madrid

Milan   Venice

Turin   Genoa

Marseilles   Nice   Leghorn

Toulon   CORSICA   Rome

SARDINIA   Naples

Palermo   Messina

Gibraltar

Tangier   Ceuta

Gomera

Peñón de Vélez   Melilla

Oran   Algiers

la Goleta

Tunis

MALTA

DJERBA

Tripoli

OTTOMAN

Black Sea

Constantinople

EMPIRE

M e d i t e r r a n e a n   S e a

Patras

Gulf of Lepanto   MOREA

SICILY

RHODES

CRETE

CYPRUS

SPAIN AND THE MEDITERRANEAN

33

commanded by Gonzalo de Córdoba, who brilliantly defeated the French at Cerignola (1503) and Garigliano (1504). So Naples fell not to France but to Spain. The victory was a sign of the times, for it was made possible by the decisive intervention of the Castilian army. This was further proof, if proof were needed, of the power inherent in the union of Castile and Aragon, and the success of their collaboration. The Castilian army was hitherto unknown outside the peninsula; now, after its apprenticeship in the war of Granada and its successful trial in the Italian campaign, it was the most powerful instrument of war in Europe.

With the conquest of Naples Spain was to remain firmly rooted in Italy and in the Mediterranean. Expansion in this direction was traditional for Aragon, whose coasts, trade, and existing possessions (the Balearics, Sardinia, and Sicily) committed her to preserving her power and her communications in the western Mediterranean. And in 1504 Naples was a valuable acquisition, not only strategically but also in revenue and agricultural resources. But possession of Naples not only involved Spain in Italy and thence in a bitter struggle with France; it also took her closer to Islam, almost to the frontier of Christendom, at a time when the expansion of the Ottoman empire had already begun to threaten the security of Italy. So Naples brought new commitments as well as new resources. It also brought new problems of defence. To move eastwards without securing the North African flank was a risky procedure, as it left communications between Spain and Italy exposed to any power which dominated the Barbary coast. Could Spain beat the Turk to North Africa? Or had she neglected her immediate interests in a vital area for too long? Before these questions could be answered the union of her own kingdoms was put to its severest test.

The conquest of Naples coincided with the end of the joint reign of Ferdinand and Isabella. On 26 November 1504 the queen died. She had never admitted the rights of her husband to the crown of Castile. Now, with characteristic stubbornness, she excluded him from the succession. In spite of the fact that their daughter and heir, Joanna, had already shown signs of the mental illness which was to render her permanently unfit to rule, she was declared successor with her husband, Philip of Austria. But even Isabella, for all her Castilian regard for the letter of the law, was not unaware that Ferdinand had thirty years' experience in the government of Castile. There-fore, in the case of Joanna's absence or inability to govern, and until her son Charles came of age to rule, Ferdinand was to be governor and administrator of Castile. In this way Isabella tried to vindicate the Castilian laws of succes-sion, which excluded Ferdinand, and at the same time give Castile the security of his government, rather than that of the alien Philip, should Joanna prove unfit to rule. The results of such folly were only to be expected. Without the title of king, Ferdinand was disarmed. The ambitious Philip was determined to oust him, and a strong party emerged in Castile hostile to 'the old Catalan', who was forced to retire like a fugitive, to be replaced by a foreign prince and his deranged queen. For the moment, thanks to the retrogressive action of Isabella, the ambitions of the Habsburgs, and the separatist attitude of Castile, the two crowns were severed again. Ferdinand had no alternative but to look to his own interests and salvage what he could for Aragon. By the treaty of Blois (1505) he allied himself with France and secured a marriage with Germaine de Foix, niece of the French king, who renounced his rights to Naples; and he threw Castilians, including Gonzalo de Córdoba, out of high office in the Italian kingdom. The risk now was that, should the new marriage yield an heir for the crown of Aragon, the separation of the two kingdoms would be complete.[26] The cause of unity, attacked on all sides, was only saved by a combination of largely fortuitous events—the death of Philip I (September 1506) shortly after the beginning of the new reign, the unequivocal madness of Joanna, and the infertility of Ferdinand's second marriage. The young Charles, heir of Joanna and fruit of Ferdinand's alliance with the Habsburgs, was left as the sole heir of both kingdoms. Meanwhile, to solve the problem of government in Castile Ferdinand was welcomed back by a Council of Regency presided over by Ximénez.

The nine years (1507–16) during which Ferdinand ruled alone were, if anything, more favourable to the cause of unification than those of his joint government with Isabella. Inevitably it was difficult to overcome the traditional lines of demarcation assigned to the respective crowns—an Atlantic policy limited to Castile and a North African policy associated with Aragon and Catalonia. America, where the crown had employed Aragonese as well as Castilian personnel and resources, was still conceived as a Castilian enterprise and a monopoly which it had to preserve for its own subjects. Similarly, in spite of the co-operation of Castile, the conquests in North Africa were regarded as acquisitions of Aragon and Catalonia.

The policy of expansion in North Africa had already begun before the death of Isabella.[27] Melilla had been won in 1497. But other enterprises, notably in Italy, had diverted the monarchs from action in Africa. This was largely Ferdinand's responsibility, though Isabella showed no more sense of urgency than her husband, and the famous dictum attributed to her in her testament—'the future of Spain is in Africa'—is an invention, like many of its kind. But in the years immediately after her death, with the collaboration of Cardinal Ximénez and drawing on the resources of Castile as well as of

---

[26] J. M. Doussinague, *Fernando el Católico y Germana de Foix* (Madrid, 1944).
[27] See P. Prieto y Llovera, *Política aragonesa en África hasta la muerte de Fernando el Católico* (Madrid, 1952).

Aragon, Ferdinand launched a series of expeditions across the Mediterranean. In 1515 Mers-el-Kebir was taken; in 1508 Peñón de la Gómera; the years 1509-11 saw the conquest of Oran, Bugia and Tripoli, and the submission of Algiers. Economically, of course, prospects in North Africa were meagre compared with those in America; Catalonia was assigned free and exclusive commerce with the new outposts and given protection against foreign competition, but the potential wealth which Castile possessed in the New World was far more attractive. This accounts in part for the failure to sustain the effort of expansion southwards. Yet strategically the area was vital for Spain's political and commercial security in the Mediterranean. To this extent her foothold in Africa—a few stations perched precariously on the coast with no penetration into the interior—was dangerously weak, and incapable of containing the combined power of the Turk and the Barbary states, soon to bestride the Mediterranean. Then it would be seen that in this direction, which was a natural and basic one for Spain, her action had been too little and too late.

Backward in the south, Ferdinand displayed greater determination in securing his frontier in the north. When the death of Gaston de Foix opened the succession question in Navarre, he reinforced the claims of his second wife with an army commanded by the Duke of Alba which quickly occupied the kingdom (1512). The acquisition of Navarre, separated from the other Spanish kingdoms since the twelfth century, completed the unification of Spain. After being briefly incorporated in the crown of Aragon (1512-15) it was then assigned to Castile; this was in keeping with Ferdinand's policy of recognising the supremacy of the larger kingdom and a sign perhaps that absolutism was prevailing over regional immunities which might have been nurtured in Navarre through association with the eastern kingdoms. Again, however, Ferdinand saw no reason why he should break traditional institutions; there was a Council of Navarre to attend to the administration of the kingdom, its own cortes continued to function, and its permanent *Diputación*, or committee of estates, operated still. These things were less important in Ferdinand's eyes than Spanish security in the Pyrenees; another blow had been struck at France, and another opportunity for French intervention removed.

The acquisition of Navarre, in fact, was the fruit not only of Ferdinand's military strength but also of his diplomacy. His skilful use of both placed Spain in a powerful position abroad and marked the direction her policy was to take for some time to come. In contemporary alliances he was usually on the winning side, first in the League of Cambrai against Venice (1508) when he redeemed the Adriatic ports of the kingdom of Naples, and then in the Holy League against France (1511-13) when he was interested less in

Italy than in Spain itself and took possession of Navarre. In these years also he sought to maintain the English alliance with his son-in-law Henry VIII, an alliance directed primarily against France and its new king, Francis I, whose expansionist aims in Italy were dangerous to Spanish interests. So Ferdinand left France enclosed within a diplomatic barrier based on Spain, England, Germany, and the Low Countries, and blocked the way southwards to Italy. His successor, Charles I, understood the meaning of this policy and sought to continue it. Charles, in fact, was to inherit not only the political unity preserved by Ferdinand but also the principles of foreign policy which he had elaborated with such success. To this extent the substance of his rule had already been prepared.

Ferdinand died on 23 January 1516. Almost immediately the anarchic instincts of the aristocracy and the towns, so laboriously repressed by the Catholic Monarchs, began to stir again. But the redoubtable Ximénez, whom Ferdinand had appointed Regent, saw Spain safely through the critical months that followed, suppressing incipient disorder, preserving the royal power intact, and transmitting to Charles his Spanish inheritance as it had been left by the Catholic Monarchs. The inheritance, like their reign, was complex. In retrospect the policy of Ferdinand and Isabella was a strange mixture of purpose and diffidence. They did not lead Spain in an undeviating line from feudal anarchy to nation state, nor was their political system a monolithic one. The monarchy they restored was far from centralised and still not absolute. The enterprise of their actions abroad, especially beyond the Atlantic, contrasted starkly with their cautious approach to domestic problems. The Spain they left to their successors abounded still in political and social anomalies, barriers deeply embedded between the constituent kingdoms, and even more rigid divisions between the different classes within each country. They had done no more, in fact, than provide the minimum conditions of order and unity. But in doing this they had solved the problems of state-building sooner than most of their contemporaries in western Europe. In the revival of royal power, in the development of instruments of government, in the creation of a powerful military machine, in the reform of the church, all of which were accomplished or initiated within a single generation, Spain had a tremendous start on any of her rivals. All these efforts, however, had been geared to the immediate demands of power, and in the interests of power some dangerous short-cuts had been taken. In particular, social and economic welfare had been ruthlessly sacrificed to political strength. Yet, in spite of this, a feeling of national euphoria and a sense of boundless optimism filled the Spain of the Catholic Monarchs. How would this spirit respond to the inexperienced rule of an alien prince?

CHAPTER II

CHARLES I OF SPAIN

1. THE BURGUNDIAN PRINCE

O N 18 September 1517, when the fleet of forty ships bringing the young Charles and his Burgundian court to Spain anchored off the coast of Asturias, the local inhabitants fled to the hills armed with staves and knives and only returned when their scouts reported the arrival not of an enemy but of their king. The incident was a strange sign of the reception that awaited Charles in his new kingdom, and as the royal party struggled across the rain-swept mountains of northern Spain towards Valladolid, the seventeen-year-old monarch, already sickened by the journey, had time to reflect on the dourness of the country and the suspicion of its people.

By a combination of dynastic marriages and premature deaths, Charles was destined to be the ruler of a world empire, but in 1517 his succession to the heart of that empire looked far from secure. From his father Philip of Burgundy, whom he had lost at the age of six, he had already inherited the first of his many dominions, the Low Countries. This included not only Luxembourg, Brabant, Flanders, Holland, Zeeland, Hainault, and Artois, but also Franche-Comté and a claim to the Duchy of Burgundy itself which had reverted to the crown of France. In January 1515 the young prince, whose Habsburg blood was already apparent in his hanging jaw and gaping look, was proclaimed ruler in the Netherlands. Within a year his maternal grandfather, Ferdinand of Aragon, was dead: as son of Queen Joanna, whose madness rendered her incompetent to rule, Charles could now claim the throne of Castile and its possessions in America, while from Ferdinand himself he inherited the crown of Aragon-Catalonia which included Sicily, Sardinia, Naples and some outposts in North Africa. As grandson of the emperor Maximilian, he was also heir presumptive to the Habsburg estates of Austria, Tyrol, and parts of southern Germany, and these he received on Maximilian's death in January 1519. 'God has set you on the path towards a world monarchy' his grand chancellor Gattinara told him in 1519, and given the extent of the dominions united under the sovereignty of Charles I of Spain, now elected the Emperor Charles V of Germany, the words seemed only appropriate.

In spite of the future imperial preoccupations of Charles V, however, the two most dominating features of his reign were his Burgundian origins and his Spanish inheritance.[1] And of all the countries he inherited, Spain proved the most difficult to claim. Born in Ghent (24 February 1500), Charles was a stranger to Spain and spoke no Spanish. There were few Spaniards among his household in Brussels. His education, in which he absorbed a mixture of chivalry, piety, and concern for his dynasty, had been a Burgundian one, and his apprenticeship in the art of government had been directed by the Burgundian nobleman, Guillaume de Croy, Lord of Chièvres, who even slept in the same room as his shy and solemn charge. Yet there was more to Charles's foreignness than language and upbringing. Already during 1516 when the young king lingered in the Netherlands while the Regent Ximénez de Cisneros was trying to extract him from the hands of Flemings and bring him to Spain in order to govern there, important Spanish offices were being granted or sold to Flemings in the king's following, and Spanish money was going to Brussels to finance the Burgundian court. There were other reasons for the Regent's anxiety. In the absence of a sovereign's hand, the Castilian nobility was restless, the towns were ready to take up arms in defence of their privileges, and there was no source of patronage with which to placate important interests and bind a following to the new king's cause. Indeed there were many in Spain who preferred Charles's younger brother, the Infante Ferdinand, who had been brought up in Spain and was popular there. The Council of Castile itself had strongly opposed the idea that Charles should take the title of king during his mother's lifetime and had yielded only because it could do little about it.

2. OPPOSITION: CORTES AND COMUNEROS

By the summer of 1517 when Chièvres, having secured relations with France and England, decided that it was time to undertake the journey to Spain, it was clear that the Burgundians had won the struggle for control of the king. After Charles's arrival in Spain this was apparent from his curt and ungrateful dismissal of Ximénez in a dispatch which the aged cardinal never lived to read. It could also be seen in the way Burgundians continued

[1] No modern account of Charles V does justice to his rule in Spain, but the outstanding work on his reign as a whole is that of K. Brandi, *The Emperor Charles V* (Eng. trans., London, 1939). Brandi was primarily interested in German problems and his account of Spanish history of the period does not supersede the careful researches of R. B. Merriman, *The Rise of the Spanish Empire in the Old World and the New*, vol. iii. *The Emperor*. For a more recent account see R. Tyler, *The Emperor Charles the Fifth* (London, 1956). A masterly survey of Charles's empire is provided by H. Koenigsberger, 'The Empire of Charles V in Europe', *New Cambridge Modern History*, ii. (Cambridge, 1958), pp. 301–33.

to receive the most valuable favours and to be retained as the principal counsellors of the silent and impassive boy whom it was impossible to approach except through Chièvres. Castilians were kept at a distance from their king and were forced to watch offices and sinecures invaded by new-comers and the national wealth plundered by foreigners who neither under-stood nor cared for the problems of Spain. Naturally they reacted. At the first meeting of the Castilian cortes in Valladolid (February 1518), the very presidency of which the king had given to a Walloon, Jean de Sauvage, indignant protests were voiced. Led by Juan de Zumel, the representative of Burgos, the cortes rejected the presence of foreigners in their deliberations. In spite of threats Zumel persisted in his resistance in the following sessions: the king was requested to respect the laws of Castile, to remove foreigners from his service and to learn and speak Spanish. Charles did indeed swear to respect the laws of Castile, but in so far as the cortes, lacking any means of constitutional resistance, granted him a subsidy of 600,000 ducats for three years without conditions, this was yet another victory for the Burgundian party.

When Charles presented himself in Aragon in the spring of 1518 the pressures on him were more complex. The Aragonese cortes were even less anxious than those of Castile to give formal recognition of the king during his mother's lifetime. Moreover, there were still separatists in Aragon, those who looked back to the times before the union with Castile, and who saw in the Infante Ferdinand an answer to their hopes. Charles had already sent his too-popular brother out of the country to the Netherlands, but now he was requested by the cortes that at the same time as they swore to Charles as king they should swear to his brother as prince-heir. Such a suggestion outraged the Castilians accompanying Charles and caused some minor dis-turbances between them and Aragonese in Zaragoza. And it was January 1519 before the cortes of Aragon recognised Charles as king, conjointly with his mother, and voted him a grant of 200,000 ducats.

In Catalonia the issues between Charles and his new subjects involved even longer and more obstinate negotiations. Here, too, there were objections to his Flemish advisers and the inevitable quarrels over procedure and money. Moreover, the Catalan cortes were a more effective instrument for resisting royal power than those of Castile, and with their right of dissent and their established procedure they could be much more difficult about money and legislation. Charles had to spend a year in Barcelona and he was there when news arrived that he had been elected Emperor on 28 June 1519.

Charles's determination to secure the imperial title arose partly from the fear of its falling to Francis I of France who, with power in Germany as well as in France, would be able to threaten not only Charles's Burgundian inheritance but also his Habsburg dominions. He was also possibly aware of his own need of the title because of the variety of his possessions which he ruled with a diversity of titles; the office of emperor would provide at least a symbol of unity. Above all, however, he believed that the imperial title was his of right, to crown the kingdoms of the most powerful ruler in Christendom, the very extent of whose dominions rendered him the one most qualified for it. Charles had to spend one million gold florins on this election in order to give the electors financial as well as political reasons for electing him, and the entire operation left him in debt to the Fuggers for half-a-million florins. But it was Chièvres, and not a Spaniard, who had negotiated his election, and if some Spaniards realised the possibilities of the empire of Charles V it was by no means certain that it pleased or impressed the majority of his Spanish subjects. What they wanted was a Spanish king of their own, not a share in a foreign emperor. Consequently, although there were signs that the Burgundian régime might be a transitory one— especially after the death of the rapacious Sauvage in June 1518 and his replacement as grand chancellor by the Piedmontese Mercurino Gattinara, humanist and Erasmist, and himself a passionate advocate of the imperial idea—there was now added a greater and more permanent cause of resentment.

This was felt above all in Castile, where hostility to the new sovereign, his ministers and his policy took the form of a collective opposition based on the towns and led by Toledo. In order to prepare to take up the imperial crown by raising money and embarking for the Netherlands, Charles returned from Barcelona to Castile and summoned the cortes to meet at Santiago in March 1520. Representatives of Toledo did not appear at this cortes and the other towns tried to bind their deputies with precise instructions: the court, on the other hand, wished them to have a free—and an open—hand. The cortes in fact refused to grant the subsidy requested by the king and against all constitutional precedent they insisted on the discussion of grievances before the granting of supply. Thereupon the cortes were prorogued to La Coruña, and it was there that Charles presented the case in which later historians have seen the germ of his imperial programme. Dr. La Mota, bishop of Badajoz, one of the few Spanish followers of Charles from his Brussels days, lectured the cortes: 'Now is returned the ancient glory of Spain . . . By God's grace our Spanish King is made King of the Romans and Emperor of the World.'[2] It was argued that Charles had accepted the imperial crown in order to undertake the defence of the Catholic Faith against its infidel enemies, and that Spain would always remain his base and

---

[2] *Cortes de los antiguos reinos de León y Castilla* (5 vols., Madrid, 1861–1903), ii. 293.

the source of his strength.[3] This looked more a desperate attempt to gain money by flattery than the submission of a considered imperial programme. On either score, however, it failed to impress the cortes, and even when a majority of the deputies had been bribed into approving the subsidy, it was against the opposition of the representatives of six towns and the abstention of all but eight out of the total of eighteen. The money itself was never collected and mobs attacked the houses of deputies who had voted for it. Moreover, the poor impression that Charles had initially made on Spaniards was now worsened.

When Charles left Spain in May 1520, surrounded by foreigners and on a mission that his Spanish subjects regarded as essentially alien, agitation had already broken out into rebellion. An accumulation of grievances against the Burgundian régime had produced the first sense of outrage: the poor impression made by the king and his foreign agents, Chièvres' contempt for Spaniards, his venal monopoly of patronage, the appointment of foreigners to Spanish offices and bishoprics, the oppression of tax-collectors, the great quantities of money taken out of the kingdom, and to crown all, the appointment of a foreign regent, Adrian of Utrecht, to govern Castile in the king's absence.[4] The climax came when Charles committed himself to an imperial idea that had little place in the traditions of Spain and found little response there.[5] The gentry and townsmen of Castile then revolted against a régime which they regarded as inimical to their interests, and which threatened to sacrifice Castile to an imperial or dynastic policy. But this was not simply a political movement. The revolt of the *comuneros* was a revolution; it occurred in a region deeply divided by opposing interests and within a society already in conflict with itself.[6]

Manufacturing industry of the artisan kind had long been established in Castile, and textiles took the lead. But the textile industry was stagnant at the

---

[3] See B. Chudoba, *Spain and the Empire 1519–1653* (Chicago, 1952), p. 20, who, however, in describing Charles's declaration to the cortes as 'the real programme of a statesman', probably exaggerates its significance.

[4] These grievances and the discontent they engendered were not confined to scholars and learned counsellors of the time as suggested by Brandi, *op. cit.*, p. 84, but were widespread and deeply felt.

[5] On the other hand see the thesis argued by R. Menéndez Pidal, *Idea imperial de Carlos V* (Madrid, 1945), who claims Charles as a very Spanish figure and bases his policy, though unconvincingly, in Spanish tradition. On the opposition of Spanish political theorists, including Francisco de Vitoria, to the imperial idea, see J. A. Maravall, *Carlos V y el pensamiento político del renacimiento* (Madrid, 1960), pp. 235–68.

[6] See the authoritative account of the subject by Joseph Perez, *La revolución de las Comunidades de Castilla (1520–1521)* (Madrid, 1977), amply seconded in its conclusions by Juan Ignacio Gutiérrez Nieto, *Las Comunidades como movimiento antiseñorial* (Barcelona, 1973).

beginning of the sixteenth century, starved of capital and short of skilled labour, deprived of protection and unable to compete with better quality foreign goods. Industry took second place to more powerful interests. The production and export of raw wool simultaneously satisfied the aristocracy whose estates produced it, the merchants who exported it, the crown who taxed it, and the foreign businessmen who bought it. The greater part of wool production thus went abroad and domestic manufacturers were too weak to compete for it or to challenge the coalition of interests which made Castile an exporter of raw materials and thwarted the development of a national textile industry. As their position worsened, manufacturers looked in vain to the crown; neither Isabella nor Charles V was inclined to assist them. Wool exports from Burgos-Bilbao flourished, as did the Indies trade of Seville, while the interior of Castile was increasingly marginalised. This was the area of the *comuneros* and these were the interests in conflict, manufacturers against wool exporters, the centre against the periphery, Segovia, which supported the revolt, against Burgos, which soon abandoned it.

The *comuneros* were members of the middle ranks of society, in revolt against the landed aristocracy and their allies. Yet it was not a simple struggle of commoners against nobles, nor a mere protest against an unpopular régime and its servants. Rather it revealed the underlying divisions in Castilian society which came to the surface after the reign of the Catholic Monarchs. While Ferdinand and Isabella distrusted the higher aristocracy and sought to curb them, they favoured and promoted the lower nobility, the *caballeros* and *hidalgos*, who came to occupy an important role in the administration, the army and local government. But many of these were rejected by the new monarch in 1517 and, in a mood of resentment, some of them joined the *comuneros*. They were not a middle class; whether they were rural *hidalgos* or urban *letrados*, they considered themselves true nobles or, like the great merchants and bankers, they aspired to nobility. On the other hand the *comuneros* included smaller merchants and manufacturers, and these did constitute an incipient middle class, though they were few in numbers in the polarised society of Castile. The succession crisis following the death of Isabella and the long vacuum of royal power in 1504–17 enabled the aristocracy of Castile to improve their fortunes and make a bid for power at the expense of the weakened state. At the same time the more vulnerable economic interests tried to improve their position, the merchants of the interior cities against the monopoly *consulado* of Burgos and the foreign merchants, the industrialists against the exporters, national manufacturers against the exporters of raw wool. During the regency of the king of Aragon Castilian textile producers received some favours against foreign importers and excessive export of raw wool, a policy continued by Cardinal Cisneros.

This was a new stage in the balance of economic power, the first protest of the central zone of Castile against the privileged periphery. The next stage was more violent.

The revolt of the *comuneros* was led by Toledo which had already, before Charles left Spain on 20 May 1520, expelled its *corregidor* and established a *comunidad*, or commune. In the course of June the revolt spread to most of the cities of Old Castile where one by one they expelled royal officials and tax-collectors and proclaimed a *comunidad*. These were spontaneous popular revolts, though the urban patriciate also participated and at Zamora the movement was headed by a fighting bishop, Antonio de Acuña. Toledo took the initiative in extending the political base of the movement and in the course of July convoked a meeting of four cities in Avila; from this emerged a revolutionary junta which drove the regent Adrian from Valladolid and set up a rival government. In September 1520 it reached the peak of its power; with a cause, an organisation and an army, it no longer requested reforms but sought to impose conditions on the king. At this point divisions opened between revolutionaries and reformers. The junta maintained that the kingdom stood above the king and that the junta represented the kingdom; it thereby alienated the moderates in Burgos and Valladolid, who were also subject to considerable pressure from the royal authorities and the higher nobility. As the junta began to claim all the powers of the state, the moderates moved away, and the royal forces moved in. With the help of the aristocracy and timely remittances from Portugal, on 5 December they took Tordesillas, the headquarters of the junta. But the *comuneros* were not yet defeated. Now their revolution was not simply a political movement but a social one; it was more than a conflict between the cities and royal power, it was a confrontation with the higher nobility and the big merchants. Charles V had been shrewd enough to associate the Admiral of Castile, Fadrique Enríquez, and the Constable, Iñigo de Velasco, with Adrian of Utrecht as co-governors of the country, and through them to associate the Castilian magnates with the royal cause. In the field the *comuneros* were no match for the royal army and the forces of the nobility, and they were defeated at the battle of Villalar on 24 April 1521. On the following day the leaders of the revolt, Juan de Padilla, Juan Bravo, and Pedro Maldonado, representatives respectively of Toledo, Segovia and Salamanca, were executed. As for the aristocracy, they now began to claim their rewards and pensions; but their presence at Villalar was not merely a service, it was a defence of their own interests. Toledo held out for another six months, with forces commanded by the last rebel chief, Bishop Acuña, who was welcomed by the whole town with shouts of 'Comunidad! Comunidad! Acuña! Acuña!'. The Admiral of Castile described this as the support of the Jews and the populace, using the two worst insults he could think of. But Acuña only lasted a month; he was captured and imprisoned in the castle of Simancas, on the battlements of which he was eventually garrotted after a violent attempt to escape. In October 1821 Toledo too had to capitulate.

By this time the social base of the *comuneros* had emerged more clearly. The rank and file came from the urban popular sectors, taking action against the traditional oligarchy of the towns; this was commons versus patricians. But the urban nobles were only part of the nobility. The grandees and the higher aristocracy also took action against the *comuneros*, on behalf of law and order and to restore their own power where that had been eroded. They were not closely concerned with the rights of Charles V, whom they did not admire, and as long as the *comuneros* confined themselves to challenging royal power most of the nobles were indifferent. But there developed alongside the political wing of the *comuneros* a radical anti-seigneurial movement which challenged the feudal power of the nobility. This was a revolution from below, a rising of the nobles' vassals. A group of great lords began to arm themselves in defence of seigneurial rights. This forced the *comunero* leaders to harden their attitude and take to arms. The movement then assumed the character of a social revolution, in which the *comuneros* fought not only against royal power but against aristocratic privilege and supremacy. In places it was a war without quarter; castles were destroyed, property sacked, and urban forces received enthusiastic support from the rural people as they struggled to free themselves from feudal burdens. Thus the grandees fought not only to serve the king but to defend their seigneurial jurisdiction.

Meanwhile, the middle sectors of the towns—small property owners, artisans, retail traders, university graduates—remained at the heart of the *comunero* movement and supplied its leadership. They were not poor; some of them had land, others professions, and they did not identify easily with the underprivileged. But nor were they rich, and they had little in common with the wealthy export merchants, allies of the nobility against the *comuneros*. So the middle sectors were not a homogeneous social class, an urban bourgeoisie, and while the *comuneros* had a social base they did not have a class base. It was a struggle between different sectorial interests, and each side constituted a coalition of groups or a political alliance. The programme of the *comuneros* offered something for most of its supporters—limitation of royal power, curbs on the aristocracy, reduction of taxes, restraints on government spending and corruption, and reform of the municipalities in order to give greater participation to the non-privileged sectors, the *comunidad*. They also demanded a reduction of the export of raw wool in favour of domestic purchasers, and protection for the Castilian textile industry. Here spoke the manufacturers and artisans of Segovia, Palencia, Cuenca and other cities of the interior, against all those who profited from the export of raw wool, the sheep farmers, the noble owners of sheep land, the merchants of Burgos and foreign businessmen. In 1520 royal power aligned itself unequivocally with this coalition of dominant interests, mindful that the customs duty derived from these exports was an important part of its revenue and that the crown's Flemish subjects wanted Spanish wool and access to Spanish markets. But, if in crushing the *comuneros*, Charles V received the collaboration of the grandees and nobles, he did not subsequently satisfy their ambitions or give them the power they wanted. It was a victory of the aristocracy over the townsmen, but the prize was taken by the king.

Meanwhile Charles V had another revolt on his hands. But whereas the *comuneros* had an organisation, leaders and ideas, the risings of the *Germanías*, or Christian brotherhoods, of Valencia and Mallorca in 1519 were spontaneous social protests making instant demands which never really developed into a political programme.[7] There was no influence from one movement to the other; the *Germanías* did not co-operate with the *comuneros* and their revolt had a different origin. The movement in Valencia began as a protest against city officials and aristocrats, and violence then spilled over into open war against the Muslims, who in turn supported their lords against the brotherhoods. The leaders of the revolt saw the advantage of invoking a religious justification for their action and giving it a more general appeal than it originally possessed. For social tensions in Valencia were not simple class conflicts, and this was not a homogeneous rebellion. It included artisans fighting for survival and perhaps for protection, peasants oppressed by feudal burdens, a few middle-sector representatives with political awareness, some lower clergy, all of these united only in their experience of poor living conditions and seigneurial abuses and also perhaps in their hatred of Muslims, whom they were only too ready to attack, plunder and convert.

In 1519 the gilds of Valencia had been armed to oppose a threatened attack by Turkish pirates. At the same time an outbreak of plague emptied the city of much of the nobility, including the governor himself. The emperor too was an absentee ruler, repeatedly postponing the meeting of the cortes of Valencia. In these circumstances, the people took the opportunity to strike at an oppressive nobility and unpopular officials. They demanded representation in municipal government, which they still did not have,

---

[7] See L. Piles Ros, 'Aspectos sociales de la Germanía de Valencia', *Estudios de historia social de Espana*, ii. (1952), 431–78, and the modern study by Ricardo García Cárcel, *Las Germanías de Valencia* (Barcelona, 1975), pp. 20–40, 62–88, 164–87.

and justice before the emperor, which was denied them by their local overlords. The early leader of the *Germanía*, Juan Llorenz, a weaver, wanted to give Valencia a republican constitution like that of Genoa and Venice. After his death, however, lesser men led the movement into violence and atrocities without a clear programme. The insurgents soon controlled the capital of Valencia, with the support of almost all the gilds, and from there they directed a rising in the rest of the kingdom of Valencia, launching armies against the viceroy and nobles, forcing the Moors to be baptised, suppressing all taxes and threatening to intervene in the distribution of property. At this point the rebellion lost some of the middle-class support from which it had drawn much of its strength and many of its leaders. This enabled the viceroy, Diego Hurtado de Mendoza, and his aristocratic supporters to retrieve the situation and destroy the forces of the *Germanía* in October 1521. The royal victory was inevitably followed by a bitter repression in which more than eight hundred rebels were sentenced—mostly to fines and confiscations—for the 'crime of *germanía* and popular union'. But it was not until December 1524 that all resistance outside the capital was overcome and a new viceroy, Germaine de Foix, published a pardon.

Although the *Germanía* of Valencia eventually clashed with royal power, it had begun as a protest against the power of the landed aristocracy and against their Moorish tenants and labourers. It also received much middle-class support and the co-operation of almost all the gilds. The movement lacked a distinct social base. It was a heterogeneous alliance of protesting groups, poor craftsmen and artisans, small farmers and labourers, lower clergy and a few merchants; it was a rising of primitive rebels; it was a peasant protest against subsistence shortage, seigneurial jurisdiction and competition from morisco labour; it was a criticism of the local administration and an attack on taxes; and it displayed a few symptoms of real revolution and opposition to existing structures. It was also indirectly a movement of resistance to the crown: the aristocracy and the higher clergy, knowing where their interests lay, gave their unanimous support to Charles V, and for this reason the suppression of the movement was yet another victory for absolutism.

3. THE SUBJECTION OF CASTILE

The risings in eastern Spain did not bring royal retribution on the institutions of those kingdoms and they managed to preserve their older rights and privileges even in the new world of the Habsburgs. Their *fueros*, or regional prerogatives, were based firmly in their cortes. The General Cortes of the realms of the crown of Aragon met six times in the reign of Charles V, as opposed to the individual cortes of each component part, Aragon, Catalonia, and Valencia, which rarely met. The former were general only in name, in that they were all held for the sake of convenience in Monzón, but even there the cortes of each of the three countries sat separately and the emperor had in effect to deal with three different bodies. Moreover, the rights of procedure, taxation, and legislation enjoyed by each of these cortes continued to restrain absolute sovereignty.[8] They were always reluctant to vote the emperor large sums of money and when a subsidy was granted one-third of the amount voted was almost invariably set aside for internal purposes and therefore left in the hands of the cortes. For this reason there existed in Aragon and Catalonia standing committees of the estates, which remained in session during intervals between cortes in order to control the administration of the revenue voted and watch over the observance of laws. Yet the influence of the cortes did not stop there. In Aragon they also exercised a large measure of control over that characteristic Aragonese institution, the office of *Justicia*, which although it was declining in prestige and in authority, was potentially one of the greatest obstacles to the exercise of sovereignty in Aragon. The *Justicia* existed to protect subjects against public and private injustice and could even intervene in trials if they were considered contrary to the *fueros* of Aragon. He was a mixture of a chief justice and a judge of appeal, whose peculiar position often made him look like an arbiter between crown and subjects, and to whom all Aragonese had the right of appeal.

It would be a mistake to regard the institutions of Aragon and Catalonia as popular or democratic ones. Many of the privileges they were defending were the monopoly of a nobility who still commanded considerable seigneurial jurisdiction and whose feudal rights survived longer than those of most nobilities in western Europe. The rising of the *Germanías* of Valencia had drawn attention to aristocratic control of local institutions. Moreover, as has been seen, if these institutions were able to defend the eastern kingdoms against abuse of royal power, it was largely because the crown had little material inducement to challenge them. From Aragon and Catalonia Charles V received the revenues of the royal patrimony and the grants voted by the cortes. The latter were careful to prevent the introduction of new taxes, it is true, but Charles was never likely to force the issue, for there was little wealth to be taxed, and certainly not enough to justify provoking a crisis. Aragon was a relatively poor country, and the commercial prosperity of Catalonia had declined with the loss of its influence in the Mediterranean and the expansion of Turkish power there.[9] The immunity of the eastern kingdoms, therefore, survived less because of their constitutional strength

[8] See above, pp. 9–10.   [9] See below, pp. 148–49.

than because of their economic weakness. Protective institutions carry little significance when there is little for them to protect. Like his predecessors, Charles V had greater resources elsewhere, especially in Castile, a very powerful reason why it was Castile that was converted into the base of his empire, or, to use the words of Bishop Mota to the unresponsive cortes of 1520, into 'its treasury and its sword', and why it was the institutions of Castile that received the emperor's closest attention. When there was wealth at stake the crown acted decisively.

The defeat of Villalar left Castile even more exposed to absolutism than it had been before. The *comuneros* had been concerned not only with objectives but also with means; the revolt was not only a protest against Spain's involvement in the European and imperial policies of Charles V, it was also an attempt, no matter how vague or rudimentary, to defend the interests of Castile by imposing constitutional checks on royal power. These were now brushed aside and from this moment Castile lay completely at the mercy of its sovereign. Municipal government was already incapable of exercising independent authority. Local elections were far from democratic, but even the elected officers of the towns had little power when face to face with the *corregidores*, those judicial officers who since the reign of the Catholic Monarchs had also been invested with administrative powers and sent to every town in Castile where they acted in effect as royal governors and controlled every aspect of municipal administration. Owing to a decline in the standards of selection, the *corregidores* were now even less popular than they had been in the previous reign and there were growing complaints that the nominees of Charles V were not university-trained jurists but ignorant favourites unable to perform their judicial functions, yet another sign that the crown now viewed them primarily as political agents through whom its authority could reach the mass of the people.

Towns browbeaten by royal *corregidores* and their ally the aristocracy could hardly be expected to send independent representatives to a national cortes. And the cortes of Castile itself were in no position to fulfil a popular function. Although they were divided into three estates—nobles, clergy, and commons—the cortes normally consisted only of the third estate, or more specifically the thirty-six representatives of eighteen towns, as the first two classes were exempt from taxation in terms of their medieval functions, military and spiritual.[10] And as the towns themselves were usually represented by *hidalgos* whose salaries were met from the taxes they voted

---

[10] *Hidalgos* in Castile were numerous. In the figures for the allocation of the subsidy of 1541 *hidalgos* (exempt) were numbered as 108,358, and *pecheros* (taxpayers) as 784,578. As these figures were for householders, the total might be 540,000 *hidalgos* and 3,923,000 commoners.

but did not have to pay, there was no one to defend their interests against royal demands. Moreover, the principle of redress of grievances before supply of money had never been effectively established in Castile. By the time of Charles V, therefore, the cortes found they had little power to do anything about his demands short of revolt. When the revolt failed at Villalar the immediate consequence of defeat was a further subjection to the sovereign, a further injunction not to withhold funds from the king or try to control their expenditure, and a further refusal to accept deputies with limiting instructions.

When he returned to Spain in 1522 the expenses incurred in his imperial journey and in the revolt of Castile caused Charles to summon a cortes at Valladolid in July 1523 in order to vote another subsidy. On this occasion the cortes made a last attempt to discuss government *before* granting supply, not on the grounds that this was their traditional right but with the naïve argument that Charles himself could authorise the innovation. Not surprisingly Charles refused: 'Yesterday I asked you for funds; today I want your advice.' He then made it clear that this was the order of business he intended to retain.[11] In this way the cortes were reduced to a tax-voting body which the crown of its own grace allowed to present petitions. Altogether the cortes of Castile were called fifteen times in the reign of Charles V, usually as soon as he returned to Spain from his foreign enterprises in search of more money. And although they usually haggled about details and might object to extraordinary demands, they invariably voted Charles the huge subsidies he demanded, as they did in 1523. Their function was only to vote taxes, as they themselves recognised in 1544 when they requested not to be summoned more than once every three years 'on account of the great costs and expense'. Even their right to petition for the enactment of legislation amounted to little, for the king was not obliged to accept their requests much less put them into effect.

Indeed the only resistance that Charles encountered in the cortes of Castile came from the nobility. In 1538 after the debts incurred in his German, North African, and French campaigns, the budget revealed that prospective revenue for the next four years would not even meet the ordinary expenses of government, much less the campaign planned against the Turk. With no new sources of income, the emperor decided to ask his Castilian subjects to impose yet another tax, the *sisa*, or tax on foodstuffs. In September he summoned a cortes in Toledo, to include all three estates on the ground that the contribution was to be a common effort to meet a common danger. The nobility had already refused to be taxed in 1527 on the occasion of the

---

[11] Merriman, *op. cit.*, iii. 125.

campaign against the Turk in eastern Europe. Then, as now, Charles made it clear that the occasion was unusual. Once again he met with opposition from the nobility who voted that they could not approve the *sisa*, as it was an infringement of their traditional privilege of freedom from taxation; to meet the financial situation the emperor should make peace with France, stay in Spain and cut down his personal spending. The other two estates were more amenable, but from the nobility Charles got nothing, and after this irritating defeat he had to be content with benevolences from his richer subjects in return for *juros*, or bonds settled on future revenues at high interest. He never again attempted to win their approval of his policies or summon them to a cortes. For their part, conscious of their financial immunity, the nobles had no reason to oppose his expensive enterprises, and consequently their concern for peace and limited objectives was confined to occasions when their own pockets were affected; indeed, by joining the growing body of state creditors they might even expect financial gains from an imperial policy which had already enhanced their military prospects. This meant that the burden of empire was largely confined not only to Castile but to the commons of Castile. To this extent Charles V could rule in Spain in alliance with a privileged class which gave him its allegiance as long as its privileges were immune. He followed in effect a policy of divide and rule. But how was that rule imposed?

4. HABSBURG MONARCHY AND ITS AGENTS

After the revolt of the *comuneros*, Charles had returned to Spain in 1522 and he spent the next seven years there. In this time he became a Spanish king and laid the foundations of his government. As he steadily grew in stature as a man and a monarch so he began to learn from past mistakes. In 1529, discussing the convenience of going to Italy for his imperial coronation, he remarked with disarming candour that there was much less chance of a rising now than when he had left for the Netherlands in 1520, 'for then I was managed and governed by M. de Chièvres, and I was not old enough to know these kingdoms or experienced enough to govern them. And as I left immediately for Flanders, having spent very little time here, and what is more, being still unmarried and without an heir, it is not surprising that there was scandal and disturbance'.[12] Since that time, however, Charles had made a real effort of adaptation. The language of the monarch and his court became Spanish. His marriage in 1526 to his cousin, Isabella, sister of the

---

[12] In J. Sánchez Montes, 'Actitudes del español en la época de Carlos V', *Estudios Americanos*, iii. (1951), 193.

king of Portugal, was pleasing to his Spanish subjects, and on 21 May 1527 the empress bore him a son, the future Philip II. Spaniards came to appreciate the human qualities of their king and to recognise the growing authority with which he spoke and acted. And even when they disapproved of his preoccupations with wider interests than their own, they sympathised with him for the enormous burden that he carried. Indeed from some of his subjects he received not only loyalty but gratitude. For he had begun to compromise over foreign advisers, and gradually Spaniards, who had begun as a minority in his service, came to monopolise the fruits of office not only in Spain but also in the constituent parts of his empire.

Yet although Spain was part of a larger empire, it was governed by a Spanish and not by an imperial organisation. Charles V's empire, or *monarquía* as contemporaries called it, united a number of countries under the rule of one person who was king of many kingdoms rather than emperor of the whole. As the great Spanish jurist, Juan de Solórzano later put it, 'the kingdoms have to be ruled and governed as if the king who keeps them together were only the king of each of them'.[13] Each component part of his empire had a separate administration as well as its own laws, institutions and taxation, and no part was constitutionally subordinate to another. This federal structure was not embraced by any imperial administration. It is true that Gattinara had visions of an imperial system of government and he himself, as Burgundian grand chancellor, exercised an authority for all of Charles's dominions; but this development came to nothing. Equally, Charles's Council of State, which contained a mixed membership of Italians, Spaniards, and Burgundians, and had an advisory function in imperial affairs, was too ineffective to constitute a common policy-making body. Indeed, without a comprehensive financial policy and organisation, in which each state could give and receive its allotted quota of revenue and expenditure, there could be no imperial government. After Gattinara's death and the abolition of the office of grand chancellor, the only unity in Charles V's empire was provided by the person of the emperor himself and stemmed from his exclusive responsibility for policy and decisions.

Charles ruled his domains as head of a dynastic organisation. He was represented in each state by a regent or a viceroy, sometimes a member of the Habsburg family, as in Spain when he was absent, sometimes chosen from the Spanish nobility, as in Italy. Charles had viceroys in each country of the monarchy—Aragon, Catalonia, Valencia, Sicily, Naples, Sardinia, and Navarre, as well as in Peru and New Spain. In the Netherlands he was

---

[13] See the introduction by J. M. Batista i Roca in H. G. Koenigsberger, *The Government of Sicily under Philip II of Spain* (London, 1951), pp. 9–35.

represented by a governor general, first by his aunt, Margaret of Austria (1518–30), then by his sister, Mary of Hungary (1531–55). Germany was also delegated to a Habsburg, his brother Ferdinand.

Even in Spain itself there was no formal unity and no single institution by which he could impose his rule. Charles was king of Castile and king of Aragon rather than king of Spain, and he did not have the same power in Aragon as he did in Castile. What unity there was came from the *de facto* hegemony of Castile, which was the main source of his wealth and his troops, and from the activities of the Inquisition, whose jurisdiction applied to the whole of Spain regardless of legal frontiers. In Spain, as elsewhere, Charles V's method of government was personal monarchy exercised through centralised but not unified institutions, and the chosen instrument of Habsburg monarchy was the royal council which Charles had inherited from Ferdinand and Isabella. The Catholic Monarchs had reorganised conciliar government by restricting membership and by introducing bureaucracy and specialisation, which had produced specialised councils for different functions of government. These reforms were carried even further by Charles V, so that conciliar government, or administration by committees, became the characteristic feature of Habsburg monarchy. These councils were not assemblies of noble advisers, as they had been originally, but were bureaucratic committees, staffed largely by jurists, for the administration of royal policy.

There were two main types of council. First, there was the Council of State, an honorific and formal body, consisting of grandees and officials, which theoretically existed to advise the monarch on high matters of state policy. Apart from a brief tenure of office of the Duke of Alba and the Duke of Béjar, however, Charles did not trust grandees in political positions and his council consisted of ecclesiastics and administrators, about seven in number. Even so, it was not regularly consulted by Charles, who took decisions himself with the advice of his chief secretaries. Consequently the Council of State had no political influence and little administrative significance. On occasions, reinforced by military experts, it turned itself into a Council of War which Charles could consult for *ad hoc* purposes. Secondly, there was a much larger group of councils, which can be recognised as genuine administrative bodies and divided into two categories according to the territory they governed and the function they performed.

Each unit of the monarchy had its council. The Council of Castile had originated from the medieval Royal Council of the kings of Castile and had already been organised into a more bureaucratic body by Ferdinand and Isabella. Charles V completed the process of modernisation, by further excluding the aristocracy and staffing it with officials from the gentry and jurist classes, and by reducing its membership from sixteen to about half that number. Its jurisdiction, like that of most Spanish councils, combined legal and administrative functions. As a court of law it heard appeals from the *audiencias*, and if the complaints of the cortes are to be believed it assumed too much judicial business and caused interminable delay. As an administrative committee it dealt with most of the internal affairs of Castile, including some ecclesiastical jurisdiction, and even at times gave advice on foreign policy.

For the administration of his eastern kingdoms Charles V inherited the Council of Aragon which under the reforms of Ferdinand had, like that of Castile, become a modern bureaucracy, from which the nobility was excluded. In addition to the administration of justice, the Council of Aragon also exercised general administrative functions. For this purpose it had a highly organised Chancellery and Treasury, staffed largely by jurists from the three eastern kingdoms.[14] When Charles V came to rule in Spain he preserved the structure of the Council of Aragon, and although it was royal policy to appoint a Castilian as treasurer, offices in Aragon were in general preserved for native incumbents. The same could not be said for royal administration in Italy, which was traditionally the sphere of Aragon. Ferdinand had already brought more Castilians than Catalans into the administration of Naples, and it was Castilians who profited from Charles V's acquisition of Milan. This process went even further when in 1555, in the interests of efficiency and specialisation, Italian affairs were taken from the jurisdiction of Aragon and given a council of their own, modelled on that of Castile. The affairs of Spain's colonial empire had already been assigned to a special council, the Council of the Indies, in 1524. All these territorial councils, however, were territorial only in name. They were in fact central institutions, located not in the countries they administered but at the side of the monarch.

Finally, there was also a group of councils which can be classified separately according to the specialised functions they performed. Of these, the most important were the Council of the Inquisition whose jurisdiction extended beyond the confines of Castile into the length and breadth of Spain, and whose functions amounted almost to those of a council for ecclesiastical affairs; and the Council of Finance, originally created in 1522 for the management of the finances of Castile but gradually supplying more and more of the resources for Charles's foreign wars.[15] The functional councils also inclu-

---

[14] See F. Sevillano Colom, 'La cancillería de Fernando el Católico', V. Congreso de Historia de la Corona de Aragón (*Estudios* I), 217–53.

[15] On the Inquisition see above, pp. 20–29; on the Council of Finance see below, pp. 59–60.

ded such subordinate ones as the Councils of Military Orders, of the *Cruzada*, and, for a time, of the *Hermandad*.

In spite of its overhaul by the Catholic Monarchs and Charles V, conciliar government was not an efficient instrument for getting things done. The cumbersome procedure of the councils in which dispatches were read and commented upon with all the formality of a court of law, and above all their confusion of administrative and judicial functions, stored up large arrears of unfinished business and threatened to bring administration almost to a halt. In fact, Charles V did not normally communicate directly with his councils. He communicated with his secretaries. It was the secretaries who rescued his government from stagnation and enabled the conciliar system to work, and it was they who answered the need for a more efficient executive by providing the link between the crown and its councils. Consequently they must be regarded as key agents in the Habsburg system of government.

The office of secretary grew in status and in power in the reign of Charles V. Charles's secretariat, like the rest of his government, was organised on a national and not on an imperial basis, and within Spain his most important secretariat was based on Castile. Aragon, however, already possessed a highly organised bureaucratic Chancellery which the reforms of Ferdinand had brought within the framework of the Council of Aragon.[16] The administrative head was the Vice-Chancellor who countersigned all royal documents and was assisted by a Protonotary who was in charge of the three secretaries and their procedure. When Charles V came to rule in Spain he preserved the structure of the Chancellery in Aragon. Castile, on the other hand, had a different system. Here, as has been seen, the Council of Castile was the main government committee, and the signature of at least three of its members was required on all official documents. The royal secretaries, however, were the medium of communication between the sovereign and the council; they prepared the agenda for council meetings and were responsible through their assistants for the redaction of all royal documents, which had to be countersigned by one of the secretaries. In general the Castilian administration was much more loosely defined than that of Aragon, which made it liable to confusion or abuse of authority yet at the same time suitable for the emergence of a powerful co-ordinator. The council resented the exercise of independent authority by the secretaries and their issue of royal decrees without conciliar approval; it also resented their control of patronage and offices. But the need for quicker decisions and the anxiety of the king to exercise authority unrestrained by the councils, caused the office of secretary to grow in authority; within the secretariat two secretaries

[16] See Sevillano Colom, *op. cit.*, pp. 217-53.

emerged who might more appropriately be described as secretaries of state in order to distinguish them from the larger group of secretaries whose subordinate functions rendered them little more than clerks. The first of these was Francisco de los Cobos.

Born in poverty and obscurity in the small Andalusian town of Ubeda, and with no formal education, Cobos had served a fifteen-year apprentice-ship in the secretariat before his appointment as royal secretary in 1516; and although he shared duties with a number of other secretaries, he soon became the principal member of the secretarial staff and, with the reforms of 1523, the controlling figure in the new Council of Finance, as well as member and secretary of most of the other councils; all of which gave him an impor-tant co-ordinating function.[17] The rise of Cobos reduced the other secretaries to minor rôles. It also produced rivalry with older officials, particularly with the grand chancellor, Gattinara. From the time that Charles returned to Spain in 1522, Gattinara and Cobos were competing for control of the machinery of government. As Cobos gained in influence with the king and placed his assistants in key administrative posts, Gattinara fought back and began to claim a position as head of the entire administration with control both of appointments and of the business of the councils. The emperor himself made it clear that this was not the function of the chancellor, whose office was a Burgundian one, but belonged to the administration of Castile.[18] From 1527 it became obvious that it was the secretary Cobos who enjoyed the chief position of responsibility and trust, while Gattinara's influence was beginning to wane. Indeed Gattinara was no longer even the leading adviser in foreign affairs. In 1529 Nicholas Perrenot, Lord of Granvelle, son of a modest Burgundian family who had risen through service in the Netherlands and diplomacy, was appointed member of the Council of State and began to take a leading part in the conduct of foreign policy. After the death of Gattinara in 1530 the office of grand chancellor was allowed to lapse and the emperor himself assumed personal responsibility for policy, using Cobos and Granvelle as his chief agents and advisers, with an agreed division of labour between the two, Granvelle specialising in foreign and imperial affairs, and Cobos in the government of Castile, where his office was now clearly based. When Charles left for the Netherlands in the autumn of 1539, Cobos remained behind, with the special responsibility of bringing order out of financial chaos, which was then the chief problem of government in Castile. And again, in 1543, when the emperor sailed from Barcelona not to return for fourteen years, he left Cobos, with Archbishop Tavera and the

[17] See below, pp. 60–61.
[18] See H. Keniston, *Francisco de los Cobos, Secretary of the Emperor Charles V* (Pittsburgh, Pa., 1960), pp. 99–103.

Duke of Alba, as the chief counsellors of his young son Philip, whom he had appointed Regent, and Cobos fulfilled this function until his death in 1547.

Cobos can be regarded as one of the creators of the Habsburg bureaucracy in Castile. He it was who recruited and trained for Charles V a staff of officials who gradually developed a corporate and professional spirit and looked upon Cobos himself as their *patrón*, or chief.[19] At first he selected his staff not from the large group of secretaries who had begun their service under the Catholic Monarchs but from his own protégés who had experience in other branches of the administration and on whom he knew he could count. Then, once he was established in control of most of the administration of Castile, he began to train men for office, such as his nephew, Juan Vázquez de Molina, Gonzalo Pérez, who succeeded the humanist Alfonso de Valdés, and Francisco de Eraso, all of whom he made assistant secretaries. Among these men there were no younger sons of nobility and, with the exception of Gonzalo Pérez, no men of learning or university training. They were, like Cobos himself, minor gentry from small towns, with a bureaucratic training and outlook as well as an eye to profit and preferment.

The organisation of business became more closely defined under Cobos. From the beginning of his service his office was responsible for the affairs of Castile, Portugal, and the Indies. After 1530 it also handled Italian affairs. He took care, however, not to interfere with the secretariat in Aragon. If he intervened to take the control of Italian affairs away from the Aragonese service that was because he believed that Castile should be responsible for Italian affairs and that the time had come to end the feeling that Naples and Sicily were Aragonese rather than Spanish kingdoms. He also refrained from interfering with the secretariat of Granvelle, who after 1530 was in charge of the rest of the empire and foreign relations. The secretary was the key figure in the distribution of incoming correspondence, either assigning it with a memorandum directly to the king or referring it to its appropriate council. Official business therefore came to the emperor thoroughly sifted by Cobos and the councils. Except for matters of international interest he rarely read correspondence himself, and his decision was usually taken down by the secretary who would prepare the document for signature and dispatch. In this way the creaking machinery of conciliar government was gradually made to work.

Yet the secretaries could not work miracles. Owing to the variety of Charles's interests and to his growing practice of depending on his own judgement in matters of policy, there was an accumulation of business which the bureaucratic machine, assiduous as it was, could not control. Moreover,

---

[19] Keniston, *op. cit.*, pp. 9–12, 332–55.

the bureaucracy itself became a vested interest and grew to parasitic proportions. Secretaries were not only important as a means of access to the king
and therefore the recipients of favours from anxious suitors, they were also
close to the source of patronage in the distribution of which they could amass
large fortunes and estates, as Cobos himself did, as well as build up a following
which would be expected to support its patron's policy. Cobos tended to
employ only his own creatures, and gradually came almost to monopolise
the control of offices. Moreover, he spent an inordinate amount of time
observing the tactics and the policy of his rivals.

The emperor himself was aware of the manoeuvring for power and
influence and of the search for wealth within his administration. In the
'Secret Instruction' which he sent to his son Philip in May 1543 when leaving
him as Regent in Spain, Charles penned an acute analysis of the factionalism
in his government.[20] He knew of the rivalries between the men whom he
left with his son as advisers in matters of state. Of Cardinal Tavera and
Secretary Cobos he wrote: 'Though they are heads of rival cliques, nevertheless I decided to appoint them both, so that you might not be left in the
hands of either one of them.' He was suspicious of the Duke of Alba's
ambition and warned Philip not to give him or any other grandee an important place in civil government, though in military affairs he could be relied
upon. Philip was also warned not to use Cobos exclusively and to watch
his accumulation of privileges which the emperor considered to be already
too many.

Yet Charles V also knew a good administrator when he saw one, and he
had no doubt of the loyalty and efficiency of Cobos. By the end of his life,
largely due to his ability, experience, and the trust the emperor had in him,
rather than through any formal definition of his office, Cobos had reached
a position of power and influence and presided over a large and dutiful
administration. He had taken the office of secretary with him in this ascent,
and he was clearly a secretary of state rather than a clerk. It is significant,
therefore, that this vital figure in Charles V's administration showed no
interest in the great intellectual, political, and religious problems of the age
of the Renaissance and Reformation. In his correspondence there was no
discussion of the great issue of the church and the empire, and no concern
for the imperial mission of his master to which Gattinara and some of
Charles's other followers were so passionately devoted. He was a Spanish
administrator and typified a more realistic and perhaps a more representative
point of view. In fact, the emperor himself considered that the greatest
service rendered by Cobos was in the field of finance.

[20] Printed in J. M. March, *Niñez y juventud de Felipe II* (2 vols., Madrid, 1941-2),
ii. 23-39.

5. THE 'SINEWS OF WAR'

Charles V's policy was based financially on Castile. As he himself gratuitously explained to the cortes of Castile in July 1523, he regarded 'these realms as the head of all the rest' and he intended to use their resources not only to sustain the others which God had given him but also to gain new ones and carry his frontiers even further for the advancement of the holy Catholic faith.[21] The cortes of Aragon, Catalonia, and Valencia provided him with occasional and modest grants, but there was a limit to their capacity, as has been seen. The Netherlands, with their trade, shipping, and industry, were a greater source of wealth, and the centralising process continued by Charles enabled him to tap that wealth more effectively than he could that of his Aragonese kingdoms. Consequently he ruthlessly exploited the financial resources of his subjects in the Low Countries until they could pay no more. In addition, he also had his possessions in Italy, and he could draw on the great financial markets like Genoa, Augsburg, and Antwerp, and on international bankers like the Fuggers and the Welsers. Yet even in terms of loans he borrowed four times as much in Castile as he did in Antwerp. By the end of his reign the quota of Castile was easily the biggest, and it was on Castile that the burden of imperial policy fell.[22] Gradually, and probably before 1550, the Low Countries could not support the financial weight which imperial policy assigned them. Less and less was coming from Naples, Milan, and Sicily; and essential as they were to the strategy of the emperor his Italian dominions were not fulfilling an imperial rôle in finance. The major effort was now coming from Spain, and within Spain from Castile, and behind Castile from America. The exhaustion of his European revenues made Charles increasingly dependent upon treasure shipments from the Spanish Indies. It was from the late 1520's that this treasure began to reach Spain in rapidly increasing quantities, yet even this did not lessen the burden on the tax-payers of Castile or decrease their quota of imperial finances.

In Spain the crown's financial position had already deteriorated before Charles ascended the throne, but it was certainly not improved by the rapacity of his Burgundian followers, the expenses of the imperial election, and the revolt of the *comuneros*. One of his first tasks on his return to Spain in 1522 was to reorganise the royal finances, and it was now that he created a new council, the Council of Finance, to supervise and control all income

---

[21] Merriman, *op. cit.*, iii. 122.
[22] See F. Braudel, 'Les emprunts de Charles-Quint sur la place d'Anvers', *Charles-Quint et son temps* (C.N.R.S., Paris, 1959), pp. 191–201.

and expenditure and to prepare a yearly budget. The new council, which began to function in February 1523, was similar to that with which he was already familiar in the Low Countries, and indeed Charles placed at its head Count Henry of Nassau who had been his chief of finances there. Soon, however, the body became exclusively Spanish in accordance with Charles's new practice and was dominated by its secretary, Francisco de los Cobos.

The optimism induced by the new service, however, was soon dispelled. Far from improving the emperor's position, Cobos in fact presided over the financial collapse of Spain during Charles's reign. Yet this was hardly the fault of the administration itself.[23] Cobos administered the treasury carefully and honestly and he managed to keep the nobles at bay in their search for sinecures and pensions. The council drew up its yearly budget estimates without fail, and while they were not always realistic and did not include debt repayment as part of expenditure, the source of the trouble lay in the fact that the demands of a new campaign or the negotiation of a heavy loan by the emperor himself without their knowledge made any attempt at a valid estimate impossible. No one knew better than Cobos the realities of the financial situation. The main cause of collapse was the emperor's foreign wars which were financed by Spain. An additional cause was Charles's personal extravagance in his royal household—which took a tenth of the national income—his ceaseless travels and his reckless purchase of jewels and objects of art. Short of peace and economy there was no solution, only a series of desperate expedients which took the crown to the verge of bankruptcy.

Ordinary revenue was derived chiefly from the *alcabala*, or sales tax, which in this period was converted into a quota payment made by each town or village; supplemented by revenues from the military orders and the grants of the cortes, it rose by about 50 per cent. during the emperor's reign and still fell far short of ordinary expenditure.[24] But expenditure was rarely, if ever, 'ordinary', and Charles's foreign campaigns devoured more and more extraordinary supply. This could be obtained in two ways. Already before Charles's time, the crown had begun the practice of raising extraordinary revenue by borrowing. This took the form of selling bonds (*juros*), the buyers of which received the crown's undertaking (*juro*—I swear) to pay a stated rate of interest. These *juros* could also be pensions without the crown having received any loan. All *juros*, whether bonds or pensions, were assigned upon specific sources of ordinary revenue, the treasury receiving only the

[23] In spite of the strictures of Brandi, *op. cit.*, p. 463.
[24] On Spanish finances see the original and pioneering work of R. Carande, *Carlos V y sus banqueros* (2 vols., Madrid, 1944-49), vol. ii. *La Hacienda Real de Castilla* (Madrid, 1949).

balance left over after these charges had been met. This practice was aggravated by Charles V as he granted more and more assignations on ordinary revenue to repay the ever-increasing number of loans he raised from bankers. In this way, fewer and fewer direct revenues remained in the hands of the king. Since 1524, for example, the revenues from the three military orders of Santiago, Calatrava and Alcántara, which hitherto had been paid directly to the crown, were paid to the Fuggers who had got them as mortgages for their loans. Banking transactions like this obviously had their advantages for the emperor in so far as the bankers were not only lending money but also transferring it abroad; such credit transfers and their payment wherever they were most needed, in Germany, Italy or the Low Countries, were quick and secure while the transport of ready cash from Spain was slow and uncertain. The trouble began when the practice grew beyond the actual resources of the crown.

In addition, however, there was also the income from the Indies—revenue from taxes, monopolies, and Indian tribute, together with the royal fifth, the crown's share of all precious metals mined. Rising sharply from 1529, the emperor's American revenue averaged roughly 252,000 ducats a year from 1534 to 1543.[25] But following the disturbances in Peru, receipts of treasure declined to about 118,000 ducats a year from 1544 to 1550. Even allowing for fluctuations, however, Charles's American income can be exaggerated. Public imports from America in the period 1503–60 totalled 12·6 million ducats: an average income of some 220,000 ducats annually. The crown's ordinary revenues in Spain at this time were estimated at a little over one million ducats annually, without making allowance for the prior charges on those revenues, which as the reign wore on came to devour the entire normal revenue and more. The income from America, therefore, was not a large proportion of the emperor's total revenue and it bore even less relation to his expenditure. To take one item from many: the disastrous campaign against Metz in 1552 cost him more than two million ducats. Alongside expenditure like this, what he derived from America each year even during the five years 1551–55 when, just before another slump, shipments were largest, was not impressive.[26] Even so, it could have great emergency value in the feeding, equipping, and payment of his restless armies and enable them to take the initiative against his enemies.

It is from the 1540's that the serious, as opposed to the normal, financial difficulties of the crown can be dated. After the Algerian campaign of 1542,

[25] E. J. Hamilton, *American Treasure and the Price Revolution in Spain, 1501–1650* (Cambridge, Mass., 1934), pp. 32–45.

[26] In the period 1551–55 shipments averaged 1·2 million ducats a year, dropping to half of this for the next five years. See Hamilton, *op. cit.*, pp. 34–5.

those in France in 1543–44 and in the Empire in 1546–47, the position
deteriorated so badly that for the rest of the reign ordinary revenue was
always completely exhausted for several years in advance; moreover, expenditure was also several times higher than extraordinary revenue, for these
major military operations coincided between 1542 and 1547 with a falling
off in shipments of American treasure. The crisis can be illustrated with an
example taken from the period. In April 1546 the emperor wrote from
Ratisbonne to his son Philip who was then Regent in Spain that he had made
up his mind to take the field against the Protestant princes of Germany.
For this he would need large sums of money, and Cobos was to undertake
the raising of loans from the agents of the German and Italian bankers in
Spain. But Cobos found it almost impossible to raise loans. Most of the
royal income had been sold or pledged up to the end of 1549 and even
part of 1550; part of the income of the Indies was already committed, and
there was not even enough money to pay the current interest on outstanding
loans. The only suggestion Cobos could offer was that the emperor should
make peace, and he advised his master to 'remember the importance of
finding a remedy and relief for these kingdoms, because of the extreme
need, for otherwise there could not fail to be serious trouble, because the
need is so notorious that not only are the natives of the kingdom aware of
it and are refusing to take part in any financial transactions, but even
foreigners . . . are doing the same thing, because they know that there is no
source from which payments can be made'.[27] But peace was the one remedy
that Charles did not consider and in these circumstances Cobos and the
Council of Finance, against their better judgement, had recourse to a last
desperate remedy—the confiscation of all treasure from the Indies and the
seizure of all specie in Spain and its shipment to the emperor. This financed
Charles's victory against the German Protestants at Mühlberg, but it left
a terrible legacy for the economy of Spain, particularly for the Indies trade.
Sequestered treasure was in theory a loan which was repayable, but repayment was highly speculative and the whole transaction impeded legitimate
trade and encouraged fraud; in March 1557 the emperor himself was com-
plaining that his officials in Seville had allowed 90 per cent. of a treasure
shipment to escape registration.

The death blow was delivered after the resumption of hostilities with
France in 1551. In order to meet the French emergency in 1552 Charles
borrowed over four million ducats; the Metz campaign alone cost 2·5
million; and he borrowed 2·5 million in each of the following years. Shipments of treasure from the Indies totalled over two million for 1552–53, but

[27] Keniston, *op. cit.*, p. 302,

Charles's foreign policy continued to be so expensive that in September 1554 the cash deficit for the current year was calculated at over 4·3 million ducats, even after all receipts for the six ensuing years had been pledged and the proceeds spent in advance. The terms on which Charles was still able to borrow worsened rapidly as the bankers had ever greater trouble in obtaining payment. Credit was now costing the crown 43 per cent. and more, when credit could be found.[28] Some creditors were tempted to remain in the game because if they refused they might lose all. For this reason Charles was unwilling to adopt the course of complete suspension of payments, and instead he had recourse to the expedient of a unilateral scaling down of payments due to his creditors. All that was left now was treasure from the Indies. Although much of this was owed in advance, by 1557 the crown was refusing even this to its creditors because it was needed immediately for the war against France. This enabled Philip's armies in the Low Countries to take the offensive and win the battle of St. Quentin in August 1557, but the effort exhausted his resources and forced him to bring the policy of his father to a halt. Paralysed by lack of money and unable to borrow more, he had to make a long overdue peace and settle with France in 1559.

Finance was the key to much of Charles V's policy and of the history of Spain during his reign. Yet the absence of political events in Spain and the silence of his subjects there after 1522 should not be interpreted as enthusiasm for the Habsburg cause. Spanish society was split between a large and privileged aristocracy which was the ally of the crown and the rest of the people who were passive spectators. Thwarted in their attempt to share the legislative power with the crown, the Castilian people lost all effective mediation in the control of taxation, and they could do nothing but watch the painful process of exploitation in the interests of a policy which was hardly their own. Divided and defenceless, Castile was in no position to oppose the creation of a superstructure which monopolised political control and dictated its destiny—the Habsburg monarchy, the aristocracy, the higher clergy, the army, and some of the intellectuals. These groups supported and could profit from the great enterprises undertaken by Charles V and his successors.

Yet there were many signs which indicated a divorce between the Castilian people and its ruling class. The emperor and some of his advisers might proclaim the ideal of a great Christian empire extending over two hemispheres with its base in Spain. Philosophers and men of letters like Alfonso de Valdés and Fray Antonio de Guevara might provide the imperial ideal with an intellectual justification. The struggle against Protestantism and the

---

[28] Carande, *op. cit.*, ii. 208.

Turk might appear as the supreme mission of Spain and her empire. But whenever popular sentiment could make itself heard, either in some collective impulse like that of the *comuneros*, or in the writings of chroniclers, or in the protests of the cortes, or in the advice of his Spanish administrators, then it was obvious that the urgent preoccupations of Spaniards were nearer home, more national in their objectives and more economical in their cost; the safety of Navarre and the outposts of North Africa, the struggle against the Turk, but in the Mediterranean and not on the Danube, the defence of the coasts, and peace with France and other Christian countries.[29] Francisco de los Cobos, the emperor's Spanish secretary, was constantly advising peace, 'that we might have a breathing space'. Even the Admiral of Castile wrote in 1531: 'Your Majesty's protracted absence from your Spanish kingdoms, though indispensable perhaps for the safety of threatened Christendom and the furtherance of your own political views, is a thing to which your Spanish subjects can hardly reconcile themselves'.[30] 'The safety of threatened Christendom', however, involved the emperor's presence in Germany, and here he received some sympathy from his Spanish subjects, for Lutheranism was hated in Spain.

6. Reformers and Humanists

Although it was quickened by the growing challenge of Protestantism, the Counter-Reformation had its roots in a movement of reform within the Catholic church which predated the revolt of Luther. And the example was set by Spain. Even before the efforts of Contarini, Giberti, Caraffa, and other early reformers grew to fruition and made their impact in Rome, the Spanish church had begun to take stock of itself and to put its house in order. And just as the Reformation itself was more than an attack on clerical abuses, so the Catholic Reform, in Spain as elsewhere, was accompanied by an intellectual and spiritual revival which went beyond a negative correction of faults. In Spain 'reform was demanded by everyone of virtue and learning; it began in the time of the Catholic Monarchs and continued throughout the sixteenth century; it was promoted to a great extent by the Inquisition, acting with the utmost severity; but it owed its principal glory to the magnanimous Isabella and to Fray Francisco Ximénez de Cisneros'.[31]

---

[29] See J. Carrera Pujal, *Historia de la economía española* (5 vols., Barcelona, 1943–47), i. 101–203.

[30] Merriman, *op. cit.*, iii. 122.

[31] M. Menéndez Pelayo, *Historia de los heterodoxos españoles* (8 vols., Santander, 1946–48), iii. 32.

Confessor of Queen Isabella from 1492, provincial of the Franciscans in Castile, archbishop of Toledo and primate of Spain from 1495, Inquisitor general from 1507 and twice regent of the kingdom, Ximénez dominated the religious life of Spain during the twenty years before the outbreak of the Reformation.[32] Having renounced the life of a recluse with some reluctance, he quickly became a man of power and influence, ruthless with opponents and inflexible in his objectives. As a bishop he was a true pastor: setting first an example himself and in his household, he then sought to reform his diocese, attacking clerical concubinage and attempting to give some meaning to the term 'cure of souls' by admonishing his clergy to reside in their parishes, to explain the gospel of each Sunday to their parishioners, to teach Christian doctrine to the children. In spite of its continuation by later prelates, his programme for the secular clergy met with only limited success. Immoral and worldly priests continued to be found in Spain as in other parts of Christendom, and among the episcopacy dignity was often more highly regarded than austerity; Ximénez, whose practice of Franciscan poverty and penance as archbishop of Toledo was notorious, found himself reproached by Pope Alexander VI for not maintaining a due episcopal state. In general the secular clergy were not equal to their mission. This was one of the reasons for the progress of the religious orders, especially of the mendicants, who came to form a spiritual élite to whom laymen looked as the true representatives of the Christian ideal. There was need of reform here, too, but the prospects were more hopeful and resistance less obstinate. Supported by the crown and with the sanction of Rome, Ximénez began to improve the standards of religious houses; with some difficulty in the case of the Benedictines, but with more success among his own Franciscans where his methods took the form of installing Observants in place of Conventuals. The Dominicans had already undertaken a programme of reform based on stricter observance of the rules of the order and accompanied by an educational and theological revival which was reflected in the opening of the College of San Gregorio in Valladolid in 1496 and of the University of Avila in 1504.[33] Thanks to these efforts the standards of monasticism in Spain—and the number of its adherents—were superior to those found elsewhere in Europe, and it was no coincidence that in the reigns of Charles V and Philip II it was her missionaries who carried the Christian faith to new frontiers.

Ximénez was a man of vision as well as of zeal, and it was mainly under his inspiration that the new learning was placed at the service of the church.

[32] See M. Bataillon, *Erasme et l'Espagne* (Paris, 1937), pp. 1–75.
[33] On the Dominican reform see V. Beltrán de Heredia, *Historia de la reforma de la Provincia de España, 1450–1550* (Rome, 1939).

The fusion of his religious and his cultural interests, together with the opportunity provided by the immense revenue of the see of Toledo, led to the foundation of the University of Alcalá, which he began in 1498 and opened ten years later. This he intended to be an institution which would provide a complete ecclesiastical training—elementary, intermediate and advanced—and which would produce a clerical élite for promotion to benefices in the Spanish church. The statutes he gave the university were modelled on those of Paris, and many of the professors, such as Pedro de Lerma, the first chancellor of the university, had studied at the Sorbonne. But it was its faculty of theology which distinguished Alcalá from other universities in Spain; by providing chairs not only in Thomist but also in Scotist and Nominalist theology, Ximénez strengthened theological studies in Spain and gave them a new status.[34] The new university grew rapidly, and what had begun as a kind of seminary soon emulated Salamanca and became one of the most brilliant centres of learning in Europe, distinguished not only for its theological and canonical studies, but also for its promotion of the humanities, languages, and medicine. Ximénez also laid the foundations of a good university library, enriched with many Arabic scientific works saved from the burning of Arabic literature in Granada, which he himself had ordered, as well as from the sack of Oran. A printing press already functioned in Alcalá from 1494, but even here the influence of Ximénez was decisive, for it was he who brought the distinguished printer, Arnaldo Guillermo de Brocar, to the university town and gave him his most important commissions; these included the printing of spiritual texts for the Christian formation of clergy and laity, and above all of the Polyglot Bible.

The adoption of Christian humanism in the service of the Spanish reform movement was best seen in the promotion of Biblical studies, which were proceeding at the highest level in Spain before Luther and the Protestant reformers began to claim the Bible as their own. In order to give sacred studies a firm basis in the sources of revelation, Ximénez organised a critical edition of the Bible by means of a collation of texts. For this purpose he collected manuscripts, obtained permission for his collaborators to consult the codices in the Vatican Library, and assembled at Alcalá a group of Spanish and foreign scholars. Convert Jews like Alfonso de Zamora, Pablo Coronel and Alfonso de Alcalá were given the task of collating the Hebrew and Chaldean texts, and establishing a correct version, while the Cretan, Demetrio Ducas, and Spaniards like Hernán Núñez, Juan de Vergara, Diego López de Estúñiga and Antonio de Nebrija worked on the Greek text. The result was the Polyglot Bible, five volumes of which contained the

[34] Bataillon, *op. cit.*, pp. 17–18.

Old and New Testaments printed with the original languages and the Latin Vulgate in parallel columns, while the sixth volume provided a vocabulary and grammar. The whole work—a great feat of printing as well as of scholarship—was completed in 1517, although it was not actually published until 1522. And while its scholarship was not impeccable, it embodied far more research than the earlier and more publicised New Testament of Erasmus, who had an imperfect knowledge of Greek and based his work on insufficient manuscript material.[35]

The religious renaissance promoted by Ximénez, supplemented at a local level by men like Hernando de Talavera, archbishop of Granada, and continued later in the sixteenth century by reformers like St. Peter of Alcántara, St. Teresa of Avila, and St. John of the Cross, had profound and permanent results. It improved the monastic orders and the higher clergy in Spain to such an extent that in the crucial years of the Reformation the Spanish hierarchy and religious were in a position to play a powerful rôle in the councils of the church, and particularly in the Council of Trent. At the same time the theological revival led by the Dominicans of the Salamanca school such as Francisco de Vitoria (1480–1546), Melchor Cano (1509–60) and Domingo de Soto (1494–1560), and developed still further by the newly formed Society of Jesus, enabled Spanish theologians not only to expound Catholic doctrine in the great contemporary debate with Protestantism but also to make important contributions to the problems of empire, race relations, and international law, which were posed by Spain's unique position in the world. More immediately, the fact that the Spanish church had already undertaken to reform itself, deprived Protestantism of much of the reforming justification it claimed in northern and central Europe and helped to make Spain less accessible than other countries to Protestant propaganda. On the other hand, the Spanish reform was initiated under royal auspices and independently of Rome, whose own religious revival it anticipated by many years. This helped to increase the power of the crown in ecclesiastical affairs, nurtured Spanish suspicions of Rome, and had lengthy repercussions on relations between Spain and the papacy.[36] It was an interesting portent that before Luther protested against the preaching of Indulgences Cardinal Ximénez had forbidden them to be preached in Spain, not on doctrinal grounds, but because he thought there were more pressing needs than the rebuilding of St. Peter's in Rome. In the opinion of the Spanish ecclesiastical authorities, orthodoxy was secure enough in their hands, without the intervention of Rome. Yet the spiritual revival which they patronised at the beginning of the sixteenth century soon produced further offshoots which

[35] For a criticism of the Polyglot Bible see *ibid.*, pp. 43–46.
[36] See below, pp. 273–86.

they themselves began to suspect, and had effects which they had hardly intended. The rush into religious life recklessly increased the number of clergy, both regular and secular, many of whom lived in conditions of squalor on the fringes of religion and beyond ecclesiastical control. Furthermore the evangelical tendencies which animated the Franciscan and Dominican reform movements, especially the enormous growth of the Franciscan Observants, allowed the intake of many erratic recruits whose enthusiasm made them prone to the exaggerations of Illuminism, and, in the opinion of some, even to Protestantism. At the same time, Ximénez' chastisement of monastic disorder gave a vague sanction to attacks on friars in general, and this was one of the features of the success of Erasmus in Spain.

The instrument for dealing with heterodoxy, actual or potential, was the Inquisition.[37] Between about 1510 and 1520 its prestige was lower than at any time since its foundation; its ruthless campaign against the New Christians had crushed whatever threat to orthodoxy came from that quarter and reduced one of the main justifications for its own existence, while its arbitrary and absolutist methods were the target for a growing body of criticism. Those who opposed the Inquisition looked hopefully to the new monarch, Charles I, and for a time its fate was in the balance. Known to be opposed to the tribunal's methods of secret accusation and confiscation of property, the young king was pressed to reduce its powers and its functions. But as far as Charles was concerned the case against the Inquisition was spoilt when its Aragonese critics appealed to Rome in order to strengthen their hands. No less than his predecessors the emperor rejected papal intervention, especially as it threatened to remove crown control of the tribunal, and for this reason he dropped his projected reform of the Inquisition and silenced its opponents. From 1523 it was clear that the Spanish Inquisition had survived the crisis with royal support and with its power intact. Indeed, it now had new targets at which to aim: not only did it continue its relentless pursuit of Judaism, but, in the age of Luther, it directed its attention increasingly to two groups, Illuminists and Erasmists.

The sect of Illuminists, or *alumbrados*, was purely Spanish in origin, as can be seen perhaps in its peculiarly mystical character. Born independently of Protestantism, it existed as early as 1512 in Guadalajara and Salamanca, and had its beginnings among a group of Franciscans, some of whom were *conversos* of Jewish descent.[38] Illuminism was an aberration of mysticism. Its creed was the abdication of the will to God and the ability, or the claim, of the faithful to put themselves in personal communication with the divine

[37] See above, pp. 20–29; on the movement to restrict the power of the Inquisition see Lea, *A History of the Inquisition of Spain*, i. 216–23.
[38] Bataillon, *op. cit.*, pp. 65–75, 179–242.

essence through ecstasy, on which occasions they believed themselves incapable of committing sin and often drew the inference that good works were useless. Some of its devotees found these doctrines a convenient pretext to indulge their sexual passions, and it was no coincidence that one of the unofficial leaders of the movement was the amorous Francisca Hernández 'of whom the men spoke with fanatical veneration, and the women with not so much respect'.[39] Others simply posed as saints and prophets, often with sufficient success to attract aristocratic patronage. In the early 1520's a flourishing group of Illuminists was discovered in Toledo, confined mainly to nuns and friars. The Inquisition had little difficulty in rooting it out, and by an edict of 23 September 1525 it condemned the entire doctrine of Illuminism. Henceforth the movement had little significance, but the Inquisition kept a close check on suspected devotees, with the result that anyone fired with religious enthusiasm was likely to be suspect: Ignatius Loyola, the future founder of the Society of Jesus, was jailed in 1527 and submitted to three examinations for suspected Illuminist leanings.

Although Spanish Illuminism predated the Lutheran revolt, many of its doctrines—such as the inefficacy of external works—were similar to those of the German reformer, and it served to pave the way for the entry of Protestantism into Spain.[40] In 1520 a Spanish translation of Luther's Commentary on Galatians was published in Flanders, followed by his *Freedom of the Christian Man*. At this stage little was known of Luther in Spain beyond a general rumour about a 'heretic who was rising in Germany'. But, warned by Rome, Inquisitor general Adrian issued on 7 September 1521 the first directive against Lutheran books in Spain. From then onwards the ecclesiastical authorities kept an anxious guard against the entry of Lutheran literature and missionaries, especially in the northern ports, but not with complete success. After a decade of the Lutheran revolt, new names, unknown to most Spaniards, had been added to the list of Protestant reformers, and their writings were making their way into Spain unmolested. The Inquisitors themselves were not always sure of their targets, and their inability to identify heretical doctrines with any accuracy partly accounts for the clumsiness of their methods and the wildness of their accusations. Isolated trials of alleged Lutherans in the 1520's and 1530's failed to reveal the existence of organised heresy in Spain, but demonstrated all too clearly how easy it was to use the Inquisition as a means of exacting personal vengeance and how ignorant many Spanish laymen were of the simplest

[39] A. Selke, 'Algunos datos nuevos sobre los primeros alumbrados', *Bulletin Hispanique*, lxiv. (1952), 125–52.
[40] On the early history of Protestantism in Spain see J. E. Longhurst, 'Luther in Spain: 1520–1540', *Proceedings of the American Philosophical Society*, ciii. (1959), 66–73.

Catholic doctrines. Here and there a few Spaniards and foreigners were claimed as victims. In 1523 the Inquisition tribunal of Mallorca executed one Gonsalvo the Painter, because he was a suspected Lutheran.[41] In 1524 a German named Blay Esteve was condemned as a Lutheran by the tribunal of Valencia, and in 1528 a certain Cornelis, a painter from Ghent, was found guilty of Lutheranism by the same tribunal and sentenced to life imprisonment. In the same year the tribunal of Toledo began the trial of Diego de Uceda on a charge of Lutheranism. This case was unique among the early trials, partly because it was the first case of Lutheranism tried at Toledo, and also because Uceda was not in fact a Lutheran but an enthusiastic devotee of the teachings of Erasmus.[42]

The entry of Erasmus opened a new phase in the Spanish renaissance. To a certain extent the ground had already been prepared. The esteem in which scholarship was held in Spain created an intellectual climate which was propitious to a favourable reception of his writings; in 1516, after the publication of his New Testament, he himself was invited to Spain—though unsuccessfully—by Cardinal Ximénez.[43] At the same time the attack on monastic abuses begun by Spanish reformers, though it had a more positive content than the ridicule heaped on religious orders by Erasmus, provided another point of contact. Advocating a general reform in the church, Erasmus satirised those whom he considered responsible for corruption, urging a return to the simplicity of the apostolic era. In the initial stages of Luther's break with Rome he refused to commit himself and advised moderation on both sides; his own view was that the church should reform itself before it began to condemn doctrines. In 1521, however, his own principles forced him to repudiate Luther over the question of free will, and from then onwards Spanish misgivings over his orthodoxy were dispelled. It mattered little to Spaniards that there were reservations about his doctrines in Rome, for the policies of Clement VII were suspect in Spain and inimical to Charles V. Indeed the views of Erasmus were welcome to those who wanted Christian concord and sought it under the auspices of the emperor rather than the pope.[44] In the court of Charles V there were influential supporters of Erasmus, including the emperor's Latin secretary, Alfonso de Valdés; from 1522 the court was in Spain and Spanish Erasmists were thus stra-

---

[41] As Lea points out, *op. cit.*, iii. 413, it is difficult to give credence to such an accusation at that date.

[42] See J. E. Longhurst, *Luther and the Spanish Inquisition: the case of Diego de Uceda, 1528–1529* (Albuquerque, 1953).

[43] Bataillon, *op. cit.*, pp. 77–8.

[44] See below, pp. 75–76; on the relation between Erasmism, the Hebraic tradition, and Illuminism see E. Asensio, 'El erasmismo y las corrientes espirituales afines', *Revista de Filología Española*, xxxvi. (1952), 31–99.

tegically placed to promote and protect the writings of their master. At the University of Alcalá the followers of Erasmus were even more numerous than those at court, while Juan de Vergara, who had worked on the Polyglot Bible, brought to the support of Erasmism the prestige of his learning and the influence of his position as secretary of Archbishop Fonseca. This was significant. The two most important ecclesiastical posts in Spain were held by enthusiasts of Erasmus: Alfonso de Fonseca, archbishop of Toledo, gave him a pension of 200 gold ducats while he was at work on his edition of St. Augustine, and Alfonso Manrique, archbishop of Seville and Inquisitor general, protected him when Edward Lee, Henry VIII's ambassador in Spain, was prompting Franciscans to attack him as a heretic.

The years 1522 to 1525 saw the Erasmist movement successfully established in Spain. Welcomed by humanists and with the approval of Fonseca and Manrique, many of his writings were published in Spanish translations.[45] Erasmus himself, who had begun by suspecting the climate of opinion beyond the Pyrenees, was· soon conscious of his popularity there and expressed his gratitude for it: 'I owe more to Spain than to my own country, or any other'. Yet he also had his enemies. In Spain, as elsewhere, the controversy about his orthodoxy raged, and as the religious struggle in Germany grew more uncompromising, so the tension increased. As they were the main butt of his jibes, the monastic orders naturally hit back and assailed him as a heretic, especially after the appearance of a Spanish translation of *Enchiridion* —with a dedication to Manrique—in 1527. To further their attacks they enlisted the support of the Inquisition, few of whose judges were as broad-minded as their general, and some of whose officials were friars themselves. To settle the issue of Erasmus's orthodoxy, Manrique convoked at Valladolid in 1527 an assembly of thirty-two theologians to examine a list of Erasmian propositions, and after six weeks of discussion had failed to produce agreement forbade attacks on the scholar, a decision which a papal brief sought to modify by exonerating only his criticisms of Luther.[46] Charles V himself, inspired by Alfonso de Valdés, sent Erasmus a friendly letter indicating that he need have no fear of any unfavourable decision and expressing his personal conviction of his piety.[47]

During the next two years, while translations of Erasmus's writings were multiplying in Spain and enjoying a vogue among the educated public unequalled in any other European country, some of his followers were turning out humanistic literature of their own. In 1527 and 1528 Alfonso de Valdés wrote two popular dialogues in Spanish attacking clerical abuses, justifying the sack of Rome on grounds of papal perversity, and praising

[45] Bataillon, *op. cit.*, pp. 172–77, 253–57.   [46] *Ibid.* pp. 260–84.
[47] *Ibid.*, pp. 298–99.

Erasmian proposals.[48] The papal nuncio in Spain, Baldassare Castiglione, author of *The Courtier*, demanded that all copies of the anti-papal polemic be seized and destroyed, but this the Inquisitor general refused to do. At Augsburg in the summer of 1530, Valdés was in personal touch with Melancthon, and although opposition to him in Spain was gathering force he continued to enjoy Charles V's favour to the last. In 1529 Alfonso's brother, Juan de Valdés, published his *Dialogue of Christian Doctrine*, in which he not only extolled the virtues of Erasmus but also described the latter's opponents as fools without knowledge of real Christian piety. This time the Inquisition moved in quickly, and began a series of examinations which resulted in the flight of Valdés to Italy and his subsequent conviction of heresy, along with the prohibition of his works in Spain.[49]

The conviction of Juan de Valdés was a sign of the times. Aware of the progress of Protestantism abroad, the Spanish church became more sensitive to criticism and less capable of tolerating dissent, however orthodox. Acting on a loose interpretation of heresy, the Inquisition renewed its campaign with increasing vigour and suddenly it broke through the defences of the humanists, at court and in the universities.[50] In June 1529 Charles V left Spain for Italy, taking with him many of the influential Erasmian courtiers. In December of the same year Inquisitor general Manrique, a staunch supporter still of Erasmus, was banished from court for displeasing the empress on a trivial matrimonial affair. By the time of Charles's return to Spain in 1533 the Inquisition had successfully associated in the public mind the teachings of Erasmus with the heresies of Luther, and Spain's leading Erasmists were either in jail as proto-Lutherans or else had fled the country. Juan de Vergara, a man of wide culture and learning, and—a fact which was always significant in the eyes of the Inquisition—a New Christian, was jailed in 1533, despite the efforts of his employer, Archbishop Fonseca. The technique employed against Vergara was typical and effective: he was smeared with accusations of Lutheranism, Illuminism, and Erasmism, all three being linked in such a way as to make them part of the same heresy.

Scholars at the University of Alcalá were also investigated. Its Chancellor, Pedro de Lerma, was an old adherent of Erasmus. In 1537, at the age of seventy he retired from the university, but in the same year he was jailed by the Inquisition for heresy. After a long trial, during which he was accused of introducing some of the teaching of Erasmus into his sermons, he was

[48] See below, pp. 75–76; Bataillon, *op. cit.*, 373–93, 395–414, 417–19.
[49] J. E. Longhurst, *Erasmus and the Spanish Inquisition: the case of Juan de Valdés* (Albuquerque, 1950).
[50] Bataillon, *op. cit.*, pp. 467–532.

forced to make public recantation in all the principal towns of Spain where he had preached of eleven propositions declared to be heretical, scandalous, and wicked; he was also required to declare that the false doctrines which he had preached in his sermons were diabolically inspired to sow evil in the church. Lerma left Spain at the first opportunity and returned to the Sorbonne, where he had once been Dean of the Faculty of Theology. There he remained, refusing to return to his native country where, he said, learned people could not live among such persecutors. In 1538 the death of Inquisitor general Manrique removed the last remaining Erasmist from a position of ecclesiastical authority in Spain. The fact that Erasmus had long since publicly avowed his opposition to Luther made little difference. From abroad Luis Vives wrote to the Dutch scholar: 'We live in difficult times, in which we can neither speak nor remain silent without danger. In Spain Vergara and his brother Tovar have been imprisoned, and other learned men as well. In England the bishops of Rochester and London and Thomas More. I pray you may have a tranquil old age.'[51] By 1538 overt expression of Erasmism was on its way to extinction in Spain.

The Erasmist movement, an early example perhaps of the tendency of Spanish intellectuals to inflate the products of foreign culture, had been orthodox in intent, and its adherents had never sought rupture with the Catholic church. Indeed there was no real danger that heresy would take root in Spain or that Protestantism would touch the mass of the people there. For the next twenty years Spain caused Rome no anxiety on account of the new doctrines coming from northern Europe. There were occasional incidents of isolated persons accused of Lutheranism being imprisoned by the Inquisition; all appear to have recanted and few of the penalties were drastic. In France, Germany, and the Low Countries a number of Spanish émigrés embraced the Lutheran faith, and Miguel Servet, a heretic to Catholics as a pantheist and one who denied the Trinity, was sufficiently objectionable to Calvin to be lured to Geneva and there burnt over a slow fire in 1553. In Spain itself up to 1558 there were only 105 cases of Lutheranism, of which 66 concerned foreigners.[52] The Spanish Inquisition, having silenced the Erasmists, was confident enough of religious security not to initiate any great heresy hunts, and comparative calm returned to the Peninsula. Outside, however, the king of Spain was fighting a losing battle.

[51] Quoted *ibid.*, p. 529.
[52] E. Schäfer, *Beitrage zur Geschichte des spanischen Protestantismus* (3 vols., Gütersloh, 1902), ii. 1–271, 342, 352.

CHAPTER III

THE EMPEROR CHARLES V

1. UNIVERSAL MONARCHY AND ITS OPPONENTS

THE unity of Christendom under imperial rule and its defence against Moslems and heretics appeared to Charles V and many of his contemporaries as the supreme mission to which he had been called. He alone, it seemed, had the will and the means to impose peace on Europe and dominion over its enemies. *Un monarca, un imperio y una espada*—the ideal expressed in the noble verses of Hernando de Acuña remained an unfailing attraction to many people in a divided and threatened world. Among some of Charles's subjects, however, there were reservations; many Spaniards believed that his accession damaged the national interests of their country. The diversity of his inheritance, whatever power it brought to his international mission, would inevitably increase the pressures on Spain from foreign commitments, doom her prospects and diminish her resources. Spanish opinion, therefore, favoured a national policy, not an imperial one, and Charles's Spanish administrators regarded their master as primarily king of Spain and not the emperor of Europe.[1] Yet contemporaries did not use the word 'imperial' to describe their monarchs' policies: that is a concept added by later historians and imputes a consistency and deliberation to Charles's policy which it never contained.

The formula 'peace among Christians and war against the infidel' does, it is true, give unity and purpose to the emperor's policy and has, moreover, the support of his own statements. His declaration to the cortes of La Coruña was not an isolated one. In April 1521, exasperated by the attitude of Luther, he wrote a personal statement of principles for the Diet of Worms: 'In defence of Christendom I have decided to pledge my kingdoms, dominions and friends, my own body and blood, my soul and my life.' A few days earlier, in the same assembly, he had referred to the subject of imperial organisation in Germany and the obstacles presented by the particularism of the princes, and declared: 'It is not my desire and will that there be many lords, but one lord alone, as is the tradition of the Holy Empire'.[2] Eight

---

[1] See P. Rassow, *Die Kaiser-Idee Karls V* (Berlin, 1932), pp. 232–33. For a Spanish view of the international policy of Charles V see J. M. Doussinague, *La política exterior de España en el siglo XVI* (Madrid, 1949), pp. 123–290.

[2] Brandi, *The Emperor Charles V*, pp. 128–33.

years later, he delivered his famous discourse in Madrid (16 September 1529) in which he announced his departure for Italy in order to be crowned by the pope and to convince him of the need for a general council which would restore Catholic unity; in addition to its religious mission he even seemed to see the empire as a political entity, though one which only sought to preserve its own inheritance and not to extend itself by conquests. It is debatable, however, whether the ideas expressed in his Madrid speech—many of which were the stock-in-trade of most monarchs at the time—were Charles's own or simply derived from the influence of Gattinara.

In any case, the words of rulers are not necessarily the best guide to their policies. In practice Charles never considered the implications of an imperial policy or produced a system of priorities that might give meaning to his words. Indeed he had too many preoccupations, many of them conflicting, to be able to do justice to them all or integrate them into a coherent programme. With his particular interests, there could not be an imperial, or universal, or supranational policy, and without an imperial organisation there could hardly be an empire.[3] Charles V was essentially an inheritor, not a creator, and it is in the defence of the particular items of his inheritance that the motives of his policy must be sought.

Yet there were 'imperialists' at the court of Charles V. His grand chancellor Gattinara lectured him on his imperial destiny and tried to give him an imperial organisation. Gattinara, however, saw Italy—yet another particular interest and a source of conflict not of peace—as the centre of a new Christian empire and tried to persuade his master to stake all on his domination there. And the influence of Gattinara can be exaggerated; it had already begun to wane before his death in 1530. Moreover, even during Gattinara's administration, the highly realist policy of Charles V, particularly with regard to France, had little to do with a 'Universitas Christiana' which some historians have attributed to him immediately after the sack of Rome by imperial troops in 1527.[4] The expression of such a philosophy was not Charles's own but came from the pen of his Latin secretary, Alfonso de Valdés, one of the many Spanish humanists who wrote for the imperial cause.

In reply to the papal protest against the excesses of Charles's troops, Valdés wrote a bitter attack on the policy of Clement VII, in which he argued that the sack of Rome was God's punishment on the sins of the pope and his vice-ridden court, while the emperor wished to re-establish peace among Christian kingdoms in order to fight the Turk and restore concord in

---

[3] J. Vicens Vives, 'Imperio y administración en tiempo de Carlos V', *Charles-Quint et son temps*, pp. 9–21, provides a brilliant analysis of the limitations of Charles V's concept of empire.

[4] See Menéndez Pidal, *op. cit.*, for example.

the church. But these were not specifically Spanish ideals and they hardly reflected the calculating policy of the emperor himself. They were the propaganda of humanists and Erasmists, many of whom sought to restore Christian
unity by means of a universal monarchy and looked for the salvation of
Christendom to the emperor rather than the pope.[5] In 1527, with yet another
reference to Charles's victory in Italy and the sack of Rome, the émigré Spanish humanist, Luis Vives, wrote to Erasmus: 'Christ has given an extraordinary opportunity to our age to realise this ideal, thanks to the great victory of
the emperor and the captivity of the pope.' Some of the Spanish men of
letters defended the imperial idea with their swords as well as their pens:
Boscán took part in the relief expedition to Rhodes in 1522; Garcilaso de la
Vega was wounded in Africa and died in the assault on the castle of Mai in
Provence in 1536; Hernando de Acuña fought in France and Germany and
took part in the battle of St. Quentin in 1557; and later in the century Diego
Hurtado de Mendoza fought in the war against the moriscos of Granada as
well as writing its history.[6]

Compared to these heroic figures, an administrator like Francisco de los
Cobos, counting the cost, advocating a return to immediate Spanish interests,
and urging Charles to stay in Spain and rule his people in peace and prosperity,
might appear prosaic indeed. But the administration reflected realities, while
the humanists purveyed dreams. This was apparent not only in the absence
of an imperial organisation, which has already been noticed, but also in the
distribution of the costs of empire and of its fruits. The major portion of
both was assigned to Castile, but the empire that Castile valued was in
America not in Europe. In spite of a brief interval of relaxation authorised
by Charles V, the American empire was a monopoly of Castile. Between
1524 and 1538, it is true, Charles tried to extend permission to trade and
reside in the Indies to all the subjects of his empire, and in these years
foreigners, particularly Germans, took part in colonial trade and enterprises.[7]
But the reasons for this were financial and technical ones and corresponded
to Charles's search for the naval and capital resources needed in colonial
expansion. They were certainly not influenced by the supranational ideas of
the humanists or their faith in the universal mission and opportunities of the
empire. In any case Spaniards had their own commercial interests to consider
and were not prepared to share them with other subjects of the emperor who

---

[5] M. Bataillon, *Erasme et l'Espagne*, pp. 243–53.

[6] See J. Sánchez Montes, *Franceses, Protestantes, Turcos. Los españoles ante la política
internacional de Carlos V* (Madrid, 1951), and its review by M. Bataillon in *Bulletin
Hispanique*, liv. (1952), 208–11: also Sánchez Montes, 'Actitudes del español en la época
de Carlos V', *Estudios Americanos*, iii. (Sevilla, 1951), 169–99.

[7] R. Konetzke, 'La legislación sobre inmigración de extranjeros en América durante
el reinado de Carlos V', *Charles-Quint et son temps*, pp. 93–111.

Charles V by Titian (detail)

happened to be associated with Spain simply because of a dynastic inheritance. Even Spain's Christian mission in the New World was national rather than universal in character, at least as far as personnel were concerned, for Charles V followed the policy of his Spanish predecessors in excluding from the Indies not only foreign traders but also foreign missionaries. This provides further proof that in the empire of Charles V the particular forces were stronger than the collective ones and that Spain was emerging as the strongest of all the particular forces.

The idea of one ruler and one empire, however, was not only viewed with reserve by Spaniards but was inevitably rejected by other rulers and other nations who regarded it as an affront to their sovereignty. In practice, of course, Charles V was not faced with a simple choice between empire and national state, and it is understandable that he should strive to preserve the possessions which his unique dynastic position had brought him. No sixteenth-century ruler voluntarily gave up an inheritance. Indeed to whom could Charles have conceded his more distant possessions? Conditions in Europe at the beginning of the sixteenth century still favoured the existence of super-states, which could now be ruled by even greater administrative and military power than was available to medieval rulers, and it would be an anachronism to insist that at this date universal states were doomed to die. There were still areas of Europe not yet ready for national sovereignty, and in view of French policy in Italy from 1494 and the aspirations of Francis I to the Empire in 1519 the suspicion remains that had not Spain claimed them as its own then France would have done so. The French kings too had dynastic ambitions not very dissimilar to those of the Habsburgs. As it was, France was now on the defensive.

The constant hostility of France can be explained as a defence mechanism of a centralised and united state that found itself surrounded by the power of Charles V. Franco-Spanish rivalry, it is true, predated the accession of Charles V, and the idea of a diplomatic encirclement of France had already occurred to Ferdinand of Aragon who had forged the Spanish–German–English alliance, which the emperor continued. Rivalry was also in part inevitable, given the fact that two great powers were neighbours. But Charles V added a new dimension to the conflict with France. From the time of his accession to the throne of Spain, the Spanish frontier with France was no longer confined to the Pyrenees but extended to many other parts of Europe. Indeed, the power of Charles V pressed France on almost all her frontiers: in the north from the Low Countries and Artois, in the east from Franche-Comté, in the south-west from Spain and the Mediterranean. In these conditions France was faced with the alternative of a struggle for independent life as a major power or acceptance of satellite status with constant risk of intervention. For France this was a national issue, and the question of Italy, important as it was in aggravating the rivalry, was of secondary interest. The main object of French policy was to resist the enormous power of the Habsburgs by striking simultaneously with its other enemies, the Germans and the Turks, and as strongly as possible, at its most sensitive point, whether that happened to be Germany, Italy or the Mediterranean. The ubiquity of Habsburg power meant that allies against it were not difficult to find. One of these was the Turk.

In the Ottoman empire Charles V faced not only a formidable land power but also his greatest maritime rival. Once again, this was a conflict which he inherited, but whereas under his predecessors Spain had faced Islam virtually on her own, now two similar but incompatible imperial systems confronted each other across the Mediterranean. At the same time, because of the wider interests of Charles V, his responsibilities lay in the defence not only of Spain but also of other parts of Europe. For the striking power of the Turk was directed against three areas—eastern Europe, the Mediterranean, and Spain itself. The Turkish move northward towards the centre of the Balkan peninsula had already begun before the capture of Constantinople in 1453, but after that date the frontier between the Ottoman empire and Christendom was pushed deeper into Europe, and with the capture of Belgrade in 1521, the year which saw the beginning of the great conflict between Charles V and Francis I, the Turk was poised to enter Hungary. The capture of Constantinople, however, had added another factor to Turkish expansion: with possession of the deserted quays and arsenals and easy access to the timber supplies of the vast forests of the Black Sea area, the Ottoman empire became a major naval power and began to menace the lines of western commerce with the eastern Mediterranean. Consequently it was no longer the land frontier along the Danube that had to be defended but also a new sea front in the Levant and the Adriatic, where even Italy was threatened.

To reach across the Mediterranean and strike at Spain itself was beyond the resources even of the Ottoman empire, and there was no real danger of the Spanish coasts being attacked by squadrons from Constantinople.[8] The Turkish fleet could not reach Spain directly but needed a base either on the Barbary coast of North Africa or on the Mediterranean coast of France. The danger for Spain lay in the fact that the Turk had allies in both these places and might find yet another ally within Spain itself. The naval power of Islam was now doubled by the combined strength of the small but numerous fleets of the Mohammedan pirates of North Africa, who began to work in close alliance with the Turk and had the support of the Sultan himself. The

[8] On the problems of Spain in the Mediterranean see the great masterpiece by F. Braudel, *La Méditerranée et le monde méditerranéen à l'époque de Philippe II* (Paris, 1949).

strength and hostility of the Moors of North Africa had been increased in the last years of the fifteenth century following the fall of Granada. Those Moors who quitted Spain took refuge on the nearby coast of North Africa and many of them continued the struggle against their hereditary enemy, not only by the capture of vessels at sea but also by raiding expeditions on the Spanish coast. In the latter event there was the additional danger of their finding allies among the *moriscos*, or those Moors who had chosen to remain in Spain and whom the Spanish authorities regarded as a subversive element. Then, in 1516 pirates of Turkish origin established their domination over Algiers, and a great number of their Moorish friends found refuge there. The new state, enriched by plunder, began to construct fleets and to make itself a Mediterranean power, a menace to Christians who were enslaved for ransom money and a source of basic insecurity in what had once been the sheltered waters of the western Mediterranean. In this area Spanish interests were directly involved, as were the interests of Europe as a whole; and it was on Spain that fell most of the responsibility for defence and counter-attack, in a war that was damaging not only financially but also in prestige. As this coincided with the war against France, the two enemies of Spain co-operated and produced the Franco-Turkish alliance, the scandal of Christendom but an irresistible temptation for French diplomacy. Another temptation was Germany.

In the same year as Charles V arrived in Spain, 1517, Luther published his Thesis against Indulgences. The crisis of religion, together with the political obstacles in the way of imperial government in Germany, increased the pressures on Charles and on Spain. In spite of their imperial title the Habsburgs had little power in Germany outside their own domains and they found they could make little headway against the particularism of the German princes. Moreover, owing to his distance from events Charles was forced to abandon personal action in Germany, though he retained control of policy: in 1521 he made his brother Ferdinand his permanent representative in Germany; in February 1522 he ceded his Habsburg domains to Ferdinand who now became archduke of Austria and was thus compensated for the loss of his prospects in Spain itself. The Protestant revolt removed Germany yet further from the emperor's control and opened yet another gap in his defences. Here was a point of weakness that many of his enemies could exploit, and France in particular began to look for an ally in Protestantism as well as in Islam. Charles himself found it extremely difficult to separate the political and the religious issues in Germany. Quite apart from his own orthodoxy, Charles valued religious peace in his empire as a condition of political union. In its political aspect Lutheranism might mean further independence of the princes of the Empire and reinforce the development of autonomous units in which the ruler would be head of both church and state. In the event, the princes gained little from the Reformation, for their penury forced them to sell church lands, and the estates used their ever-increasing demands for money to gain new privileges and some say in church affairs.[9] But whoever gained from it, Charles was forced to oppose Lutheranism, for it was a denial of an imperial Germany under a central government and another blow to his hopes of giving some substance to the idea of the Holy Roman Empire.

Charles's own religious views, however, though not deeply developed, were never anything but orthodox, and it was in religion that he came nearest to reflecting public opinion in his Spanish kingdoms, which was intensely anti-Lutheran. He himself seems to have appreciated this, for he usually met complaints about his long absences from Spain with the argument that he was putting down Lutherans. Even here, however, Charles had his own interests to think of as well as the views of his Spanish subjects. Owing to his political objectives in Germany, which had little to do with Spanish interests, he had to preserve communications with the German princes. Consequently his policy towards Lutheranism wavered between the desire to suppress it and the desire to prevent it from entrenching itself more deeply: to accomplish the second objective he was ready to negotiate. This, however, brought him into conflict with yet another power—the papacy.

The emperor's international objectives never received the papal support to which he considered they were entitled. Like other rulers in Europe, the pope was conscious of the ubiquitous presence of Habsburg power. In Italy it held a particular menace for him: if the same king possessed Milan and Naples then the independence of the papacy, caught between these two states, could be threatened. Papal reserve towards the emperor, however, was not simply the distrust of one statesman for another. It was also derived from religious reasons. No one in Spain, and certainly not the crown, challenged the spiritual authority of the pope; but every effort was made to limit papal intervention in temporal affairs and even in ecclesiastical matters like church appointments and jurisdiction. Charles V inherited this tradition and strengthened it. In 1523, for example, he secured from his former tutor and regent, Adrian VI, a perpetual grant of the right to present to bishoprics. But later popes were less compliant, and disputes over ecclesiastical jurisdiction were a constant source of tension between Spain and the papacy. Moreover, the papacy suspected some of Charles's religious objectives and believed that he either misunderstood Luther's doctrines or underesti-

[9] F. L. Carsten, *Princes and Parliaments in Germany from the fifteenth to the eighteenth century* (Oxford, 1959), pp. 431, 437.

mated their distance from Catholic orthodoxy. Suspecting the emperor's objectives, the papacy also suspected his means. In particular it believed that his criticism of the moral decadence of the curia and his plea for a general council of the church reflected his political as well as his religious interests. Charles V inherited the medieval idea that it was the duty of the emperor to call a council when the critical state of Christendom demanded it. But his own interests demanded it too. In the first place, a likely difference of opinion between the council and the pope made it possible for the emperor to use the threat of a council to put pressure on the papacy, and Charles valued such a weapon in his anti-French diplomacy. Secondly, Charles wanted a council in which Protestant opinion might be freely voiced in order to reach a compromise by means of some relaxation in church discipline, such as permission for clerical marriage and services in the vernacular. In this case he was more concerned with politics in Germany than with a revival in the church. Spain itself had never been really affected by conciliar theory, though even in Spanish opinion[10] at the beginning of the sixteenth century the question of church reform included the idea of a general council. The Spanish church, however, was more concerned with the practical problem of making sure that reform councils would be convened at frequent intervals and their decrees carried into effect than with the question of papal authority as such, and the Spanish church remained implacably hostile to Lutheranism wherever it showed itself. Yet Charles could not procure the papal alliance he wanted even on Spain's account. His Spanish counsellors believed no less than Charles himself that Paul III should abandon his position of neutrality in the conflict between their master and Francis I, and they based their position on the ground that the pope should support an orthodox nation like Spain rather than a dubious one like France. When the papacy did abandon its neutrality, however, it was not always in favour of Spain.

Indeed, in the Habsburg–Valois rivalry the king of France could count on numerous allies who would offer him material or moral support—the Ottoman Turk, the German Protestants, Denmark, the pope and many Italian princes, all of whom were more or less hostile to Charles V. The European possessions of the emperor, on the other hand, scattered and unintegrated as they were, were exposed to numerous enemies and could count on few friends. Only the king of England and the Shah of Persia favoured the Habsburg cause from time to time, the first against France, the second against the Turk. In a hostile world, the English alliance could

[10] See H. Jedin, *A History of the Council of Trent*, vol. i. (Eng. trans., London, 1957). Also R. Burgos, *España en Trento* (Madrid, 1941); C. Gutiérrez, *Españoles en Trento* (Valladolid, 1951); F. Cereceda, *Diego Laínez en la Europa religiosa de su tiempo, 1512–1565* (2 vols., Madrid, 1945–46).

be very useful to Charles V. The future maritime-colonial struggle between Spain and England had not yet developed, though its origins were already being prepared; in any case, England was not yet a first-rate power. But Charles appreciated that England had great diplomatic value and even greater strategic value. One of the first acts of foreign policy which the emperor undertook on his own initiative was to confirm the English alliance by the Treaty of Canterbury with Henry VIII in 1520 and by the project of a marriage between Charles himself and Mary Tudor in 1521. The marriage never took place but the alliance lasted almost without interruption for the whole of the reign and culminated in another marriage, that of Charles's son, Philip, with the same Mary in 1554. By that time the emperor regarded the English alliance as vital for the defence of the Low Countries and of their communications with Spain.

2. THE ARMED FORCES OF EMPIRE

To preserve diplomatic communications and defend his many interests Charles V had a network of resident embassies which he inherited from Ferdinand of Aragon and which were filled by one of the most accomplished diplomatic staffs in Europe.[11] In the last resort, however, the sanction behind his policy was his armed forces and the money with which these could be provided.[12]

One of the vital needs of Charles V's widespread empire was the maintenance of political and commercial communications by sea power. He also had to defend it against a powerful maritime rival in the Mediterranean. Yet the weakness of his empire was exposed precisely at sea. This was partly a question of manpower. Compared with the human resources of the Turk and the pirates of Algiers, Charles was woefully short of trained seamen capable of manning the galleys of his Mediterranean fleet. In default of sufficient oarsmen, the Spanish navy had to rely heavily on convicts and prisoners-of-war and was still unable to meet its commitments. With the discovery of America and the growing maritime demands that this involved, more and more Spanish seamen, especially from Biscay and Andalucía, were engaged on the Atlantic crossing. Catalonia, on the other hand, could not fulfil a similar function in the Mediterranean. The decline of Catalonia, already apparent in the fifteenth century, was virtually complete by the time Charles V began to rule. Its maritime activity was now reduced to minor trade with Marseilles and the Balearics, and Catalan ships rarely ventured to Sardinia or Sicily or the outposts of North Africa. Remote from

[11] G. Mattingly, *Renaissance Diplomacy*, pp. 138–52.
[12] On the money available for warfare see above, pp. 59–64.

the fisheries of northern Europe and bereft of an active trade in the Mediterranean, Catalonia was in no position to provide a 'nursery' of trained seamen for the Spanish fleets. Another consequence of the loss of trade was the decline of the Catalan merchant fleet and this in turn produced a decline in shipbuilding and with it the loss of skilled labour and management. Once the tradition of shipbuilding had gone, it was difficult to replace it, and Charles V never attempted to. So dead was the Catalan coast that when in 1562 Philip II decided to undertake a vast programme of shipbuilding and naval armament he had to give the contracts to Italian shipyards; and in order to try and revive the arsenal of Barcelona he had to import Genoese technicians.[13]

The final obstacle to the maritime power of Spain was the shortage of vital naval stores. Compared with the Turk, whose timber supplies from the Black Sea area were almost inexhaustible, Spain was at a grave disadvantage. Like her neighbours, she suffered from the general deforestation in the western and central Mediterranean and lacked sufficient timber for her masts and oak for her hulls. More and more throughout the sixteenth century Spain was forced to procure her timber supplies from the Baltic, but with greater distances to cover and more obstacles to encounter than her enemies in northern Europe.[14] To the basic conditions of Spain's maritime position the government of Charles V paid little attention. On the other hand, the emperor occasionally disposed of large sums of money. Like most rulers in the sixteenth century he raised his naval forces as he needed them by contracts with private shipowners, rather than by developing a permanent royal navy. In Spain the state's biggest contractor was Alvaro de Bazán, father of the Marquis of Santa Cruz, who conceived the idea of the Invincible Armada. And without the vessels he could hire from his Genoese ally, Andrea Doria, the emperor's position in the Mediterranean would have been desperate indeed.

While Spain could not provide Charles V with a powerful navy, she could supply him with the best army in Europe. The long struggle with the Moors in Spain itself had established a military tradition which survived the fall of Granada in 1492. Soldiering had become a fashionable and a profitable occupation not only for the gentry but for the whole population. Recruitment, therefore, was not an insuperable problem, and after the experience of the war of Granada a modified form of national conscription was introduced in 1496 which was the first step in replacing feudal levies by a national army, recruited, paid and controlled by the central government.

The Spanish army excelled above all in its infantry, whose superiority was observed by Machiavelli and survived to the period of the Thirty Years War. Indeed her infantry forces for foreign wars were the only ones seriously

[13] Braudel, *op. cit.*, p. 114.   [14] Braudel, *op cit.*, pp. 108–10.

organised by Spain in the sixteenth century. In the peninsula itself militia or police forces were the only ones used, and their main task was to keep public order and security. The cavalry was regarded merely as a subordinate arm, accompanying each infantry regiment. These regiments had been originally organised by a brilliant young officer of Ferdinand and Isabella, their 'Great Captain', Gonzalo de Córdoba.[15] In the Italian wars at the beginning of the sixteenth century he had improved the efficiency of the Spanish units by introducing radical changes in their organisation, which took the form of an increase in armament by the addition of pikes and arquebusiers and an improvement in tactics by attention to mobility. Combined with the introduction of the *tercio* in 1534, which became the standard regimental unit, the reforms of Gonzalo de Córdoba effected a revolution in infantry fighting which made the reputation of the Spanish army for the next hundred years. The essence of this method consisted in the integration of the various arms. Of the 3,000 men in a Spanish *tercio*, there were 1,500 pikemen, 1,000 swordsmen and 500 arquebusiers.[16] In battle formation the pikemen would form protective squares, with the swordsmen in the centre so that these might surprise the enemy when it came to hand-to-hand fighting. These squares were very difficult to break, especially as they were given supporting fire from the arquebusiers and artillery separately positioned.

The Spanish *tercios*, probably so called because of the three elements of which they were composed, first made their appearance in Italy and they were named after the regions where they were stationed, Milan, Naples, Sicily or Sardinia. Later, when Philip II decided to send an army into the Low Countries, he established the *tercio* of Flanders. They were recruited from the various nationalities of which the empire was composed, but Charles V and his successor were most partial to the Spanish soldier, the one in whom they had most confidence, and as far as possible the Spanish regiments were kept homogeneous. In Spain, the ten or twelve companies of which a *tercio* was composed were recruited by means of volunteers; the royal treasury made a contract with a captain whose reputation would guarantee his ability to raise a sufficient number of troops. Government inspectors then made sure that the company was complete to the number specified in the contract before paying the captain.

Among these volunteers were often the younger sons of noble families who preferred a military career to a court or ecclesiastical one and who wanted to serve their apprenticeship under officers with the best reputations.

---

[15] Piero Pieri, 'Gonsalvo di Cordova e lo origine del moderno esercito spagnolo', *Fernando el Católico e Italia*. V. Congreso de Historia de la Corona de Aragón (*Estudios*, III), 207-25.

[16] Later in the century the size of the *tercio* was reduced to under 2,000 men.

There were also recruits who were escaping from justice: later in the century, when Philip II was desperate for troops for the war in Flanders, he recruited a *tercio* from Catalan bandits whom he pardoned on condition that they enrolled in the Spanish army. And always there were those who volunteered because they could not find a living in Spain except by manual work, and for some Castilians a military career was infinitely better than working. Indeed it offered prospects of earning sufficient money with which to buy a landed estate at a time when there were few other ways of making a fortune in Spain; the careers of some of Charles V's greatest commanders, such as Antonio de Leyva and Fernando de Alarcón, both of whom acquired wealth as well as glory, provided striking examples of the profits available in the military profession and a compelling reason for the support which universal monarchy could claim among some of the emperor's subjects. But if the Spanish army reflected social conditions in Spain, it also frequently reflected the state of the royal treasury. Mutiny, often highly organised, was endemic in the Spanish army of the sixteenth century and could usually be traced to a bankrupt government's inability to pay its troops. Prolific as she was in soldiers, Spain could still not supply sufficient recruits for the emperor's many campaigns and he had to rely also on mercenaries recruited from various parts of his dominions, such as Germans and Walloons. Less reliable than Spanish troops, the discipline of these regiments depended entirely on the payment of their wages, and this in turn depended on the emperor's ability to raise money. Nevertheless, Charles V was not the only monarch with financial difficulties, and although his resources were never equal to his commitments, he usually disposed of greater money power than his most powerful European rival, Francis I of France.

3. The Struggle with France

The relative strength of Charles V and Francis I, and its relation to their financial power, was first tested in the contest for the imperial crown, which was decided in Charles's favour. From then onwards the French king was alert to the possibilities of strengthening his own position by attacking the weaknesses of his rival. Anxious to exploit the revolt of the *comuneros* in Spain, Francis I declared war on the emperor (22 April 1521) and so began a new period of conflict. A French army invaded Navarre but was too late to take advantage of the disorders in Castile where the rebels in fact joined with the royal army to repel the French and ended the attempt of Navarre to restore its independence under French protection. This kind of hostility, however, was largely accidental: the main theatre of war, and the permanent struggle, was in Italy.

Whereas the policy of Chièvres, who died in May 1521, had aimed at the protection of the Low Countries by understandings with England and France, Gattinara wished to make Italy the centre of the emperor's interests, with the argument that, once the French had been turned out of Italy, he could make terms with the pope and control all Europe. The influence of Gattinara gave a new direction to Charles's policy, but this was partly because his advice also coincided with the strategic interests of the Habsburg empire. Milan, the former fief of the German empire, held a key position in the Spanish-Austrian axis: as it was easily reached from Genoa it was a vital link in the line of communications between Spain and Franche-Comté and between Spain and the Tyrol.[17] Once Charles was convinced of the importance of Milan, he acted quickly and sent an expedition into Lombardy which took Milan for the emperor in November 1521. In January 1522 Charles's former tutor, now Regent of Spain, Adrian of Utrecht, was elected pope as Adrian VI. Consequently, Gattinara's two conditions for the success of Charles's empire—domination in Italy and alliance with the papacy—were on the point of being fulfilled, and by August 1523 the emperor and his vassal states, together with the pope, Venice, Florence, and England, were allied against Francis I. But Adrian VI, the keystone of the alliance, died in September and was succeeded by Clement VII, whose election initiated a series of Italian popes all anxious to hold the balance between the two great powers, and thus removed one of the basic conditions for the success of Gattinara's policy.

Meanwhile, however, Charles had been looking after his northern flank. At Windsor on 16 June 1522 he had concluded an alliance with Henry VIII which had been followed by a secret treaty.[18] By this Charles was betrothed to Henry's daughter, Mary, then aged six, and the allies agreed on a plan for the complete conquest of France by armies led by the monarchs in person; out of the subsequent division of spoils Henry was to receive the crown and the western provinces, while the emperor was to recover all the former Burgundian territories and add to them Languedoc, Provence, and the valley of the Rhone, thus providing another link between Spain and Italy and the northern lands of the Habsburgs. In spite of its fantasy, the Treaty of Windsor is a telling commentary on the dynastic and chivalric nature of Charles's policy at this stage and provides yet a further justification of French resistance to Habsburg power. Both monarchs were serious, and within his aggressive intent Charles was pursuing an objective that was

---

[17] On imperial Milan see F. Chabod, *Lo Stato di Milano nell' Impero di Carlo V* (Milan, 1934).

[18] See *Calendar of State Papers, Spanish, Further Supplement to vols. 1 and 2 (1513–1542)* ed. G. Mattingly (London, 1947), pp. xvii–xviii.

always dear to his heart—the recovery of his Burgundian patrimony. The plan itself, however, was unrealistic and doomed to failure: it underestimated the military and financial weakness of the allies and the great defensive strength of France.

With England a diplomatic rather than a military ally, and with a pope who began to loosen the coalition formed under his predecessor, the prospect of uniting Italy against the French looked as distant as the conquest of France itself. Francis I reconquered Milan in October 1524, and in December Clement VII concluded an alliance with France and Venice. In these circumstances, Charles decided that the English match was not worth concluding: a Portuguese bride would bring him a bigger cash dowry, and armed with this he could settle Italy before returning to the grand plan against France. At this point, on 10 March 1525, he received the news that his generals, Pescara, Leyva, and Lannoy had routed the French at Pavia and taken Francis I prisoner. Charles could now dictate the terms of peace without reference to England. He found it much more difficult, however, to follow up his victory over France. Indeed, the captivity of the French king in Madrid, sensational as it was to contemporaries, could not in itself solve the problem of power posed by Charles's relations with France or reduce the dilemma whether to give priority to Italy or to Burgundy. His Spanish counsellors were urging him to abandon the Italian mirage, and he himself, against Gattinara's advice, refused Francis I's offer to pay a huge ransom, leave Italy and renounce all claims to Flanders and Artois, for he wanted above all the Duchy of Burgundy. In any case, what were such offers worth? By the Treaty of Madrid (15 January 1526) Francis I undertook, in return for his freedom, not only to renounce his claims to Italy and Flanders, but also to hand over Burgundy to the emperor. But Charles himself realised that to implement the treaty would require armed force and considerable expense.

Indeed, far from fulfilling the Treaty of Madrid, Francis I organised the League of Cognac against the emperor. Whether Charles V aspired to a universal empire or not, the fact remained that even without counting any of the territories in dispute—Milan and Burgundy—his dominions were already too universal and injured too many interests not to provoke widespread resentment: and as for his pursuit of Christian concord, there was little sign of that in his demands in the Treaty of Madrid. It was not difficult, therefore, for Francis I to find allies in Italy, beginning with the pope himself and including Venice, Florence, and other cities, while even Henry VIII momentarily abandoned the Spanish alliance. Such a widening of the enemy front in Italy was dangerous to Charles V. In order to defend himself he decided to strike at the weakest link in the chain, the pope. But shortage of money was beginning to tell; unpaid armies were difficult to control, and the assault on Rome in May 1527 by Spanish and German troops was followed by looting and sacrilege that lasted for a whole week.

These campaigns, however, like the victory of Pavia itself, could not win Charles the balance of power in Italy or fulfil the programme that Gattinara was still urging on him. From 1526 his Spanish administrators had been advising him to avoid all plans of further involvement in Italy, largely on financial grounds. In fact the stalemate of 1527 was caused by the fact that neither Charles V nor Francis I had money to do more. Gradually, however, an improvement in Charles's material prospects began to give him the advantage of power against his rival. Treasure from the Indies was now arriving in appreciable quantities. In July 1528 Andrea Doria defected from France and transferred his service and his fleet to the emperor who now had a major naval base at his disposal and greater security of communications. The French army which had invaded Milan and Naples was defeated, and in July 1529 pope and emperor were reconciled in the Treaty of Barcelona and Clement VII at last agreed to receive Charles in Italy. Outmanoeuvred and outfought, Francis I was now forced to come to terms. By the Peace of Cambrai (3 August 1529) he recognised Charles's sovereignty over Artois and Flanders and surrendered all claims to Milan, Genoa and Naples; for his part Charles renounced his immediate claim to Burgundy while still protesting all his rights there. This was shortly followed by Charles's recognition of Francesco Sforza, duke of Milan, as his imperial feudatory.

Now that he was reconciled with the pope, Charles decided to undertake the journey to Italy to receive the imperial crown from his hands. At this moment, just before his departure from Spain, he delivered his 'imperial' speech in Madrid, in which he publicised his ideal of a Christian empire.[19] Superficially, Gattinara's policy had triumphed: Charles followed up his political victory in Italy by reaching an understanding with the pope, symbolised by his coronation in Bologna by Clement VII. But Gattinara's position in the emperor's administration was beginning to decline, and his policy was destined to bring Charles more problems than it solved. The dominant position in Italy, which Gattinara had promised would make him master of Europe, in fact prevented him from pacifying Europe and using his Christian empire against the Turk, with whom France had already established diplomatic relations. Feeling the pressure of Habsburg power on all its land frontiers, France would strike out whenever the opportunity occurred. The death of the Sforza duke of Milan in 1535 reopened the question of Italy by producing demands of the French government for the succession of one of its candidates, and when in March 1536 a French army

[19] See above, pp. 74–75.

invaded Savoy and Piedmont and occupied Turin the threat to Milan became acute. Consequently, Charles's successful African campaign of 1535, which culminated in the capture of Tunis, could not be followed up because he was then forced to turn his attention back to France. Returning in triumph from Tunis and filled with ideas for the unification of Christendom and an attack on the Turk, only to find Francis I still in the way, the emperor met the pope in the presence of two French ambassadors (17 April 1536) and gave vent to his exasperation in a speech in which he denounced Francis I's failure to keep his promises and his subversive activities among Charles's states, and declared that unless he accepted his conditions for peace he was prepared to make war. The only alternative he could offer was a personal combat between himself and Francis: if Charles was victorious then his prize should be Burgundy, while if Francis won he should receive Milan. Paul III could not take such a performance seriously—in view of the state of Christendom the emperor's obsession with Burgundy was little short of stubborn—but Charles was serious about one thing, the renewal of war.

Yet he himself had aggravated the situation by allowing negotiations to proceed for a French candidate for Milan when in fact he had no intention of compromising. The negotiations themselves produced a direct conflict of opinion between Charles and his own ministers. Both Cobos and Granvelle urged a policy of peace even at the cost of compromising; Cobos because of his awareness of the emperor's financial position, Granvelle because of his desire to free Charles for a settlement of the conflict with the German Protestants by preserving peace on the Italian and Flemish fronts. Charles himself, however, never intended to make concessions, and it is difficult to avoid the conclusion that he allowed his ministers to negotiate simply in order to gain time. Eventually, against the advice of his civilian counsellors but encouraged by his two chief commanders, Andrea Doria and Antonio de Leyva, Charles decided to resume hostilities. Following the success of his combined operations against Tunis in the previous year, he planned a joint attack on France by sea and land: this meant a complete redeployment of the troops that had originally been assembled for the projected invasion of Algiers in the following year and their dispatch to the front in northern Italy. Of the multiple attacks that converged on France, the invasion of the north from the Low Countries had to be abandoned for lack of money, but Charles personally advanced in the south by way of Provence in the summer of 1536, with the intention of relieving pressure on Milan by a combined operation aimed at Marseilles. The campaign itself was an unrelieved disaster and by October Charles was back in Genoa, deeper than ever in debt and militarily ruined. The war was equally costly for France, and it was mutual exhaustion that brought major operations to a halt. After peace negotiations had failed over the emperor's demands for Milan, for French aid against the Turk and for French support for a general council, the pope managed to arrange a summit meeting at Nice between king and emperor in which neither met each other but each negotiated separately with the pope. Out of this came the Truce of Nice (18 June 1538), on the understanding that it should last ten years and with a programme of a league against the Turk, war on the Protestants, and co-operation in a general council.

Given the prevailing conditions of power, however, co-operation was the last thing to be expected, and the struggle was renewed before the truce expired, again over the question of Milan. Taking advantage of the exhaustion of the emperor's available resources in the Algiers expedition of 1541, Francis renounced the ten years truce in July 1542 and sent an invading army into the Low Countries where Charles's administration was already beset by the presence of heresy and discontent over financial exactions. Threats of this nature, however, brought the best out of Charles and he acted decisively. In order to deal an overwhelming blow against France, he renewed the English alliance (11 February 1543), ordered Cobos to scrape together all available funds in Spain and went in person to Germany to arrange a religious compromise and raise funds and troops for an attack on France from the east. Once he had contained the danger in the Low Countries, Charles then assembled an army at Metz; and while an English force invaded Normandy he himself penetrated by Champagne to within a short distance of Paris. With this advantage, and anxious to be free to tackle the Lutherans in Germany, Charles decided to negotiate at once without the participation of his English ally. By the Peace of Crépy (19 September 1544) the French king renounced his claims to the Low Countries and Naples, while the emperor offered one of two marriages to the Duke of Orleans, second son of the king of France: either his daughter Maria, with the Low Countries after Charles's death, or his niece, Anne of Hungary, with Milan a year later. Charles himself opted for the second alternative, but whether this was a serious attempt to rid himself of the burden of Milan and liquidate the Italian problem or a desperate expedient to pacify Francis I while he himself dealt with Germany cannot be certain, for the Duke of Orleans died before the plan could materialise.[20]

In view of the long prevarication of the emperor during many years of discussion about Milan, he probably at no time seriously considered alienating it or ever regarded it as anything but a fief that belonged to his dynasty.

[20] For the problem of priorities involved, however, see the authoritative discussion by F. Chabod, 'Milan o los Paises Bajos? Las discusiones en España sobre la "alternativa" de 1544', *Carlos V (1500–1558)*. Homenaje de la Universidad de Granada (Madrid, 1958), pp. 331–72.

Here as elsewhere the objectives of both monarchs remained the same as before, and the collapse of the Crépy settlement left the issues between them unsettled. Peace was welcome to the emperor because he had urgent problems to settle in Germany, and the two monarchs were at peace when Francis I died on 31 March 1547. But if the rivalry of the monarchs was now ended there remained the conflict of power and the territorial disputes between France and the Habsburg ruler. Meanwhile, Charles himself remained an intransigent dynast. In a political testament dated 18 January 1548, drawn up for his heir's guidance, he advised Philip never to abandon his claim to the Duchy of Burgundy, 'our country' (*nuestra patria*).[21]

4. Defence against the Turk:
the Danube and the Mediterranean

During the later stages of the emperor's struggle with Francis I a third power, the Ottoman Turk, had intervened on the side of France to increase the pressure on Charles in western Europe just as it was already threatening his position in eastern Europe and the Mediterranean. Turkish power, like his own, was ubiquitous and Charles found it impossible to resist it with equal strength in every area. In 1526 Soliman the Magnificent began his great attack on Hungary and with a huge army he defeated and killed Louis II of Hungary and Bohemia at the battle of Mohács (29 August 1526). A few days later the Turks were in Buda, the capital of Hungary, and within striking distance of the eastern frontier of Austria, Charles's Habsburg inheritance. Towards the defence of the Danube, however, the emperor's contribution was negligible.[22] Even his Spanish subjects, compliant as they were to most of his demands, drew the line short of Habsburg interests in eastern Europe and were usually unwilling to supply troops and money for this area. Charles himself realised that he would have to delegate power here to his brother Ferdinand: he had ceded his eastern possession to him as archduke of Austria in 1522 and he continued to assist his defence preparations with some of his own revenues from Naples. Now, following the death of Louis II, Ferdinand was elected king of Bohemia and Hungary and thus extended his appanage in eastern Europe. Whether he was powerful enough to resist the Turk, however, remained to be seen.

In 1529, two years after Charles had been refused a subsidy in Spain for an expedition to Hungary, the Sultan began a second invasion. He recovered

---

[21] See B. Beinert, 'El testamento político de Carlos V de 1548. Estudio crítico', *Carlos V (1500–1558)*, pp. 401–38.

[22] On Charles V's policy in eastern Europe see B. Chudoba, *Spain and the Empire, 1519–1643*, pp. 61–67, 70–78.

Buda and laid siege to Vienna: this was the greatest threat the Habsburgs had yet faced. As the fate of Austria itself was at stake, Charles was forced to take direct action. In 1532 he managed to raise an army in Germany, commanded by his best generals, including Antonio de Leyva and the marquis of Vasto, and send it to the assistance of his brother. A small contingent of Spanish troops took part in the defence of Vienna and the emperor himself was present in the campaign. As a result, the Turk was forced to fall back on Buda, though he kept up a relentless attack on Hungary and Austria for many years to come. While Charles was ready to defend the Habsburg inheritance in Austria, however, he refused to commit himself to the defence of Hungary. At this point, therefore, there was a divergence of interests between himself and Ferdinand. Even during his short stay in Vienna in the autumn of 1532 the emperor made it clear that he only sought the defence of the capital of the Danube and not the liquidation of the Hungarian question, for he had other commitments which forced him to seek a pacification in eastern Europe. But although Charles considered that the fate of Hungary did not concern him directly, he did not abandon his brother completely for, on leaving Vienna, he assigned him some troops. In the course of the heavy fighting during the 1530's more units of Spanish troops arrived, but the Habsburgs had to content themselves with the defence of a narrow frontier in Hungary, and with their commitments elsewhere they were glad to accept a truce in November 1545.

Some of these commitments were also against the Turk and they too were part of a losing battle. But whereas the Spanish contribution to the defence of the Danube was on a small scale, the emperor commanded greater support for the defence of the Mediterranean where the interests of Spain were directly involved. In 1522 Soliman captured Rhodes, the island of the Knights Hospitalers, and thus secured another base from which he could direct his operations against Charles V. To attack him more directly he had an incomparable ally in Kheirredin Barbarossa, a renegade Christian and the most relentless of the African pirates. In the name of Islam and as a vassal of the Sultan, Barbarossa could direct the struggle in the western Mediterranean where he was the leader of a new power—Algiers. Spain, too, had a foothold in Africa. As outposts for the defence of her own coasts she had a chain of forts in North Africa which had been established in the reign of Ferdinand of Aragon. But the Italian diversion had caused Ferdinand to neglect to extend his African defences by seizing the interior of the Maghreb, and the opportunity once missed never occurred again. From 1516 the Barbary pirates established themselves at Algiers and through their colonisation of the interior of the Maghreb made themselves a new state in the western Mediterranean. In 1518 they placed themselves under the protection

Empress Isabella by Titian

of the Sultan and became his greatest asset in the naval war with Spain. And gradually they began to free themselves of the rival Spanish fortresses on the North African coast.

The danger was rendered even more acute by the attacks on the coast of Spain itself and by the problem of the moriscos within Spain. After the fall of Granada in 1492 and the forcible conversion of the Moors of Castile in 1502, Spain was possessed of a large alien minority, nominally Christian, never assimilated, and always regarded as a threat to internal security and a potential ally of her Islamic enemies in the Mediterranean. As large numbers of moriscos inhabited the remote and largely undefended coastal regions of southern and eastern Spain and were known to be sympathetic to the cause of Islam in North Africa, there was some justification for Spanish fears. As an act of thanksgiving for the victory of Pavia, and with an eye to internal security, Charles V decided in 1525 to extend the Castilian decree of 1502 to Valencia and to give the moriscos of that kingdom the alternative of expulsion or conversion.[23] This provoked an armed revolt in the Sierra de Espadón in 1526, and after negotiations the Moors accepted baptism in order to avoid expulsion. But the question was complicated by that of the Barbary pirates. In 1529 one of the captains of Barbarossa led a fleet of galleys in a sacking expedition against the coast of Valencia, carrying off many Spanish prisoners. And meanwhile the piracy continued as the Algerians swooped on western shipping and coasts in search of the supplies that North Africa could not afford them. Spain, having failed to complete the North African conquests of Ferdinand and Isabella, was now paying the price of neglecting her naval resources: faced by a maritime power, Charles V still produced no programme for reviving the naval strength of Catalonia, while all efforts to base an efficient navy on the south of Spain were ineffective.

It was not until the early 1530's that the emperor was able to reply to the naval power of Islam, and this was because he now had the help of his new ally, Genoa. The value of the Genoese reinforcements was seen in the success of the powerful fleet led by Andrea Doria into the Gulf of Corinth in 1532: there he was able to take Patras, while in the following year he captured Coron in the Morea, though the occupation of both was only temporary. This expedition may have had the effect of distracting the Sultan's attention and relieving the pressure on Austria, but it also provoked Soliman to greater efforts. He allied himself more closely with Barbarossa who was now appointed commander-in-chief of the Turkish fleet and showed his prowess by attacking the Italian coast and capturing Tunis from Spain's Moorish ally, Muley Hassan, in August 1534. At the same time Soliman also began

[23] See below, pp. 218–24.

to seek a closer alliance with France. It was now a struggle for control of the central Mediterranean.

From Charles and from Spain a supreme effort was necessary. Turkish naval strength was growing, and the threat was approaching closer to the coasts of Naples, Sicily, and Spain itself. To cut the Mohammedan naval front in the Mediterranean and establish a Spanish base between Algiers and Constantinople, Charles decided to strike at Tunis. The opportunity came from peace with France in 1535, while the means were supplied by an extra subsidy voted by the cortes of Castile and the seizure of private revenue from the Indies. A large, though hastily prepared, expedition—and one in which his Castilian advisers had little faith—left Barcelona and assembled in Sardinia before sailing for North Africa. In the heat of mid-June it reached Tunis, and after heavy fighting, during which Charles himself was in the front line, first La Goleta then Tunis itself were captured (21 July 1535). A fleet of eighty-two galleys was taken, thousands of Christian captives were freed, and Muley Hassan was restored to his throne. Barbarossa himself, however, escaped to take refuge in Algiers and continue the struggle from there.

Although the emperor's success in North Africa produced a profound impression in Europe and was followed by a famous winter of royal festivities in Naples, the conquest of Tunis could not in itself alter the balance of power in the Mediterranean. Charles did not have the naval strength necessary to follow up his victory and pursue Barbarossa to Algiers. Consequently, the pirate chief was able to organise new raids against the Balearic Islands and the coast of Valencia in 1536 and another large-scale attack against southern Italy in 1537, in combination with the renewed offensive by France who had already concluded her first alliance with the Turk in February 1536. Indeed Charles's war with France from 1536 to 1538 was itself a diversion from the Mediterranean campaign, which could not be renewed until after the Truce of Nice in 1538. In February of that year Charles tried to organise a new offensive against the Turk by concluding an alliance with the papacy and Venice; but the forces of the league were defeated by Barbarossa at Prevesa in September 1538 and the league itself disintegrated when Venice, always anxious for her trade and grain supplies in the eastern Mediterranean, made a separate peace with the Turk in 1540. Without the Venetian fleet the western coalition could not face the Turkish navy, and consequently Charles decided to concentrate all his available resources in the west in order to conquer Barbarossa's stronghold of Algiers and so complete the programme he had begun at Tunis. The emperor himself led a large expedition which included the conqueror of Mexico, Hernán Cortés, and which reached Algiers in October 1541. But the season was late for such a campaign and

150 of his ships were lost in a storm; although Charles landed and attacked Algiers, he was forced to re-embark and abandon the operation in order to avoid yet greater disaster.

Algiers was one of the greatest catastrophes of the emperor's career and the last of his major naval actions. From now on his position in the Mediterranean deteriorated rapidly. When the struggle with France was renewed (1542–44), the Turk was able to be of great service to his ally and French galleys reinforced the Turkish navy. Barbarossa co-operated in the siege of Nice and in 1544 the Turkish fleet wintered in Toulon together with its cargo of Christian slaves. On the death of Barbarossa in 1546 another experienced pirate, Dragut, took his place and continued his campaign. In August 1551, forty years after its conquest by Spain, Tripoli was attacked by the Turk and had to be evacuated by the Knights Hospitalers; in the hands of the Turk it became another useful base and another link in the chain with Algiers.[24] Other outposts on the North African coast fell gradually into Moslem hands and the Sultan continued to send out powerful fleets to attack the coasts of the central Mediterranean. There was a point, however, beyond which the Sultan could not press his advantage: distracted by war with Persia and weakened by the growing uncertainty of French co-operation once his fleets had crossed the vast distances of the Mediterranean, he was unable to achieve naval supremacy in the west. It was the factor of distance rather than the strength of Spain, or indeed of any Christian power, which earned a short respite for the west. Nevertheless, the Sultan's North African allies continued to menace the security of the western Mediterranean and to harry trade and shipping between Spain and Italy. The Barbary pirates infested that part of the Mediterranean between Sardinia and the African coast, thus forcing Christian shipping to keep to the safer routes near Cape Corsica; but the French occupation of Corsica, undertaken with the help of the Turk, threatened communications between Spain and Italy even here, and there was no respite for Charles in the defence of the maritime routes of his empire.

Consequently, far from accomplishing the great crusade against Constantinople which was the dream of his younger years, Charles V was unable to provide even for Spain's immediate interests. It is true that he never obtained the full co-operation of Aragon and Catalonia, an essential condition for Spanish supremacy in the western Mediterranean.[25] But the fact remains that he himself diverted national resources and efforts to remoter imperial interests.

[24] See Braudel, *op. cit.*, pp. 739–42.
[25] J. Vicens Vives, 'La Corona de Aragón y el ámbito del Mediterráneo Occidental durante la época de Carlos V', *Karl V. Der Kaiser und seine Zeit* (Cologne, 1960), pp. 211–17.

For naval power depends not on hastily prepared expeditions but on a long and arduous process of building, recruiting, and training. Such a programme was never undertaken by Charles V and had to await the initiative of Philip II.

5. Princes and Protestants in Germany

For the emperor the problem of Protestantism was even more complex than that of the Turk, and it was this which finally reduced his policy to ruins. Not only was it linked with his struggle against France, it also affected his relations with the papacy. Above all, it undermined his already precarious position in Germany. Yet even without its political content Protestantism already had profound significance for the emperor and for Spain. Although Charles V was not a man of the Counter-Reformation, or the leader of a spiritual revival in the Catholic Church, he was totally hostile to heresy and if he had possessed the means he would have destroyed it, as he attempted to do in Spain and the Low Countries where he disposed of more power than he did in Germany. This was also the Spanish position and here the coincidence of views was spontaneous. Troops and money for the battle against heretics came above all from Spain, and many of the great intellectual leaders combating the Reformation, such as Ignatius Loyola, came from Spain. The assembly of a council, to which Lutherans would be summoned to have their doctrines condemned and where the dogma and traditions of the Catholic Church would be reaffirmed, was an idea canvassed by Spanish theologians as well as by their king. After the sack of Rome in 1527, and in reply to a protesting brief of Clement VII, Charles already used this threat and spoke of appealing to a general council if the pope did not change his policy, which the emperor regarded as disastrous for Christendom. But he could not overcome the reluctance and the suspicion of the papacy until the pontificate of Paul III, and even then complications arose to delay decisive action. This was due not only to the fact that the conciliar movement traditionally aroused papal susceptibilities, but also to Rome's awareness of the extent of Charles V's power. The Catholic concord that the emperor was seeking was to be a concord under his inspiration and his hegemony, and implied the preservation and perhaps extension of a European empire which was unacceptable to his neighbours and inevitably aroused the suspicion of France, which in spite of imperial and Spanish opinion was also a Catholic power. And without denying the sincerity of the emperor, it is necessary to take into account the contemporary tendency to adopt religious justifications, especially in official statements, for secular policies. There is also the fact that in spite of the divine mission that the emperor claimed to fight infidels and heretics, he did not give priority to the Protestant revolt, any more than he did to the threat from Islam. He himself argued that he could not do this until he had pacified western Europe and reached an understanding with the pope and with France. But apart from the fact that he himself was an obstacle to such an understanding, his long preoccupation with the means prevented him from accomplishing the end.

In spite of the declaration made by the young emperor before the Diet of Worms in April 1521, the first of the great policy statements written by himself, in which he declared his resolve to undertake the defence of Christendom and the doctrines of the church, the fact remains that Charles underestimated the differences between Luther and the church, and delayed committing himself to decisive action. Admittedly the situation was difficult. Charles already had a political problem in Germany deriving from the sovereignty of the estates and the independence of the princes, both of which frustrated his desire to give meaning and sanction to imperial government; and with his commitments elsewhere, Charles had to delegate responsibility in Germany to his brother Ferdinand. Religion reinforced politics. Although Luther was declared an outlaw by the Edict of Worms, he was able to live under the protection of the Elector of Saxony while what Charles regarded as a temporary schism hardened into a lasting breach, the political advantages of which were exploited by reformers and princes alike. In June 1526 a vague declaration by the Diet at Speyer was interpreted as allowing each prince to decide religion in his own state. In 1529, in another Diet at Speyer, a Catholic majority reaffirmed the decision of Worms against Lutheranism, and while denying any rights to reformers, demanded toleration for Catholics in reforming states. This decision, which appeared successful on the surface, was the beginning of the road to disaster for Charles and for the Catholic cause. The Lutherans protested against it and began to improve their political organisation. At this point Charles decided to take personal action; freed from war with France since the Peace of Cambrai (1529) and fresh from his coronation at the hands of the pope, he returned to Germany after eight years' absence and was present at the Diet of Augsburg in 1530. In the emperor's party at Augsburg there were numerous Erasmists, including his secretary Granvelle, and although it is doubtful whether he himself was influenced by the ideas of Erasmus, Charles exercised the greatest patience during the long disputations and attempted to find a solution which would not compromise Catholic dogma. But his arbitration failed, and even his offer to arrange a general council was rejected by the Protestants, as it was by the pope. The Protestants emerged from Augsburg with their own formula rejected but intact—the profession of faith presented by Melancthon and known as the Confession of Augsburg— and this now managed to survive. Short of force, there was nothing Charles could do, and he did not wish to use force. Threats without sanctions, therefore, had little effect except to encourage the Protestants to improve their political position by forming the League of Schmalkalden (February 1531), directed by the Elector of Saxony and the Landgrave of Hesse, and a potential ally of Charles's other enemies in northern Europe.

But the Empire was also threatened by the Turk. Charles's brother Ferdinand, who had just received the title of King of the Romans (January 1531), desperately needed the help of the German princes to defend his dominions against Soliman. The Turkish invasion of Austria in 1532 forced Charles to make a temporary settlement in Germany, known as the Peace of Nuremburg (May 1532), by which a general peace was established within the Empire where no one would be condemned for religious beliefs until a council be held. The measure was effective for its purpose, and with Protestant support Charles was able to raise a powerful army which liberated Austria and forced the Turk to retreat.

Throughout the 1530's Charles V had to continue the policy of temporising with the Protestants, partly because of the Turk, whose pressure was relentless in this period, partly because of France, but above all perhaps because of his desperate financial position. For all these reasons the emperor wanted a united front in Germany, and to secure this he was ready to compromise still further. Moreover, both Charles and Granvelle were convinced that the emperor had the right to resolve religious problems, if necessary without the intervention of the pope, and they believed that a Catholic restoration ought to begin with the suppression of abuses in the church. Theoretically, therefore, Paul III should have been the answer to their hopes, for he was a reforming pope and anxious for a council.[26] But now it was discovered that this was merely a further embarrassment to Charles, for it raised the problem of Protestant participation in a council. In default of a council, therefore, and anxious for the help of the imperial estates against France and the Turk, Charles decided to impose his own solution in Germany—the Declaration of Ratisbonne (July 1541). This guaranteed safety to adherents of the Augsburg Confession, sanctioned some secularisation of ecclesiastical property, granted the Protestant princes the right to reform monasteries and other religious institutions, and increased the influence of Protestants in the imperial chamber.

The pope condemned the Declaration of Ratisbonne, and events condemned it too. The emperor gained nothing from it, except the knowledge that the more he yielded to the Protestants, the greater his weakness was exposed and the higher their demands were raised. Yet still he was not ready to act. In June 1542 Paul III published a bull calling the Council of

[26] See L. von Pastor, *History of the Popes* (Eng. trans., London, 1894–1953), xi. 41–217.

Trent for 1 November; but at this point Francis I broke the Truce of Nice and prepared to attack the emperor; consequently no council was possible at that date. The pope tried to reconcile the two rivals, but Charles was playing for time, anxious for the assistance of Maurice of Saxony, Albert of Brandenburg, and other German princes against France, and knowing that the Protestants were opposed to a council called by the pope. But having signed the Peace of Crépy with Francis I in September 1544, Charles was in a position to attack Protestantism more firmly. Yet it was still not to be a theological attack. When the Council of Trent finally opened in December 1545, the emperor's representatives tried to prevent any dogmatic definition of the problem of justification, because he did not want to alienate the Lutherans whom he still hoped would accept the invitation to join the council. The council did in fact define the doctrine of justification and of the sacraments, and the emperor's state of mind when he decided to join battle with the Protestants was one of resentment against the pope and other bishops.

Many Catholics in the following of the emperor, including his own confessor, the Spanish Dominican Pedro de Soto, had long been advocating war, without, however, resolving the dilemna of how to deal with a religious movement by military means.[27] But the Protestants themselves had a political and military organisation, and it was this which the emperor hoped to overcome when an alliance with the papacy (June 1546) and the efforts of Cobos in Spain gave him sufficient funds to raise an army. The imperial troops, commanded by the Duke of Alba and headed by the emperor himself, won the battle of Mühlberg on 24 April 1547, a victory in which the confusion on the imperial side—redeemed as usual by the bravery of Charles's Spanish troops—was only slightly less than that of the Protestants. Charles's triumph over the League of Schmalkalden at last put him in a position in which he could attempt to impose his own political and religious settlement in Germany. The result of both, however, was another setback to the imperial cause.

Harmful though it was to the Protestants, the emperor's victory at Mühlberg also increased dissensions within the Catholic camp. The church itself was fearful of Charles's power, and the Council of Trent scattered after the emperor's victory; those prelates who supported Charles remained in Trent, while the rest reassembled in Bologna according to the pope's instructions; later the entire council was prorogued owing to Charles's opposition. Acting independently of the papacy and on the assumption that

[27] On de Soto see V. D. Carro, *Pedro de Soto y las controversias político-teológicas en el siglo XVI* (Salamanca, 1931); and the same author's *El maestro Fr. Pedro de Soto, O.P. (confesor de Carlos V)* (Salamanca, 1931).

he himself could exercise ecclesiastical functions, the emperor imposed another compromise known as the Interim (30 June 1548), a document drawn up by his theologians, among them Pedro de Soto, which preserved Catholic doctrine and the authority of the pope but made every possible concession to Lutheran opinion in matters of discipline and worship. There were signs that the emperor's religious policy was not entirely acceptable to Spanish opinion, and the Jesuit Bobadilla, who circulated a criticism of the Interim under the very nose of Charles, had to be censured. Indeed the Interim suffered the fate of most religious compromises: it was attacked simultaneously by Protestants and Catholics alike, and it failed to secure the objective for which it was intended—religious peace in Germany.

While Charles's religious settlement caused dissension within the church, his political aims caused dissension among the Habsburgs themselves. Francis I had already died before the battle of Mühlberg, and after it the emperor had his hands free in Germany. Here was the opportunity to secure his political ideal and the interests of his family by realising a wish that was dear to his heart: he would obtain the imperial succession in Germany for his son Philip, and so bind the German heritage with the Burgundian and Spanish ones. Such a solution, however, was not acceptable to German opinion, either Catholic or Protestant: in November 1550 even the Cardinal of Augsburg was moved to protest against the intolerable presence of Spaniards in Germany and to declare that Germany would only accept a German prince at its head. Furthermore, Charles also encountered the inflexible opposition of his own family.

Summoned by his father from Spain, where he had been Regent since 1542, Philip had left Valladolid in October 1548. He was twenty-one, and it was his first tour of Europe. He joined his father in Brussels in April 1549 and was there recognised as inheritor of the Low Countries. He was then paraded in Germany. At Augsburg during the winter of 1550–51 the Habsburgs had a family conference lasting more than six months, during which Charles's plans were frustrated by the ambitions of his brother Ferdinand and the hostility of his nephew Maximilian, Ferdinand's eldest son. The power of the eastern Habsburgs, based in Austria, extending to Bohemia and Hungary, and crowned with the title of King of the Romans, an appanage which Charles himself had helped to create, was now turned against him, in circumstances which made him helpless to resist it. For the growing independence of the eastern Habsburgs coincided with powerful interests in Germany. In so far as Germany refused to accept political subordination and Catholic laws, it refused to accept a Spanish régime which personified both, and further rejected the prospect of being held by Spanish and Italian troops. Therefore, German opinion turned towards the princes of Vienna, whom it believed could be managed more easily than a Spanish successor could be; it was Ferdinand it wanted as emperor, with Maximilian, not Philip, to succeed him. Ferdinand's growing influence in central Europe and his determination to keep the empire, already implicit in his title of King of the Romans, forced Charles to compromise in the agreement of 9 March 1551, by which Ferdinand would succeed Charles as emperor but in turn would support Philip as his successor, with Maximilian coming a poor third. The agreement, however, remained a dead letter, not because of the poor impression the young Philip made in Germany, as he did everywhere outside of Spain, but because facts were against it. The determination of the Austrian Habsburgs and the hostility of Germany combined to frustrate Charles's aspirations for his dynasty. It only remained for the events of 1551–52 to push him right out of Germany.

France played the major rôle in the growing offensive against the emperor, seeing in his difficulties in Germany the vital opportunity to reduce his power once and for all. The Protestant princes of Germany reached an understanding with Henry II and consented to his taking Metz, Toul, and Verdun which were part of the Empire: and the enemies of Charles were now joined by another German prince, Maurice of Saxony, who in spite of being a Protestant had hitherto fought on the side of the emperor. France also renewed her link with the Turk and urged the Sultan to break his truce with the Habsburgs. In August 1551 the Turk took Tripoli. Beset by dangers on many fronts and by worse financial difficulties than he had yet experienced, Charles saw his world disintegrating. Unable to cope on every front and fearing above all for the Mediterranean, he took one of the most momentous decisions of his career: he ordered his Spanish and Italian troops to evacuate Württemberg in August. By withdrawing his forces of occupation, Charles indirectly prepared the way for the German explosion of 1552. To garrison Germany he now had to rely on his brother Ferdinand, whose commitments in Hungary left him little resources or enthusiasm for Charles's cause and whose relations with the rebels in Germany itself were an object of great suspicion to the emperor. In these circumstances it would have been wiser for Charles to take refuge in the comparative safety of the Low Countries and strike at France from there; instead he continued to expose himself in Germany, and when Maurice of Saxony made a sudden raid against him near Innsbruck in May 1552 he had to take to flight across the Alps to Villach in Carinthia. The second session of the Council of Trent was quickly closed; Metz, Toul, and Verdun fell to France; and the Turk was threatening Austria. There was little to salvage from the disaster in Germany, and the Treaty of Passau, negotiated by Ferdinand and Maurice and ratified by Charles on 15 August 1552, merely ratified the emperor's defeat. In its recognition of

Protestantism as the equal of the Catholic religion in the Empire on a basis of *cujus regio, ejus religio*, the Treaty of Passau foreshadowed the Peace of Augsburg three years later (25 September 1555), when constitutional form was given to these concessions. Augsburg was the logical culmination of the emperor's policy and weakness in Germany, though he bitterly regretted it and left its negotiation to Ferdinand.

After his defeat in Germany, Charles also failed against France. Encouraged by the Duke of Alba and anxious for his communications between the Low Countries and Franche-Comté, he attempted to recover Metz in the winter of 1552; again and again his army attacked until in January 1553 he was forced to raise the ruinous siege and retire to the Low Countries where he remained until his return to Spain in 1556. For now he had reason to fear for the security of his first inheritance. If Germany were lost, and with it a Catholic and imperial frontier beyond Flanders, and if France were threatening, then it was necessary at least to secure the Low Countries. In his later years this became one of the greatest anxieties of the emperor, his return to the point of departure. Love for his native land and concern for his son caused him to separate the Low Countries from the Empire. But how could he defend them, distant and isolated as they were, and how could he secure their communications with Spain, now more clearly than ever the base of his power?

6. The Low Countries and the English Alliance

In the Low Countries, unlike Germany, Charles had a Regent whom he could trust. After the death of Margaret of Austria, he appointed another Habsburg, his sister Mary of Hungary, as governor in the Low Countries in 1531. For the rest of his reign she applied his rule with as much firmness and tact as the circumstances permitted. These, however, were not propitious, for Charles was faced by mounting religious and economic discontent.

Lutheranism had a foothold in the Low Countries from about 1518. Much as he disliked Lutheranism, however, Charles also disliked papal intervention, and for the rest of his reign he sought to keep religious policy in his own hands. Two months after the Bull excommunicating Luther, the emperor issued an edict ordering the burning of all Lutheran books (20 March 1521). A year later (23 April 1522), without consulting the pope, he appointed an Inquisitor general of the Low Countries, Van der Hulst, who as well as being a layman was also a member of the Council of Brabant and therefore an official of the king. Charles's attempt to establish exclusive control of the Inquisition, however, was checked when in 1523 Adrian VI appointed Van der Hulst papal Inquisitor for the Low Countries, and although he was soon deposed by Margaret of Austria on account of the reckless persecution in which he indulged, this ended the emperor's attempt to introduce imperial Inquisitors in the Low Countries; in 1524 three native priests were appointed papal Inquisitors with full powers, though later Charles insisted on the agreement of a member of the provincial council before any sentence could be passed. From 1525 Charles V published new and various edicts against Lutheranism, accompanied by severe sanctions; indeed, from 1550 the only penalty prescribed for all religious offences was death. At first judicial power rested with city councils, but later Charles transferred this jurisdiction to provincial councils and so kept the persecution of heretics in his own hands.[28]

While he managed to contain, though not terminate, the progress of heresy, the emperor could make little headway against the political and fiscal particularism of his various provinces. Of all his possessions the Low Countries enjoyed the greatest prosperity, based on the secure foundations of trade and industry, and they were, with Spain, his greatest source of money and one which he ruthlessly tapped. As it was their own wealth which the emperor's wars were devouring, they had even more urgent reasons than Spain for demanding peace, and they never ceased to demand it. The prosperity and liberty of the Low Countries under Charles V, however, which are invariably contrasted with the misery and oppression prevailing under Philip II,[29] were the monopoly of a small class, and the fortunes made by a few in the earlier period were accompanied by desperate poverty for the mass of the people especially in the towns, whose wages lagged far behind prices during the entire period from 1521 to 1556.[30] These social conditions bred discontent and erupted in the agitation of the Anabaptists, whose movement was essentially a proletarian one, with social as well as religious implications, and who received the relentless attention of the authorities on both accounts from 1535 onwards. There were no Anabaptists among the propertied classes, whose approval of the government's policy of repression prevented the movement from becoming a popular challenge to state authority as Calvinism later did.

Such an alliance, however, did not sustain every aspect of Charles's policy. The trading and industrial communities of the Low Countries were careful to exercise their autonomous rights against the attempts of the emperor to complete the process of unification and centralisation begun by his Burgundian

[28] Léon-E. Halkin, *La Réforme en Belgique sous Charles Quint* (Brussels, 1957); M. Dierickx, S.J., 'Fue cesaropapista la política religiosa de Carlos V en los Paises Bajos?' *Hispania*, xix. (1959), 378–85.

[29] See below, pp. 288–97, including a fuller treatment of subject.

[30] C. Verlinden, 'Crises économiques et sociales en Belgique à l'époque de Charles-Quint, *Charles-Quint et son temps*, pp. 177–90.

predecessors. To the organs of central government—the Council of State, the Council of Finance and the High Court of Appeal—the provincial Estates and the Estates General maintained a stubborn resistance, haggling over money, insisting on redress of grievances and exercising their right to report back to their provinces and towns. Charles never attempted to introduce Spaniards into his Burgundian administration, but even with native officials he found he could not be so absolute in the land of his birth as he was in Castile and that his relentless financial demands might strain the alliance with the propertied classes on which his rule depended. In 1539 resistance in Ghent broke out into violent revolt—firmly suppressed—when the citizens overthrew the authorities who had complied with Charles's demands.

Resistance to the religious, financial, and administrative policies of the central government made the Low Countries a useful field of intervention for the emperor's enemies, particularly for France, who on occasion could co-operate effectively with his opponents in the north-east. Charles had his most harrowing experience of this danger in the duchy of Guelders where he encountered some of his bitterest enemies, who, with French money and support, kept up a steady attack on his position in the Low Countries. It was 1543 before he could annex Guelders and secure his north-eastern frontier in the Low Countries. By 1552, however, with Germany lost and France hostile and his rule in Flanders far from absolute in spite of his personal popularity there, he had reason to fear not only for his north-eastern frontier but for the whole of his Burgundian inheritance.

It was in these circumstances that the English alliance became the solution to the German disaster, to French threats, and to the danger to the Low Countries.[31] For the purposes of defence and communications with Spain, it could secure an English port and the Channel passage. But it might secure much more than that. By marrying Philip to Queen Mary, England itself could be brought into the Habsburg orbit. The marriage between Philip and Mary (25 July 1554) meant much to both parties. Mary sought in Philip a support for her plans of a Catholic restoration in England and looked for an heir to continue her régime. The emperor and his son saw England as a compensation for the loss of Germany and a security for the Low Countries. By the marriage, England and the Low Countries were associated in a personal union. As Philip was to inherit Spain as well as the Low Countries, this meant that the crowns of Spain, Burgundy, and England would be temporarily joined in one person. If Philip and Mary had an heir, he would inherit not only England but also the Low Countries and Franche-Comté,

---

[31] For a good treatment of the English marriage and alliance see Royall Tyler, *The Emperor Charles the Fifth*, pp. 180–231.

while Spain and its dominions would pass to Philip's son by a previous marriage, Don Carlos. This would enable England to guard the Low Countries, especially against France, while Spain could concentrate on the defence of Italy and the Mediterranean. And if Don Carlos died without an heir, then the entire inheritance would go to the heir of Philip and Mary.

In envisaging a possible separation of the Low Countries from the crown of Spain, though with the intention of keeping it more firmly within his family, Charles V evidently did not regard the union of the two to be inevitable and sacrosanct, from the point of view either of Spanish interests or prestige. It was only later, in the reign of Philip II, that the separation of the two came to be regarded as inconceivable and that the determination to possess the Low Countries at all costs became a ruinous obsession which lasted until the end of the Habsburg régime. But when the moment of decision came, Charles V did in fact preserve all those territories united to the crown of Spain for the inheritance of his son. By then, however, the possibility of leaving them to a grandson had disappeared and he had no desire to leave them to Ferdinand of Austria. For the son whom Philip and Mary desired never came, and the only result of the match was to make Spaniards highly unpopular in England; soon national and religious sentiment combined with maritime rivalry to ruin relations between the two nations.

Meanwhile, the waning prospect of an eventual Anglo-Spanish empire was a profound relief to Henry II of France and reinforced his opposition to the emperor. The accession of Paul IV to the papacy brought another enemy of the Habsburgs to the international scene and heralded new difficulties for them in all parts, especially in Italy. Charles V could take no more. For years, sick and disillusioned and prematurely old, he had been waiting for the time to renounce his heavy burden to his son. Better to give Philip his inheritance now, during his father's lifetime, than to risk an improvised accession amidst the disorders of war after his death.

Already in January 1548 the emperor had recorded his political testament for his son.[32] In 1550 he had begun to dictate his memoirs. Five years later he judged the time had come. On 25 October 1555, before the assembly of the Estates General in Brussels and after recording his life work in a speech which moved himself and his audience to tears, Charles abdicated to Philip the sovereignty of the Low Countries. Three months later (16 January 1556), in the house in which he lived on the outskirts of Brussels, he handed to his secretary the abdication of all his Spanish dominions in the Old World and the New. The renunciation was made in three different documents and corresponded to the nature of the Habsburg monarchy. In one he renounced the crown of Castile and León, together with the kingdom of Navarre and the

[32] B. Beinert, op. cit., pp. 401–38.

Indies; in another he renounced the crown of Aragon-Catalonia, with the kingdom of Sardinia; in the third he renounced the crown of Sicily. The kingdom of Naples and the duchy of Milan were already in the hands of Philip since the time of his marriage with Mary Tudor when Charles had given them to him in order to increase the value of the new husband and give him a royal title. As a last gesture—though it had little significance apart from reflecting his financial difficulties—he even managed to sign a truce with Henry II of France (5 February 1556) and to transfer Franche-Comté to his son. Now he only had the Empire, where in reality his brother Ferdinand had ruled from 1553. This, too, he renounced, in September 1556, though it was not until February 1558 that the electors accepted his abdication and elected Ferdinand in his place. In September 1556, leaving Philip in the Low Countries, Charles sailed for Spain and in February of the following year reached Yuste, the remote and peaceful monastery in Extremadura where he chose to spend his last years, hardly in retirement, for he was still nominally emperor, retained a keen interest in international affairs and continued to advise and help his son. There he died on 21 September 1558.

In returning to Spain to die, a Spain that he had already detached from Germany, Charles V recognised the direction his empire had been taking for many years. Imperial dreams had died with the loss of Germany and the division of Italy. The Low Countries and Spain remained the twin pillars of Habsburg power in Europe, and of the two Spain was the richest source of money and troops and the natural base of the Habsburg monarchy. The administration and the finances of the monarchy, which had never succeeded in becoming imperial, were now clearly Spanish. The Council of Italy, created in 1555, was a sign that Mediterranean policy was ceasing to be that of an empire and becoming part of Spanish foreign policy, or perhaps of *Spanish* imperialism. The decision revealed the presence of a new generation —of Philip II, who was not an emperor but an absolute monarch, and of Castilians, whose near monopoly of viceregal and conciliar government underlined the preponderance of Spain. While this corresponded more closely to the realities of power, it also meant that the varieties of choice available under Charles V were replaced by a monolithic régime that was Spanish in personnel and in objectives. Nevertheless the mark of imperialism left on Spanish policy by Charles V could never be effaced, and the legacy of overseas commitments, especially in the Low Countries, remained to haunt Spain for a century and a half to come.

CHAPTER IV
SPAIN DURING THE PRICE REVOLUTION

1. THE PEOPLE

To sixteenth-century observers the most striking feature of the Spanish landscape was its emptiness.[1] Not far from the Ebro, for example, with its irrigated fields, its lines of trees and its industrious moriscos, were the barren heaths of Aragon stretching monotonously to the horizon. Francesco Guicciardini, envoy of Florence to Ferdinand of Aragon, travelled across this region in the spring of 1512 and was depressed by the 'utterly deserted country, where there is not a lodging to be found nor a tree to be seen, only vast stretches of rosemary and heather, for this is arid land'.[2] Even fruitful Andalucía had its deserts, inhabited not by human beings but by wild beasts, the terror of mules and their riders. It was no coincidence that Don Quixote and Sancho travelled most of the time in solitude along deserted routes. Much of Spain was, indeed, deserted, and if its land was ill-cultivated it was partly because it was under-populated.

At the beginning of the sixteenth century Spain had a population of over seven million, and although this was higher than that of England (barely three million) it was much smaller than France's fifteen million and smaller still than the twenty-two million of the Ottoman empire and its satellite states.[3] Yet after her civil wars and during a period of relative prosperity, Spain's population increased steadily throughout the sixteenth century and suffered no catastrophic decline until the years around 1600. In Castile the population rose from 7,414,000 in 1541 to 8,485,000 in 1591–94, an increase of about 15 per cent. The recovery of Catalonia was slower: the figures available for 1553 indicate a population of less than 40,000, which was only a tenth of that of 1359, but here too there was an improvement in the second

---

[1] The composite work edited by J. Vicens Vives, *Historia social y económica de España y América* (5 vols., Barcelona, 1957–59), supplies the previous lack of a good general account of Spanish economic and social history; the sixteenth century is covered in vol. iii with contributions by J. Reglá and G. Céspedes del Castillo.

[2] Quoted in Braudel, *La Méditerranée et le monde méditerranéen à l'époque de Philippe II*, p. 350.

[3] Population figures for the sixteenth century have become increasingly clear, thanks to modern research: see Jordi Nadal, *La población española (siglos xvi a xx)* (3rd ed., Barcelona, 1973), pp. 16, 28–37.

half of the century and recovery lasted longer than that of Castile.[4] The population of Spain, however, was not evenly distributed among the various regions: Castile was much more densely populated than the peripheral areas, and in 1591, with 6,910,000 inhabitants, it had a density of 18·2 inhabitants to one kilometre compared with 11·8 among the 1,180,000 inhabitants of Aragon, and 12·1 among the 145,000 inhabitants of Navarre.[5]

Even within Castile the distribution of population underwent important shifts in the sixteenth century, symptomatic perhaps of the increase in the number of inhabitants. Internally, there was the movement of northerners towards the south, drawn by the Andalusian monopoly of the Indies trade; in the course of only sixty years (1530–90) Seville doubled the number of its inhabitants from 45,000 to 90,000, while many towns of Castile, like Medina del Campo and Valladolid, whose prosperity had been based on their commercial and financial relations with northern Europe and suffered during the war years in the second half of the century, experienced a considerable loss of population from about 1575.[6] Another shift of population occurred as a result of the rebellion of the Alpujarras between 1566 and 1571, which was followed by the dispersal of the moriscos of Granada throughout northern Castile; in this case the vacuum was partly filled by settling colonists from northern and central Spain. Finally, sheer lack of subsistence might force people to migrate to other parts of the country, in Castile from rural areas to the towns, in Catalonia from the Pyrenees to the plains. In addition to internal movements of people, however, there was also the factor of emigration, some of it compulsory as in the case of the Jews in 1492, some of it voluntary, to America. The number of Spaniards who emigrated to America in the course of the sixteenth century was much lower than has been supposed, under 150,000 by the 1550's.[7] For contemporary states, however, this was a considerable exodus of manpower, and raises the question—to which there is still no answer—did Spain become a colonial power because she had the manpower to sustain her discoveries, or even because the growth of her population beyond her domestic resources forced her to expand?

On the other hand, the departure of Spaniards from the mother country

---

[4] J. Vicens Vives, *Apuntes del curso de Historia Económica de España* (2 vols., Barcelona, 1956), i. 289–91; J. Nadal and E. Giralt, *La population catalane de 1553 à 1717: l'immigration française et les autres facteurs de son développement* (Paris, 1960), p. 19.

[5] Bartolomé Bennassar, *Valladolid au Siècle d'Or* (Paris, 1970), pp. 152–208.

[6] On Seville see Ruth Pike, 'Seville in the Sixteenth Century', *Hispanic American Historical Review*, xli. (1961), 1–30.

[7] See below, p. 157.

was accompanied by the immigration of many foreigners into Spain.[8] The number of Frenchmen crossing the Pyrenees, lured by the wealth of Seville and the Indies trade, and in eastern Spain even by the prospect of manual work, increased steadily in the sixteenth and early seventeenth centuries; in Catalonia Gascons formed 20 per cent. of the population at the end of the sixteenth century and provided an important labour force in the rural areas. But the most powerful group of foreign immigrants was that of the Genoese. From the thirteenth century they had a substantial colony in Seville, while in the Mediterranean they were commercial rivals of Barcelona. All the privileges acquired during this time and revoked by Ferdinand of Aragon in 1500 were restored by Charles V as a reward for the spectacular volte-face of Andrea Doria in 1528, when he took his service from France to Spain. From that year Genoese bankers played a major rôle in Spanish state finances, together with the Welsers and Fuggers, acquiring the most remunerative revenues, *juros*, monopolies and commercial privileges in return for their numerous loans to the crown. Their situation was further improved after the separation of Spain from the German Empire, and they ended by supplanting their rivals from the north, including the Fuggers. In addition, they took a large share of American treasure, partly as a return on their loans to the crown, partly from their own participation in the Indies trade, which included valuable contracts for the supply of negro slaves. Taking root in Spain, hispanised Genoese entered the councils and the church and commanded Spanish armies and fleets. Indeed, owing to their economic and thus indirectly their political power, they could almost be regarded as part of the Spanish ruling class. For few Spaniards took part in industry and commerce; the majority of them lived on and from the land.

The social structure of Spain was based almost exclusively on ownership of land, most of which was in the hands of the nobility and the church. The virtual monopoly of landed wealth enjoyed by the aristocracy was legally protected by the device of *mayorazgo*, or entail, which, combined with the principle of primogeniture, tied estates in perpetuity to the same family and prevented alienation. Ruthlessly exploited, the system tended to concentrate land in the hands of a few powerful families, some of whose estates in Andalucía survive to the present day. The Laws of Toro (1505)

---

[8] On French immigration see J. Nadal and E. Giralt, *La population catalane de 1553 à 1717: l'immigration française et les autres facteurs de son développement* (Paris, 1960); on the rôle of the Genoese in Spain see R. S. Lopez, 'Il predominio economico dei Genovesi nella monarchia spagnola', *Giornale storico e letterario dell Liguria*, xii. (1936), 65–74. The general topic is covered in A. Girard, 'Les étrangers dans la vie économique le l'Espagne au XVIᵉ et XVIIᵉ siècles', *Annales d'histoire économique et sociale*, v. (1933), 567–78.

regulated and extended the process by making what had previously been an exclusive privilege of the nobility into an institution of civil law. Commoners, or those who could afford to, took advantage of the measure to establish small *mayorazgos*, and while this possibly reduced the monopoly of the older aristocracy, it also increased the immobility of landed wealth in Spain and its stagnation.

Based on their vast latifundia and protected by the law of entail, the Spanish aristocracy were also favoured by economic conditions in the sixteenth century. In an age of rising prices landowners were sheltered from the effects of inflation by their ability to profit from it. Agricultural prices rose much faster than non-agricultural prices during the first three-quarters of the sixteenth century, and from 1575 to 1625 the two groups remained together.[9] Unlike the industrial exporter, however, whose goods were eventually priced out of the foreign market, the agricultural producer in Spain could increase his income not only by exploiting his land and selling its vital produce—corn, wool, and cattle—but also by raising his rents at a time when land was appreciating in value. The income from rents increased with the rise in prices, with the result that the nobility, who despised work and regarded business as debasing, was one of the few sectors of Spanish society that did not suffer from the price revolution.

The aristocracy's loss of political power, therefore, must be seen in the context of its economic strength. It had surrendered its feudal rôle to the demands of absolute monarchy and was now content to serve the crown in the subordinate fields of war, diplomacy, and viceregal administration. For this it was compensated by the extension of its economic power, a process in which the crown itself was a willing ally. And although the feudal power of the nobles declined at a national level, it survived in their own districts in the form of seigneurial jurisdiction over their vassals, which enabled them to collect feudal dues, appoint local officials and even render justice. Such power originated in natural conditions which still prevailed in sixteenth-century Spain, whose vast and arid plains needed a large and disciplined manpower to cultivate them. Spain inherited its machinery of irrigation intact from the Moors, together with the personnel necessary for its operation. In the sixteenth century it was still the moriscos, protected but virtually owned by their aristocratic masters, who cultivated the plains of Lérida, Valencia, Murcia, and Granada.[10] Seigneurial jurisdiction survived in its most primitive form, however, in Aragon, where it was protected against the crown by the *fueros*, in which aristocratic privileges sheltered

---

[9] E. J. Hamilton, *American Treasure and the Price Revolution in Spain, 1501–1560*, p. 261; Braudel, *op. cit.*, pp. 631–32.
[10] Braudel, *op. cit.*, 64.

under territorial autonomy. An Aragonese lord could rule his vassal almost absolutely, and in certain cases had power to condemn him to the garrotte or sell him to the galleys. And although the harshness of this régime was assuaged by the increasing castilianisation of Aragon and the occasional intervention of the crown, even Philip II in 1591 dared not abolish their sacred *fueros*.[11]

In Castile, on the other hand, the aristocracy was tamed. Philip II continued the policy of his predecessors and governed with the help of humble commoners, posting the more powerful members of the nobility, such as the Dukes of Medina Celi, Alcalá, Albuquerque, and Medina Sidonia, to distant viceroyalties or other assignments. An administration staffed by university-trained jurists strove with increasing success to replace seigneurial by royal justice, which would usually support a vassal against his lord. Private franchises were attacked; in 1559 the crown resumed by purchase the enormous privileges of the Admiral of Castile, whose jurisdiction had extended to all the 'dry ports' of Castile and the customs houses of the Biscayan ports.[12] Gradually, in spite of exceptions like the Duke of Alba and the Duke of Feria, the Castilian nobility was deprived of political significance. Yet a vestige of its power survived even under the weight of royal absolutism. In 1538 all the authority and persuasion of Charles V could not obtain from the noble estate of the cortes of Castile the grant of an additional tax.[13] And the crown never disputed the landed wealth of the aristocracy or attempted to strike at the source of its power. Consequently, under the feeble successors of Philip II the Spanish aristocracy was to make yet another bid for political supremacy.

The landed wealth of the nobility and their immunity from taxation made their class the ideal to which all Spaniards aspired. In 1520 Charles V established a distinction between grandees and *titulos*: the number of the former was reduced to twenty, and the two corps together had no more than sixty members in 1525. By 1581, however, the number had risen to a hundred, while the hordes of claimants to gentry status were innumerable. For titles of nobility could be bought, and the financial needs of the crown drew it to sell more and more *hidalguías* to those capable of buying them —merchants, *nouveaux riches* from the Indies, and *letrados* in the royal administration, whose humble origins bred a burning ambition to noble status. The practice was constantly attacked by the cortes of Castile on the grounds that titles of nobility procured for the buyer exemption from taxation and increased the burden on the remaining commoners. At the same time, the success of middle-class buyers in acquiring estates and titles

---

[11] See below, pp. 357–64. [12] Merriman, *The Rise of the Spanish Empire*, iv. 441.
[13] See above, pp. 50–51.

aggravated class distinctions and further increased the gulf between the aristocracy and the mass of the people.

In Spain a middle class hardly existed. There was, it is true, a merchant class in Castile, for even Spaniards were not averse to acquiring wealth. The merchants of Burgos and Medina del Campo had long been enriched by the wool trade, while the wealth of the Indies made the fortunes of many Spanish as well as foreign merchant houses; and while the Spanish creditors of the state were in a minority, they were by no means absent, for the Benaventes, the Encinas, the Haros and the Lermas often appeared in the contracts signed with the Council of Finance.[14] For these reasons the traditional opinion that Spaniards had little aptitude for commerce needs to be modified. On the other hand large-scale commercial operations could hardly be expected in a country insufficiently urbanised and among a people lacking the traditions of business enterprise. Indeed, the notable exceptions ended by proving the rule. Simón Ruiz, for example, was a successful and enterprising businessman.[15] At Medina del Campo he operated at the centre of commercial affairs, corresponding ceaselessly with the greatest merchants of Lisbon, Antwerp, Lyons, and Genoa, and he was well known in the entourage of Philip II. Beginning from about 1550 as an importer of Breton linens, he gradually extended his operations and acquired sufficient capital to speculate—with enormous success—on the exchange; by 1576 he was lending money to Philip II and was participating in numerous *asientos* for the payment of the army in Flanders, either furnishing the capital himself or working for a commission. From his considerable fortune he spent large sums on poor relief, including the endowment of a hospital at Medina del Campo, a sign that charity was not dead in sixteenth-century Spain. Merchants like Ruiz, however, were a small minority: there were about twenty Genoese houses comparable to his, and only five or six that could be classified as genuinely Castilian. Moreover, there was a lack of staying power in Spanish firms, which can be seen in the career of the Ruiz family itself; the second generation dissipated the wealth created by the first and sought to abandon business for nobility. There were, it is true, economic factors operating against Spanish businessmen in the sixteenth century. The favourable conditions after the influx of precious metals and the opening of the American market gave new opportunities to Spanish industrialists and merchants, but these did not last long beyond 1550. The stimulus created by rising prices and colonial markets then turned to a disadvantage as it drew more and more foreign manufacturers and merchants into the colonial

[14] H. Lapeyre, *Une famille de marchands: les Ruiz. Contribution a l'étude du commerce entre la France et l'Espagne au temps de Philippe II* (Paris, 1955), 118–21.

[15] *Ibid.*, 46–47, 60–73, 95–103, 597–98.

trade. In spite of her attempts to monopolise the American market, Castile could not resist the pressure of foreign competition; other European countries, less affected by the price rise than Spain, could produce cheaper goods, against which Castilian manufacturers were unable to compete and to which they eventually lost the colonial market, But while this might explain the demise of Spanish manufacturers, it hardly accounts for the retreat of Spanish merchants, for foreigners in Spain, such as the Genoese, were operating successfully in similar conditions, and many Seville merchants managed to survive by acting as commission agents for foreign manufacturers.

There was, in fact, a further reason for the absence of a middle class in Spain—a social prejudice against trade and towards nobility which found expression in the conviction 'que el no vivir de rentas, no es trato de nobles'. The odium attached to manual work and to business—*el deshonor de trabajo*, in the contemporary phrase—operated against the emergence of a middle class from the very beginning, for merchants aspired to leave trade and invest their money in a landed title. In view of the aristocratic structure of Spanish society and the security of land as an investment, this was a natural tendency and not merely the result of empty vanity, for it was clear to everyone that the noble had all the advantages—honours, exemption from taxation, and a territorial wealth which was infinitely more secure than commerce.[16] Consequently, the ambition of most of those who had made their wealth in business, especially the second generation of a family firm, was to abandon the merchant class, which was only regarded as an intermediary stage in the social hierarchy, and live as gentlemen.

The mania for aristocratic status need not have been damaging to Spanish society and economy if the newly ennobled, like those of the English gentry who came from merchant backgrounds, had remained faithful to business. But it produced a contempt for trade and restless anxiety to join the aristocracy which were ruinous for Spain and her people. According to the theologian Bartolomé Albornoz, 'no one wishes to inherit the profession of his father' in the country which only esteemed 'arms and letters'.[17] Merchants, he argued, did not appreciate the qualities of the state to which God had called them, nor the imperfections of that to which they aspired: 'ravian y mueren por la caballería'. The starving *hidalgo* of Lazarillo de Tormes was, indeed, a symbol of a real situation. It was not surprising, therefore, that a whole sector of Spanish life was colonised by Italians who

---

[16] This is the process which Braudel calls 'la trahison de la bourgeoisie', *op. cit.*, 619–24.

[17] *Arte de los contractos*, 1573, quoted in Lapeyre, *op. cit.*, pp. 117–18; see also Carande, *op. cit.*, i. 102–104.

were not paralysed by aristocratic prejudice and who had, in any case, the advantage of superior techniques acquired over many centuries of large-scale commerce. The predominance of Italians and their enrichment at the expense of the state caused alarm and resentment, and the unpopularity of the Genoese, those 'anticristianos de las monedas de España' as Quevedo called them, was notorious. But the Spanish crown and its people could hardly have managed without the Grimaldis, Dorias, Spinolas, Lamellinis, and others, who virtually monopolised trade and assisted the monarchy with enormous loans.

In a society where standards were set by the landed aristocracy there were few prospects for labourers and artisans. The Spanish working class of the sixteenth century, confronted by a prosperous nobility whose estate was a magnet for manufacturers and merchants, had visible evidence for the view that work was degrading. In the absence of an identifiable middle class, possible entry to which might have acted as a stimulus, the tenant and the craftsman lost confidence in work as a means of progress. They worked because there was no alternative, or because the alternative was hunger. The notion that the typical Castilian was the idle *hidalgo*, too proud to work, is a myth that would hardly need contradicting were it not repeated so often. Except in the extreme north, in Asturias, *hidalgos* formed a minority of the population; the Basques believed they were all nobles, but that did not prevent them cultivating the land and building ships. The further inference—that in Spain only the moriscos worked—is equally false, for there were hundreds of thousands of hard-working peasants and the extensive public and private building that was done in the sixteenth century could only have been performed by an army of artisans. Indeed for a miserable subsistence, which barely covered vital provisions, they had to work hard indeed. A contemporary report of the tavern-keepers of Barcelona recorded that the workers of the city ate a midday meal consisting of a piece of bread and garlic.[18] If by any chance the worker had a surplus from his wages, heavier and heavier taxation took it from him. But usually he had little to start with. Peasants and tenant farmers found the pressure on them growing daily as exploiting landlords intensified their production or raised their rents. In the first half of the century, when industry appeared to be flourishing, the peasants tried to find a way of escape from the destitution of the countryside by flocking to the cities in search of work. But once this brief boom had passed and the middle classes were beginning their exodus from trade and industry, there was nothing in the cities for them either, so the number of unemployed increased, wandering from one monastery to another in search of free soup. In these conditions the only

[18] Vicens Vives, *Apuntes del curso de Historia Económica de España*, i. 297–98.

solutions open to them were to enrol in the army, to enter the religious orders, or to resign themselves to a life on the margin of society. The inarticulate masses of the sixteenth century had few spokesmen, but the hordes of vagabonds, beggars and unemployed who infested the roads of Spain, especially those leading to the court, were eloquent testimony of the increase of destitution in a society where the aristocracy monopolised the ownership of land.

This was the situation in Castile. In eastern Spain poverty had a different origin. The pressure of population on a mountainous region which could not sustain it forced highlanders in the Catalan Pyrenees to descend towards the neighbouring plains of Ampurdan and Lérida.[19] But in their search for a living on the land or pasture for their herds they came up against the Catalan peasants who were already in possession, often sustained by wealthy speculators in Barcelona. Unable to find a living either in the mountains from which they came or in the plains to which they were drawn, they became outlaws and lived by contraband or brigandage; highland raiders, in search of loot, terrorised the lowland villages and lay in wait to rob travellers and couriers in a frontier district where the king's writ hardly ran yet near which passed one of the vital routes of imperial Spain, linking her to Italy via Barcelona. But Aragonese and Catalan adventurers were to be found in all parts of Spain and the empire and they were drawn to any war. In 1570, during the war of Granada, they flocked in hundreds to the camp of Don John of Austria; and Philip II himself raised a *tercio* from Catalan brigands for the war in Flanders. Their homeland, moreover, was adjacent to France and presented a political and religious problem which took many years to liquidate.[20]

Spanish society in the sixteenth century was permeated at every level by the church.[21] The religious estate comprised about 100,000 members in the sixteenth century and was said to take half the national income. In spite of their privileges and wealth, however, the Spanish clergy could hardly be considered as a separate social class. The vocation and the composition of the church transcended class distinctions: its ranks included sons of artisans and peasants as well as representatives of the gentry and nobility, while its mission was shared by aristocrats like St. Teresa of Avila and commoners like St. John of the Cross. Yet it would be surprising if the church did not reflect in some degree the aristocratic structure of Spanish society. With rare exceptions, the most important dioceses, as well as the best benefices, were in the hands of men from aristocratic families; a tendency which was due not only to social prejudice and influence but also to

[19] On Catalan brigandage see the brilliant passages in Braudel, *op. cit.*, 46–48, 648–59.
[20] See below, pp. 210–17.   [21] See also below, pp. 251–86.

the fact that until the decrees of the Council of Trent became effective ꞊eminaries were not provided for the education of priests, and thus candidates of humble origin found their uncultured backgrounds a liability in the process of preferment. Moreover, the church owned a disproportionate amount of the country's wealth and shared the aristocratic monopoly of land. The cortes protested frequently but in vain at the accumulation of property in mortmain and criticised it as one of the causes of the economic distress of the country. But the church absorbed manpower as well as land. In the last decades of the sixteenth century when economic pressures on most sectors of Spanish society were increasing, the security offered by the church and its income helped to swell the ranks of the clergy as destitute families put their sons into the priesthood and the younger sons of the nobility competed even more intensely for the better benefices.

Nevertheless, although the clergy were just as zealous as the nobility for their privileges, immunities, and wealth, they had different ideas about their use. In the first place, the religious revival associated with the Counter-Reformation included a renewed emphasis on charity, and many of the resources of the Spanish church were directed towards the relief of the poor and the maintenance of hospitals, which rendered it a welfare as well as a religious organisation. Secondly, the higher clergy identified themselves completely with the policy of the state, especially in the reign of Philip II. The church provided the crown not only with useful administrators but also with many financial subsidies, which compensated to some degree for the clergy's partial exemption from ordinary taxation. Therefore, the crown's interest in the church inevitably extended to appointments to benefices, for it wanted a hierarchy distinguished not only for its piety and learning but also for its readiness to co-operate with the state. In some cases immense wealth was at stake. The see of Toledo, for example, was the richest in Christendom outside Rome. Its incumbent during much of Philip II's reign was Gaspar de Quiroga, who was a fervent supporter of the king's foreign policy.[22] In 1586 he made the king a grant of 200,000 ducats to be spent entirely on the war against England. Again, in February 1588, he donated 100,000 ducats for the Spanish Armada. After its defeat he sent another 100,000 ducats and gave generously towards shipbuilding in 1589 and 1594. Moreover, grants of this kind were independent of the regular revenue which the royal treasury received from the church and which gave the crown a vested interest in supporting the extension of ecclesiastical property.

The wealth of the church, however, was unequally distributed between

[22] M. Boyd, *Cardinal Quiroga, Inquisitor General of Spain* (Dubuque, 1954).

the higher and the lower clergy, who were already separated, as has been seen, by differences of background and culture. In spite of the vast revenues of most of the Spanish dioceses, the lower clergy were often destitute and their social position was more akin to the underprivileged outside their ranks than to their aristocratic superiors. In social conflicts in Catalonia the Dominicans and Franciscans aligned themselves with the common people against the nobility, while the latter could usually count on the support of the Benedictines who were themselves great landowners. Indeed, in view of the different social attitudes of the clergy in Spain and of their frequent clashes over race relations and missionary methods in the Spanish colonies, the Spanish church of the sixteenth century was much less monolithic than it often appears. And in a society rigidly divided into classes, it was the only institution that bridged the gulf between rich and poor and took its message to all Spaniards, regardless of their social position.

2. AGRICULTURE AND INDUSTRY

Agrarian conditions in Spain were not the same in every region: the prospects of the Catalan peasant, with his relative security of tenure, were much brighter than those of the landless labourer of Castile, and in a country made up of local economic units, isolated from each other and often living on a subsistence agriculture, conditions could vary almost from one village to the next. Nevertheless, the dominant feature of the agrarian régime in Spain was the existence of vast latifundia, held in rigid entail and mortmain and worked by a rural proletariat.[23] This not only withdrew large tracts of land from circulation and prevented investment and improvement, but also had pernicious social effects. In Castile the peasant rarely owned the land he worked, and if he was fortunate enough to have a tenancy it was usually insecure, expensive, and burdened with debt; in order to buy supplies and meet his obligations he often had to sell his produce long before harvest at very low prices.

Yet the rise in agricultural prices in the sixteenth century and the consequent increase in revenue from the land sometimes and in some places made agriculture a lucrative business which occupied not only farmers and labourers but also investors. The new interest was seen in the cultivation of new lands and in the more extensive exploitation of land already under cultivation, for both of which capital had to be assembled. This was often done by farmers borrowing money and paying an annual interest, which was secured by a mortgage on his farm. In this way, land was turned into

[23] There are few modern works on the agrarian history of Spain. See C. Viñas Mey, *El problema de la tierra en la España de los siglos XVI–XVII* (Madrid, 1941).

an object of speculation. The extremely high rates of interest involved—sometimes as much as 50 per cent.—encouraged capitalists to engage in agricultural loans; these included not only the wealthy, such as nobles and religious communities, but also smaller people with modest amounts of capital. In other words this was yet another process converting owners of capital in Spain into a parasite class living on rents and interest from investments in land rather than on industrial or commercial enterprises. The comment of a seventeenth-century *arbitrista*, Manuel Caxa de Leruela, indicates that the system was well known at the time: 'As people saw that you gave two thousand ducats and received each year two hundred, and that after six or seven years the two thousand were recovered, it was obviously an interesting kind of loan'. By the end of the sixteenth century a vast amount of capital was invested in agricultural *censos*. To the farmers themselves such investments were a mixed blessing. For a time, under favourable conditions of price and demand, the supply of capital assisted the development of agriculture, and the higher yield of the land allowed the peasant to meet his payments to the owner of the mortgage. But whenever agricultural prices dropped, even temporarily, the farmer found himself without enough money to pay the interest. The mortgage was then surrendered, causing a transfer of property which increased the concentration of land in the hands of a few *latifundistas*, and drove more people from the country to swell the ranks of unemployed in the towns. At the same time, the divorce between capital and labour helps to explain the technical poverty of Spanish agriculture and the apparent contradiction between an underpopulated countryside and the cultivation of new lands. To improve agricultural production uncultivated land on the plains and in the hills was brought into use by drainage or irrigation, while the countryside surrounding many towns like Valladolid, Toledo, and Madrid was converted, often with the help of the local authorities and sometimes of the crown, into fertile fields and gardens. Some of the reclamations, however, consisted of inferior land, and although the first crops were remunerative and there was an initial increase in production, this was followed by a gradual decline in the quality of the product and a drop in the yield per unit of land in general. In other words, the extension of the area cultivated was the means adopted by the poor farmers of Castile to obtain what is better achieved by the adoption of improved techniques.[24] Moreover, as will be seen, the extension of arable agriculture was small indeed compared to the effort and the territory assigned to pasture farming.

Andalucía, nestling under the prosperity of Seville, was an exception to the situation in Castile in general. From capital made in the Indies trade

[24] Vicens Vives, *Apuntes del curso de Historia Económica de España*, i. 300–01.

and with the incentive of high prices on the American market, investments were made not merely in the form of loans but directly in production.[25] The cultivation of the vine and the olive—a sign of capitalist agriculture— was extending over the whole basin of the Guadalquivir, to whose ports ships from northern Europe came to seek not only the wool of Castile and the products of the Indies but also the oil and wine of the fertile plain of Andalucía. Other parts of Spain were also capable of responding to a market demand. Although industrial crops like flax and hemp were neglected, the production of raw silk flourished in Granada and Valencia, while saffron, which was used in cooking and dyeing, was produced in great quantity in Aragon and competed in the European market with the product of Languedoc and Provence.[26]

The most important item of agricultural production, however, was grain, for bread was the principal food of Spaniards in the sixteenth century.[27] Old Castile produced the greatest volume of cereals and in good years had a surplus for export. During the course of the sixteenth century, however, the good years became less frequent and Spain experienced a real crisis of production, with increasing dependence on foreign imports. Even in Castile adverse weather conditions could reduce crops to famine level; Aragon produced enough only for its own needs, while Catalonia and the Basque country had to supply their own deficiencies with foreign imports. In this important commodity, therefore, the state employed a policy of price control: in times of shortage prices would tend to rise, so a ceiling price was fixed by the government. The years after 1502 were a period of bad harvests, so the ceiling price, already introduced by the Catholic Monarchs, was continued. The period from 1512 to 1539 was relatively productive— though there was famine in Castile in 1521 and a serious drought in Andalucía in 1525—so the ceiling price was lifted. From 1539, however, a series of poor crops caused a return to a policy of price control, and in the second half of the century this was the normal system, for the growing distress of the rural population reacted unfavourably on grain production, as can be seen perhaps in the constant rise of agricultural prices. The problem of grain supplies occupied a large part of the correspondence of Philip II, for these were needed not only for the civilian population but also for troops and sailors in their campaigns abroad. The system of ceiling prices was the government's way of protecting the consumer—including itself—against the producer. For the farmer, however, there was no assistance, though in

[25] Viñas Mey, op. cit., 16–20.
[26] Lapeyre, op. cit., 589.
[27] E. Rodríguez y Ibarra, *El problema cerealista en España durante el reinado de los Reyes Católicos* (Madrid, 1944). On grain supplies in the western Mediterranean see Braudel, op. cit., pp. 277–84, 447–64.

practice the policy of price control often broke down. In any case, the anxiety of the state for the provision of its armed forces often conflicted with the interests of the towns who were determined to feed their own populations and thus to preserve the supplies of their own countryside; in 1582, for example, Bilbao protected its supply in the plain of Burgos against the great government requisitions which were becoming more and more pressing.

Spain, it is true, possessed sources of grain outside the Peninsula. Milan and Naples occasionally produced enough for export, and Sicily was one of the biggest granaries in the western Mediterranean, which Spain preserved by a policy of taxing foreign buyers and restricting permits for purchase. But the Turkish advance across the eastern Mediterranean and control of grain supplies there increased the strain on western sources, especially in time of war; without the corn of Sicily, provided by Philip II on cheap terms, Venice could never have survived the war culminating in Lepanto. Moreover, Sicily itself, for reasons which are still obscure, was drying up, and there was a noticeable decline it its grain exports in the period 1532–78.[28] It was in these circumstances that the Mediterranean was opened to grain from northern Europe in the second half of the sixteenth century; English and Dutch shippers broke into the Mediterranean trade primarily as carriers of grain from the Baltic; and even while she was fighting her rebel subjects in the Low Countries Spain depended on Dutch imports of vital grain supplies to remedy her own deficiencies.

The acute shortage of cereals in Spain can be attributed to two basic conditions in her economic life. As the population was increasing, so there were more mouths to feed, and domestic production could not keep pace with the growing demand. This failure was due, in turn, to the neglect of arable resources in favour of pasture farming.

The predominance of stock-farming in the Castilian economy and its preference to agriculture had already been made explicit by the Catholic Monarchs, who declared their conviction that 'the breeding and preservation of livestock ought to be the principal substance of these kingdoms'.[29] This was also the policy of the first Habsburgs whose interests coincided with those of the Castilian aristocracy. As pasture farming demanded less labour, its extension at the expense of agriculture released men for recruitment into the armies constantly required by their foreign policy, while the nobles saw that the easiest and most profitable use to which they could put their land was to turn it into sheep runs. Yet sheep farming was a response to

[28] Braudel, *op. cit.*, 466–67.
[29] J. Klein, *The Mesta. A Study in Spanish economic history, 1273–1836* (Cambridge, Mass., 1920).

natural conditions as well as to official support. The dry climate of the Meseta of Castile and the poverty of its soil were hardly suitable for arable agriculture, but admirably adapted for the rearing of sheep. Moreover, the contrasts of temperature between the sierras and the southern plains had, from time immemorial favoured migration of flocks. Towards October the herds of sheep left the mountains and high plateaux of Old Castile to winter in Extremadura, Andalucía and the region of Murcia, returning north from the beginning of April. In their travellings they followed the routes which had been reserved to them, known as the *cañadas*, at certain points of which they were obliged to pass royal agents who collected the tax called *servicio y montazgo*. Since the thirteenth century the sheep breeders had been organised in a powerful corporation, the Mesta, which organised their affairs and defended their privileges. In Castile grazing rights were superior to all other land rights, and the crown usually defended the sheep-owners in their conflicts with the farmers, upon whose lands the sheep encroached. From early in the sixteenth century the privileged position of the Mesta was directly related to the incessant demands for subsidies made on it by Charles V, especially from 1525 when the ratification of its prerogatives converted the assistance it gave to the crown into a species of open and permanent credit.

In the second half of the century, however, the blow delivered to Spanish exports by the price revolution also hit the Mesta. Sheltered by royal support, sheep-farming had been good business while the wool it produced could be exported without difficulty. But the steep rise of Spanish prices beyond those of the rest of Europe after 1550 diminished the sale of wool and with it the herds of sheep. In little over ten years, between 1552 and 1563, the total number of sheep declined by 20 per cent.[30] While it was incapable of maintaining its own progress, sheep farming also had a harmful effect on the rest of the Spanish economy. This was felt above all by agriculture, for farmers lived in constant dread of the yearly migrations of the herds, which overflowed from their legal passage, damaging crops and causing soil erosion, and producing a continuous struggle between farmers and shepherds over encroachments. And while the Mesta had the right to pasture its flocks on waste land, town land and even town commons, it effectively prevented the enclosure of common land for arable agriculture. But industry also felt the impact of Mesta privilege: while the sheep breeders wanted to export the maximum amount of wool, the cloth manufacturers were anxious to retain the quota they needed for domestic industry. In the fifteenth century the latter had obtained the right to buy one-third of the wool produced; during the reign of Charles V, coinciding with increased

[30] *Ibid.*, p. 27; Hamilton, *American Treasure and the Price Revolution in Spain*, pp. 228-29.

industrial output in Spain, they tried to increase their quota to one-half, and their failure was yet further proof of the state protection given to the Mesta.

In the disputes between the Mesta and industrialists, the methods employed by both sides reflected the organisation of the Spanish economy in general and of Spanish industry in particular. There was an extraordinary development of craft gilds in Spain in the sixteenth and seventeenth centuries, and their over-regulated and antiquated methods dominated manufacturing processes. Far from showing concern for methods of production, training and technique, they were more concerned with trying to remove competition, both regional and foreign.

Yet under the stimulus of the price revolution and the American market Castilian industry made some progress in the sixteenth century. The abundance of wool placed the textile industry in a position to exploit the new conditions, and the production centres of Barcelona, Valencia, Segovia, and Toledo increased their output. The boom, however, did not last long beyond the middle of the sixteenth century, nor did the level of production ever reach that of England, the Low Countries, and Italy; in fact the time came when it could not even supply the domestic market. One reason for this was the traditional and facile orientation of the Castilian economy towards the rearing of sheep and the export of raw wool. A further cause was the protection given by Charles V to Flemish manufacturers. Yet the industry itself was strangled by over-regulation, which tended to remove decision and initiative from the producer. In contrast to this was the slight concern shown for the instruction of weavers and the improvement of technique, with the result that Castilian textiles lost the market not only because they were dearer than those of foreign competitors but also because they were inferior in quality.

In contrast with the development of the cloth industry, modest as it was, the production of yarn and spun flax was low; hemp was cultivated in Aragon and Valencia, but not enough was manufactured for the needs of the Spanish navy. On the other hand the production of silk and silk goods made some progress and their export eventually outstripped that of cloth. The industry had a Moorish tradition and the silk itself was produced in Valencia, Murcia, and Granada.[31] In spite of the fact that much of it was exported in a raw state, especially to Italy and France, whose products then competed with those of Spanish looms, the manufactured article also had a market abroad. Another industry in which the Moors had specialised was leather, and this was given an added impetus in the sixteenth century when

[31] F. Bejarano Robles, *La industria de la seda en Málaga durante el siglo XVI* (Madrid, 1951).

the famous hides of the Spanish Indies provided the raw material on advantageous terms. Ornamental leather goods, jackets, and above all the gloves of Ocaña and Cuidad Real, scented with musk or amber, were sold in the principal centres of Europe.

While Castile specialised in wool, the economy of Biscay rested on iron.[32] Easy access to foreign markets through the port of Bilbao was an important asset to the industrial potential of the region; foreign vessels came to load great quantities of iron, bringing in exchange foodstuffs which the mountainous interior did not produce for itself. Although some of the ore was exported abroad, however, it was obviously more profitable for the Basque provinces to work it in their own forges first. A large portion of the metal was, in fact, used in domestic production of nails, agricultural tools, anchors and arms. Estimates of the number of forges, mainly in Guipúzcoa, in the sixteenth century vary between eighty and three hundred, but whatever the number the technique of metallurgy had certainly advanced. At the beginning of the century the use of water-power caused a minor industrial revolution.[33] The old methods, which involved enormous expenditure of wood and human energy, were gradually abandoned in favour of more efficient ones. On most of the coastal rivers forges, called *masuqueras*, were established: hydraulic wheels motivated huge bellows which maintained the furnaces, while others worked powerful hammers to forge and stretch the iron and steel. And in addition to the revenues which they brought to the proprietors and lessees, the forges gave a livelihood to a large working population—muleteers, carters, timber workers, and even producers of cider, large quantities of which were consumed by the ironworkers.

The Biscayan coast was productive not only in metallurgy but also in ships. Unlike the Catalan shipyards, which lacked the stimulus of an active trade and whose local timber supplies were of inferior quality, those of the Basque country had a good supply of local timber and iron and were favourably situated on the trade route between Castile and the Low Countries, where Biscayan-built ships were to be found in large numbers. Yet in spite of their situation on the Atlantic coast and the needs of the Spanish empire the Biscayan shipyards did not take the initiative in the development of new types of ships beyond those known in the Mediterranean.[34] Basically the galleon was a modified merchantman armed with cannon, and although both were used extensively on the Atlantic crossing

[32] See T. Guiard Larrauri, *Historia del Consulado y Casa de Contratación de Bilbao y del comercio de la villa (1511–1880)*, (2 vols., Bilbao, 1913–14).

[33] Lapeyre, *op. cit.*, p. 588.

[34] A. P. Usher, 'Spanish ships and shipping in the 16th and 17th centuries', in *Facts and Factors in Economic History. Essays presented to Edward Francis Gay* (Cambridge, Mass., 1932), 189–90.

they were simply variations of types already common to the Mediterranean and of Venetian origin; the caravel, on the other hand, was developed by the Portuguese. But what they lacked in originality of design and, compared to the Dutch, in technical progress, the Spanish shipyards made up in the volume of tonnage they produced. During the greater part of the reign of Philip II production on the northern coast of Spain was stretched to its limit.[35] How much was due to royal and how much to private initiative is difficult to determine. The profits to be earned in the Indies trade made shipping a good investment and in the sixteenth century most of the ships employed in the Atlantic crossing were built in Basque shipyards. But the demands of war, especially in the 1580's, were also one of the factors giving added stimulus to Spanish shipbuilding. In 1583 there were 15,000 *toneladas* of shipping under construction in Biscay, and in the next three years fifty vessels were ordered on the royal account. The defeat of the Spanish Armada did not bring mercantile activity to a halt, but brought further employment to local shipyards in an effort to replace the losses suffered. The pressure of the state, however, sacrificed genuine merchant vessels to big ships which were only useful in wartime.[36] The vessels most useful in European trade were small ones, capable of reaching inland ports, like Bilbao and Seville, and operating economically with modest cargoes on frequent and regular voyages. Philip II, on the other hand, tried to force shipowners to build large vessels because of their military value, and although this was not necessarily in the interests of civilian shippers it was a tradition which dated from the navigation acts of the Catholic Monarchs who not only prohibited the shipment of Spanish merchandise in non-Spanish ships when native vessels were available but also introduced subsidies for the construction of larger vessels. A report dating from the end of Philip II's reign explained the naval decline of Spain, already apparent at that date, in terms of the measures taken in favour of heavy shipping which remained subsequently inactive and ruined the shipowners and their seamen; the author contrasted the complete liberty prevailing in other maritime nations and concluded that 'all the naval power of the northern countries has had its origin in our ruin'.[37] But this was only a partial view: on the most important Spanish trade route—the Indies—big ships were not only needed but commercially profitable, as can be seen by the heavy civilian orders placed in Basque shipyards for this type of vessel, predating the naval programme of Philip II. Spanish shipping and shipbuilding, in fact,

[35] T. Guiard Larrauri, *La industria naval vizcaína* (Bilbao, 1917), pp. 53, 64–72.
[36] Lapeyre, *op. cit.*, 212–14.
[37] C. Fernández Duro, *Armada española desde la unión de los reinos de Castilla y de Aragón* (9 vols., Madrid, 1895–1903), ii. 443–48.

were the victim of many circumstances. The high costs of materials and labour, due partly to the price revolution, compared unfavourably with those of shipyards in northern Europe; in any case the naval supplies of the Basque interior eventually proved insufficient and imports from Scandinavia —highly vulnerable during the war with England and the Dutch—raised the cost of Spanish-built ships still further. State requisitions were another blow to the industry. In the sixteenth century there was not a rigid distinction between the royal navy and the merchant marine, and Philip II continued the traditional system of *asiento, flete y embargo*, by which the state contracted with private shipowners to hire or requisition merchant vessels in time of emergency; in this case, the difficulty of securing repayment and compensation for deterioration or damage, especially after a disastrous campaign like that of the Spanish Armada, deterred shipowners from investing in further building programmes. Meanwhile, the technical stagnation inherent in the industry prevented any improvement of its ships which might have revived the flagging demand, and thus during the last two decades of the sixteenth century the Basque country was undergoing an industrial decline that had already begun in Castile.

Indeed, the existence of textile, silk, leather, metallurgical and shipbuilding industries in Spain and the growth of population in many urban centres, cannot disguise the fact that Spanish industrial enterprise in the sixteenth century was weak and growing rapidly weaker, and there was nothing comparable to the minor industrial revolution then beginning in England. This decline is easier to describe than to explain. Castilian industry in general was technologically less advanced than that of northern Europe and its products were less competitive in quality. Industrial progress can hardly be made without efficient organisation; Spanish manufacturers showed little aptitude for management and were in any case hampered by the restrictive regulations of the gilds. The state itself did little to encourage productive activities or investment in productive enterprises. Industry needs capital, and this must be earned—usually by foreign trade. Spain had an adverse balance of trade in Europe, and like most countries whose basic exports are raw materials which do not cover the costs of foreign purchases she had to pay for vital imports in cash.[38] In the New World, on the other hand, Spain acquired immense wealth. But this was not productively invested. On the contrary, American treasure—the one source of surplus wealth she undoubtedly possessed—was squandered in foreign wars, or used to defray the adverse balance of trade with foreign countries, or lavished on grandiose building and luxury goods. Spain's industrial difficulties, however, can be attributed above all to the price revolution and the burden of taxation.

[38] See below, pp. 148–55.

Inflation, which was at first a stimulus to Spanish manufactures, ended by pricing them out of the international and even out of the domestic market. In the mid-sixteenth century the price inflation and the increase in the cost of essential goods—although understood by some Spanish theorists—were attributed by the authorities not to the influx of treasure and insufficient production, but to over-export and excessive demand, especially from America. In 1548 the cortes of Castile demanded the application of a radical solution—a prohibition of exports, even to the Indies, and encouragement to the import of foreign goods. The crown refused to prohibit exports to the Indies but decreed that foreign cloth could be imported and sold in Spain. Then by an edict of 25 May 1552 it ordered a virtual prohibition of the export of goods made from wool, silk, and leather, except to the Indies. By another edict of 23 April 1552 it tried to stimulate the entry of foreign linen and cloth by ordering these textiles to be imported to the same value as the wool exported. Even allowing for the usual evasion, these edicts were as harmful as they were inept, a fact which was recognised by the cortes themselves when, under pressure from merchants who had suffered from foreign competition, they admitted in 1555 that the prohibitions had caused a depression and unemployment and requested a return to the export of textiles and the dropping of the obligatory returns policy. In 1558 the latter was, in fact, removed and export of cloth to Portugal allowed. But the prohibitions on the export of silk and hides, both raw material and manufactures, remained in operation, though from 1567 certain articles were excepted. Meanwhile, the mid-century crisis of the Castilian economy, wrongly diagnosed and treated as usual with an eye to the consumer rather than the producer, had given foreign importers immense opportunities at the expense of Spanish industry and commerce.[39] From then on they were fighting a losing battle with foreign competition, and although Segovian cloths managed to stay in the market in some substance, by the 1590's Castilian industry was near the brink of bankruptcy.

Inflation, however, was not the only enemy. Heavy taxation both raised the cost of Spanish manufactures and deterred businessmen in Castile from investing in enterprises that were the target of the state's financial policy when they could invest their capital in land and an aristocratic way of life and thus escape the main burden of taxation. Industry was hit not only by export duties but also by the *millones* and the alcabala, the two great indirect taxes of the time. The latter was a sales tax which added to the price of an article almost every time it changed hands and was one of the main grievances of all industrial interests. From 1575, when the curve of the tax

[39] See J. Larraz, *La época del mercantilismo en Castilla, 1500–1700* (2nd edn., Madrid, 1944), pp. 50–57.

index rises considerably above that of the general price index, the royal treasury increased the pressure of taxation still further, both to compensate itself for the decline in the purchasing power of money and to meet the rising cost of war, and thus placed an intolerable burden on the already weakened remnants of Spanish industry. The rising demands of the state, therefore, played their part in the ruin of productive enterprises in Spain. Foreign commitments drained her capital resources, and this affected not only government revenue but also private capital which was diminished by taxation and by the frequent expropriations of revenue from the Indies.

3. AMERICAN TREASURE AND THE PRICE REVOLUTION

Before the arrival of American treasure in the sixteenth century, European trade was fed primarily by gold from the Sudan. But Portuguese expeditions along the Atlantic coast of Africa to the Gulf of Guinea between 1460 and 1470, and the establishment of direct trade relations between Portugal and the East Indies at the beginning of the sixteenth century, diverted the route of Sudanese gold away from the Mediterranean and caused a great scarcity of gold in Europe. This was supplied in part by the German silver mines, which enjoyed a period of relative prosperity between 1470 and 1530, coinciding with the shortage of precious metals. From 1530, however, this shortage was unexpectedly eased when American treasure began to replace the old sources of supply and gave Europe an immense stock of money, the origin of grave alteration in prices, especially in Spain, the country where the treasure arrived and from which it was distributed.

The influx of treasure consisted almost entirely of silver. Up to 1550, it is true, imports were mixed, but American gold was never sufficient, even in the best years, to produce an appreciable effect on prices, and after 1550 it was relatively insignificant. Silver receipts, however, expanded enormously.[40] They began most effectively about 1530, and remained at a relatively modest, though steadily rising, level until 1550. From then the galleons began to import silver in vast quantities, which became vaster still from 1580 and caused a profound revolution in prices. Behind the flood of silver lay a technical revolution in America itself. The new method of amalgamation devised in Germany and consisting of the treatment of silver with mercury was introduced in the mines of New Spain by Bartolomé de Medina in 1557. From 1571 it was applied to the Potosí deposits in Upper Peru.[41] This process increased the exports of treasure tenfold, and they reached their peak in the period 1580 to 1630, the great age of Spanish imperialism. 'The king has reason to say', wrote one of Philip II's

[40] See Appendix II, Table A.   [41] See below, pp. 169–71.

secretaries, 'that the emperor never disposed of as much money as himself for his enterprises'.[42]

The interest of the state in precious metals derived not merely from mercantilist prejudices but from their ability to buy what it most needed—the means of power. Spain was already a protectionist country, barricaded with customs, and a government which theoretically controlled everything entering and leaving its frontiers was unlikely to allow the new-found treasure to escape its grasp. But the monopoly, and the attempts to preserve it, were not perfect: there were frequent complaints from the cortes that the continual exit of precious metals—'as if we were Indians'—was impoverishing the country, and it was commonly said that Spain was 'the Indies of other countries'. Yet there were many reasons why the precious metals should escape from Spain and circulate abroad. Spain was primarily an exporter of raw materials and an importer of manufactured goods; with an unfavourable trade balance, she had to settle her payments with ready cash. This accounted for much unlicensed export of specie by Spanish merchants or by foreign merchants resident in Spain, all of which made its way to the great production centres of Europe. In a sense the precious metals were the crutches which enabled the Spanish economy to move. But alongside clandestine export, the state had to authorise some foreign payments in specie, for imports of vital food supplies and naval stores had to be bought with cash. The greatest remittances of all, however, were made by the crown itself in order to pay for its overseas commitments. Instead of investing their money in productive enterprises at home, as the Fuggers did at Augsburg with the money from their mines at Schwaz, the Spanish Habsburgs lavished more and more on foreign enterprises, the price not merely of ambition but of the very existence of the Spanish empire and its defence. The routes by which the precious metals left Spain all converged on northern Europe, either directly from Bilbao or via France and Italy, for it was here that Spain's political and military interests were most exposed and her balance of payments was most adverse. The money itself was vital not only in the conflict with France and the war in the Low Countries but also in the economy of northern Europe, for from Antwerp it made its way to Germany and England, while the latter also profited from the smuggling of specie by Spanish merchants in wool ships.

[42] Quoted in Merriman, *The Rise of the Spanish Empire*, iv. 438 n. 2. The total registered imports (which does not, of course, allow for smuggling) of public and private treasure between 1503 and 1660 was 447,820,932 pesos, which has been estimated at about £257,488,418. See C. H. Haring, 'American Gold and Silver Production in the first half of the Sixteenth Century', *Quarterly Journal of Economics*, xxix. (1915), 433–79, and Hamilton, *American Treasure and the Price Revolution in Spain*, pp. 35–38. On the routes by which the precious metals left Spain see Braudel, *op. cit.*, 377–98.

In spite of its rapid departure from Spain, however, American treasure had profound effects on the Spanish economy. The 'extremely close correlation between the increase in the volume of treasure imports and the advance of commodity prices throughout the sixteenth century, particularly from 1535', has been so well established that the products of the American mines must be regarded as the principal cause of the price revolution in Spain.[43] The Spanish government, like its neighbours in the rest of Europe, did not understand the causal connection between the influx of precious metals and the rise of prices, and was thus hampered in its economic and financial policies. On the other hand, contemporaries were certainly aware of the price revolution, for it was reflected in the cost of living, and although there was much uncertainty and confusion about its causes, individual economists began to appreciate the rôle of American treasure. Of these the most distinguished was the French theorist, Bodin, who established a connection between treasure imports and inflation in 1568. The views of Bodin, however, had already been anticipated in Spain. Twelve years previously, in 1556, Martín de Azpilcueta Navarro, a canon lawyer, produced the first clear statement known to exist that the high cost of living was a result of treasure imports:

We see by experience that in France, where money is scarcer than in Spain, bread, wine, cloth, and labour are worth much less. And even in Spain, in times when money was scarcer, saleable goods and labour were given for very much less than after the discovery of the Indies, which

[43] Hamilton, *American Treasure and the Price Revolution in Spain*, p. 301. Hamilton's thesis and the statistical evidence with which he sustains it are unassailable, but criticism of some of his methods and interpretations has been growing; see P. Vilar, 'Problems of the formation of capitalism', *Past and Present*, x. (1956), 15–35; Ingrid Hammarström, 'The "Price Revolution" of the Sixteenth Century. Some Swedish evidence', *The Scandinavian Economic History Review*, v.[2] (1957), 118–154; and especially, J. Nadal, 'La Revolución de los Precios españoles en el siglo XVI. Estado actual de la cuestión', *Hispania*, xix. (1959), 503–29. The criticisms of later commentators can be summarised as follows: 1. Hamilton worked on town prices, but a complete study ought to take account of rural prices, paid in local markets and more closely tied to crop yields. 2. A third of Spain is omitted from his investigation, including Catalonia and the Basque country, both of which perhaps were more closely related to the European economy than the rest of Spain. 3. Not all of the regions can be fitted consistently into his thesis: Valencia, after being in front up to 1530, then drops behind, but takes the lead again from 1581 to 1620. Moreover, although it is true that in general prices rose more quickly in Seville than in Valencia, that does not tell us whether at any given time the cost of living was higher in Seville than in Valencia, or vice versa. 4. His figures for entry of American treasure are defective in that he does not indicate the criterion adopted for separating royal income from private income or include unregistered receipts. 5. His price figures suffer from a defect of origin: they are of uniform provenance—hospitals and charitable establishments. In spite of the criticisms, however, no one has offered to replace Hamilton's work, which remains indispensable.

flooded the country with gold and silver. The reason for this is that money is worth more where and when it is scarce than where and when it is abundant.[44]

Other Spaniards of the Salamanca school showed similar awareness. The Dominican, Fray Tomás de Mercado, published his *Tratos y contratos de mercaderes y tratantes* in 1569—it was completed by the previous year and owed nothing to Bodin—and although it was full of ethical analysis in the traditional style it also contained some acute economic observation, including the quantity theory of money and the relation between American treasure and the current inflation.

An adequate understanding of the problem, however, had to await modern scholarship. The causal relation between the influx of precious metals and the rise of prices is to be distinguished by regions and by periods. Broadly speaking, the price rise was greatest in Andalucía, which through its monopoly of the Indies trade always received the first impact of treasure imports; this was followed by New Castile, then by Old Castile and León on the one hand and Valencia on the other, corresponding to their distance from the receiving centre. The general price level in Spain slightly more than doubled in the first half of the century. In this period the rise occurred largely in the first, third, and fifth decades. Prices continued to rise in the second half of the century, with plateaux of relative stability in the years 1551-56, 1562-69, and 1584-95; but from 1596 prices soared, reaching their apogee in 1601 with an index number of 143·55 on a 1571-80 base. By 1600 prices had risen to a level four times as high as that of 1501. From 1601 the process was checked, and after a period of oscillations ended in a temporary decline from 1637 to 1642 when there was a drastic drop in remittances from America, but prices never fully descended from the peak attained at the close of the sixteenth century.[45] To this factual description, however, two considerations should be added. First, although prices reached their apogee in the second half of the sixteenth century, the price rise was proportionately greater in the first half of the century. From 1501 to 1550 the advance was 107·61 per cent., while in the last half of the century it was 97·74 per cent. Moreover, the rhythm of acceleration of the price revolution slackened in the middle years of the century. Between 1549 and 1560 prices increased only 11·9 per cent., and the year 1562 marks the transition from a rapid rise (2·8 per cent. half yearly increase) to one more moderate (1·3 per cent.). This mid-century phenomenon can be related to the contemporary depres-

[44] In M. Grice-Hutchinson, *The School of Salamanca. Readings in Spanish Monetary Theory, 1544-1605* (Oxford, 1952), p. 95; see also Larraz, *op. cit.*, pp. 109-131.
[45] Hamilton, *American Treasure and the Price Revolution in Spain*, pp. 190-92, 199-203. See Appendix II, Table B.

sion in the Indies trade (the channel of American treasure) and indicates that the economic depression of the seventeenth century and its relation to the influx of treasure were already foreshadowed at the beginning of Philip II's reign.[46] Secondly, it would be wrong to ascribe the difference between the economic progress of Spain and that of northern Europe uniquely to prices. In general, it is true, the rise of prices was later and less intense in the rest of Europe than in Spain, because of the time required for American treasure to circulate there and the dilution suffered in the process; first France then England felt the impact. But this does not give us a complete picture of the cost of living in these different countries: grain, for example, was always dearer in France than in Spain during the great inflationary period.

Moreover, treasure in itself was not the only cause of the price revolution. The quantity theory of money, by which an increase in the quantity of money in circulation brings a proportionate increase in the level of prices, is too crude to account for all the factors involved in the history of Spanish prices. Prices are also affected by conditions of supply and demand. Industrial and agricultural production, therefore, must also be taken into account. An increase in the amount of money in circulation without a corresponding increase in the production of goods means that the same amount of goods is chasing more and more money, and therefore prices rise. The money pumped into Spain from America was not used to increase domestic productivity, and higher prices were the inevitable result. After an increase in industrial production in the first half of the sixteenth century, though one which did not keep pace with the increase of money, Spanish output then fell off and money sought products abroad. From the side of demand, there were now more people to be fed and clothed and housed. The growth of population enhanced the demand for goods, including foodstuffs. Agricultural producers, like industrial producers, were unable to respond to the rising demand, and new and less fertile lands were cultivated; in this way marginal costs increased, and *per capita* yields became smaller, while demand continued to rise. The pressure of population on food supplies thus increased the price of agricultural produce, and further helped to raise the cost of living.

The consequences of the price revolution are perhaps even more difficult to elucidate than its causes. It certainly caused a general rise in the cost of living, but what this meant for the different classes and for the economic development of the country as a whole is by no means clear. According to the classical explanation, the economic backwardness of Spain

---

[46] See below, pp. 169–70; see also Nadal, 'La Revolución de los Precios españoles en el siglo XVI', *op. cit.*, 512.

was related directly to the results of inflation there.[47] The lag of wages behind prices in Europe aided the accumulation of capital; the diminishing price of labour gave entrepreneurs the opportunities of exceptional benefits which could then be further invested. Spain, on the other hand, was claimed as an exception to this general rule, for although there was a lag of wages behind prices it was not enough to afford extraordinary benefits and therefore give great impetus to capitalism. A further refinement of the argument was to note the close correspondence between periods of inflation and deflation of benefits and those of national rise and decline; in these terms the greatness of Spain coincided with the inflation of 1520 to 1600 and its eclipse with the deflation of 1600 to 1630.[48] For there was a close relation between inflation of benefits and accumulation of capital; as wages in Spain were higher than those elsewhere, so there was less opportunity to accumulate capital, and this was the principal reason for Spain's economic inferiority. But these monetary theories leave many questions unanswered. Apart from the fact that inflation of profits does not necessarily imply an industrial boom, there is no ground for arguing that all Spanish wage-earners were better off than their foreign counterparts during the price revolution. From a comparison of the wages of builders in England and France with those in Valencia, it is clear that the latter underwent at least the same progressive losses as the former throughout the sixteenth century.[49] In any case, builder's wages, unaccompanied by those of industrial and agricultural workers, are not representative enough to justify generalisation. It is true that the Spanish inflation did not produce an accumulation of capital for investment. But this was because those who profited from it used their wealth unproductively, either in buying a title and an estate, or in extravagant building, in the purchase of luxury consumer goods, or in simple hoarding.

How, then, did the price revolution affect the various sectors of Spanish society? Conditions in sixteenth-century England support the view that the divorce between constantly rising prices and fixed rents could impoverish the land-owner.[50] But this does not apply to Spain, where rents were not fixed and where the greater power of landowners enabled them to raise rents and replace their tenants by those better able to pay. There is also abundant evidence that in Spain the rich were getting richer and the poor poorer.[51] A possible inference from this is that the opening of the American

[47] E. J. Hamilton, 'American Treasure and the Rise of Capitalism, 1500–1700', *Economica*, ix. (1929), 338–57.
[48] Lord Keynes, *Treatise on Money* (London, 1930), ii. 154–55, 161.
[49] Nadal, 'La Revolución de los Precios españoles en el siglo XVI', *op. cit.*, 523–24.
[50] Hamilton, 'American Treasure and the Rise of Capitalism', *op. cit.*, 350.
[51] Viñas Mey, *El problema de la tierra en la España de los siglos XVI–XVII.*

market and the rise of population in the peninsula itself produced an increase in demand for agricultural products, an extension of cultivation, and a rise in the value of arable land, all of which coincided with the added stimulus of inflation. If, at the same time, the concentration of property in the hands of a few extremely wealthy families is taken into account, together with power to raise rents, then it would seem that the inflationary period was not unfavourable to the great landowners in Spain and did not deter people from investing in land. But landowners were not the only ones to gain from the price revolution. Anyone with something to sell or trade could reap the benefit of inflation, as many manufacturers and merchants did in the first half of the century. When conditions then became more difficult, and constant inflation began to make Spanish enterprise less competitive in the international and colonial markets, only the more powerful merchants were able to survive foreign competition, but those who did so undoubtedly prospered. Enormous fortunes were to be made in the Indies trade, whose expansion was related directly to the rise in prices; when prices rose in Spain there was a strong presumption of an even greater rise in America, and this encouraged further investment.and more profitable returns.[52] The latter were distributed beyond the merchant houses of Seville to entrepreneurs in other parts of Spain, for the American market took the oil and wine of Andalucía, the wool of Castile, the metallurgical products and ships of the Basque country. To at least the end of the sixteenth century there was still money to be made in Spain. On the other hand, the price revolution brought impoverishment to those who lived on fixed incomes and small rents, for these did not keep pace with prices. Small landowners of the *hidalgo* class, the lower clergy, government officials and many others all found their standard of living reduced as the price of commodities rose beyond their means. The situation of the peasant is less clear, for it is difficult to reconcile agricultural prosperity and the great rural emigration to the towns, which in turn makes it difficult to explain the alleged extension of cultivation in Spain. But one thing is certain—wages lagged behind prices, and the difference between the two was worse in the first half of the century. Even if the money value of wages subsequently picked up, their purchasing power continued to fall. By 1550 real wages were roughly 20 per cent. lower than the average for 1501-20, and they continued to fall steadily from 1551-60 to 1591-1600, the decrease being now about 12 per cent.[53] Throughout most of the sixteenth century life was difficult for the Spanish poor; indeed, for the mass of

[52] See below, pp. 168–75.
[53] Hamilton, *American Treasure and the Price Revolution in Spain*, p. 280. See Appendix II, Tables C and D.

Spanish wage-earners the price revolution was a grievous blow which reduced their already low standard of living still further.

The crown, on the other hand, like its ally, the aristocracy, was less
crippled by these developments than the majority of its subjects. Certainly
the cost of administration, and of paying, feeding, and equipping its armed
forces, rose for the crown just as the cost of goods did for the private
consumer; for war was an industry like any other, and one that was more
costly to Spain than to other countries because of her higher level of prices.
But as the aristocracy could raise its rents, so the state could increase its
revenue; this enabled it to keep up with prices, while inflation alleviated
the burden of the loans which formed such a substantial part of its income.

4. The Cost of Government

While the Spanish crown's expenditure in the sixteenth century was
immense and increasing, it also had enormous and growing resources.
The figures available in contemporary budgets lack precision, but are
sufficient to show the general trend. The revenues of Charles V tripled
during his reign.[54] Those of Philip II doubled in the period 1556–73 alone,
and more than redoubled by the end of the reign.[55] Debts, however, were
also increasing. Philip II inherited from his father a debt of at least twenty
million ducats, and seems to have left to his successor a debt of five times
that amount. But all the desperate financial expedients of the reign, the raising
of loans secured on future revenues and the two decrees of suspension
of payments in 1575 and 1596 point to the same conclusion: expenditure
was soaring beyond revenue. In 1588 the expenses of the Armada preparations alone were costing 900,000 ducats a month, as Philip himself
admitted to the cortes in June of that year. During the last ten years of his
reign, the crown's insolvency could hardly be disguised.

Of all the items of revenue possessed by the Spanish crown that from
the Indies was the one which most impressed Spaniards and foreigners
alike. Compared with receipts from other sources, however, it was not
spectacular.[56] The sums derived from the Indies—consisting of the royal
fifth, the alcabala, customs duties and the *cruzada*—increased rapidly during
the last two decades of the reign of Philip II, and between 1590 and 1600
they reached an annual average of more than four times as much as in the
early 60's. Even so, they still formed a smaller proportion of total revenue
than used to be supposed. The crown's American revenue rose from about

[54] See above, pp. 59–63.
[55] Modesto Ulloa, *La Hacienda Real de Castilla en el reinado de Felipe II* (Madrid,
1977); Felipe Ruiz Martín, 'Las finanzas españolas durante el reinado de Felipe II',
Cuadernos de Historia. Anexos de la Revista Hispania, 2 (1968), 109–173.
[56] See above, p. 61.

11 per cent. of total income in 1554 to about 20 per cent. in 1598. At its highest this was no more than Philip II's revenue from ecclesiastical sources and much less than the amounts extorted from the unfortunate taxpayers of Castile. Yet receipts from America were invaluable windfalls by any reckoning, and their sheer size gave Spain the extra power which she possessed in the sixteenth century. Moreover, the considerable returns derived by individual Spaniards from the Indies—averaging two-and-a-half times those of the crown during Philip II's reign—played an important part in enabling the king's subjects to pay the various domestic taxes at rates which would otherwise have been impossible. For Spain was no parasite on its dependent states. All the other European possessions of the crown had long ceased to be positive sources of revenue: in the Low Countries, Milan, Naples, and Sicily the revenues were progressively absorbed on the spot. There only remained Spain, or rather Castile, and the permanent presence of Philip II in the Peninsula together with comparative domestic tranquillity enabled him to organise more effective demands on taxpayers, even on the grandees, than the emperor had ever been able to do. In the course of his reign the list of Castilian taxes was ruthlessly increased, with the imposition of new duties or the modification of old ones. The master tax was the alcabala, which took one-tenth of the price of all sales transactions and rose in the second half of the century to 14 per cent. This too was a rising revenue (from 1,200,000 ducats in 1561 to 3,700,000 in 1574), and one which hit the consumer as well as the producer. Naturally there were complaints, as towns, cortes, and theologian-economists protested against the monstrous growth of taxation. In 1563 Cadiz declared that rising impositions were ruining its commerce. In 1571 the cortes blamed the disturbing rise of prices not on American treasure but on the facts which they had before their very eyes: 'it is due to these taxes and the high cost of all the necessities of life that so few people can live without difficulties'.[57] But the state was blind to all difficulties except its own, and, faced with inflation and the cost of war, knew no other policy than to raise its demands.

Some of these demands fell heavily on the church. Philip II's revenue from ecclesiastical sources was a permanent and major item in his budget, comparable with his income from America. The most valuable ecclesiastical revenue, and one which bankers regarded as the best security for their loans, was the *cruzada*, or crusade subsidy, granted by the papacy to the crown in the form of a bull of crusade in which spiritual benefits were conferred upon the faithful in return for a money offering. Long after its original justification—the war against the Moors—had gone, the *cruzada*

[57] Cortes of 1571, *Actas*, iii. 357.

continued to be renewed, partly because of the Turkish threat in the Mediterranean and partly because it was regarded as granted to the king of Spain for the purpose of promoting Catholicism. In the reign of Charles V the *cruzada* ceased to be an emergency measure and became a regular source of royal revenue, renewed—though sometimes reluctantly—by the pope at three-yearly intervals for the rest of the century. In the course of Philip II's reign its yield was roughly doubled.[58] Whereas the *cruzada* was a direct contribution from the laity, the *subsidio*, or subsidy, was a tax on the rents, lands, and other forms of income enjoyed by the clergy. Finally, there were the *tercios reales*, or royal tithes, and the rents of the military orders. Philip II inherited all this revenue and added to it. In 1567 Pius V granted him a new tax called the *excusado*, which was a tax upon the property of each parish and was intended for the war in Flanders. There was, therefore, a financial reason why the crown should encourage the enormous growth of church property in Spain, because the church was a rich source of taxation. It is difficult to assess the amount of Philip II's revenue from ecclesiastical sources and its proportion to his total income, but clearly it was considerable; it was, moreover, a rising revenue and one which, by the end of the reign, probably amounted to 20 per cent. of his entire income. In 1574 Don Sancho Busto, acting bishop of Toledo, complained to Philip II that more than half of the church's revenue was being taken by the state for its own use, and that the Spanish king was a poor example for Lutheran rulers to follow, as his methods were no better than theirs.[59] It might be added, indeed, that his methods were probably more effective than those of Protestant rulers who confiscated church property. The English crown sold monastic land for ready cash and failed to derive a long-term revenue from it. Philip II, on the other hand, by maintaining and extending church property and then taxing a prosperous institution ensured that the Spanish state possessed yet another source of revenue, and one that was permanent and sheltered. It was not only the Indies which gave Spain greater financial power than her English rival; the Spanish church also played its part.

While these enormous taxes never caught up with expenditure, they soon outstripped the primitive means available for collecting them. One of the weaknesses of the Spanish state in the sixteenth century—a weakness which it shared with most of its neighbours—was that it did not have the agencies capable of establishing perfect communication with the mass of the taxpayers. The obstacles arose not simply from the constitutional

[58] E. Pacheco y de Leiva, 'Relaciones vaticanas de Hacienda española del siglo XVI', *Escuela Española de Arqueología e Historia en Roma. Cuadernos de Trabajo*, iv. (1918), 67. See also J. Lynch, 'Philip II and the Papacy', *Transactions of the Royal Historical Society*, 5th Series, ii. (1961), 26–28.

[59] Lynch, 'Philip II and the Papacy', *op. cit.*, 27.

prerogatives of the eastern kingdoms of Spain but also from a defect in central administration. Charles V and Philip II had no state bank, and thus they were utterly dependent on private bankers. When Philip II returned to Spain in 1559 his greatest preoccupation for the next ten years was to bring order into his finances. Advice was pouring in from all sides, but in the final analysis he was invariably recommended to turn to the Fuggers, or the Genoese, or the Malvendas. The dispersion of his states and his many overseas commitments involved a dispersion of revenues to be collected and of payments to be made, and only the international merchant houses had the means of doing this. The transfer of money, one of the basic financial needs of an empire like Spain, alone demanded recourse to merchant-bankers. But the latter fulfilled another rôle: they advanced money, and thus mobilised government revenue before it was due. To do this they often had to be given the actual collection of taxes or the right to administer their mortgages. The Genoese had the monopoly of the sale of playing cards in Spain and control of certain salt works in Andalucía. The Fuggers were given the administration of the mercury mines of Almadén and the silver mines of Guadalcanal in southern Spain, as well as of the property of the military orders; the latter concession meant that vast grain lands, pastures, tolls, and peasant dues were placed under foreign control, to exercise which the Fuggers introduced their own agents, German, methodical, and zealous. Even when the collection of revenue escaped the hands of foreign firms, it was often given to intermediary agencies such as the towns or the cortes, because the state itself was not equipped for such a task.

Most of this revenue was spent faster than it was collected, and most of it went on naval and military expenditure, especially for the maintenance of Spanish troops in the Low Countries and for financing the war there from 1567 onwards. Here the problem was one of getting money to the spot where it was needed. To keep the Low Countries supplied there was an apparently simple solution—the king could send cash directly on his own account, limited only by the regularity of treasure imports from America. For a long time the sea route through the Atlantic and the English channel was open and fairly secure, and it was simply a question of shipping money at Bilbao or Santander and sending it without any intermediary to financial agents in Antwerp.[60] There were operations of this kind under Charles V and in the early years of Philip II's reign. From 1567, however, with the menacing arrival of the Duke of Alba in the Low Countries, England turned hostile; her piracy increased and her blockade

[60] Braudel, *op. cit.*, 377–98. H. Lapeyre, *Simón Ruiz et les 'asientos' de Philippe I* (Paris, 1953), 13–14.

of the Channel was begun, as could be seen in the seizure of the Duke of Alba's pay ships in 1568.[61] When better relations were resumed, Spain had then to reckon with another enemy—Dutch pirates, whose operations were intensified after the capture of Brill by the Sea Beggars in 1572. In these circumstances the transport of money to the Low Countries by the Atlantic route was becoming too risky and could only be undertaken occasionally by convoys or skilful blockade running.

Another route had to be found. The most direct one was through France; but although this had the advantage of being shorter it was also subject to interruption during the wars of religion and to the inconvenience of transporting heavy loads of metal in cumbersome convoys of beasts and vehicles, accompanied by large military escorts. In any case, the French government disliked operations of this kind in its own territory, especially as they were directed to financing a policy with which it was not necessarily in agreement. Between 1566 and 1581 one of the objects of Spanish diplomacy was to secure safe conduct for transport of money across France. The need was urgent; by 1572 the position of the Duke of Alba, who had been short of money almost since his arrival in the Low Countries, was desperate. But at the end of that year the first great land convoy of precious metals got through; 500,000 ducats reached him with the help of French visas. There were further convoys, and assignments were also made across France through merchants or by smuggling. But the French route was never more than a makeshift one and had little importance after 1578.

By then a new route had been established, across the western Mediterranean from Barcelona to Genoa, in conditions of relative security and dependent on no passport. This route was probably initiated in the early 1570's when Spanish capital was needed in Italy for the war against the Turk. But it was also a means of supplying the Low Countries, for from Genoa the money could be taken by land via Milan and across Savoy, Franche-Comté and Lorraine, territories which were either subject to the Spanish crown or belonging to friendly princes. The security of the route enabled royal remittances to be increased, and vast sums of money reached Farnese via Milan in 1584, 1586, and 1588. But in spite of these direct assignments from the treasury, Philip II could not dispense with private merchant-bankers, and more money was sent through them than by his own account. Between 1586 and 1588, when plans for the invasion of England from the Low Countries were reaching their crucial stage, there was a series of enormous *asientos*, or loan-contracts, many of them amounting to more than a million ducats and one of them reaching two-and-a-half millions. For Spanish policy, and the war supplies which fed it, could not

[61] See below, pp. 152–53.

await the annual and often overdue treasure imports from the Indies. Only the businessmen could provide regular deliveries of funds and effect their necessary transfer, thanks to their international network of fairs and exchanges. And if the government had to seek the assistance of financiers in Spain itself, it was even more dependent on them for the supply of the Low Countries, where the Spanish authorities were beset with ever-increasing difficulties and constantly hampered by lack of money. The financiers rescued the crown from many of these difficulties, and in the last years of Philip II they were making payments from month to month. From the services they rendered, of course, they received immense advantages, profiting from an improving rate of exchange, from the interest on the debt—especially as there was usually delay in repayment—and from the licence to export cash which they could then resell at a profit.

The Spanish and Flemish *asientos*, therefore, brought together demand and supply.[62] After trying to make payments through Italian and German financial centres, which were too far removed from the Low Countries, the Spanish Council of Finance found the correct formula in 1589 in the *asiento* of 2,400,000 écus made with Agostino Spinola. This huge operation assured the governor of the Low Countries monthly payments on the spot, and was followed by many others which carried similar clauses; that of four millions in 1595 marked the determination to pursue a yet more vigorous policy in the Low Countries. Repayment terms varied, according to the state of the Spanish treasury: the account was settled in Spain itself, some of it in cash, and the rest in charges on income from the Indies or on other revenues of the crown at future dates.

In providing for the Netherlands, the Spanish Council of Finance certainly made progress in the art of using businessmen for the service of the state, but financiers charged heavily for their advances. No one was more aware of the financial damage than Philip II himself, but in view of the demands on Spanish policy there was no alternative short of liquidating many of his imperial interests. Indeed, these *asientos* were the largest financial operations in Europe in the period 1580-96.[63] This was due in the first place to the influx of precious metals from America; these benefited not only Spain but also Italy, the Low Countries, and even France, which in spite of being outside the Spanish political system received a share of Spanish money, representing the surplus of its favourable balance of trade with Spain. Secondly, the increase in the amount of funds at the disposal of financiers was also due to the fact that it was only in the service of the state that capital could be used. The

[62] Lapeyre, *Simón Ruiz et les 'asientos' de Philippe II*, pp. 17–20, 41; Carande, 'Un banquero de Felipe II en Medina del Campo', *Moneda y Crédito*, num. 49 (Madrid, 1954), 13–23. [63] Lapeyre, *Simón Ruiz et les 'asientos' de Philippe II*, pp. 103–4.

reason for this was the decline of commerce, which was particularly notice-able from 1585, the year in which Spain reoccupied Antwerp. The situation was similar in the Peninsula itself where there was a general decline in the activity of commercial towns. As a result of the war which Spain was waging against England and the Low Countries, the Atlantic ceased to be a trade route and became a theatre of war. The decline of commerce left businessmen with increased funds at their disposal at the very time when the Spanish government needed more and more money. This coincidence led to an increase in the number of *asientos* and made them the principal source of revenue for large merchant houses. Under the impact of war and the pressure of Spanish foreign policy, commerce declined while finance prospered. This prosperity, however, was artificial, since it was founded on a decadent econ-omy. And the crushing burden of war led to a suspension of payments by Spain in 1596 and forced even Philip II to consider a policy of peace, a sign that political forces were being overwhelmed by economic ones.

Indeed the financial position of the crown was growing unbearable. The vast increase of American silver production from 1580, it is true, gave further impetus to Spanish imperialism: American silver not only provided its quota for the Portuguese war but also paid for the success of Farnese in the Low Countries, the preparation of the Armada, and the ruinous intervention in the affairs of France from 1589. But this constant influx of precious metals still remained insufficient to meet the enormous cost of Habsburg policy. Consequently, as neither ordinary nor extraordinary revenue was sufficient, the state was forced to fall back on other devices, first of all on further credit, which only aggravated the problem by its crippling rates of interest, then on unilateral declarations of bankruptcy, repeated in 1557, 1575, 1596, 1607, 1627, and 1647. When the time came to liquidate its debts, the crown proclaimed its inability to pay and thus suspended payments. This inevitably deterred many bankers, yet not to the point of outright with-drawal. For by suspension of payment they did not lose everything, nor did the state *annul* its debts: in a sense this device was a conversion of debts into long-term credit titles to future revenues. These *juros*, however, expanded beyond the actual resources of the crown; at the end of Philip II's reign they represented the enormous sum of 100 million ducats and came to form a paper currency which quickly depreciated and caused wild speculation. Therefore, although it was in the interest of bankers to continue to co-operate with their client, they would charge much higher rates of interest—70 per cent. was not unknown. Meanwhile, the state itself was involved in a vicious circle, for the only remedy it knew was to mortgage the future.[64]

[64] Braudel, *op. cit.*, 397–98, 783–84; see also, Carande, *El crédito de Castille en el precio de la política imperial*. Discurso leido ante la Real Academia de la Historia (Madrid, 1949).

CHAPTER V

COMMERCE AND EMPIRE

1. COMMUNICATIONS

THE political and economic interests of the Spanish empire and its relations with the outside world were utterly dependent on the efficiency of its communications. Here it had to contend not only with the hostility of France and England but also with the obstacles of distance. For Spain was situated not in the heart of Europe but on its periphery, and while this was a vital asset in its rôle as a colonial power it was a hindrance to the integration of its European possessions and to commercial relations with outside states. The factor of distance was felt by the state as well as by merchants; Spanish troops and naval units were usually operating far from their base in the Peninsula, and their transport and supply added greatly to the budgetary difficulties of the crown, just as the distance from markets added to the freightage costs of Spanish merchants. But communications were slow as well as expensive; and this, too, affected not only the actions of administrators but also the decisions of merchants and their knowledge of the market. Nevertheless, Spanish transport was not overwhelmed by these problems, and it managed to provide a relatively efficient service: within Spain, certainly, the isolation of the various regions from each other was to some extent overcome.

The Royal Association of Carters covered the country with a network of commercial links. In the sixteenth century, of course, sea transport was superior to that by land because it was much quicker. There were times, however, when it was not only safer to carry goods by land but also unavoidable. Internal waterways played little part in Spanish transport, for the Tagus and other rivers were not navigable. Consequently, the carriage of goods within Spain was limited to beasts of burden and the *carretas* (long, narrow ox-carts); the latter were four-wheeled vehicles and difficult to use in a land so rugged and mountainous as Spain, where, except in the Basque country, roads were neglected by the state, local authorities, and merchant gilds alike. The principal method of transport, therefore, was provided by horses and even more by mules, whose qualities of strength and endurance made them not only useful for agricultural labour but also indispensable for carrying freight across the vast and roadless distances of the Iberian peninsula. In the reign of Charles V the royal surveyor, Alfonso de Herrera, calculated the number of mules operating in internal transport as 400,000, and fortunately for Spanish economic interests their number increased throughout the sixteenth century. The mule convoys crossed the peninsula in all directions and gave Castile access to the peripheral states and to the outside world. The two principal routes were from Castile to the Mediterranean ports, especially the wool ports of Cartagena and Alicante, and from Castile to Bilbao, via Burgos and Medina del Campo, for trade with northern Europe. On the other hand, the Spanish government, under pressure of the horse-breeders of Andalucía, had forbidden the use of mules for riding, and that was the reason why the infirm Christopher Columbus, for whom a horse's gait was too rough, had to petition King Ferdinand in 1505 for special permission to ride a mule in order to go to court in pursuit of his claims against the crown. By the mid-sixteenth century, the breeders needed little protection, for the supply of horses—of which the best came from Andalucía—could not keep pace with growing civilian and military demands. So precious was this commodity that Philip II considered it necessary personally to examine all requests for licence to export horses, and in this matter he entrusted the frontier guard not to his customs officials but to the most efficient agency he had, the Inquisition—which then justified its anti-smuggling operations with the argument that it was preventing the export of horses to Huguenots and Lutherans. In spite of formal prohibition, however, there was a thriving horse trade from Spain to France.[1]

Spain had the second largest merchant marine in Europe in the sixteenth century, surpassed only by the Dutch. The main routes of maritime commerce lay in the Mediterranean and the Atlantic.[2] With the expansion of the Turk and the decline of Catalan trade, the Spanish routes to the eastern Mediterranean had fallen into virtual disuse, and there only remained the trade to Italy, from Alicante via the Balearics and the south of Sardinia, carrying wool to the ports of Genoa, Leghorn and Venice, supplemented from the 1570's by the Barcelona–Genoa route which was used for transit of government money and supplies. In the Atlantic, too, traditional Spanish communications were threatened by foreign enemies. The principal route, from Bilbao, Laredo or Santander to Antwerp—the bridge between Castile on the one hand and England and the Hanse towns on the other—was one of the most frequented shipping lanes in Europe until the period 1568–75, and Spanish ships carried a large portion of the maritime trade between the peninsula and northern Europe.[3] By 1575, however, the hostility of England

[1] Braudel, op. cit., 353; Lapeyre, Une famille de marchands: les Ruiz, p. 593.
[2] The trans-Atlantic route is discussed below, pp. 161–68.
[3] G. Connell Smith, Forerunners of Drake: a study of English trade with Spain in the early Tudor period (London, 1954), p. 14; Usher, 'Spanish ships and shipping in the 16th and 17th centuries', op. cit., 212.

and the Dutch, together with the economic collapse of Antwerp and the bankruptcy declared by the Spanish crown, badly hit commercial communications between Castile and the Low Countries. But there still remained the routes to France, though Huguenot pirates rendered these insecure, too. From Lisbon, Sanlucar, Seville and Cadiz ships sailed to Rouen, which became the most active Atlantic port of France, for in addition to exporting the products of Brittany it also substituted for Antwerp when the Dutch corsairs made the Channel and the North Sea route too risky. From Nantes, at the mouth of the Loire, there were two other routes, one to the Andalusian ports, based on the interchange of French wheat against Spanish salt and irregular in its traffic, and another to Bilbao and Santander, carrying French wheat and textiles in exchange for iron and treasure.

These two areas of shipping had their own distinctive vessels. The traditional Mediterranean vessel was the *galera*, or galley, a long and rapid boat driven by oars, an instrument of war against the Turk and the Barbary pirates as well as of commerce. But from the beginning of the sixteenth century the galley was being challenged by the *carraca*, which was round and short and possessed greater resistance to waves. The round type of vessel with a wide bottom was more characteristic of the Atlantic and its heavier seas, and here trade was served by a variety of ships—the *carabelas*, of Portuguese origin and the instrument of the great discoveries; the *galeones*, with their high sides, round rig and great castles on the prow for military purposes, slower in speed but equal in fame to the *carabelas*, used for conveying the treasure of the Indies and in the Invincible Armada; and the Biscayan *zabras*, small, rapid vessels, and very useful for active commerce.

Commerce was also served by an efficient postal service. The Spanish postal system was not originally a public service, nor was it a state monopoly. The crown had organised its own postal service for government needs, but it was not the only one. The universities, the towns, the associations of merchants, all had their own, though in the sixteenth century the royal post tended to eclipse its rivals and it received a lot of private patronage, especially when it was officially opened to the public in 1580. The official post was in the hands of the Taxis family, one of whose members had acquired the office of postmaster-general of Castile at the beginning of the sixteenth century. By the end of the century they were running six main routes from Madrid—north to the French frontier via Burgos and Irun, north-east to Barcelona via Zaragoza, east to Valencia, south to Seville, south-west to the Portuguese frontier via Toledo and Caceres, and west to Valladolid. The royal mail also ran an international service, the most rapid line of which was to Flanders across France, taking seven to eight days from Burgos to Brussels; there was also a regular service to Italy which left Madrid once a fortnight for Irun, Lyons, Genoa, Milan, Rome, and Naples, and took about 24–27 days to reach Rome.[4]

These communications were vital for commerce; the house of Ruiz, for example, averaged seven or eight letters daily in the years of its greatest activity. But the organisation of trade was also highly developed in other directions. The commercial classes of Burgos, Bilbao and Seville formed powerful merchant gilds, regulating and protecting their own interests, and had their agents in key-places abroad, like Antwerp, Rouen, and London.[5] Spanish commercial technique of the sixteenth century showed no significant advance on that introduced into Spain in the middle ages by Italian merchants, who were already familiar with double-entry book-keeping and bills of exchange. There was some improvement of method, and Spanish merchants were at least as up to date in their ways as their colleagues abroad, but this was still a far cry from the joint stock companies of the seventeenth century. The mentality was still medieval too, and merchants were reluctant to break canonist doctrine, especially on the question of profit and usury; as the church opposed the taking of interest on credit, lenders—with the help of theologians—had to disguise it in a complicated system of contracts in which the notion of risk always entered. Yet this hardly handicapped Catholic businessmen against their Protestant colleagues, for the great European bankers of the time—the Fuggers, Spinolas, Bonvisis, and Capponis—were all Catholics and probably led their Protestant rivals in financial and commercial affairs.[6] On the other hand, their regard for religion tended to make businessmen in Spain more scrupulous than many of those in other countries. In 1586, for example, the governor of Brittany, who had been the victim of English piracies, seized goods belonging to some English merchants and sold them to the agent of the Ruiz who despatched them to his firm in Spain. There, theologians were consulted, and they judged that the purchase was unacceptable on the ground that the governor could not administer justice himself in time of peace—England was at war with Spain but not with France—or make good a robbery by one Englishman by taking from another, without having letters of marque from his sovereign.

When the sixteenth-century merchant had accumulated sufficient capital he often turned to credit operations as a more lucrative source of profit, without necessarily abandoning trade. The career of Simón Ruiz was probably the best example in Spain of such a process. The deposit banker,

---

[4] Lapeyre, *Une famille de marchands: les Ruiz*, pp. 165–70; J. Devos, 'La poste au service des diplomates espagnols accrédités auprès des Cours d'Angleterre et de France, 1555–1598', *Bulletin de la Commission Royale d'Histoire*, ciii. (Brussels, 1938), 205–467.

[5] See R. S. Smith, *The Spanish Guild Merchant. A history of the Consulado, 1250–1700* (Durham, N.C., 1940).

[6] Lapeyre, *Une famille de marchands: les Ruiz*, pp. 126–37, 230–361.

on the other hand, was officially excluded in Spain from engaging in lending. However, deposit bankers at the Medina del Campo fairs engaged in speculation, and the banking houses of Seville often used their customers' funds in investments in the colonial trade or loans to merchants, charging their depositors no commission and permitting them overdrafts.[7] Banking in Seville prospered in the third quarter of the sixteenth century, though bankruptcies were not infrequent, owing to the uncertainties of the arrivals of treasure, its frequent confiscation by the government, the regular suspension of payments by the state, and the generally speculative nature of the banks.

The main centres for exchange operations and for financial relations with foreign markets were the fairs of Castile—Villalón, Rioseco, and Medina del Campo—which had originated in the middle ages as centres of domestic and foreign trade but now became chiefly centres of exchange, reaching a notable prosperity in the first half of the sixteenth century.[8] As they were financial markets, at which debtors, including the state, fulfilled their obligations, the fairs were dependent on the arrival of treasure in the Indies fleets, and as the latter could not keep to a fixed date there was great difficulty in synchronizing the two. The integration of all the fairs into that of Medina del Campo in 1567–68 afforded some improvement, but in the following years delays in payments increased; some Spanish merchants went bankrupt, causing a further hold-up in transactions, and the general difficulty in cashing bills restricted the exchanges effected by foreign merchants on the Medina fairs. In 1575 the disastrous suspension of payments by the crown, together with the enormous increase of the alcabala tax, caused the collapse of financial and commercial operations, and the Medina fairs remained in abeyance until 1578. In that year the guarantees given by the crown to creditors tempted back the Genoese and others, and Medina recovered a little of its former activity, especially from 1590, during the period of highest silver imports from America. But again, from 1594 to 1598, delay in the arrival of the fleets prevented fairs from being held. Meanwhile, Madrid had been taking much financial business from Medina, and with the definite establishment of the court there in 1606 it became the financial as well as the political capital of Spain. The policy of the government, therefore, and the wars in which it was involved, had their effect on the money market. They were also harmful to commercial activity in general and aggravated the problem of balance of payments.

[7] Ibid., 263; Carande, Carlos V y sus banqueros. i. La vida económica de España, pp. 198–206, 223.

[8] See C. Espejo and J. Paz, Las antiguas ferias de Medina del Campo (Valladolid, 1912); Carande, Carlos V y sus banqueros. i. La vida económica de España, pp. 211–34; Lapeyre, Une famille de marchands: les Ruiz, pp. 476–99.

2. Foreign Trade and the Balance of Payments

In spite of the contempt for trade and the shortage of merchant vocations among Spaniards, Castile underwent remarkable commercial progress under Charles V and Philip II, assisted principally by the exploitation of the New World. This experience, however, was not shared by eastern Spain, whose foreign trade had already become increasingly sterile.[9] The pact of 1528 between Charles V and Andrea Doria gave the Genoese considerable privileges, with the help of which they were able to introduce their cloths into Sicily and Naples, the traditional markets of the Catalan industry. Even before this, however, the expansion of the Turk, the difficulty of trading with the infidel, and the decay of the Catalan merchant marine, had hastened the commercial decline of eastern Spain. Subsequently, the southern ports of Málaga and Alicante eclipsed Barcelona and Valencia, because they were nearer to the Atlantic trade and also positioned at the opening of the route via the Balearic islands to Italy; here were loaded the diverse products of Spain's overseas empire—cochineal, pepper, American hides and sugar—for re-export in the Mediterranean.[10] On the other hand, a modest trade between Barcelona and the nearby ports of Marseilles, Genoa, and Leghorn survived, for they were the entrepôts for the Catalan export–import trade with those distant countries of the eastern Mediterranean which had previously traded directly with Barcelona. In Genoa Catalan merchants bought the spices and silks of the East, a trade which was hit but not destroyed by direct Portuguese access to the East Indies: and in the second half of the century they bought in Leghorn the wheat which had been imported from northern Europe by Hanseatic, Dutch, and English shippers.

Having lost its traditional position in the Mediterranean, however, the obvious reaction of Catalonia was to attempt to acquire a new one in the Atlantic by participating in the trade of Castile with the Indies. In 1522 the first petition of Barcelona to trade with America was refused, just as the requests of other foreigners within the Spanish monarchy were refused. So the Catalan merchants then tried to practise indirect trade by getting a foothold in Seville, where fraud and contraband were rife, and so into the American market. But there was opposition here too, and in 1534 the Catalans were refused permission to have a consul in Seville or Cadiz. They then directed their efforts to markets in Castile, the gateway to America,

[9] On Aragon see I. de Asso, *Historia de la economía política de Aragón* (new edn. by J.-M. Casas Torres, Zaragoza, 1947); on Catalonia see J. Carrera Pujal, *Historia política y económica de Cataluña (siglos XVI–XVIII)* (Barcelona, 1947); also, H. Lapeyre and R. Carande, *Relaciones comerciales en el Mediterraneo durante el siglo XVI*, Ponencia del VI Congreso de la Historia de la Corona de Aragón (Madrid, 1957).

[10] Braudel, *op. cit.*, 167–68.

and in the 1530's were selling Catalan cloths in Medina del Campo, the principal supply centre of Spanish cloths for the trans-Atlantic market. Again, however, there were difficulties, this time in the form of severe competition from Flemish, English and French clothiers, for while the latter could place their goods directly in the ports of Seville or Cadiz, on payment of moderate customs duties, the Catalan exporters to Castile suffered from the fiscal barriers between the constituent states of the empire and had to pay three sets of duties—the Catalan customs, transit dues across Aragon, and entrance duties at the 'dry ports' of Castile. Finally, as the century progressed, Catalan industries and exports suffered from the same vicissitudes as those of Castile.

Yet Castile itself enjoyed considerable commercial prosperity in the sixteenth century.[11] Without transforming a society which was still thoroughly rural, military, and religious, and where most trade was still domestic and local, the influx of silver from America gave a vigorous impulse to its economy. Desire for gain animated merchants and increased their number, and led them to more daring speculations. The literature of the time is full of allusions to the frantic scramble for wealth, which astonished and scandalised contemporaries. The limitless enterprise of the Gradas of Seville was recorded by the Dominican theologian from Mexico, Tomás de Mercado, in a remarkable passage:

> First they deal in all parts of Christendom and even in Barbary. To Flanders they ship wool, oil and wine, and bring therefrom every kind of haberdashery, tapestries and books. To Florence they send cochineal and hides, and bring back strings of gold, brocades, silks, and from all these countries a great quantity of cloth. At Cape Verde they trade in negroes, a business which demands large capital and gives considerable returns. To all the Indies they ship great cargoes of every kind of merchandise, and return with gold, silver, pearls, cochineal and hides in vast quantities. Finally, to insure their cargoes (which are worth millions) they have to take out insurances in Lisbon, Burgos, Lyons and Flanders, because so vast are their shipments that neither the merchants of Seville nor of twenty cities like Seville are capable of insuring them.[12]

The part played by genuine Castilians in this commercial expansion is more difficult to determine. Spaniards were not necessarily averse to trade, as long as its returns were lucrative and rapid. Indeed, as far as the wool

[11] See L. Reitzer, 'Some observations on Castilian commerce and finance in the sixteenth century', *Journal of Modern History*, xxxii. (1960), 213–33; Lapeyre, *Une famille de marchands: les Ruiz*, p. 120.

[12] *Suma de tratos y contratos de mercaderes*, quoted Lapeyre, *Une famille de marchands: les Ruiz*, pp. 118–19.

trade was concerned, although the Genoese dominated all the south of
Spain—New Castile and Andalucía—Spaniards held their own in the north
—Old Castile and the Cantabrian coast. In this region the powerful city of
Burgos, which had been enriched by the wool trade even before the discovery of America and became a great centre of maritime insurance, had a
substantial group of Spanish merchants, and these established colonies everywhere Castilian wool was sold, at Bruges, Antwerp, Rouen, Nantes, and
Florence. Medina del Campo, animated by its fairs, was the meeting point
of the merchants of Burgos, Valladolid, Segovia, Salamanca, and Madrid,
and some rich businessmen lived there, the most illustrious being Simón
Ruiz. At Seville, which was more cosmopolitan and contained less prejudice
against commerce, Spaniards faced powerful competition from the Genoese,
but there too the Burgos merchants posted their factors, emulating the
foreigners. Though Spanish merchants could not compete in status' or substance with Italians and Germans, they were probably in advance of all
other nations in the sixteenth century. Ruiz operated on an international
scale. English traders may well have learned double-entry book-keeping in
Spain.[13] French merchants of Nantes and Rouen probably acquired the
practice of drawing up bills of exchange from Spaniards.[14] Nevertheless,
these developments could not disguise the fact that there was an abnormally
large number of foreign merchants operating in Spain, as has been seen—
the Genoese, who engaged in trade, shipping, and finance; the Germans,
who dealt in mining and milling; the English, who were numerous and
prosperous in Seville and other southern cities.

Apart from the American trade, the commerce of Castile in the sixteenth
century was based principally on the export of raw materials and precious
metals against the regular import of manufactured goods and occasional
import of provisions. The primary exports were wool, salt, oil, cochineal,
iron, hides, and sugar. Cochineal, a magnificent scarlet dye, and hides were
re-exports from the Indies, as also was sugar; although the latter could not
compete with Portuguese supplies, it made an important contribution to
the European market. Iron, of course, came from the Basque country.[15] In

---

[13] Connell Smith, op. cit., p. xvi.

[14] Lapeyre, Une famille de marchands: les Ruiz, pp. 122, 162–63. On the Spanish
commercial colony in Antwerp see J.-A. Goris, Étude sur les colonies marchandes meridionales
(Portugais, Espagnols, Italiens) à Anvers de 1488 à 1567 (Louvain, 1925); on the French in
Spain see A. Girard, Le Commerce français à Seville et Cadiz au temps des Habsbourgs
(Bordeaux, 1932).

[15] See T. Guiard Larrauri, Historia del Consulado y Casa de Contratación de Bilbao y del
comercio de la villa (1511–1880); H. Lapeyre, 'El comercio de Bilbao en el siglo XVI',
in Curso de conferencias sobre cuestiones históricas y actuales de la economía española. Universidad de Valladolid, Facultad de Ciencias Políticas, Económicas y Comerciales de Bilbao
(Bilbao, 1957).

spite of the repeated prohibitions on export, it departed in great quantities, especially to France—a necessary contraband because it balanced the purchase of grain for the Basque provinces and also because the local metallurgical industry, in spite of its proportions, did not absorb the entire output of ore. Oil, which was used in textile manufacture as well as for food, was produced for export mainly in Andalucía. The latter also had one of the best supplies of salt in Europe, a vital preservative which drew a constant stream of foreign ships to Puerto de Santa María. But the most important export commodity of Castile was wool.[16] The best product came from the herds that had wintered in the warmer pastures of Andalucía and Extremadura, and was known as *merina* or *extremeña*; this was the quota that was reserved almost exclusively for export. The market was dominated by a few great merchants, in the north by those of Burgos and Segovia, in the centre and the south by the Genoese who bought the greater part of the wool sold in the markets of Cuenca, Toledo, and Granada. Purchasing their wool directly from producers or from Mesta warehouses, the merchants shipped it from Bilbao to northern Europe, from Málaga to Italy, and from Seville to the Indies. Although Spanish wool had markets in Italy, France, and England, the principal buyers were the manufacturers in the Low Countries, where it enjoyed a near-monopoly, an economic link which reinforced the political union.

These were the basic exports of Castile. Against them she imported woollen and linen cloths, quality fabrics, books and paper, and occasionally—though becoming more regular—corn and fish. From the Low Countries she took cloth and tapestries; from England cloth, cereals, and tin; from France linen, cereals, hardware, paper, and books; from Italy and Germany cloth and metal products; from Scandinavia fish and timber; from East Prussia naval stores; from Poland and Russia cereals.

These trading conditions obviously bred an adverse balance of payments. In general, the merchandise going from Spain was of small value and consisted of raw materials. She had nothing comparable to the textile trade of France, Flanders, and England, which earned these countries considerable returns in cash. The combined influence of the Mesta and the merchants, who found the export of raw wool more profitable than that of Castilian cloth, ruined any chance of an export trade in textiles. Consequently, the total value of Spanish exports was much less than that of imports, and she had to settle the difference in cash. Contemporaries were well aware of these facts. In 1558, shortly after the great revolution in Spanish prices pre-

---

[16] H. Lapeyre, 'Le commerce des laines en Espagne sous Philippe II', *Bulletin de la Société d'Histoire Moderne*, 11e série, lix. (1955), 5–8 (Suppl. of *Revue d'Histoire Moderne et Contemporaine*, ii. (1955).

cipitated by the influx of American silver had initiated a heavy outflow of treasure, Luis Ortíz, an accountant in the government service, presented a report to Philip II in which he clearly formulated the balance of trade doctrine.[17] Spain, he argued, was simply exporting raw materials and relied on foreign imports for manufactured goods, which cost much more than primary products and were often made from the raw material that Spain had originally exported. On the basis of relative costs, Ortíz estimated that the value of imports was eight to ten times that of exports, and that Spain was enriching other countries with the ready cash she had to pay for the adverse balance. And he might have added that the balance was rendered even worse by the fact that in many cases Spain had to pay the cost of foreign shipping to bring in vital imports, for she herself did not have the necessary vessels for carrying cereals and naval stores from northern Europe.

Yet Spanish trade was affected not only by conditions of production and exchange but also by the impact of war in a century when Spain had more enemies than friends. After the classical period of the Habsburg–Valois conflict, which had hit Spanish commerce but not ruined it, the peace of Cateau-Cambrésis improved Spanish commercial prospects, for although Huguenot piracy continued, it concentrated on the Indies trade rather than on trade with northern countries. Nevertheless, it could still damage the latter. During the first French war of religion in 1562 the Huguenot rebels seized the two great commercial towns of Rouen and Lyons, and delivered Le Havre to the English. This became a base for privateering against Catholic vessels of every nation; the Channel passage grew increasingly hazardous, and Spanish trade with Rouen was completely interrupted. The second war of religion (1567–68) and the third (1568–70) also paralysed Spanish trade with France. Yet there were further obstacles to come.

In 1566 the revolt of the Netherlands initiated a long political and religious struggle which was also grievous to Spain's economic interests. The export of Spanish wool to the Low Countries became more and more risky, though in years of peaceful conditions in France Rouen began to act as an intermediary market between Spain and her northern dependencies. From 1568, however, Spain had to reckon with another enemy in northern Europe—England—and was beset by an unofficial alliance of Protestant maritime units, the Rochelois, the Sea Beggars, and the English. And in December of that year Spanish pay ships seeking refuge in English ports from French privateers were seized by the English government.[18] The Duke of Alba clumsily

---

[17] E. J. Hamilton, 'Spanish Mercantilism before 1700', in *Facts and Factors in Economic History. Essays presented to Edward Francis Gay* (Cambridge, Mass., 1932), pp. 230–33; Carrera Pujal, *Historia de la economía española*, i. lvii–lxii.

[18] See below, pp. 313–14.

retaliated by seizing the goods of English subjects in the Low Countries, but while this immediately worsened relations it hardly compensated for the loss suffered by Spain; it merely produced an English embargo on Spanish and Flemish goods which amounted to a sum estimated at one-and-a-half million ducats. Moreover, English privateers profited from this providential conflict to emulate their French colleagues, and it became even more difficult for Spanish shipping to penetrate the Channel. In these circumstances trade could only survive by devious means; relations between Spain and the Low Countries were conducted at Rouen or St. Malo, and those with England at St.-Jean-de-Luz. The crisis in Anglo-Spanish relations lasted until 1572 and brought great disorganisation in its wake. And there was no sign of respite. On 1 April 1572 the Sea Beggars seized Brill and increased their operations on the Channel and Baltic routes. In the same month, by a commercial agreement with France, England transferred the staple of her merchandise from the Low Countries to Rouen and Dieppe. And throughout the 1570's privateering continued.

From 1582 to 1585, however, there was a short and fruitful respite for Spain.[19] The organisation of the League in France and the subsequent need of the Huguenots to turn their efforts from the Atlantic towards their enemies inland relieved one of the pressures on the Spanish trade routes. At the same time, the ultimate crisis in Anglo-Spanish relations did not begin until 1585, when Farnese's capture of Antwerp was followed by England's decision to intervene directly in the Low Countries. The years immediately before the sailing of the Armada, therefore, were preceded by a period of relative calm and by one of the most propitious periods of Spanish trade, especially with the Indies; this, in turn, produced a prosperity which helped to make the Armada and to retrieve its loss.

The Anglo-Spanish struggle, however, was even more crucial for Spain and her economy than the conflict with France and the Low Countries, for the English attack was directed primarily at the Spanish Indies and their trade routes. Although English intervention in the Low Countries was one item in the series of provocations which caused Philip II to accept the project of invading his enemy, the Armada was regarded primarily as part of the defence system of the Spanish empire, which would repulse the English attack on it by striking at its roots. The expedition was based on the decision to throw the Indies fleets as well as other units into the assault, and was a response not only to the needs of state but also to the demands of Spanish public opinion, especially of the merchant class, which was the one most hit by English policy. All Spanish commercial interests wanted to destroy Elizabeth I. Their hopes, of course, were dashed, but the defeat of the Spanish

---

[19] See below, pp. 172–73.

Armada did not give England absolute mastery of the Atlantic, for fleets continued to trade with the Indies and bring back its treasure, as will be seen. Some Spanish trade even managed to survive with northern Europe. French ships succeeded in getting through to Spain in convoy, and Spanish merchants continued to export their wool from San Sebastian in well-armed convoys which reached the Lower Seine.[20] Indeed, a limited trade survived with the Dutch and even with England, for war was not total. During the period of the cold war both the Dutch and the English had traded with Spain.[21] England, it is true, had long enforced a policy of excluding vital war supplies from Spain even in neutral shipping, but her Dutch allies took a more lenient view of strategic materials and continued to take grain to the Peninsula.

If her northern enemies continued to provide commercial services for Spain, they did so because they wanted the vital specie which was yielded. The decline of Antwerp prevented it from meeting the credit demands which had previously been made on it and forced merchants to go direct to Spain for bullion. This trade was criticised by some members of Philip II's administration. Don Luis de Requesens, his governor in the Low Countries after Alba, was opposed to Spain trading with her enemies and in 1575 he advised Philip II to exclude Netherlanders, Englishmen and even Frenchmen from Spain and her dependencies, at least for six months. Concern for his vital supplies caused Philip II to defer a decision, and meanwhile he requested further opinions. The reply of an anonymous minister gave various reasons why the proposed measure was impossible: if Spanish ships were prevented from trading to France, England, and the Low Countries, shipowners would end by selling their ships at a time when Spain needed to increase her fleet; in any case, there was no alternative to English, French, and Flemish merchants, and lack of essentials would be serious for Spain and her colonies; finally, if foreigners were prevented from trading openly with America via Spain, then they would do so either clandestinely or via the Canaries.[22] For reasons of this nature trade managed to survive during the unofficial war and even after 1585, though on a limited scale. The Dutch went openly to Spain with cereals in spite of English protests and the increasing opposition of the Spanish authorities. An indirect Anglo-Spanish trade also survived, English merchants buying Spanish goods—oil and cochineal—in Rouen.[23]

A limited trade under war-time conditions represented, of course, a decline from the prosperity of more peaceful years. But this was not the end of the damage caused by state action. The fiscal policy of the crown was another

[20] Lapeyre, *Une famille de marchands: les Ruiz*, pp. 424–25.
[21] For trade between Spain and England before the Elizabethan war see John Brown, *The Marchants Avizo* (first published 1589, ed. P. McGrath, London, 1957).
[22] Quoted in Braudel, *op. cit.*, 490.
[23] Lapeyre, *Une famille de marchands: les Ruiz*, pp. 425–26.

blow to Spanish trade. This policy was not yet animated by the mercantilist object of protecting national production. In fact, the export of certain products—essential foodstuffs, arms and horses—were forbidden. Imports, on the other hand, were presented with few obstacles, except for certain luxury goods which were forbidden by the sumptuary laws. In short, the state paid more attention to taxing exports than imports, for customs duties were regarded primarily as means of raising revenue and not of economic planning. At the beginning of Philip II's reign Spanish customs were moderate, but they were soon augmented, partly from a new duty on wool in 1558 which was further increased in 1564, and partly from the duties on exports from northern ports which were increased in 1565. These additional burdens raised the costs carried by Spanish commerce and were certainly one of the causes of its decline. Indeed, when the government did attempt economic planning it was usually disastrous because based on faulty information and mistaken analysis; this was the case when steps were advocated and taken to discourage the export of goods which were thought necessary to meet domestic requirements.[24] Not content with this, the government positively encouraged imports, as has been seen, and gave further opportunities to foreign producers and merchants, at a time when Spanish prices, by making Spain a good market and a poor supplier, were already operating in favour of importing and against exporting.

Starved of native production, hit by war, and damaged by fiscal policy, Spanish commerce began to limp badly in the second half of the sixteenth century. This, however, did not apply to the Indies trade, the greatest trade in the world and the economic life-line of its owner.

3. Spain and the Indies

Trade between Spain and Spanish America throughout the sixteenth and the first half of the seventeenth century, both in the value and the volume of goods carried, was easily the biggest trans-Oceanic trade in the western world. Together with its principal content—American silver—it became the most important single item in Spain's economy, and without it her position in the second half of the sixteenth century would have been immeasurably weaker. Subsequently, there was an intimate connection between the contraction of the trade from 1630 to 1640 and the decline of Spain under the later Habsburgs. As soon as American sources of wealth ceased to irrigate the Spanish economy, the metropolis began to experience a period of acute difficulties.

Such a prize was not acquired by chance. Spain had political, geographical,

[24] See above, p. 128.

and technical assets which made her more fitted than any other nation in western Europe not only to seize the opportunities of empire but to create them. Portugal, it is true, had opened the way in the fifteenth century, pushing farther out into the Atlantic and south along the African coast in search of negroes, spices, and gold. And the economic and technical progress which made expansion possible were available to other nations than Spain. The existence of merchant bankers and bills of exchange placed instruments of international exchange and above all of credit at the service of overseas commerce, and, during a period of acute shortage of precious metals, assembled capital without which the enterprises would have been impossible. The new methods were perfected first in Italy, as early as the thirteenth century, but Spain was the quickest to learn from them and in this respect was certainly superior to the countries of northern Europe.[25] Nor was she slow to profit from the technical revolution in ships and the art of navigation. In other respects her progress was unique and her experience first-hand. In the art of warfare she led Europe, and this she had learned in the long struggle against the Moors, followed by her campaigns in Italy. The superiority of her arms, particularly of her firearms, were basic factors in the rapid and overwhelming conquest of the Aztecs and the Incas. But Spain had administrative as well as military power. The effective sovereignty of the crown and its agents, as developed by Ferdinand and Isabella, gave Spain the first modern state machinery in Europe and equipped her not only to administer an empire from the metropolis but to export her institutions and officials to new territories.

Spanish colonisation differed in kind from that of Portugal, the only rival in the race for empire. Portugal was less conscious of the political and religious advantages of expansion than her neighbour. Columbus, of course, and his sovereigns, were not uninterested in the gold and spices of the Far East, and Portugal was not unaware of the advantage of turning the flank of Islam. But the search for alliances against the expansion of the Ottoman Turk in eastern Europe and the Mediterranean, and awareness of the power to be derived from imperialism, were far more dominant in Spanish policy than

[25] On Spanish expansion see Francisco Morales Padrón, *Historia del descubrimiento y conquista de América* (Madrid, 1971). On the Spanish empire in America see C. H. Haring, *The Spanish Empire in America* (New York, 1947); J. H. Parry, *The Spanish Seaborne Empire* (London, 1966), and Charles Gibson, *Spain in America* (New York, 1966). On the meaning of conquest and settlement for Spain and for Europe see J. H. Elliott, *The Old World and the New 1492–1650* (Cambridge, 1971). On the Indies trade the classic modern account is by C. H. Haring. *Trade and Navigation between Spain and the Indies in the time of the Habsburgs* (Cambridge, Mass., 1918); but all previous works have been virtually superseded by the monumental work of H. and P. Chaunu, *Séville et l'Atlantique (1504–1650)* (8 vols., Paris, 1955–59) which is itself a mine for further research.

in that of Portugal.[26] This difference of emphasis was reflected in the actual process of expansion. The means adopted by Spain in the first years of discovery and conquest—especially the rapidity of operation and the choice of routes—were particularly important in determining the future policy of empire. The search for a western passage to the Far East gave way from the time of the second voyage of Columbus to a desire to exploit the new lands, which he had discovered incidentally, for their own sake; in other words to a policy of colonisation which would at once extend Christianity and yield gold. Once this decision had been taken, the only limit was the amount of territory available. At this point, Spanish policy differed from Portuguese in yet another respect—in the adoption of a relay system of colonisation. Between 1492 and 1498 the exploration of the New World was limited to the Antilles and a few portions of the coast of Tierra Firme, and was controlled exclusively by Columbus. In the second period, 1498 to 1506, Columbus lost his monopoly and exploration turned more to Tierra Firme, with Santo Domingo used as a secondary base for further colonisation. In the third period, 1506 to 1516, Columbus was dead, and although expeditions of the old type continued to leave Spain, the greatest efforts of exploration and conquest were made from the colonies themselves, first from Santo Domingo then from Cuba. Finally, from 1517 to 1535, the massive conquest of the continent was undertaken, of Mexico and Peru; operations which were also launched from existing colonies.

Spanish colonisation was unique not only in purpose and method but also in quantity. From as early as the second voyage, in 1493, Spain threw an unprecedented volume of men and materials into the enterprise—seventeen ships and 1,200 to 1,500 emigrants.[27] In the first eight to nine years about 5,000 or 6,000 men emigrated. This was a sign that Spain had the manpower for expansion, partly because her population was growing, partly because the fall of Granada and the completion of the *reconquista* released

[26] Chaunu, *op. cit.*, viii. 1, pp. 76–85.

[27] On the policy and methods of colonisation see J. Pérez de Tudela Bueso, *Las Armadas de Indias y los orígenes de la política de colonisación* (Madrid, 1956). Complete statistics do not exist to show the exact number of Spaniards who emigrated to the Indies during the colonial period. See C. Bermúdez Plata, *Catálogo de pasageros de Indias durante los siglos XVI, XVII, y XVIII*, (2 vols., Seville, 1932–40); on the first volume, which covers the period 1509–34 and gives 5,320 names, see C. Pérez Bustamente, 'Las regiones españolas y la población de América (1509–34)', *Revista de Indias*, vi. (1941), 81–101; on the second volume, which covers the period 1535–38 and gives 5,600 names, see J. Rodríguez Argua, 'Las regiones españolas y la población de América (1535–1538)' *Revista de Indias*, (1947), 698–748. For a considered modern estimate see Magnus Mörner, 'La emigración española al Nuevo Mundo antes de 1810. Un informe del estado de la investigación', *Anuario de Estudios Americanos*, 32 (1975), 43–131, who suggests a maximum of 250,000 emigrants for the period 1506–1600, and 200,000 for 1601–50.

forces which had previously been tied down in the Moorish war. Gold was the only possible justification for this enormous operation, and the second expedition of Columbus was financed by expectation of it. The mining and slave-labour characteristics of the colonial economy thus appeared from the very beginning. This form of exploitation presupposed effective occupation of extensive territory and mobilisation of a large labour force. With her powerful military machine and administrative technique Spain had the means to accomplish both.

Yet the search for gold was tempered by a religious mission, without which Spanish expansion would have been inconceivable, or else would have taken a very different form. For the discovery and conquest of America were animated by a spirit of missionary expansion and sustained throughout by all the resources of the church. Here again, Spanish assets were unique. Spain possessed the first reformed church in Europe.[28] The standard of her hierarchy, the quality of her theologians, and the zeal of her missionaries were unequalled in the western world. Moreover, the Spanish church had direct experience of contact with the infidel in the Peninsula itself, and while this accounts for some of its intolerance it also helps to explain its anxiety to extend the faith to those who knew it not. Thus it had the confidence and the personnel to play a vital rôle in colonial expansion. It also had the ideals and the strength to restrain the rampant colonialism of the settler class and to give some features of order and justice to the new empire. For the motives which drove Spain to colonise were mixed. In the classical words of Bernal Díaz, soldier and chronicler of Cortés' expedition to Mexico, Spaniards went to the New World 'to serve God and His Majesty, to give light to those in darkness, and also to get rich'. The church and the crown took the condition of serving God seriously, and the proof is their efforts to convert the Indians and to protect them. But the mass of the colonists were indifferent to these things. As Pizarro explained to a priest who protested at the spoliation of the Indians in Peru and exhorted him to bring them instead to knowledge of God and the faith: 'I have not come here for such reasons. I have come to take away their gold.'[29] Men like Pizarro went to the Indies as a ruling class, to extort labour and money from the natives, and to wage war on them if necessary. The missionaries, anxious to save the souls of the Indians, found their efforts frustrated, and some of them began to offer positive alternatives to existing relations between Spaniards and natives. It was important that the church had the vigour to produce such men and

[28] See above, pp. 7–8, 64–73.
[29] Quoted in L. Hanke, *The Spanish Struggle for Justice in the Conquest of America* (Philadelphia, 1949), p. 16, a basic work for the question of race relations in the Spanish empire.

Hernán Cortés

that the crown gave them the opportunity to experiment with their alternatives, such as the peaceful evangelising of Las Casas, the hospital-villages
of Vasco de Quiroga in Mexico, and the reductions of the Jesuits in Paraguay
and elsewhere. The dilemma, of course, was irreducible. As secular rulers
the Spanish kings desired dominion and revenue, and in this the church was
compromised too. As Christian monarchs and patrons of the church in
America they were committed in conscience to the work of winning the
Indians to the faith. But the fact that both objectives were taken seriously
meant that royal policy was ambivalent and vacillating. This gave the
idealists—bishops, missionaries, and lawyers—the opportunity they were
looking for to insert their ideas and their influence in the struggle for
justice for the Indians. These Christian humanitarian ideals permeated
Spanish colonial legislation, and though they were not always effective in
practice they prevented Spain's dominions in the New World from de-
generating into a mere robber empire.

The diverse qualities needed in a colonial power were combined uniquely
in Spain; she had the objectives and the means. It was no accident, therefore,
that Columbus attached his fortunes to those of Castile.[30] He had tried other
powers first. Portugal refused his services, because the very progress of geographical speculation and the experience acquired in political and business
circles there caused her to refuse to commit herself to a mistaken hypothesis.
In any case, Portugal had invested too much in African expeditions and in
a search southwards for a direct route to eastern spices to interest herself in
the plans of a man whose distances were so patently wrong. Too late for
Portugal, Columbus was too early for northern Europe, for whereas
Portugal rejected his plans because she knew too much, powers like France
and England rejected them because they did not know enough. In Castile,
however, where the genius and tenacity of Columbus met the intuition and
imagination of Isabella, the ground was almost ready for such a project,
though it needed seven years' effort before it finally came to fruition in
1492. These long years of delay are significant. If Columbus had not spent
ten years of his life submitting his plans to the whole of western Europe, then
the rôle of Castile might be regarded as accidental. But the reply of Isabella,
and the financial support of the shippers and businessmen of Niebla, rule
out the possibility of chance, because the choice had been offered all round
and for a very long time. Moreover, from one compelling point of view,
that of geography, Spain was ideal for Columbus's purpose.

Indeed, of all the conditions favouring Spain geographical ones were
probably the most important. Andalucía, the spear-head of the *reconquista*,
was already a frontier region, with long experience of contact and friction

[30] On Columbus see S. E. Morison, *Admiral of the Ocean Sea* (2 vols., Boston, 1942).

with Islam, and ready to turn reconquest into conquest. More than this, Andalucía was situated at the intersection of the Mediterranean and the Atlantic, and at the right latitude; winds and currents made Seville—and Lisbon—the best places from which to take ships out into the Atlantic and bring them back again.[31] From the very beginning, therefore, Andalucía enjoyed a virtual monopoly of communications and commerce with the Indies. Trade was soon confined at the Spanish end to Seville and its satellite ports on the Guadalquivir, and was a monopoly in the hands of a corporation of Seville merchant houses, known as the *Consulado*. In establishing these restrictions, of course, the crown was moved by political, religious, and strategic considerations, as well as fiscal and economic ones. But although this was a legal monopoly—and an object of criticism ever since—it was founded in reality and corresponded to technical and geographical conditions.

In 1495, it is true, Cadiz was *named* as the port of exit; and by the edict of 14 February 1503 which organised at Seville the *Casa de Contratación*, or House of Trade, an agency which administered economic relations between Spain and the Indies, an obligation was imposed on colonial shipping to use only the port of Seville, thus defining permanently the monopoly of Seville and the exclusive right of Castile to relations with the new discoveries.[32] But the orders of 1495 and 1503 simply registered existing facts. In its contracts with entrepreneurs, of whom Columbus was the first, the state confined itself to the rôle of registration, guarantee, and arbitration against future claims. The choice of ports originally depended on private enterprise, and Columbus chose Cadiz and Seville; all the expeditions between 1492 and 1510 left from Andalucía. In other words, it was the experts of the time who chose Andalucía, first Niebla and then, because of the growing size of the expeditions, the Guadalquivir ports of Cadiz, Seville, and Sanlucar. In favour of Seville there was a decisive factor—it was already a centre of commerce, finance, and administration, and therefore contained the personnel and the agencies by which the state could control the new enterprises, using Cadiz and Sanlucar as its ports on the Atlantic coast. It was not, therefore, a question of assuring a monopoly to a single port, but to a whole complex of ports and an entire region, of which Seville was the inland capital.

The monopoly solution, then, was chosen by experts and stood the test of time and of experience. But why, in addition to excluding other states—

---

[31] 'Le plus Atlantique des pays mediterranéenes, le plus mediterranéen des pays Atlantique', as Chaunu describes Andalucía, *op. cit.*, viii. 1, p. 52.

[32] J. de Veitia Linaje, *Norte de la contratación de las Indias occidentales* (Seville, 1672); R. Antúñez y Acevedo, *Memorias históricas sobre la legislación y gobierno del comercio de los españoles con sus colonias en las Indias occidentales* (Madrid, 1797); Chaunu, *op. cit.*, viii. 1, pp. 182–84.

a universal practice at the time—and other kingdoms within Spain—a sign of the hegemony of Castile—did Spain also exclude other ports like Valencia, Barcelona, La Coruña, and Bilbao? The answer is that before the state excluded them, nature herself did. It would have been unreasonable to add to the difficulties of an already difficult Atlantic crossing. Shipping from the Mediterranean ports was excluded by its dependence on favourable wind and current conditions to navigate the straits of Gibraltar—an extra journey, moreover, in a region which was directly exposed to the Barbary pirates. The Cantabrian coast was better situated, but still could not compete with the advantages of wind and current enjoyed by south-western Spain, at a time when speed and timing were vital and skilled pilots in short supply. And just as the Barbary pirates threatened the junction between the Mediterranean and the Atlantic, so the French, and later the English and Dutch, corsairs infested the routes between Spain's northern and southern Atlantic coasts. Before the means of measuring longitude were available, any vessel from northern Spain wanting to make America would have to cling to the coast as far as Cape St. Vincent, and it was precisely along the coast that the northern pirates directed their attacks, for they had little chance of meeting their prey in mid-ocean. If the Indies trade had gone north, it would have been wide open to attack, and an even more tempting target than Spain's European commerce because it was much more valuable. Finally, economic conditions reinforced geographical and tactical ones. In agricultural potential the mountainous northern coast was much inferior to the south. The three main agricultural commodities were grain, wine and oil, and although it was not always possible to export them, when it was they came from Andalucía, which thus provided for the sustenance of crews, emigrants and settlers from sources that were easily accessible to its port.

The state, of course, had its interests too. Faced with the natural facts of monopoly, it found it convenient to underwrite them. For political as well as fiscal reasons, the Spanish government desired to exercise exclusive control over relations with the New World, in order to prevent the emigration of elements dangerous to political and religious security. In the sixteenth century the two things were almost inseparable, and in view of Huguenot pretensions to Florida and English collaboration with the Islamic-led *cimarrones* of Tierra Firme, Spanish policy was no more than realistic. It was equally vital to exercise control over the passage of arms and subversive literature, and to concentrate all the means of defence in order to make them more effective. The crown's interest in a single-port policy, therefore, was obvious, and it soon fashioned a monopoly administration, beginning with the embryo bureaucracy assisting Bishop Juan Rodríguez de Fonseca, Isabella's colonial adviser; in 1503 this blossomed into the *Casa de Contra-*

tación, which found its natural base in Seville. The *Casa*, dependent on the crown, was the vital instrument of monopoly, for it controlled the fleets, shipments, and personnel involved in trade and colonisation. In 1524 it was made dependent on the Council of the Indies founded in that year; the latter ended the personal management of colonial administration exercised by Fonseca and became the crown's central agency for colonial government, with the *Casa* specialising in economic affairs.

Yet the policy of the crown was, if anything, more flexible than that of private shippers and merchants. An edict of Charles V in 1529 opened the outward journey to other ports than Seville and for a time there were prospects of a modification of the rigid monopoly.[33] But this policy was never effectively applied, partly because of opposition from the monopolists, partly because the government itself soon found it necessary to control treasure imports, and above all, perhaps, because the very ports which might have benefited from it did not seriously try to—it was hardly feasible. The law, therefore, was dropped, and in any case the gradual emergence of the convoy system reinforced the channel of monopoly. This is not to say, of course, that it was ever completely effective. There was considerable fraud, and on the return journey in particular much trade and treasure escaped via Galicia, Gibraltar, and Portugal. On the whole, however, the monopoly was observed—up to 97 per cent. on the outward journey for more than a century, and up to 96–98 per cent. on the inward journey.[34] This was *within* the Spanish monopoly. From without came the foreign interloper, plying his unofficial and illegal trade, resistance to which varied in America in proportion to the amount of official trade which the colonies were receiving from the mother country. If the latter was inadequate, then the colonists—often with the connivance of local officials—were ready to break the laws and trade with the foreigner, as happened in the 1540's and 1560's when French, Portuguese, and English interlopers were all active in the Caribbean. However, although the presence of interlopers was almost permanent, it was only from 1620 and still more from 1630 that they really began to make nonsense of the monopoly. Up to that time the rule of Seville was supreme, and Spain preserved for herself the major share of returns from America.

Yet to speak of the 'Seville monopoly' is to ignore the part played by other regions of Spain. While Seville had a monopoly of trade, the north of Spain, especially Biscay, had a monopoly of shipping, for it supplied almost all the Spanish vessels in the Indies trade.[35] Indeed, the northern provinces in general played an important rôle in colonial expansion. The ports of

---

[33] See above, pp. 76–78.   [34] Chaunu, *op. cit.*, viii. 1, pp. 201–03.
[35] *Ibid.*, viii. 2, 1, p. 405.

Ferrol and La Coruña were defence bases against northern maurauders. The wealth of the north, built, as has been seen, on fishing, metallurgy, shipbuilding, and the export of wool, supplied capital, equipment and goods for the trade, as well as many of its personnel. For much of the sixteenth century this supply was substantial. From 1520 to 1580 the northern coast provided at least 80 per cent. of the shipping on the Indies route. From 1580 to 1610 this fell to 50 per cent., and from the second quarter of the seventeenth century it was only one element among many—a decline which also involved the supply of seamen and was reflected in the depopulation of northern towns, which lost many of their inhabitants to those of the south. For these regions were most exposed to Anglo-Dutch privateering and maritime power, and their prosperity suffered once the route from Bilbao to Antwerp had been cut.[36] But they were only one part of Spain. The early eclipse of a limited sector of the peninsula has been one of the reasons for the tendency to pre-date the economic decline of Spain. The Indies trade itself, however, continued to flourish and to bring great wealth to its owner long after the 1580's. This was due, among other things, to the increasing efficiency with which Spain defended it against her rivals.

The defence of the colonial monopoly was based essentially on administrative control and naval cover; in addition there were military installations at key points in America itself.[37] Every ship sailing between Seville and the Indies was required to register for each voyage out and back with the *Casa de Contratación*, which kept a record containing a detailed account of the ship, company, and cargo. The officials of the *Casa*, however, were allied by many ties of family, friendship, community of interests, and more or less clandestine financial deals, with the great merchant houses of the *Consulado*, the corporation to which the Seville monopolists belonged. Their duty was to regulate trade; the actual collection of the customs—the *almojarifazgo* collected at the Spanish and the American ends of the trade— was separately farmed. Accordingly, the registration of shipping was rigorously enforced, because it was a means of maintaining the Seville monopoly. The registration of merchandise on the other hand, being the basis for the assessment of duties, was systematically arranged to conceal the nature and value of goods. The over-all quantity of goods could not, of course, be readily concealed; but containers were merely counted, formal statements of their contents were accepted, and the *Casa* regularly and successfully opposed requests of the *almojarifes*, or customs officials, to be allowed to open them for inspection. The basis of assessment was thus arbitrary, formal,

[36] *Ibid.*, vi. 1, pp. 160–67; vii. pp. 36–37; viii. 1, pp. 256–66.
[37] V. E. Chatelain, *The Defenses of Spanish Florida* (New York, 1941); J. A. Calderón Quijano, *Las fortificaciones en Nueva España* (Seville, 1952).

and largely fictitious, and by shipping goods on the warships which escorted the merchant convoys consigners could escape registration altogether. Because of this 'psychosis of fraud', the nature of shipments to the Indies can be ascertained only in the roughest quantitative fashion and it is impossible to estimate the growing quantity of foreign goods being shipped to the Indies within the monopoly.[38] The monopoly itself, however, was also under attack from without.

From an early date communications between Spain and the Indies had to be protected against privateers and pirates, and soon the colonial market itself had to be preserved from foreign interlopers; by Spaniards these were all described by the generic term of *corsarios*. The most dangerous area for shipping in the early decades of trade was between the coast of Andalucía and the Canaries and Azores: here the French and Barbary corsairs operated, lying in wait for Spanish vessels returning from the Indies. Soon, however, the European corsairs extended their operations to the other end of the route and began to prey on the Caribbean. In the first half of the sixteenth century the greatest menace came from France, for not only were the recurrent Franco-Spanish wars also fought in the Atlantic but the Huguenot pirates always regarded Spanish shipping as fair game. In the second half of the century the greatest attack came from English seamen, who, led by Hawkins, first tried to force their way into the Spanish trading system, and then under Drake ended by raiding it outright. Defence was urgent and it was soon provided. From 1512 the *Casa* was under orders to send two caravels to the Canaries to protect ships from the Indies against French corsairs. From at least 1521 a squadron of three to five ships was ordered to patrol between the coast of Spain and the islands; this squadron, which was eventually included in the fleet system, foreshadowed the future *Armada de la Guardia de la Carrera de las Indias*, which became the classical armed escort across the Atlantic. For some years, however, Spanish defence had to be content with its modest beginnings, though in 1513 the *Casa* had been instructed to send two caravels across the Atlantic to patrol the coasts of Cuba and protect shipping at the other end of the crossing.[39] Then, as the danger increased, the defence organisation became more efficient—and more expensive. From 1528 another line of defence appeared, the *armada* called 'para la guardia de costa y navios de Indias'; its exact station is not known, but it evidently provided a defensive bridge between Andalucía and the New World.

These efforts were increased at different times throughout the 1520's and

[38] Chaunu, *op. cit.*, i. pp. 70–88, 97–121.
[39] Haring, *Trade and Navigation*, p. 87; on the French threat see H. Folmer, *Franco-Spanish rivalry in North America, 1524–1763* (Glendale, Calif., 1953).

1530's, according to the incidence of war with France or the amount of piracy, and in this period the origins of the ultimate organisation of the Indies trade can be observed: independent sailings gradually gave way to sailings in convoy, protected by warships. It was in these years, too, that the *avería*, first imposed about 1518, began to operate, at first intermittently for immediate needs and finally as a regular tax; in this way the trade itself was made to bear the costs of defence, particularly of the armed fleets which escorted the convoys.[40] In the 1540's, as the temptation to marauders increased with the amount of trade, larger and more powerful ships were used in the interests of security, and this development was linked with the obligation to sail in convoys of at least ten vessels, escorted by warships which were also growing in size and armament. The system was further developed in the difficult years of war with France during the 1550's, which produced bigger and stronger convoys sailing biannually. Although the war with France officially ended in 1559, Spain was then faced with the new and ever-growing danger from northern Europe, and after many hesitations the convoy system was given its definite form. In 1564 the double convoy —that is, the grouping of two fleets right up to their point of separation in the lesser Antilles, begun during the 1540's—was replaced by two separate annual convoys.[41] Under this reorganisation all ships leaving Spain for the Indies had to sail in convoy, except those that had sufficient armament, the slave ships from Angola, and the *avisos*, or dispatch vessels which maintained communications in the interval between annual sailings. The convoys themselves assembled in Seville, Cadiz, and Sanlucar, and left in two groups: the *flota* sailed in April or May for Veracruz in New Spain, and the *galeones* in August for Nombre de Dios on the isthmus of Panama; from their rendezvous at Havana the combined fleets returned to Spain in the following autumn. In spite of its rigid and clumsy appearance, the convoy system was a successful piece of adaptation. Had Spain been able to develop her imperial communications in peaceful conditions, of course, a swifter and more efficient means of trade would have been necessary and possible. But in view of the refusal of other powers to recognise her monopoly of trade and occupation in America, this was the only possible answer. No doubt the limitation of trade to convoys was partly an attempt to compensate for the shortage of skilled pilots, but the most compelling reason was the search for security; it was no coincidence that the convoys were given their most permanent form at a time when Hawkins was rampant in the Caribbean. The system itself functioned fairly well, in spite of the fact that escort vessels

[40] G. Céspedes del Castillo, *La Avería en el comercio de Indias* (Seville, 1945); Chaunu, *op. cit.*, i. pp. 169–75, 185–94.
[41] Haring, *Trade and Navigation*, pp. 1–20, 123–54, 201–30.

sometimes carried merchandise in the mouths of canons. And it was a powerful reply to Spain's enemies and rivals. To capture or destroy a fleet was extremely difficult; only on rare occasions, in the course of two centuries, was an entire fleet destroyed, as in the disastrous battle of Matanzas in 1628. Normally, casualties were due to the poor condition of ships, to the weather, or to accidents. Indeed, from the 1560's, when the Indies fleets came to be composed almost entirely of larger and more powerful vessels, sailing in convoy, Spain dominated the Atlantic, and this vital channel of imperial communications functioned, if not smoothly, at any rate effectively. The cost, of course, was high—shortages of goods in the colonies which provided further opportunities for the interloper, and a crippling defence tax on the trade itself which only encouraged fraud. And there was little defence of the Pacific coast route between Panama and Lima. But the convoy system was not Spain's last word on defence.

Naval patrols eventually developed into three main units—the *Armada del Mar Océano*, which had a roving brief in the Atlantic, the *Armada de la Guardia de las Indias*, which escorted the convoys, and the *Armada de Barlovento*, which covered the Caribbean area. To these were added squadrons of galleys. The latter were already used for the coastal defence of southern Spain, and although they were costly in manpower and supplies and unsuitable in northern waters, they were effective because of their independence of wind and useful enough to be sent in 1574 to the Indies, where they were used to patrol the coasts of Tierra Firme from Cartagena to Nombre de Dios, of Cuba and of Hispaniola. Yet it was not a successful transfer: shortage of men, an unsuitable climate, and the inability of the vessel itself to cope with ocean waters, all reduced the efficiency of the galley in its new world. But this in turn produced a more successful piece of adaptation—the *galizabra*, a hybrid vessel combining the features of the galley and those of the ocean warship.[42] Finally, in the last decades of the sixteenth century the authorities produced yet another answer to enemy attacks. From 1588, owing to the temporary disorganisation of the regular convoy system caused by the heavy demands of the Spanish Armada on the Indies fleets, squadrons of *zabras*, small, rapid, and well-armed ships, sacrificing everything to speed and chartered at the expense of the crown, were put into service on the trans-Atlantic route to bring back the treasure on which Spanish policy depended. The *zabras* were not meant to combat assailants, for they were not heavy enough, but to escape from them by their speed. In this sense they were an admission of weakness as well as a costly expedient, for they carried no merchandise. But they served the purpose for which they were intended, and were yet another

[42] On the use of galleys at Cartagena de Indias see Chaunu, *op. cit.*, viii. 1, pp. 1035–39, 1042–54.

example of Spain's resilience and a further warning to her northern enemies not to underestimate her defensive power.

Organised, controlled, and protected, the Indies trade expanded with remarkable vitality. Essentially it consisted in placing consumer goods at high prices in the American market and receiving money in exchange. Spanish exports consisted primarily of wine and oil from Andalucía, cloths from central Spain, tools from the Basque country, mercury for the amalgamation of silver, and men. Colonial production which might compete with that of the mother country was prohibited—though not always effectively —but this still left room for the import of the animal and vegetable products of the Indies, some of which Spain herself had transplanted there, such as hides, dye-woods, and sugar, all of which earned money in re-export. But Spaniards placed greatest value on the mineral wealth of the Indies. The great deposits of silver in New Spain and Peru were the economic justification of empire, the magnet of emigrants and merchants, the hope of a bankrupt government; and they were the ultimate reason for the rigour of the monopoly and the care with which it was protected. The material does not exist from which to estimate the production of each mining zone or the total production of America; the only gauge is the amount of metal received in Spain, but this is a defective figure because it does not account for the treasure left in America, that going to the Far East on the yearly Manila Galleon, and that disappearing through channels of fraud and contraband. Nevertheless, even declared imports point to the immense proportions of silver disgorged from the Indies.[43] These imports primed the trade still further and were one of the chief factors in its powerful expansion.

This expansion was not regular but subject to various fluctuations.[44] There was a long period of trade expansion from 1504 to 1610, and a long period of decline from 1610 onwards. Within the first period there were two phases of expansion, one from 1504 to 1550 and one from 1562 to 1592, separated by a mid-century recession of twelve years.

The first great period of expansion, from 1504 to 1550, saw the number of outward–inward sailings increase from 35 in 1506 to 215 in 1550, with the volume of trade increasing by 800 per cent. from 3,309 *toneladas* at the beginning of the period to 32,355 at its end.[45] This was the age of the conquistadores, of rapid colonial expansion, of the first shipments of treasure,

[43] See above, p. 130 n. 42.
[44] The discovery, dating, and analysis of these fluctuations are among the most important contributions of Chaunu to the subject; see his figures and tables, *op. cit.*, vols. ii–vii, and his interpretation, first on a geographical and then on a chronological basis, vol. viii. See especially, viii. 2, 1, pp. 15–25, and Appendix II, Table E.
[45] *Ibid.*, viii. 2, 1, pp. 49–50.

which acted as a stimulus to investment and further conquests. From 1504 to 1510 Spain was sending men, foodstuffs, materials, and animals to the Indies and getting back gold, and in these early years she was running the colonies at a loss for they were absorbing more than they returned. From 1510 to 1522, with the exploitation of the islands—Hispaniola, Cuba, Puerto Rico—returns on investments began to mount, not only in gold but also in sugar. But this expansion was checked during the period 1522–32 when the resources of the island colonies were invested in turn in the colonisation of New Spain.[46] Then, from 1533 to 1544, New Spain began to deliver its wealth, followed by Peru, both of which vastly increased the flow of precious metals. Trade ceased to be insular and became continental in scale; larger ships and more of them began to be employed as expansion made them necessary and made them pay. The greater part of their cargoes was no longer agricultural products but manufactured goods such as textiles and equipment for the mines and sugar mills. At this point the relation between prices and expansion became more direct. When prices rose, everything rose, including the trade. Merchants wanted a return on their investments; producers in America wanted a market for their products in Spain and in the rest of Europe. Correlation depended on merchants and shippers *knowing* the price level and being aware of the financial relationship between Spain and the Indies. From the period 1535–40 this was the case: merchants sent large quotas of goods to the Indies when prices were high in Spain, and less when prices were lower. Therefore, the Indies themselves were the stimulator, causing an inflation in Spain which facilitated the financing of trade with the Indies. The Seville merchants, knowing from experience that a rise of prices in Spain created a presumption in favour of a rise of prices in the Indies, increased their exports in the expectation of heavy returns. Heavy returns of bullion in turn raised prices and trade still further.[47]

The expansion of the first half of the century reached its peak in the six years from 1544 to 1550. By this time territorial expansion was virtually complete, though not yet fully exploited. In 1545 prospectors discovered the mineral wealth of Potosí in the bleak Andes of Upper Peru, and this was to become the biggest source of silver in the world.[48] The number of ships and the volume of trade increased as prices rose further still. In the interests of security against pirates and privateers larger and larger ships were being used, and they were obliged to sail in convoys of at least ten vessels escorted by powerful warships. There were, therefore, two factors

[46] *Ibid.*, viii. 2, 1, pp. 81–141.   [47] *Ibid.*, viii. 2, 1, pp. 142–85.
[48] See Hamilton, *American Treasure and the Price Revolution in Spain*, passim; C. H. Haring, 'American Gold and Silver Production in the first half of the sixteenth century', *The Quarterly Journal of Economics*, xxix. (1915), 475–79; L. Hanke, *The Imperial City of Potosí* (The Hague, 1956).

in expansion—trade and the ships to carry it. As trade expanded so did shipping, and as the supply of shipping could not keep pace with the demands of trade so freightage became dearer. Shortage of ships combined with the attraction of higher freightage prices stimulated more shipbuilding and drew more foreign vessels to Seville. The profits earned from high freight rates then enabled shippers to make further investments and increase the size of their fleets. The time came, however, when the Indies themselves could not respond quickly enough to the commercial demands of the metropolis. This lag of returns to Spain behind exports caused a stock of ships to accumulate in the Indies, not yet ready to return because of the shortage of profitable freight. In Spain, meanwhile, as freight was expensive only costly goods capable of paying it were being consigned. Rapid expansion, therefore, was blocked by two bottle-necks; ships piled up in the Indies and goods in Seville, just at the time when the additional investments in shipbuilding began to bear fruit. As long as high prices gave an incentive to export, all was well. But once prices dropped, or halted, then crisis followed, for on their return to Spain vessels exceeded the demand of a reduced export, and this in turn would hit the shipyards.[49]

These repercussions, of course, took time to make their impact, but from 1550 they were certainly being felt, and expansion was brought to a halt for more than ten years. The outward traffic for 1554—23 vessels compared with 133 in 1550—was the lowest since 1522, and there was an equally drastic fall in the volume of tonnage and its value. The conditions of trade had now changed: the plundering economy of the conquistadores had come to an end, and the expanding frontier of conquest had halted; wealth was no longer available for the mere taking, it had to be created. At the same time prices slumped, and without the prospect of certain profits merchants drew back. When prices began to pick up again after 1554 there was still the mounting war with France to put a brake on trade. It was between 1554 and 1556 that the menace of French privateers was most acute and Spanish shipping losses were heaviest. The merchants in Seville reacted by refusing to consign cargoes, and no convoy left the Guadalquivir for twenty-two months. When sailings were resumed in 1555 they took the form of yet bigger convoys, and while this improved security it also hampered trade, for until the convoy system was perfected it retarded traffic by preventing vessels from turning round quickly for return journeys; this diminished the profits on shipping investments and immobilised commercial capital. And war did further damage. The enormous military effort made by Spain in the 1550's on behalf of Charles V and his son was one of the principal causes of the state bankruptcy in 1557; the subsequent sequestration of money

[49] Chaunu, *op. cit.*, viii. 2, 1, pp. 247–50.

remittances from America encouraged merchants not only to seek to evade it by fraud but also to keep their money in the Indies. As less money was coming in, so less investments were going out, and this reinforced the existing depression.[50]

From 1559, however, there began a long period of expansion which was clearly under way from 1562; between then and 1608 the number of ships on the Indies route increased by 176 per cent., and the volume of tonnage by 238 per cent. There were other signs of prosperity—new exports, such as timber for American shipyards, more manufactured goods in proportion to agricultural products, new types of ships, more foreign ships, and more foreign merchants at Seville. And the whole trade now enjoyed more efficient protection, for the convoy system was finally perfected in 1564. The revival began slowly, and it was not until 1566–70 that the volume of trade characteristic of 1546–50 was attained. Nevertheless, the conditions in which expansion could begin were already operating. For a brief period after the Treaty of Cateau-Cambrésis (1559), Spain was at peace. Although the seamen of the west coast of France continued to wage war on Spanish shipping almost independently of their government's policy, France herself was weakened by the wars of religion, while Spain was free from heavy military commitments until the war with the Turk in 1571 and the renewed outbreak in the Low Countries in 1572. In the Caribbean, it is true, Hawkins was probing Spanish trade and defences from 1562, but it was another ten years before Drake made his spectacular and much more ominous assault on Panama. Meanwhile, the main lines of conquest and occupation had been accomplished, and the settling and internal development of the colonies could proceed apace. Shortly before 1560 German methods of silver production by amalgamation with mercury were adapted to the mines of New Spain, with marked improvement in production; and from the time the Huancavelica mercury mine went into operation, especially from 1576, Potosí had a local source of this vital commodity, and Peru began to furnish proportionately more metal even than New Spain.[51] The rapidly increasing output of the silver mines, with consequent renewed demand for European commodities and renewed flow of treasure to Spain, promoted the second long period of expansion, by inducing merchants to invest in trade. The investments were particularly lucrative in manufactured goods, which continued to replace agricultural products in the holds of the galleons. Other sectors of the Spanish economy benefited from the new boom, especially the Biscayan shipyards, for it was they and not their foreign rivals who supplied most of the vessels for the

[50] *Ibid.*, viii. 2, 1, pp. 261–344.
[51] G. Lohmann Villena, *Las minas de Huancavelica en los siglos XVI y XVII* (Seville, 1952), pp. 452–53.

Indies trade. Finally, there was a marked rise in prices, at once a result and a cause of more intensive trade.

Yet progress was not without its setbacks. The organisation of convoys, made necessary by the shortage of pilots and the needs of security, was itself an obstacle, for the convoys and their escorts had to be paid for by the trade, while they also prevented ships from being used economically by immobilising them for long periods and restricting the returns on the capital invested in them.[52] But the greatest problems arose outside the trade. The expeditions and devastating raids of Hawkins and Drake opened a new era in the Spanish Atlantic. Their effects cannot be gauged simply by the losses suffered by Spanish trade and shipping, for these were relatively small; even Drake's sensational descent on Panama in 1572 caused losses of only one-twentieth of the annual value of exports from Spain to the Indies.[53] But though the prizes gained and the destruction wrought by the English enemy were insignificant, the creation of insecurity, especially on the important Pacific route from Callao to Panama, was enormous. For Drake was not only a pirate; he was also a national enemy striking at strategic positions within the imperial economy, and the subsequent loss of confidence among Spanish merchants was profound. Meanwhile, the extension of Spain's commitments in Europe prevented her from putting a total effort into imperial defence. The war against the Turk culminating in Lepanto (1571) claimed many of the smaller vessels which had previously operated in the Indies fleets, and gave shippers an incentive to keep their vessels in America rather than expose them on the Guadalquivir to royal demands. Financial demands were even heavier, and merchants ran an even greater risk of having their treasure sequestered in order to pay for the campaign in the Mediterranean or the army in the Low Countries. Thus they had powerful motives for keeping their cargoes and their treasure in the Indies as well as their vessels. Hampered by the demands of its government and the threats of its enemies, the Indies trade was also hit by conditions within America itself. The epidemic of 1576 in New Spain wiped out 40–50 per cent. of the Indian population and greatly depleted the labour force.[54] The Mexican quota of precious metals fell from 61 per cent. (1571–75) to 35 per cent. (1581–85), and trade with New Spain suffered accordingly.

But the Indies trade had its own resilience, and there was a further upswing from 1578, with years of great prosperity between 1584 and 1586. Compared to 114 ships engaged in 1576 there were 213 in 1586, and an

---

[52] Chaunu, *op. cit.*, viii. 2, 1, pp. 436–41.
[53] *Ibid.*, viii. 2, 1, pp. 514–15.
[54] W. Borah, *New Spain's Century of Depression* (Berkeley, 1953), 18–19; Chaunu, *op. cit.*, viii. 2, 1, pp. 518–19, 560–63.

increase in the volume of trade by 50 per cent.[55] At the same time the most
decisive progress yet made in the import of precious metals took place
between the half decades 1576–80 and 1581–85, and was immediately reflected
in the rise of Andalusian prices by 18 per cent. in the six years from 1576 to
1582.[56] Conditions in this period, especially between 1582 and 1585, were
most favourable to commercial expansion. The union of the two crowns of
Spain and Portugal provided an additional base in the Azores and thus
greater security for imperial communications, at a time when the convoy
system itself was beginning to work more efficiently and with quicker
rotations. The relative military calm between the relaxation of Huguenot
pressure from France and the beginning of real war with England gave
Spain a breathing space which she used to great effect. Trade and treasure
multiplied, and it was in these years that Spain earned the great surpluses
which financed the Armada and its rapid replacement. The convoy for
New Spain in 1585 was one of the record convoys in the entire history of
the Indies trade—51 vessels, 17,000 *toneladas*—in a year when Spain had many
other commitments and could not relax her defences against Drake.[57] In
spite of the danger, merchants were investing capital in the high price years
of 1582–84 in further trade, tempted by the recovery of the Mexican market.

But expansion was never limitless, and the reckoning came from 1587.
Excess of exportation during years of prosperity brought its own reaction
in a glutting of the market both in Spain and America. Again, however,
the greatest obstacle came from without. The mounting action of the English
offensive from 1585 to 1589 struck again at the security of Spain's interests
and the confidence of her merchants. This could be seen in the greater
number of warships used for escorting the convoys and of *avisos* for the
transmission of news and directions. Drake's raid on Cadiz in April 1587,
when he caught and destroyed the New Spain fleet in port itself, not only
reduced the stock of vessels available but also demolished their cargoes; in
one blow he struck at the state and the trade, prevented the departure of a
convoy, and caused such panic among Seville merchants and shippers that
they hesitated to invest further. The last line of defence was now the Spanish
Armada, and in this they placed all their hopes. Consequently, there was a
pause in the Indies trade while they awaited the success of Spain's great
enterprise. The Armada had already absorbed a great portion of Spanish
shipping. This was justified on the ground that it was designed to serve not
only the needs of the state but also of those merchants whose interests English
policy so grievously damaged. As the defence of the Indies was at stake, it

[55] Chaunu, *op. cit.*, viii. 2, 1, pp. 585–88.
[56] Hamilton, *American Treasure and the Price Revolution in Spain*, pp. 107–08.
[57] Chaunu, *op. cit.*, viii. 2, 1, pp. 726–28. See above, p. 153.

was logical that the powerful Indies fleets should be thrown into the assault; indeed, they furnished the major part of the invasion force, which accounts for the predominance of huge vessels in the Armada. More than this, the Indies trade supplied most of the personnel for the English campaign, either directly by levies in the ports of the Guadalquivir, as in the case of the escort fleet of Diego Flores de Valdés which was diverted from its journey to Tierra Firme in 1588 to join the Armada, or indirectly by levies among the reserves of Biscay, the nursery of Spanish seamen, which supplied most of the manpower on the American run.

The Indies trade, therefore, had the greatest stake in the Spanish Armada. Its men, its ships, its vital interests, all were involved. Inevitably, the subsequent disaster was a shattering blow to its confidence and its prosperity. Shipping losses alone were damaging. Out of an Atlantic fleet of 100,000 tons, the losses of 1588 amounted to 50 per cent.; counting those in Cadiz of the previous year, they reached 60 per cent.[58] The Indies trade felt the impact more than any other section of the Spanish economy, not only because of the number of ships it had committed to the campaign but because they were its biggest, youngest, and best ships—precisely those on which it had relied so much. Even more grievous were the human losses. Of the 8,000 officers and men who sailed, very few returned to active service. With her many overseas commitments, Spain was already short of seamen, and it took much longer to make a good seaman than to build a ship. These disasters had an immediate effect on the Indies trade. The demands of the Armada and then its losses prevented normal fleet sailings, and from October 1586 to March 1589 no convoy left for Tierra Firme. The break in the seasonal rhythm of sailings raised the incidence of shipwreck due to hasty or late departures from the Indies. In the early 1590's the ships available for the Atlantic crossing were so old and so small that merchants hesitated to commit their goods to them, especially in view of their exposure to English privateers.[59] Shortage of ships and of manpower raised freightage rates and added to the burdens the trade had to carry. Seamen, conscious of their strength, were demanding higher wages and heavy advances, and refusing to sign until the very moment of departure. Meanwhile the war continued to depress trade, as merchants preferred to leave their returns in the Indies out of reach of English privateers and of their own government—a useful safety device but one which caused private treasure imports to drop. All these difficulties had their origin in the English offensive, and the abrupt rise in the rate of the *avería*, from 1·7 per cent. in 1585 to 8 per cent. in 1591 reflected an enormous

---

[58] *Ibid.*, viii. 2, 1, p. 769.
[59] *Ibid.*, iii. pp. 398–400, 412–13, 437 n. 59, 420 n. 10; vi. tables 200 and 201; on shortage of seamen and rise of wages see iii. p. 420; viii. 2, 1, pp. 795–96.

increase in the costs of defence, and thus in the overheads of trade. The destruction of the New Spain fleet in Cadiz in 1587 and of the armed escort which was swallowed up in the Armada of 1588 were particularly ominous for the *avería*, especially as they coincided with the period when the campaign against England depleted the Spanish fleets, when the demands of the Indies weighed heavily on Spanish shipping, and when mounting costs made ships as expensive as they were rare.

Yet all was not lost. Indeed, the most remarkable event of these years was not the disaster to the Armada but the rapidity with which Spain recovered from it. Drawing on the resources accumulated in more prosperous years, especially in the first half of the decade, she began to fight back, and to give yet further proof of her immense staying power. The state itself led the revival, anxious for its own treasure supplies. Expert engineers were sent to reorganise fortifications in the Indies. In the absence of regular armed convoys, the government, at its own expense, devised a new method of transporting treasure and valuable goods—in small squadrons of *zabras*, those extremely rapid frigates which were capable of outstripping most pursuers.[60] The system was first adopted in 1588, was renewed in 1589 and 1590, and then prolonged until 1592. But the whole of the Indies trade reacted rigorously to the emergency. New vessels were rapidly built in Spanish shipyards, and old ones were retained beyond their normal life. Smaller ships than were usual on the American run were pushed into service. Convoys and their armed escorts were reconstituted from as early as 1590, an amazing recovery by any standards. Some of the signs of the revival were ominous, it is true; attracted by the high freight prices and by Spain's need to relax her regulations in order to procure shipping, many foreign vessels, most of them from northern Europe, entered the Indies trade, and their proportion rose from 5·9 per cent. of the total shipping in 1579–87 to 21·25 per cent. in 1588–92.[61] But this development was not yet beyond control, and Spain continued to monopolise the greater part of the returns. By 1592 the worst was over, and the Indies trade could return to its normal rhythm and methods, with regular fleet sailings and vast receipts of treasure. From the wreckage of the Armada, therefore, Spain salvaged much more than a few vessels. She preserved her richest possession and continued to exploit it remorselessly.

---

[60] *Ibid.*, iii. pp. 412, 437 n. 59, 450, 468. See above, p. 167.
[61] *Ibid.*, viii. 2, 1, pp. 772–73.

Julián Romero, commander of Spanish tercios by El Greco

CHAPTER VI
PHILIP II AND THE GOVERNMENT OF SPAIN

1. Peace and Recovery

PHILIP II, whom tradition encloisters in the Escorial directing the forces of the Counter-Reformation, began his reign far from Spain and at war with the pope. Left by his father in the Low Countries in 1556, it took him three years to liquidate the sorry remnants of the emperor's affairs beyond the Pyrenees and to extricate himself from the old quarrels with the old enemies. Political and jurisdictional disputes with Paul IV in Italy suddenly erupted into war in September 1556; Henry II of France automatically seized the opportunity to strike at his Habsburg enemy, and so within a year of his accession Philip was confronted by a Franco-papal alliance—the recurrent nightmare of his father—and a war on two fronts. The military operations followed the pattern of stalemate characteristic of the entire Habsburg–Valois conflict, as the two exhausted and bankrupt powers went through the clumsy motions of attack and counter-attack. Philip won the battle of St. Quentin, and the French took Calais from his English allies. Had anything changed in forty years?

If old prejudices remained, circumstances were rendering them increasingly outmoded. By September 1557 the veteran Paul IV realised he was out of his depth and, besieged in his own states by the Duke of Alba, withdrew from the war. On 21 September 1558 Charles V died at Yuste, and Philip was now urgently required in Spain. On 17 November Philip's wife, Mary Tudor, died, and the union of England and Spain, so ominous for France, was abruptly dissolved. By this time both France and Spain had learnt the folly of fighting a useless war on ever-worsening credit, and were ready to come to terms. These were signed in the Treaty of Cateau-Cambrésis on 2–3 April 1559. The settlement was neither a triumph for Spain nor a disaster for France, but simply reflected the existing balance of power in Europe, confirming Spain's hegemony in the south and her weakness in the north. France virtually abandoned her aspirations in Italy, not only by restoring Savoy and Piedmont to their duke and thus sanctioning a barrier against future intervention south of the Alps, but also by relinquishing Corsica and thereby depriving herself of one of the key strategic positions between Spain and Italy in the Mediterranean. But France had not lost all. Her withdrawal from a policy of military extravagance abroad enabled her to concentrate on national interests, and these she advanced by recovering Calais and retaining Metz, Toul, and Verdun; in this way she threw Spain's English ally out of France and preserved her own conquests in the northeast, conquests which were an obstacle to communications between the Spanish dominions of Franche-Comté and the Low Countries. France could still not feel secure while Spain was installed in the Low Countries with an English ally across the Channel. But the marriage of the Dauphin to Mary Stuart in 1558 threatened to enclose England within the Auld Alliance and to isolate the Low Countries still further.

England was equally important to Spain. Charles V had staked the security of the Low Countries on the English alliance and had expressed his wish 'that at all costs England and the Low Countries should be bound together, so that they can provide each other with mutual aid against their enemies'.[1] Philip II tried his utmost to salvage what he could from this policy, and before he reached a settlement with France he waged an intense diplomatic campaign to keep the English base in his hands. But circumstances were against him. The fall of Calais ruined the little reputation he still possessed in England, while the death of his wife severed the formal ties of alliance. In desperation he then tried to marry Elizabeth, but she was elusive and noncommittal, and it took Philip about two months to realise that she had no intention of marrying him. In default of England he turned to France, and the peace treaty was concluded with a marriage alliance. In June 1559 Philip married by proxy his child-bride, Elizabeth of Valois, eldest daughter of the king of France. In this way he brought to a close the policy of his father. Germany had long been irretrievably lost; now the dream of an Anglo-Flemish state bestriding the Channel was shattered, and Philip inherited the burden of the Low Countries without the English base to sustain it. He did not yet despair of England, as can be seen in the diplomatic support he gave to Elizabeth against France and against the papacy. But his own empire was thrown back unmistakably on Spain, away from the north to the south of Europe, and the Peace of Cateau-Cambrésis, in reinforcing Spain's grip on Italy, only completed the process.

There was something symbolic, therefore, in Philip's return to Spain in September 1559. From now on the king of Spain remained in the Iberian peninsula, surveying Europe from behind the Pyrenees. Spain, which had

---

[1] Quoted in M. Fernández Alvarez, *Tres Embajadores de Felipe II en Inglaterra* (Madrid, 1951), p. 21. See also the same author's 'La Paz de Cateau-Cambrésis', *Hispania*, xix. (1959), 530–44.

long been the treasury of the monarchy, now became the source and the inspiration of its policy. Henceforth, events were seen and judged from Spain, in a Spanish ambience, by Spanish personnel, and in Spanish interests. These were natural developments, not only because of Philip's own preferences but also because he could not govern his empire without Spain and he could not govern Spain without residing there. The Regent, the Councils, the cortes, his officials, all were anxious to have him back. In the monarch's absence seigneurial independence always tended to increase, while officials found it more difficult to apply the royal writ. Social and political tensions were aggravated by a religious crisis, and one of the first public functions which Philip attended was an *auto de fe* in Valladolid. But his greatest problem was yet another legacy from his father—the economic effects of prolonged warfare. Spain had escaped the direct blows of war, but she had supplied the lion's share of men, money, and ships. Ordinary and extraordinary revenue had long since been spent; during the war against Paul IV, Philip had to extort money from Spanish prelates, while treasure from America was not inexhaustible. Philip was forced to make peace, and in the final analysis the imperial policy of Charles V was liquidated by the Spanish state bankruptcy of 1557.

Financial reasons, then, forced Philip to return to Spain and to stay there. One after the other the peripheral states of the empire had refused, not always tacitly, to supply him with subsidies. Sicily, Naples, Milan, the Low Countries, all were unwilling to contribute to imperial defence when their own interests were not involved, and their experience of Charles V's rule had taught them that this was most of the time. Their refusal to recognise the empire as a financial unit reflected the nature of the organisation to which they belonged. The component parts of Philip II's empire continued the separate relationship with their common sovereign which had been characteristic of Charles V's reign, and there was no possibility of Philip imposing a central organisation on them even if he had wanted to. But he did wish to tax them, and their reluctance to contribute was something which he could never overcome. In the Mediterranean, it is true, Spanish imperial interests coincided with the local interests of Naples and Sicily, and consequently during times of danger from the Turk or the corsairs Philip II could count on the material co-operation of Sicily and Naples. But the Mediterranean states were indifferent to his interests in northern Europe and in the 1580's, when those interests became paramount, they declined to collaborate beyond their own needs. The king appreciated their point of view, but he also believed that the resources of his states should be shared for the benefit of which ever was in most need of them. In 1589 he told the Council of Italy: 'Except in the most urgent cases, it is not the custom to transfer the burdens of one kingdom to another. And since God has entrusted me with so many (kingdoms), since all are in my charge, and since in the defence of one all are·preserved, it is just that all should help me. . . .'[2] But his view could not overcome the concern of each state for its financial independence or the suspicion that the cases of emergency were permanent and usually those of Spain.

If Sicily objected because the cause was not her own, the Low Countries objected because they believed the cause was positively harmful to their interests, and because they were obliged to fulfil a rôle in northern Europe which they could not afford. Philip II had personal experience of the Low Countries from 1555 to 1559, and during these years he survived not on local subsidies but on the financial help he received from Spain. 'I will gain nothing by staying here', he wrote to Granvelle in June 1559, 'except lose myself and these states. . . . The best thing that can be done is for all of us to seek the remedy, as I will do as far as possible, and if the remedy is not here then I will go to seek it in Spain.'[3] For it was becoming increasingly difficult to obtain revenue from Spain at a distance; his presence was required there in order to sanction the collection of subsidies by his own immediate authority. When he reached Spain, however, he found that the costs of war which had gone on for too long had brought his finances even there to the verge of disaster. From Toledo he wrote to Granvelle in December 1559: 'Believe me, I am anxious to provide the Low Countries with everything I know they need. . . . But I give you my word that I have found here a situation worse than that there, so that it is impossible for me to help you, or even to provide here for needs so small that you would be astonished if you could see. I confess that when I was in the Low Countries I never thought that things could be like this, and for these reasons I have not found any remedy outside the money of the dowry. . . .'[4]

Philip II's first major task, therefore, was to restore his finances.[5] This forced him to settle in Spain, impose his authority, and withdraw from the widespread commitments of his father. In the process the empire he ruled changed, not in size but in character. Less ecumenical than that of Charles V, it was also more solid, firmly based in the peninsula, and essentially Spanish in character. Philip II was first and foremost king of Spain. That was what Spaniards wanted.

[2] H. G. Koenigsberger, *The Government of Sicily under Philip II of Spain* (London, 1951), pp. 55–56.
[3] C. Weiss, ed., *Papiers d'état du Cardinal de Granvelle* (9 vols., Paris, 1841–52), v. 606.
[4] *Ibid.*, v. 672.
[5] Financial policy and conditions are treated above, pp. 136–42.

2. 'The Perfect Master in the Art of Ruling'

The reputation of Philip II, more perhaps than that of most great rulers, has suffered from extremes of eulogy and disparagement. His apologists have seen him as a Catholic crusader, his critics as a reactionary bigot. Neither view is realistic; the first ignores his constant concern for national interests, the second implies that he was wrong not to be a democrat and a Protestant.[6] Contemporary observers found him equally difficult to understand—a solitary and secretive figure, who spoke in a low voice, stroking his pointed beard, with a thin smile that cut like a sword, as Antonio Pérez recalled. Few people broke through the barrier of his reserve. Ambassadors and suitors he received with courtesy, listening to their requests, but staring at them disconcertingly and replying so softly as to be often unintelligible; and he never spoke of himself. People became anxious and speechless as they faced him, overwhelmed not only by his power but also by his presence. Yet his Castilian subjects loved him with a blind affection and with an implicit confidence in his judgement and integrity, sensing perhaps beneath the mask of sovereignty the human character of their king.

For human he was. His early education had been entrusted to Juan Martínez Siliceo, bishop of Cartagena, who taught him little more than ecclesiastical Latin and whose indulgence was responsible for Philip's notorious weakness in any language except Spanish.[7] A more systematic and disciplined education was provided by his next tutor, Juan de Zúñiga, grand-commander of Castile, a man of scrupulous piety and morals, closely connected with the Jesuits like all the Requesens family. Under Zúñiga's influence the prince acquired a seriousness which never left him, but he had his share of human failings, and these his tutor reported frankly to the emperor. Certainly in his youth Philip caused his father some concern. In 1543, shortly after his son's first marriage, Charles was worried about his lethargy, his coolness towards his wife, and his apparent lack of religious devotion. But this was just a passing crisis, reflecting a reaction against

[6] For these reasons few of the general biographies of Philip II are satisfactory. Some of these are reviewed in R. B. Merriman, *The Rise of the Spanish Empire in the Old World and the New*, vol. iv., *The Prudent King*, which is itself one of the two outstanding modern works on the reign; the other is F. Braudel, *La Méditerranée et le monde méditerranéen à l'époque de Philip II*, frequently referred to in these pages. For the interpretation of a modern Spanish scholar see M. Fernández, Alvarez, *Felipe II. Semblanza del Rey Prudente* (Madrid, 1956). L. Fernández y Fernández de Retana, *España en tiempo de Felipe II*, in *Historia de España* edited by R. Menéndez Pidal, xix. (2 vols., Madrid, 1955) is a compendious narrative of events but otherwise disappointing. Recent works on Philip II and his entourage are surveyed in a useful and balanced review by H. Lapeyre, 'Autour de Philippe II', *Bulletin Hispanique*, lix. (1957), 152–75.

[7] The sources for the early life of Philip II are gathered in J. M. March, *Niñez y juventud de Felipe II (1527–1547)* (2 vols., Madrid, 1941–42).

authority which was natural in a young man of eighteen who probably resented being dragged in the wake of the emperor's policies; the attitude was to be seen even more clearly in the lack of grace with which he accepted his marriage to Mary Tudor. In other ways Philip remained strongly marked by the education he had received; from it he received his extensive know-ledge of history, his appreciation of scholarship and the arts, and the early awakening of his political judgement.

Physically Philip II had few reserves. Fair-haired, of rather less than medium height, erect of carriage, his eyes permanently reddened from overwork, he did what he could to nurture his strength, especially by his austerity of life and careful sleeping habits, but his constitution was gradually weakened by asthma, stone, and gout. His resources of mind and spirit, however, were immense. Emotionally he was completely attuned to the exercise of power, and by any standards his sang-froid was phenomenal. He was always master of himself, never showed his feelings, and never panicked; he took the disaster of the Armada with the same equanimity as the triumph of Lepanto, and the occasions on which he was seen to be moved were rare, such as the death of his third wife, Elizabeth of Valois, or the completion of the Escorial. Yet he was far from insensitive; he had a cool head but not a cold heart. To his family he was utterly devoted, and the famous letters he sent from Portugal to his young daughters between 1581 and 1583 reveal a Philip II who is simple, tender, solicitous, a good father, who eats too many melons and misses the song of the nightingales at Aranjuez.[8] If contemporary gossip is to be believed his married life was not entirely blameless. In his youth he was credited with an affair with Isabel Ossorio, lady-in-waiting to the empress; at the time of his stay in England and the Low Countries other adventures were attributed to him; after his return to Spain he was supposed to have had a liaison with Eufrasia de Guzmán, lady-in-waiting to the Princess Joanna, and the correspondence of the French ambassadors in 1561 and 1564 seems to confirm that he was not always faithful to Elizabeth of Valois.[9] But the subject is popular and the evidence suspect, and in default of proof the prudent king should be left with the benefit of the doubt.

The sincerity of his religious life could hardly be questioned; his conscience was scrupulous, his beliefs firmly based and carefully practised. And he probably placed more confidence in his confessors and theologians than he did in his ministers and officials. The affairs of the church were his daily

[8] L. P. Gachard, ed., *Lettres de Philippe II à ses filles les Infantes Isabelle et Catherine écrites pendant son voyage en Portugal (1581–1583)* (Paris, 1884).

[9] A. Gonzáles de Amezúa y Mayo, *Isabel de Valois, reina de España (1546–1568)* (3 vols., Madrid, 1949), a work which is also valuable for the study of Philip II, his court and his foreign policy.

concern, and he was known to be a friend of reform. St. Teresa wrote of him, 'Don Philip is very well disposed to religious who are known to keep their Rule, and will always help them'.[10] He also recognised sanctity when he saw it, and he was anxious to secure for his library original manuscripts of St. Teresa's own works. This religious feeling combined with his taste for literature, art, and science, gave birth to the greatest architectural monument of his reign, the monastery of San Lorenzo de El Escorial. Philip was fond of Madrid, and it was he who made it the capital of Spain, formally establishing his court there in 1561. But he also required a place of retreat, outside of Madrid yet accessible. The Escorial originated as a mausoleum for the remains of Charles V, but from the beginning Philip incorporated in it a royal residence with a monastery and a church. Begun soon after the capital had been established at Madrid, it took twenty years to build and was the king's dearest possession; during the process of construction one of his few relaxations was to sit and watch it rising among the lonely hills of the Guadarramas about twenty miles to the north-west of Madrid, its grey stone, hewn from nearby quarries, merging perfectly with the landscape. There he could go into retreat among the Hieronymite monks, attend Mass from his own austere room, and collect his Titians and Tintorettos, his rare books and precious manuscripts, procured with a scholar's enthusiasm from agents in all parts of Europe. Yet Philip II was not permanently enclosed within the walls of the Escorial; that is a legend. When it was necessary he travelled extensively in the peninsula, and he only took his court to the Escorial for a brief period during the summer. But it was his favourite residence, a place to which he could frequently retire for peace of mind and soul and for the best conditions of work, living at the same time in the atmosphere of a monastery.

Religion pervaded all aspects of Philip II's life and work.[11] In making political decisions which affected his own conscience he invariably consulted his religious advisers, and while it is difficult to pierce the secrecy of these matters it is also difficult to avoid the conclusion that they must share the responsibility for some of the more sinister actions of their sovereign. One of the essential features of his character was his high sense of justice and his concern for the impartial administration of law. But he also believed that his sovereignty gave him the right to execute private and secret justice, beyond the cognisance of any authority except God. This belief led him to acts of savage and arbitrary despotism, performed with a complacency which seems to have come from the concurrence of his theologians.

[10] *The Complete Works of St. Teresa of Jesus*, trans. and ed., E. Allison Peers (3 vols., London, 1946), iii. 142.
[11] See above, pp. 117–19, and below, pp. 251–86.

Perhaps the most brutal example of such behaviour was his action in the case of Baron de Montigny, representative of Egmont and Hornes in Spain and condemned to death by the Duke of Alba for rebellion in the Low Countries. Montigny was executed secretly in the castle of Simancas in October 1570, for Philip II decided that it would be better to strangle him quietly in order to avoid the repercussions which his execution would produce in the Low Countries and in Europe generally. Therefore the official version, prepared by the king himself, was that Montigny died a natural death. 'The affair went so well', he wrote to Alba on 3 November, 'that till now everyone has believed that he died of illness. And this must be given out there too, by discreetly showing round two letters coming from here.'[12] This kind of mentality Philip shared with other sovereigns of the time, but the distinguishing feature of his behaviour is the lengths to which he went for the satisfaction of his conscience. In this case the Dominican theologian, Hernando del Castillo, was expressly chosen by the king to be present at the last moments of Montigny, and although he seems to have disapproved of the whole business he nevertheless collaborated.

Sovereignty, of course, could be used to justify almost any royal action, and Philip's own sense of prerogative was highly developed. With it went a notion of personal duty and responsibility which made him the most hard-working monarch in history. He ruled his empire sitting at his desk, receiving his endless correspondence from all parts of the world, reading, annotating, replying, and insisting always on seeing everything himself. This was partly because of an ingrained inability to trust anyone. His father had already warned him not to give himself to any of his entourage, but Philip's distrust of his subordinates went much deeper than this. He particularly distrusted the strong: the Duke of Alba, the Marquis of Santa Cruz, Don John of Austria, and Alexander Farnese, and preferred to give his confidence to lesser personalities like Ruy Gómez, the Duke of Medina Sidonia, and his secretary Mateo Vázquez. It has been argued that this attitude betrayed a sense of inferiority and a lack of confidence in himself, to compensate for which he surrounded himself by impenetrable barriers of reserve and solemnity and erected mistrust into a system of government. Even Philip's virtues are seen as an expression of weakness. His excessive industry, for example, has been interpreted as a way of escaping from the political and personal anxieties which tormented him, and his proverbial prudence as irresolution.[13] Persons as diverse as Gonzalo Pérez, Don John

---

[12] *Colección de documentos inéditos para la historia de España*, ed. M. Fernández de Navarrete, etc. (Madrid, 1842–1931), iv. 565.

[13] G. Marañón, *Antonio Pérez (el hombre, el drama, la época)* (6th edn., 2 vols., Madrid, 1958), i. 41–51.

of Austria, and Luis de Requesens, all complained of his slowness, and Pius V wrote to him that 'Your Majesty spends so long considering your undertakings that when the moment to perform them comes, the occasion has passed and the money all been spent'. Even his confessor, Fr. Chaves, who connived at so much in his sovereign's politics, reproved him in later years for not doing justice more speedily and threatened to withhold absolution from him for not coming to a decision on the charge of peculation against his minister, the Count of Barajas.

All this may be true, but it is only half the story. The character of Philip II should not be judged in isolation from the conditions which confronted him. It was natural that he should distrust the more powerful of his subjects and prevent the crown from becoming a cipher in the hands of the aristocracy, as it had been less than a century before and was to become again under his immediate successors. Any self-respecting monarch would have done the same. And if he also withheld responsibility from his weaker subordinates that was not simply because he distrusted them—in some cases he had reason to—but also because he believed that his own judgement was best—as it usually was—and that it was his duty to give it. To this extent, and in view of the vast information at his disposal and his own tenacious memory, his attitude was plausible. He was a professional monarch doing his job. And it was a difficult job, the most difficult one of any sovereign at the time. He had to govern an immense empire, formed of constituent kingdoms, which in an age of imperfect communications depending on horse and ship were effectively more extended and scattered than they would be today. His whole life was spent fighting against distances.[14] True, he himself added to the inevitable slowness of communications by his methods of working and the slowness of his decisions. But this slowness was to some extent calculated for he had to measure the distant repercussions of his acts. Once a decision had been taken and dispatched, it was difficult to revoke it for events were beyond his reach. Philip II was handicapped, therefore, less by his personality than by the nature of his task; it was this which imposed most of his attitudes upon him. More impressive than his weakness was the way in which he faced up to his vast responsibilities. And one of the greatest of these was to provide an heir to the throne.

3. Don Carlos and the Succession Problem

Transfer of power from one sovereign to the next was never easy in the sixteenth century. Unless the monarch had an undisputed male heir,

---

[14] This has been best appreciated by Braudel, *op. cit.*, pp. 310–24.

competent to rule, there was likely to be trouble. And in Spain mortality lay heavy on the royal family, ever since Ferdinand and Isabella had lost so many of their children. Philip II, whose own accession was exceptionally free of complications, found it less easy to provide for his successor. His first wife, Maria of Portugal, he married in 1543 when he was only sixteen; within two years she had died in bearing him the Infante Don Carlos, whose own grasp on life was precarious. Nine years later he married Mary Tudor; but the union, undertaken for his father's reasons of state, was barren of children and, on Philip's side, of love. His third marriage in 1559 was also a diplomatic arrangement, but Philip grew to love Elizabeth of Valois and to cherish her dearly; yet it was seven years before she bore him a child, and this was a daughter, Isabella Clara Eugenia, who with her younger sister Catherine was the joy of Philip's life. But, after less than ten years of married life with her husband, Elizabeth died in October 1568. Her death had been preceded in the same year by that of the Infante Don Carlos. These personal bereavements were also political problems for Philip II; at the age of forty-one he was a widower again and without a male heir. Yet now his anxiety was small indeed compared to that which he had felt when his son and heir was alive.[15]

When Philip returned to Spain in 1559 Don Carlos was fourteen and had spent his youth without sight of his father. His grandfather, Charles V, appalled by his appearance and his temperament, disliked him on sight and refused to have him at Yuste. His tutors, García de Toledo and the humanist, Honorato Juan, found him hardly more prepossessing, and the latter confided to Philip his belief that the boy was going mad. His unpropitious heredity was against him from the start. His father and mother were cousins, and both were grandchildren of Joanna the Mad. The results of such inbreeding, common in the house of Habsburg, were seen perhaps in the grotesque form of Don Carlos, whose frail body could hardly support his overgrown head and who was further handicapped by recurrent fevers and a permanent stammer; by all accounts Philip II had begotten a son who was mentally and physically abnormal. In 1560, however, the cortes of Castile recognised Don Carlos as heir to the throne, and Philip made provision for his education and upbringing. His adolescent years were spent at Alcalá in the company of Don John of Austria and Alexander Farnese, but the university which produced so many distinguished alumni could make no impression on the retarded mind of Philip II's son. Only a kind of cunning emerged:

---

[15] For modern Spanish views on the controversial story of Don Carlos see E. Tormo, 'La tragedia del príncipe don Carlos y la trágica grandeza de Felipe II', *Boletín de la Real Academia de la Historia*, cxii. (1943), 161–209, and the article 'Don Carlos' by P. Aguado Bleye, in *Diccionario de Historia de España* (2 vols., Madrid, 1952), i.

in spite of the close watch on his behaviour ordered by his father he managed to evade his guardians in order to seek the company of a young girl, the daughter of a palace servant. In one of these escapades he fell down some stairs and seriously injured his head. Philip hastened to Alcalá with a doctor who performed the operation of trepanning, a treatment which the prince successfully survived. In 1562, after his recovery, the king took him back to Madrid and in the hope of leading him towards responsibility made him President of the Council of State, whose sessions the prince began to attend. His conduct only grew more erratic. Now his fellow councillors, the élite of church and state, were the targets of his temper and obstinacy, his anxiety to hurt and insult, while his political indiscretion became notorious. The question of his marriage had to be raised, and Philip toyed with the idea of trying to marry him to Mary Stuart, but soon dropped it. In any case, should he be allowed to marry at all? Philip II began to doubt it. Don Carlos also wanted to become governor of the Low Countries, as his father had promised the States General in 1559. But in view of his political incapacity, the Low Countries in the 1560's were the last place he could be sent to. Frustration only made the prince worse; openly and sarcastically he began to criticise his father, believing he denied him office and affection without any reason. And at the same time he was indulging in acts of wanton violence and sadism, some of which, like his ordering young girls to be beaten, were clear signs of sexual perversion.

The conduct of Don Carlos, which at first affected only his immediate entourage, assumed a more sinister aspect in the political context of 1567. The situation in the Low Countries was reaching a climax, and Philip II decided that the only remedy was to send the Duke of Alba on a mission of repression. One of the rebel leaders, the Count of Egmont, had been in Madrid between January and April 1565, and directly or indirectly had established contact with Don Carlos, who was then making his first deranged plans to escape to the Low Countries and try his luck there. But the prince confided his scheme to the Prince of Eboli, the most loyal of Philip II's ministers, who immediately informed his master. Philip simply noted the information. In June 1566 the Baron de Montigny arrived in Madrid to represent the interests of the rebel leaders, Egmont and Hornes; and when, in September of the following year, the Duke of Alba reported from Brussels that he had imprisoned the latter, Philip II seized their agent and executed him three years later, as has been seen. Montigny, too, had been in touch with Don Carlos. By 1567 the prince had formed another plan to escape to the Low Countries and he asked Eboli to give him 200,000 ducats for the purpose. Again Philip was informed and again he withheld his hand. Don Carlos then wrote letters to various grandees, asking their help for a great enterprise he was planning. Inevitably the king soon knew of this too. Finally, the prince asked Don John of Austria, recently appointed captain-general of the sea, to take him to Italy, promising him Naples and Milan when his cause triumphed. Don John reported the matter to the king.

By this time Philip had decided what he had to do. As a matter of duty he could not contemplate the crown going to a man who was patently unfit to rule, and would lead the monarchy back to the condition from which it had been rescued by the Catholic Monarchs. It was equally important to prevent him from marrying and having an heir, from whom little better might be expected. There were only two remedies—perpetual confinement or death. On the night of the eighteenth of January 1568, with three councillors and a detachment of guards, he entered the bedroom of his son in the Alcázar of Madrid. Don Carlos awoke, confused, and seeing his father asked if he had come to kill him. With his usual impassivity Philip II confiscated the prince's papers, put him under armed guard, and left the room. That was the last time he saw his son. While Don Carlos was in confinement Philip II communicated his decision to Cardinal Espinosa, the Prince of Eboli, and the prince's guard, the Duke of Feria, and he also asked the advice of some distinguished theologians, including Melchor Cano. Then, before he began to prepare more suitable accommodation, he gave instructions about the régime to be observed for his son in his small prison in the Alcázar. There Don Carlos died on 25 July 1568 in circumstances still unknown.

If Philip II ordered the execution of his son, it would not be out of character, for he believed the fate of the monarchy was at stake, and he also believed that he had the right of private judgement and execution, as the case of Montigny was to show. But it is not known that he did so. The various opinions on the death of Don Carlos—that his death was ordered by his father and took place by beheading, or by strangulation, or by poisoning, or that he died as a result of his own excesses in prison—all are speculation, for the evidence does not admit of certainty.[16] There is even less historical foundation for the literary and polemical interpretations of the case—that he was killed because of his sinful love for his stepmother, Elizabeth of Valois, or for his partiality to Protestantism, or because he connived at a vast 'international conspiracy' against Philip II. Even his nebulous schemes for escaping to the Low Countries or to Italy—all of them pathetically lacking in secrecy—must be considered as the outpourings of a disordered mind rather than a calculated plot to subvert the monarchy,

[16] For some of the evidence see *Documentos inéditos para la historia de España*, xxvii. 38–39.

of which he was palpably incapable. This is precisely how Philip II saw them.

Don Carlos had been accepted by the cortes as heir to the throne, and therefore his father felt obliged to justify his imprisonment. On the day after his arrest Philip II ordered his postmaster-general to place an embargo on all mail, and for two days no letter left the capital. Then, on 22 January, the king gave the world his official version, in letters to the pope, to his ambassadors, and to his officials. These messages confined themselves to the bare facts of the imprisonment, with an indication that his duty forced him to take this painful decision. Then, when rumours and scandal began to accumulate, he defended his action in more detail in confidential letters to those whose regard he valued. These need not be taken at their face value, but they give Philip II's point of view, which was the one traditionally neglected. The burden of all his explanations was that he had apprehended his son not because he had committed any crimes, much less as a punishment, but because his son could not be held responsible for his actions. In a private letter to the pope he specifically denied that his son was guilty of rebellion or heresy, and explained that the cause of his detention was

> not the passion nor the fault of the prince, nor any intention on my part to chastise or correct him, for if this had been my motive I would have taken other measures, without going to this extreme. . . . But since for my sins, it has been God's will that the prince should have such great and numerous defects, partly mental, partly due to his physical condition, utterly lacking as he is in the qualifications necessary for ruling, I saw the grave risks which would arise were he to be given the succession and the obvious dangers which would accrue; and therefore, after long and careful consideration and having tried every alternative in vain, it was clear that there was little or no prospect of his condition improving in time to prevent the evils which could reasonably be foreseen. In short, my decision was necessary.[17]

Philip II could never bring himself to use the word 'insane' in speaking of his own son, but he was aware of his condition, and he knew that it was his duty to detain him, partly in his son's own interests but above all to prevent his succeeding to the throne, and with the intention perhaps of disinheriting him. This he never needed to do, for his son died. The most likely explanation of his death may be found in his own excesses in confinement. He spoke of suicide, and he behaved as though he were attempting it; a brief hunger-strike was followed by a bout of gluttony, then massive consumption of ice, and the final break-down.

[17] Philip II to Pius V, 9 May 1568 in Fernández y Fernández de Retana, *España en tiempo de Felipe II*, i. 764–65.

The tragedy of Don Carlos was also the tragedy of Philip II. The year 1568 was a terrible year for the king, perhaps the worst of his reign. Amidst the political blows from the Low Countries and from Granada his personal grief struck him with savage intensity. He had now lost two wives and his only son, the latter in circumstances which soon unleashed a torrent of abuse all over Europe. Shortly afterwards his third and best-loved wife died, leaving him desolate. And he still had to provide for the succession. In November 1570 he married his fourth and last wife, Anne of Austria, the daughter of his cousin, the Emperor Maximilian II. Before her death ten years later she bore him four sons and one daughter; but of these only one survived childhood, and he was to succeed his father as Philip III. The king's love for his daughters, Isabella and Catherine, was that of a man clinging desperately to the last remnants of family life.

4. ABSOLUTE MONARCHY: THE ADMINISTRATION

Charles V had been a peripatetic emperor. Philip II was a national king. The difference was inevitably reflected in the working of the crown and its institutions. Theoretically Philip II was no more absolute than his father, and he continued the institutions he inherited as well as the constitutional autonomy of the component parts of his empire. But Spain, and in particular Castile, was now the metropolis, and the administration itself because more sedentary, rooted in Madrid. As Philip II did not visit his realms outside Spain he administered them through officials whose actions he controlled down to the minutest details. This presupposed that he kept in touch with them almost daily by letter, while his phenomenal memory and the constant reports he demanded of his ambassadors, viceroys, and local officials enabled him to know from his desk, not only political conditions but also the state of every town and diocese and even the curricula of the Spanish universities. This total information he shared with no one; each of his officials worked in his own department, dependent for information about the business of other departments on private sources of intelligence. Secrecy, and resultant suspicion and intrigues, permeated the entire administration, and one of the most frequent words used in official correspondence was the verb '*disimular*' which means 'to hide one's real intentions'. Even Philip's closest counsellors were informed only of limited areas of policy. Only the king had total knowledge, and he was the only co-ordinator.

Philip II preferred writing to talking. This was true even of his daily relations with his secretaries. Consequently he conducted a voluminous correspondence about correspondence—commenting upon dispatches and giving instructions for their distribution, even correcting blemishes of grammar and taste in the writings of his subordinates. Inevitably he was always submerged beneath a mountain of papers, besieged by business from his councils and from private parties, and exhausted from audiences. There was hardly time for him to see the queen and his children, while the public results of this impractical system, whereby the king was virtually his own secretary and council combined, were only too apparent. 'We will see to all this tomorrow, for now I have neither the time nor the head for it.' 'I have a lot to send you from yesterday, but it is not possible now. I will do it tomorrow.'[18] Philip II's efforts were heroic and impressive, but he set himself an impossible task and utterly failed to discriminate between matters of policy and the routine business of administration, or between the important and the trivial. At the time he was preparing the Spanish Armada he was conducting a vigorous polemic with the pope on the state of clerical dress in Spain.

As the flood of papers began to flow more abundantly problems of storage naturally arose. Due to the wandering habits of Charles V the crown and its officials had never been in a position to consult their own records. In 1547 the cortes of Monzón had established the office of Chronicler of the Kingdom of Aragon, whose duty it was to collect and compile the records of the eastern kingdom. The first and greatest incumbent was Jerónimo de Zurita, and in 1567 Philip II commissioned him to search out and collect all state documents in Aragon and the Italian dependencies and deposit them in the castle of Simancas, near Valladolid, where Philip's first secretary of state, Gonzalo Pérez, had already begun to concentrate the Castilian royal papers. In this way one of the greatest national archives in Europe was formed, and for the first time the crown could dispose of its own records with some efficiency. But not with complete efficiency, for Simancas was remote from Madrid and documents were not readily accessible for consultation. Therefore the royal secretaries tended to hoard records in their own house, partly for reference but partly as insurance against possible victimisation in the future. Thus, in spite of the methods of secrecy imposed by Philip II there was a leakage of confidential and in some cases damaging documents, and it was for this reason that the king was subsequently anxious to get his hands on the papers of his secretary Antonio Pérez, when the latter fell from grace.

Although personal monarchy was the mainspring of government, even Philip II could not dispense with institutions. On the contrary his sense of duty compelled him to improve what he had inherited. Conciliar govern-

---

[18] *Correspondencia privada de Felipe II con su secretario Mateo Vázquez, 1567–1591*, ed. C. Riba García (Madrid, 1959), vol. i. pp. 128, 205.

ment was still the essential feature of Habsburg administration, and it was still headed nominally by the Council of State. But the latter never had the opportunity of developing into a privy council on the lines of that familiar in England. The crown's anxiety to control policy meant that its competence was not defined beyond a vague commission to discuss foreign affairs and matters of state, and the size of its membership was not fixed, though the presidents of the Council of Castile and the Council of Italy usually had seats. Although the king was nominally its president he never attended meetings. Here, as elsewhere, he preferred to communicate in writing, through his secretaries, and to be informed of its deliberations by *consulta*, the document containing the council's opinion on any matter on which the king happened to consult it. The king's absence, and the fact that rival policies were apparently canvassed there, have given rise to the view that he deliberately allowed freedom of speech in the council in order to play off rival factions against one another and thus remain immune from a single pressure. But there was no need for Philip II to adopt so devious a course for a council whose composition and competence were entirely at his discretion and whose advice he was under no obligation to take. It was natural that its members should have opinions, and these were useful to the king as a means by which he could keep in touch with the policies or interests being represented. Such was the limit of its usefulness; and even this was qualified by the fact that what members said in council did not necessarily represent their opinions, for they often contradicted their public views in secret reports to the king. This was how Philip II himself preferred to do things. He had a small and exclusive group of major advisers and servants on whom he could draw for important assignments— the Castilian, the Duke of Alba, the Portuguese, Ruy Gómez da Silva and Christóvão de Moura, the Catalan Luis de Requesens, the Basque Juan de Idiáquez, and the Burgundian Cardinal Granvelle—but these he preferred to spread out over a number of offices according to his needs rather than institutionalise them in a single council, though some of them were members of the Council of State. The latter, in fact, never outgrew its amateur status and remained a group of grandees, favourites, and ecclesiastics whom the king consulted as he pleased.

The regional councils, on the other hand, which supervised the administration of particular kingdoms or areas—Castile, Aragon, Italy, Portugal, the Low Countries, and the Indies—were fully professionalised, and while they were not ministries they were the means by which central control was imposed on the whole empire. These councils, as has been seen, exercised not only executive functions, but also legislative and judicial ones. For sixteenth-century Spaniards thought of government chiefly in terms of

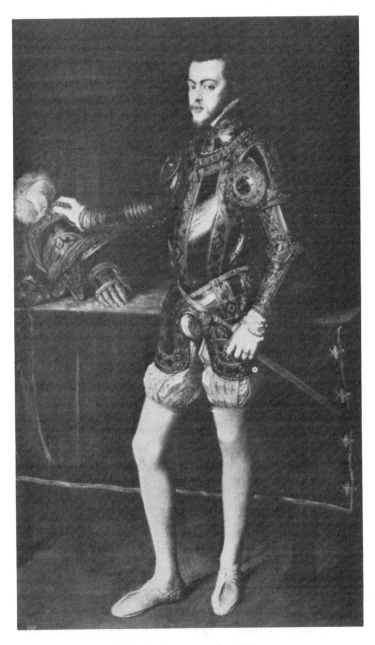

Philip II, in armour by Titian

jurisdiction; the traditional duty of their king was to do justice. But this confusion of functions meant that Spanish government did not possess a central organ specialising in administration. The defects of the system were mirrored in the Council of Castile. The decrease in the membership of the council in the closing years of Charles V's reign, together with the general neglect of internal administration at the time, resulted in an accumulation of unfinished business, especially of legal suits. In 1559 Philip II increased the number of councillors to sixteen in addition to the president, and this remained fixed for the rest of the reign. But its judicial functions continued to act as a drag on its efficiency, and it was not until 1598, the last year of his reign, that Philip II decreed a division of the council into separate departments, each with a special function of its own, one executive and administrative, the other judicial.[19] Whether the reform was actually implemented, however, is another matter, for it had to be repeated in 1608. Administration by committee, operating with all the formality of a court of law, had obvious weaknesses. The Count of Barajas, president of the Council of Castile from 1583 to 1592, complained of the confusion and inefficiency which stemmed from its defective organisation and 'which render intolerable the office of president of this Council. There is no order of precedence in the cases that come before it, save the memory of those councillors who have to deal with them . . . so that it is necessary for all who have suits to be tried to pace up and down the courtyard and struggle with one another to get nearer the door of the Council in the hope that they may be the next to be called before it. . . .'[20] In the hands of a king who preferred not to delegate responsibility, there was little hope of reform. Philip II preferred to leave the council submerged under its legal business while he rescued it from administrative stagnation by his own industry.

Aragon also had its council, though, like the other non-Castilian regional councils, it was not located in the area it administered but remained in attendance on the king, subject to central and Castilian influence. Nevertheless, Philip II respected its constitution, which provided that its president and five councillors should always be Aragonese, Catalans and Valencians. The Council of Aragon 'consulted' the affairs of the eastern kingdoms and was the organ of communication between the king and his representatives there. It was also the supreme court of justice for Valencia, the Balearics, and Sardinia; not for Aragon or Catalonia, whose *fueros* demanded that justice be administered within the kingdom, and in the case of Aragon proper this meant in the Audiencia of Zaragoza. Originally the Council of Aragon had possessed jurisdiction in the Spanish dominions in Italy, where, although the king reserved administrative powers to himself and his

[19] Merriman, *op. cit.*, iv. 415–16.   [20] Quoted *ibid.*, iv. 417–18.

governors, he allowed the council to exercise judicial functions. But the anxiety of the Castilian administration to break the Aragonese tradition of regarding Italy as an exclusively Aragonese affair, associated with a council which contained no Castilians, caused it to separate Italian affairs from the Council of Aragon and assign them to a new body. Thus, in 1555, the Council of Italy was created, of which the principal members were Castilians; it was distinct from that of Aragon and took from it the affairs of Naples, Sicily and Milan.[21] The new council, whose organisation was perfected by Philip II, was composed of six councillors, called regents, three of whom were Spaniards and three Italians, while all of them were lawyers. The office of president was usually held by a man of some political experience, a distinguished grandee like the Duke of Francavilla, or a high ecclesiastic such as Cardinals Granvelle and Quiroga. Under the president and regents were a horde of minor officials of varying importance, some of them taken over from the Council of Aragon. The most important office shared with the latter was that of the treasurer-general, occupied for much of Philip II's reign by the Count of Chinchón, and—a significant point— not confined to natives. The Council of Italy was the supreme court of appeal for the Italian dominions and supervised all aspects of administration there, including appointments, trade, and finance. But during the whole of Philip II's reign the council's judicial business was still considered its most important activity, and it was not called upon to discuss vital matters of policy.[22]

Government by committee and *consulta* probably reached its maximum efficiency in the reign of Philip II, yet still remained imperfect. The king's refusal to attend council meetings only increased the suspicion and lack of confidence which were already deeply embedded in Spanish government. As the king's policy was unknown to councillors they were afraid to speak their minds too freely or commit themselves to a definite position in case they ended up on the wrong side. The king himself often reversed his councils' decisions given in *consulta* without informing them of the fact. These conditions made it impossible for the councils to develop a consistent policy even within their own narrow limits of authority. Matters of state policy, of course, were beyond their competence and exclusively reserved for the king, who might or might not consult the Council of State upon them. But even at an administrative level they were unable to develop a policy of their own. For the king insisted on being consulted on almost every matter of council business, and especially on official appointments and on the granting of privileges or licences of every kind. Apart from

[21] C. Riba, *El Consejo Supremo de Aragón en el reinado de Felipe II* (Valencia, 1914), p. xvii.
[22] Koenigsberger, *The Government of Sicily under Philip II of Spain*, p. 68.

official appointments, he considered numerous private requests for advancement. Of the 54 *consultas* from one council alone—that of Italy—which were in the king's hands on one day in 1583, no less than 37 were private petitions.[23] No doubt favouritism and bribery existed as they did in most contemporary administrations, but the thousands of *consultas* listing and commenting on candidates proposed by the different councils for high office, both secular and ecclesiastical, are abundant testimony of the meticulous care taken by king and councils in the selection of officials. But Philip II's personal scrutiny of patronage was not limitless and it was impossible for him to satisfy his desire for absolute control over his subordinates. Given the enormity of the task there was often no alternative but to follow the advice of his councils. Moreover, Philip was in financial difficulties from the time of his accession, and for this reason he promoted the sale of many public offices, a device which his successors were to exploit even more ruthlessly. Certain classes of office were already being sold in Spain by Charles V. But Philip II began to create offices with no other intention than that of selling them, and he extended the practice to the Indies.[24] Sale of office was not necessarily corrupt, and it might be regarded as another form of indirect taxation, the candidate paying a fee for the office he would have received in any case; moreover, Philip II excluded from sale senior administrative and financial posts and all judicial appointments. But the multiplication of offices, in areas of administration where they were not necessarily most needed, set a bad precedent and lowered administrative standards generally.

Conciliar posts could not be bought, but even so they were not filled with outstanding administrators. The king's search for loyalty and his suspicion of independence in his officials encouraged mediocrity and conservatism in the councils, as in other branches of the administration. Moreover, as the councils were primarily courts of law they were naturally composed almost entirely of lawyers, whose preoccupation with the details of law and procedure made them incapable of taking initiative in administration. Like the rest of the Spanish bureaucracy under the early Habsburgs, they are often described as 'middle-class officials', but in the absence of a middle class in Spain they are best described as professional jurists, the products of the universities and the minor gentry. The Spanish bureaucracy had not always been recruited from the universities, as has been seen, but increasingly a university career and degree became a passport to ecclesiastical and civil preferment, and whatever opportunity existed in Spain for

[23] *Ibid.*, p. 63.
[24] J. H. Parry, *The Sale of Public Office in the Spanish Indies under the Habsburgs* (Berkeley and Los Angeles, 1953), pp. 1–5.

men born in poverty and obscurity lay along this path. The contemporary historian of the reign of Philip II, Luis Cabrera de Córdoba, observes that the king preferred 'virtue to noble birth and therefore in his reign all applied themselves to letters'.[25] The remark had become suspiciously like a formula, applied by the chroniclers to all good kings from the Catholic Monarchs onwards, but Philip's respect for learning makes it appropriate in his case. The growth of universities and the increase in the number of students in Spain in the sixteenth century were closely related to the fact that church and state provided opportunities for graduates, and the products of Alcalá and Salamanca were to be found in large numbers in the administration of Philip II. Another avenue to civil promotion was the church. Gonzalo Pérez, who rose from obscure and probably Jewish origin to be Philip II's secretary of state, was a priest. Diego de Espinosa was a cardinal and Inquisitor general as well as President of the Council of Castile. Diego de Covarrubias y Leyva, son of a noble family of Toledo, made his way via the University of Salamanca, where he was professor of canon law, to become a judge of the Audiencia of Granada, then bishop of Ciudad Rodrigo and archbishop of Santo Domingo in the Indies, and finally President of the Council of Castile. Gaspar de Quiroga, son of a poor though noble family of northern Castile—a characteristic beginning—was another graduate of Salamanca who secured a steady succession of civil and ecclesiastical appointments—President of the Council of Italy, primate, cardinal and Inquisitor general.[26] Philip II did not exclude the higher aristocracy entirely from the fruits of office. Like his predecessors he usually favoured them for the highest positions, the viceroyalties and governorships, as well as for the foreign embassies. He even used them sometimes for internal administration and on his councils. Luis Hurtado de Mendoza, second marquis of Mondéjar, was President of the Council of Castile from 1561 to 1563. But after Mondéjar's retirement his six successors in the Council of Castile during Philip II's reign, with the exception of the Count of Barajas (1583–92), were all either jurists or clerics.[27]

Conciliar administration, as has been seen, could not have worked without an efficient link between king and councils. This was provided by the royal secretaries, whose organisation reflected in some ways that of the councils themselves. Just as there was not a single council responsible for the whole empire, so there was not a single secretariat. To each of the regional councils a separate royal secretary was attached, while the king

[25] Luis Cabrera de Córdoba, *Felipe Segundo, Rey de España* (1619) (4 vols., Madrid 1876–77), ii. 354.
[26] Boyd, *Cardinal Quiroga, Inquisitor General of Spain*, p. 4.
[27] Merriman, *op. cit.*, iv. 417.

communicated with the Council of State through his principal secretary, who might be described as his secretary of state. Institutionally the office made no real advance on the position reached by Cobos under Charles V; that is to say its holder was more than a clerk but less than a minister, remaining essentially the king's private secretary. Indeed, Philip II's secretaries probably exercised less independence than those of Charles V, for the king attended personally to all incoming correspondence and outgoing orders and directed the work of all his secretaries. On the other hand the enormous growth of paper administration under Philip II increased the importance of the secretary, for it was he who was responsible for keeping the cumbersome machine moving. The administration worked at two levels. Routine correspondence went to the secretaries; important papers were sent directly to the king and he decided to whom to remit them. Thus the ordinary secretaries dealt with routine matters of government, while the king and his private secretary dealt with major items of policy.[28] The secretaries were the vital link with the councils; in consultation with the king they remitted papers to their appropriate council, receiving back the *consultas* which they then considered with the king. They attended council meetings, and although they might not have a vote their close contact with the king gave their views some influence, and it was they who drafted the *consultas*. Their power was certainly sufficient to arouse the resentment of the councils, as it had done under Charles V; in 1578, for example, the Council of Italy urged the secretary's replacement by three clerks entirely dependent on itself, a system which already prevailed in the Council of Aragon, whose secretariat had not produced an outstanding figure. But Philip II resisted this suggestion, for apart from considerations of security he regarded the secretary as his own official and not a dependant of the council.

The power and influence of the secretary made his office virtually the only one which attracted any political interest. Charles V had preferred a dual administration of affairs of state, and had shared them between Cobos and Granvelle. Philip II, however, began—uncharacteristically—with a single secretary of state, Gonzalo Pérez, a brilliant administrator of obscure Aragonese origin and reputed to be of Jewish descent. He had entire supervision of foreign correspondence, in much the same way as Cecil had under Elizabeth but without the English minister's influence on policy. On his death in 1566 he was succeeded by his son Antonio, whose ability outshone even that of his father. But Antonio Pérez did not get the

---

[28] For a detailed account of the working of Spanish government from the secretary's viewpoint, see A. W. Lovett, *Philip II and Mateo Vázquez de Leca: the Government of Spain (1572–1592)* (Geneva, 1977), pp. 34–38.

office in its entirety; he was secretary of state, it is true, but his duties were confined to northern affairs, France, England, the Low Countries, and Germany, while his secretaryship of the Council of Castile also gave him supervision of internal correspondence. Mediterranean affairs, however, were assigned to another secretary, Diego de Vargas, who was the sole secretary of the Council of Italy. It was after the death of Vargas that political pressure was brought to bear on the office, as factions manoeuvred for influence at court and attempted to exercise it through the secretaryship. For this reason the king himself became more wary. With the support of his friends at court, especially the Marquis of los Vélez and Archbishop Quiroga, Antonio Pérez claimed the office vacated by Vargas in 1578. But the Count of Chinchón, and all those who feared an extension of Pérez's power, resisted his claim by trying to reduce the status of the office. This Philip II refused to do, but he continued the division of responsibility, and Vargas was eventually succeeded by Gabriel de Zayas who supervised the Italian and Mediterranean correspondence.[29]

Meanwhile, Philip II's growing suspicion of his subordinates and his anxiety to divide responsibility still further led him to increase his secretariat in 1573 by appointing to it Mateo Vázquez de Leca. This assiduous and methodical cleric rose from obscurity in Seville to become Cardinal Espinosa's secretary when the latter was Philip II's private secretary, and he succeeded Espinosa in the office in 1573. He survived the shoals of Philip II's administration for eighteen years until his death in 1591, largely by his utter loyalty and his readiness to inform on his colleagues. Vázquez, in fact, became a kind of 'arch-secretary', who handled mostly domestic affairs but whom Philip also gave foreign correspondence without notice to either of his secretaries of state. On the fall of Antonio Pérez in 1579, which Vázquez himself helped to manoeuvre, he became the chief secretary, and Philip II did his most important business almost entirely through him. But the ferocious discipline of work which Philip imposed on himself was too much for others and Mateo Vázquez began to wilt under the strain, as indeed the king himself did. Therefore, from about 1580 a secretarial committee was formed which operated under Vázquez's supervision. Affairs of state were assigned to Juan de Idiáquez, a Basque who, like Cardinal Granvelle, was recalled from embassy service in Italy when Philip was surrounding himself with those he could trust at the time of

---

[29] On Gonzalo Pérez see A. González Palencia, *Gonzalo Pérez, secretario de Felipe II* (2 vols., Madrid, 1946); on development of the office after his death see Marañón, *Antonio Pérez*, i. 33–34, 87–88, 384–85, ii. App. III, XLII, and LXXXVII; Koenigsberger, *op. cit.*, p. 66.

Pérez's disgrace in 1579; the Count of Chinchón, a man of conservative instincts who had long been a familiar figure in the administration, was given Aragonese and Italian business; and Christóvão de Moura, a Portuguese favourite who had already occupied various posts at court, specialised in affairs of his own country. All three met with Mateo Vázquez to handle papers of importance including the *consultas* of the councils, and to give their opinions upon them; these were then communicated to the king by Vázquez who acted as secretary of the committee and remained the king's confidential secretary.[30]

In the second half of the 1580's, as policy became more complex and expensive, the structure of government underwent further development. A system of juntas emerged and proved to be a flexible and efficient form of administration; these were called as they were needed, from a pool of ministers and officials, to deal with particular problems. The Junta Grande made its appearance from 1586 to organise the collection of supplies for the Armada or perhaps to deal with finance in general. It was an informal gathering of officials, whose advice to the king was usually taken seriously. Soon it was exercising a co-ordinating role in government, arousing the jealousy of those who were not members, and working under the control of a secretary, usually Vázquez. The Junta Grande had a fairly large membership, and particular aspects of government were assigned to special sub-committees, smaller juntas such as the Junta de Cortes, Junta de Arbitrios, Junta de Presidentes, Junta de Población, Junta de Milicia. The Junta Grande was more than an advisory committee, less than an executive. Personal monarchy remained intact and in charge, but within the ranks of the Junta there was an inner group made up of Moura, Idiáquez, Vázquez and Chinchón, who formulated major policy and general strategy and were immediately responsible to the crown. These came to be known as the Junta of the Night.[31] Secretary Vázquez played an important part in the development of the junta system; he was the go-between linking king and juntas.

All this was a far cry from the situation in the first two decades of the reign, when Gonzalo Pérez and his son had added personal status if not constitutional stature to the office. Far from growing into a real ministry, the secretaryship had actually shrunk in importance, its functions divided among lesser men whose rôle was mute and anonymous. Caught between

---

[30] Riba, *El Consejo Supremo de Aragón*, pp. xxi–xxii; *Correspondencia privada de Felipe II con su secretario Mateo Vázquez*, passim; Lovett, *op. cit.*, pp. 11, 29–33.

[31] The details of the junta system were first established by Lovett, *op. cit.*, pp. 144–45, 201–5.

the jealousy of the councils and the suspicion of the king, it had never been able to escape from its clerkly origins. As personal status counted for so much in Spain, a secretary could only cope with the magnates of the council, who were probably contemptuous of him, by making himself as much like a great lord as possible, increasing his own household, using its members as his assistants, and generally creating an unofficial empire of his own within the royal administration. Then he would have to cultivate important figures at court, helping them with his influence in their search for privilege and preferment, and gradually forming a faction on whose support he could count. At this point he exposed himself to grave risks— the intrigues of rival secretaries, and the suspicion of the king. This was precisely the fate of Antonio Pérez, who began as a secretary, tried to act like a minister, and ended in disgrace. The experience made Philip II permanently suspicious of the office.

Yet for over ten years Antonio Pérez exercised a compelling influence on Philip II, and his rise to power was unequalled in sixteenth-century Spain. As the son of a priest, a public career might well have been closed to him, but the liability was overcome by the careful formation he was given by his father. Brought up officially as Gonzalo's nephew, he attended the universities of Louvain and Salamanca and completed his studies in Italy. Already initiated by his father in affairs of state, he was the obvious choice to succeed him as secretary in 1567. Soon the king's confidence in him was almost absolute, and suitors sought his good offices, for it was known that Philip often took his advice. But how was this vain, venal, and somewhat disreputable man able to acquire such influence over so aloof, distrustful, and demanding a king? Cultivated tastes, smooth manners, clever use of flattery, a certain servility—all these traits undoubtedly seduced Philip, who was never at ease with strong and independent personalities. But Pérez also had ability, and Philip recognised it; this was a case where talent was rewarded. The king appreciated his outstanding intelligence, his knowledge of affairs, especially of the problems of foreign policy, and his instinct for getting to the heart of a matter, all of which marked him out from the horde of mediocrities which filled the administration. Thus, confident of royal favour, Pérez advanced his career. He maintained a large establishment —a fashionable house in Madrid and a palace on the outskirts where he kept a crowd of raffish retainers and lived in a style which was the envy of other officials. He was on terms of familiarity with everyone who counted at court; the higher nobility were obliged to recognise him, for he could help them to preferment, and he also had friends among the clergy, notably Cardinal Quiroga, whom he helped to the see of Toledo and who remained his supporter almost to the end. And as his influence increased so did his affluence. His salary, of course, was not enough, even counting the large emoluments incidental to so strategic an office. But he had links with Genoese business men, especially the Spinolas, whom he helped in their negotiations with the king. Like most of his contemporaries, he made money out of the exercise of his office.

A man so close to the source of power was bound to attract friends and create enemies, and even to introduce an element of politics into the administration. Absolute though he was, Philip II could not live in complete isolation from human beings; he needed officials, he noted their views, and he might take their advice. The advisers naturally tried to monopolise the king, and with him influence and power. Consequently even in the apolitical life of Spain, where all policy decisions and most administrative ones were made by the king alone, factions formed around those who were close to the throne and in a position to gain royal favour; for favour meant office and privilege. In the first two decades of the reign there were two vague but discernible factions, towards which councillors and officials gravitated, one led by the Portuguese favourite, Ruy Gómez da Silva, the Prince of Eboli, and the other by the powerful magnate, the Duke of Alba. Conditions seemed propitious for faction. There was not yet complete agreement on the basis of policy, especially of foreign policy, and the government was still wavering between alternatives. The alternatives might be expected to follow two common approaches to political problems, one intransigent and traditionalist, the other flexible and moderate. For this reason the Eboli faction is often described as a peace party, or even a liberal one, while the Alba faction is described as a war party, and regarded as conservative. But these labels have little substance. True, the Duke of Alba urged war to the bitter end in the Low Countries, but he had no desire to take the war across the English Channel; he stood for a line of diplomatic compromise with England and in this area he exercised a restraining influence on Spanish policy. The so-called peace party, on the other hand, while it might advocate a pacific settlement in the Low Countries, did so in order to gain a breathing-space which would enable Spain to wage war on England by means of an invasion across the Channel. In any case, as policy was an unchallenged prerogative of the crown and there was no means of changing it, there could be no political parties; and needless to say there were no 'liberals' in sixteenth-century Spain. The opinions of these groups, in fact, were not consistent but changed according to the time and the problem. Their real objective was not the promotion of a policy but the conquest of power and wealth, both of which were to be found in royal grace and favour. And as power for one man usually meant loss of power by another it was inevitable that there should be rival factions; it was notorious that

Eboli and Alba automatically opposed each other on every problem that arose.[32]

The Eboli faction attracted a sizeable group of nobles—the Marquis of los Vélez, a veteran warrior and diplomat and member of the Council of State; the Duke of Sessa, a descendant of the Great Captain; the large and powerful family of Mendoza, whose members were usually to be found in viceregal or ambassadorial office; and it could later count on the support of Cardinal Quiroga.

It also comprised a number of officials, and of these the most distinguished was Antonio Pérez, who became its key figure and took over the leadership after the death of Eboli in 1573, mobilising it for his own purposes. It was then that his association with Eboli's wife became close, so close indeed that much of the political conflict of Philip II's reign has been explained in terms of an alleged love affair between the Princess of Eboli and Antonio Pérez, and attributed to the rivalry of the king and his secretary for the love of the same woman. The story, like so many others of the reign, is untrue—untrue of Pérez as well as of Philip.[33] The Princess of Eboli, who wore a black patch over her right eye, was another member of the Mendoza family, a domineering woman, pious in a theatrical way—she entered a convent the day her husband died and came out a few months later—but above all avid for influence over affairs and people. St. Teresa suffered from her attentions; Antonio Pérez was helped to ruin by them. The political objectives of this eccentric woman amounted to little more than an anxiety to interfere wherever she could, and so she cultivated Pérez whom she believed 'would go far', hoping through him to remain at the centre of things when her husband's death threatened to deprive her of influence. Pérez, of course, found her useful because of her aristocratic connections. But their relationship was purely political and financial: both needed money, and there was money to be earned by an official who had the right connections. So he revealed to her state secrets, and together they traded in royal grants and government information, helping suitors who

---

[32] Marañón, op. cit., i. 30–32, 125–28, while recognising the inconsistency of the factions and the real nature of their objectives, still calls them 'liberals' and 'conservatives', and sees their origin in the time of the comuneros, the latter being feudal and conservative, and the royalists progressive. But the evidence is vague and the argument unconvincing.

[33] Contemporary English opinion of Philip II, of course, like Spanish opinion of Elizabeth I, was quite defamatory. Giving news from Calais on 28 August 1588 Howard wrote to Burghley: 'The King's bastard son, the Duke of Pascaredo (Pastrana), came there yesterday'; in J. K. Laughton, State Papers relating to the defeat of the Spanish Armada (Navy Records Society, 2 vols., London, 1894), ii. 174. The Duke of Pastrana was in fact the son of the Princess of Eboli but his father was Ruy Gómez, not Philip II.

were prepared to buy their favours. And the intrigue was probably empty of love.[34]

The spokesman of the opposing faction was the Duke of Alba, powerful head of a powerful family, whose distinguished military and viceregal career was put to its severest test in the Low Countries. Alba was an inveterate enemy of Pérez and his group, all of whom he included in his hatred of the Prince of Eboli, his old rival in the Council of State, and in his aristocratic contempt for officials. On his side were ranged his own extensive household—the Toledos were prolific in generals, admirals, and viceroys—the secretaries Vázquez, Zayas, Idiáquez, and Moura, and the king's confessor, Fr. Chaves. The faction also included two great lords who had considerable influence in the second part of the reign, and both of whom enriched themselves shamelessly from office—the Count of Barajas, President of the Council of Castile, whom Philip was to employ in his campaign against Antonio Pérez until he in turn was investigated for peculation and deprived of office, and the Count of Chinchón, treasurer-general of Aragon and Italy, an extreme royalist who owed his preferment to Pérez's rival, Mateo Vázquez. In the 1570's, however, the faction had not yet reached its place in the sun. The Duke of Alba failed in the Low Countries; by 1572 he was out of favour with Philip II and his governorship subject to inspection. His recall in 1573 and subsequent banishment from court by a king who was tired of his pretensions coincided with the beginning of Pérez's great influence. But Pérez too overreached himself. From trading in grants and official information he passed to unauthorised interference in matters of state—in affairs of the Low Countries and perhaps of Portugal—and so to his undoing in 1579. Once administrators tried to act like politicians Philip II struck them down, and he did so with impunity. The basic weakness of factional politics of this kind was that they had no strength outside the administration. From his cortes the king had nothing to fear.

5. Cortes and Commonwealth

Spanish political theorists in the sixteenth century rejected despotism and insisted that the sovereign rule in accordance with divine and natural law. But, with few exceptions, they allowed the king absolute power. One of the exceptions was the Jesuit theologian, Juan de Mariana, who, after a brilliant career at the University of Alcalá, taught with outstanding success at his order's colleges in Rome and Paris, returning to Spain in 1574 to live

---

[34] Marañón, *op. cit.*, i. 165–213.

the life of a scholar in the Jesuit house in Toledo. There in 1599 he published his famous political treatise, *De Rege et Regis Institutione*, written for the guidance of the heir to the throne, who in the meantime had become Philip III. The book was a bitter indictment of absolutism.

Mariana, of course, like other Spanish philosophers, preferred monarchy to any other type of government; but his preference was qualified by the assertion that the king must rule not only with a council but also with the consent of his subjects expressed in a senate composed of 'the best men', and must administer 'public and private affairs in accordance with their expressed opinions'.[35] But who decided policy in case of conflict? Was the authority of the king or the commonwealth greater? 'The regal power', he argued, 'if it is lawful, ever has its source from the citizen'; this power 'they hedged about with laws and obligations, lest it . . . degenerate into tyranny'.[36] Therefore Mariana approved of the protective laws and institutions of Aragon, where he considered the law of the community, or commonwealth as he called it, was greater than that of the king. This he regarded as an ideal to which other provinces should aspire, for it was in the common interest to limit the king's power. In Castile, unlike Aragon, there was no appeal to the commonwealth. While Mariana recognised that in matters of foreign policy, justice, and appointments the king was absolute by law in Spain, he rejected the notion that he could levy taxes, or abrogate laws, as he pleased. In these matters there was, or ought to be, right of opposition, a right which had been taken away in Castile but still existed in Aragon.

Right of criticism and opposition, argued Mariana, should be embodied in the cortes, and for this reason he criticised the decline of the cortes of Castile and its neglect by the crown. Bishops and nobles had been excluded in order that decisions could be left to the king alone and to the whim of a few, while 'the procurators of the towns . . . are corrupted by gifts and expectations; since they are not chosen deliberately but by lot, a new means of corruption and a proof of a confused commonwealth'. The result had been that policy, disastrous policy, had got beyond control, while 'events prove the spread of kingly power in war and peace'.[37] The most important power which Mariana reserved for the cortes was control of taxation and legislation. But he went further than this, for he also claimed for the commonwealth, represented in the cortes, the right to decide the fate of a tyrant king. It was this which earned his book such notoriety, for he asserted

---

[35] In G. Lewy, *Constitutionalism and Statecraft during the Golden Age of Spain: A Study of the Political Philosophy of Juan de Mariana, S.J.* (Geneva, 1960), p. 53.
[36] *Ibid.*, p. 55.   [37] *Ibid.*, p. 57.

that a king could 'be removed from office and even punished with death under exceptional circumstances'.[38]

Mariana, then, rejected the kind of absolutism which he saw before his eyes in Castile, the absolutism in fact practised by Philip II. His views were not revolutionary; he looked back to what he regarded as medieval government, and he wanted the return of the bishops to the cortes even more than the return of the nobility, whom he disliked. But the monarchy he advocated was constitutional monarchy, for in his view the king was responsible not only to God but also to the people, acting through their representatives in the cortes and in accordance with the law of the land. Yet Mariana was exceptional. True, other Spanish political philosophers like Francisco de Vitoria, Francisco Suárez, Domingo de Soto, and Diego de Covarrubias also subscribed to the theory of the popular origin of sovereignty, in the sense that they derived political authority from God via the people and insisted that power was based on consent, or, as Soto asserted, that 'kings and princes are created by the people who vest in them the authority to govern'.[39] And they all rejected tyranny. But, in their anxiety to preserve law and order and the authority of judge and ruler, they invariably admitted qualifications to the limits they placed on sovereignty. Vitoria allowed for no appeal from king to commonwealth, and argued that 'it is better that the laws of the tyrant be obeyed than to live without any'; while Suárez conceded that a king could tax without consent. But the greatest weakness of arguments such as these was that they never advanced beyond abstract speculation. In spite of their scholarship, their sense of tradition and responsibility, their respect for the law, in spite of their advocacy of the right to resist tyranny, even perhaps by killing the tyrant, in the ultimate analysis the Spanish neo-scholastics were supporters of outright absolutism. For their democratic theory of the origin of sovereignty never included institutional safeguards by which a king might be judged and controlled by some human authority outside of himself. Consequently, unlike Mariana, they were incapable of providing any real check against the abuse of political authority, as long as that authority was legitimate and acting, at least theoretically, in accordance with divine and natural law and for the common good. Yet their views were probably

---

[38] *Ibid.*, pp. 61, 72. Mariana's *De Rege* was published in Spain without causing comment, but in Paris it was burnt by the public hangman in 1610 after the assassination of Henry IV. The Spanish Inquisition was more interested in other works of Mariana; see below, pp. 266–67.

[39] Lewy, *op. cit.*, pp. 62–64; see also V. Beltrán de Heredia, *Francisco de Vitoria* (Madrid, 1939); L. Sánchez Agesta, *El concepto del Estado en el pensamiento español del siglo XVI* (Madrid, 1959).

more representative of Spanish opinion than were those of Mariana, and they certainly reflected political realities in Castile.

By the reign of Philip II the cortes of Castile had lost any prerogatives they had ever possessed. After the exceptional assembly of 1538 they were reduced to a single chamber, composed of thirty-six representatives of eighteen towns, chosen not by election but by lot and sometimes in rotation from a municipal oligarchy of privileged families or groups of magistrates, and in such a way that royal intervention could be easily exercised if necessary. From the fifteenth century their right to be consulted before the crown took extraordinary taxation had been increasingly evaded, and without the means of making redress precede supply they were incapable of providing any restraint on personal monarchy. There remained little of their rights to preserve, but that little was also taken from them. At the very beginning of Philip II's reign, their last authentic prerogative, that of refusing to consent to the revocation of laws passed in previous cortes, was undermined: 'If it be my pleasure,' declared Philip in 1555, 'I shall annul, without the cortes, the laws made in the cortes; I shall legislate by edicts and I shall abolish laws by edicts.'[40] Later, to remove the last remnants of resistance, he began to attack the *poderes*, or instructions given by towns to their deputies in an attempt to prescribe their conduct in the cortes. At the opening of the cortes of 1566 he obliged the deputies to swear that their *poderes* were 'unlimited and unrestricted', and thereafter he used his local officials to obtain the same end.[41] The cortes frequently complained of the way their privileges were being ignored, petitioning against the imposition of new taxes without their consent, against the usurpation of the legislative authority by the Council of Castile, and demanding that no new law or edict be made by the king alone while the cortes were in session.[42] The king allowed them their head. In 1569 he even authorised the publication of the *Nueva Recopilación*, or revised laws of the kingdom, which actually contained laws in which the principal powers of the cortes in legislation and finance were specifically stated to be in force.[43] The difference between theory and practice, complacently accepted, could hardly be carried to greater lengths.

This was the situation which Mariana denounced—abject failure by frequently corrupt procurators of the towns effectively to defend the cortes' original rights in taxation and legislation. Yet, impotent as they were, why did Philip II continue to convoke them? Partly because of his perverse

---

[40] *Cortes de los antiguos reinos de León y de Castilla*, v. 677. See Merriman, *op. cit.*, iv., 422–33.
[41] *Actas de las Cortes de Castilla* (Madrid, 1877–91), ii. 13.
[42] *Ibid.*, iv. 529–31; vi. 311–22.   [43] Merriman, *op. cit.*, iv. 427.

respect for the technicalities of the law, and partly because of his anxiety to remain in touch with outside opinion. His method of government depended on his possession of detailed information of his states which he could not acquire himself; so he used the cortes to keep himself informed of affairs and opinions. It was a one-sided arrangement, for he refused to be consulted personally by deputations of procurators, and his answers to their petitions were non-committal or negative, and sometimes given after the assembly had been closed. The petitions themselves are revealing. Except for occasional criticisms of the foreign policy of Philip II, mainly in the last years of the reign, the cortes usually left matters of policy well alone. They were more interested in local affairs, especially in the financial and economic state of the country, in the security of foreign commerce, the state of coastal defences, the attacks of Moorish and English corsairs, the moriscos, the excesses of the Inquisition, student behaviour, and the proliferation of obscene literature. Even Philip II could only have regarded most of their petitions as innocuous.

Monarchy, then, was absolute. But its absolutism was qualified by conditions, and its power was less imposing in practice than it was in theory. It was restricted in the first place by inefficiency; the bureaucracy, which was not large by present-day standards, never entirely succeeded in overcoming the obstacles of distance involved in governing Spain and in applying central decisions over the length and breadth of the country. It was also restricted by the existence of local forces; the aristocracy with their feudal jurisdiction, and some of the towns with their privileges, had traditionally demanded a share in royal control of the country or some degree of independence from such control. These forces were less vigorous in Philip II's reign and more vulnerable to royal pressure exercised through local officials. In Castile, at least, his sixty-six *corregidores*, extensively endowed with judicial and administrative functions, dominated the town councils and took his authority to the mass of the people. But there were further constraints on central government. As the state sought to share the increasing costs of war with its wealthier subjects, so it had to share public functions with private or provincial interests. Philip II began his reign with direct control of the machinery of war; he had an army recruited by royal captains and a navy directly administered by the crown. The drift from state control began when the pressure of war, the accumulation of military commitments, the unprecedented demand for men, money and supplies forced the monarchy to re-allocate the burdens and re-distribute the costs of the state.[44] Military

---

[44] This process has been identified and studied by I. A. A. Thompson, *War and Government in Habsburg Spain* (London, 1976).

administration was then devolved from direct royal control to private contractors and local authorities, from central to local government, from public to private sectors. Military financing came to rely more and more on independent financiers. Then other branches of military administration—the operation of the galleys, construction of shipping and maintenance of fleets, supply and manufacture of arms and munitions, provisioning and recruiting of troops—were delegated to localities or individuals. As the central bureaucracy lost control of this area of government, so contractors, provinces, lords and cities came to enjoy monopoly rights and fiscal and judicial immunities. This led in turn to a revival of aristocratic power and a reinforcement of seigneurial privilege. It also increased the influence of the foreign *asentista* in Spanish government. But while the process can be observed in the middle and later decades of Philip II's reign, it was not complete until the time of Philip IV when the unitary state founded by his predecessors was seriously eroded under the pressure of war.

Outside Castile there were regional immunities, in Granada until 1570, in the Basque country permanently, and above all in Aragon. To travel from Castile to Aragon was to cross a frontier into a different social and political world, where semi-independent lords exercised numerous feudal rights to the detriment of the crown and of their vassals, where Castilians were debarred from office, where laws were different and independently administered, and where taxation was checked by the cortes. Philip II experienced the difference at the very beginning of his reign, when he himself was absent in the Low Countries. In 1556 the viceroy of Aragon, Diego Hurtado de Mendoza, Duke of Francavilla, had an Aragonese garrotted on a charge of complicity with brigands. The sentence was regarded as an infringement of the *fueros* and produced a violent reaction: the cortes assembled without royal summons, the people of Zaragoza started rioting, the viceroy was forced to take refuge, and the Regent in Valladolid disavowed him.[45] For the next three years Aragon was without a viceroy, and appeared to have won its point.

There were reasons for the crown's diffidence in Aragon. It was partly a question of security: the proximity of France meant that any disturbance on the eastern periphery of Spain was liable to be exploited by enemies from across the Pyrenees, so it did not pay to alienate Aragon, especially in time of war with France. But the greatest reason has already been noticed.[46] The Aragonese block of states had few resources to offer the crown, either in men or in money, so there was little temptation for the

[45] See J. Reglà Campistol, *Felip II i Catalunya* (Barcelona, 1956), 17–18.
[46] See above, pp. 9–10, 47–49.

crown to claim those resources by absolute methods. This could be seen in Philip II's relations with the cortes of Aragon. The eastern cortes assembled in two ways—in particular cortes held within each kingdom, Aragon, Catalonia, and Valencia, and in general cortes when all three met in one place simultaneously, though still sitting separately. But the king rarely visited his eastern kingdoms, and so he held few cortes there. As their taxable capacity was much less than that of Castile there was little inducement for him to do so. Therefore, apart from the meeting of the separate cortes of Aragon in 1592, for which there were special reasons as will be seen, Philip only held two cortes in his eastern kingdoms, and these were general cortes which met at Monzón in 1563 and 1585. Both were empty of incident and both were characterised by the assembly's obsessive concern with legal and constitutional matters, many of them of a trivial nature. And the material stagnation of the region was reflected in the lack of legislation, or even of complaint, on financial and economic affairs, though they voted the moderate subsidies which the king requested. Consequently for most of his reign there was no reason for Philip to change the principles of his predecessors with regard to the eastern kingdoms. With their voluntary co-operation, he levied troops and taxes on the few occasions he required them, but there was no temptation to do more. The constitutional obstacles, in fact, can be exaggerated. The crown was never faced by a block of opposition from the states of Aragon; none of them felt a unity of interests with the others, any more than they did with Castile, and they never rallied to the other's defence. Consequently Philip was able to deal with each one separately. With Aragon he took issue in 1591 when his authority was seriously challenged there.[47] With Catalonia he had already reached an understanding.

6. CATALONIA: SECURITY RISK OR NATIONAL ASSET?

Catalonia was not secessionist in the sixteenth century. On the contrary it collaborated with the central monarchy and played its part in imperial defence. According to its means, it provided Philip II with men, materials, and money.[48] Troops could be raised in Catalonia, not by conscription it is true, but by voluntary recruitment and often from criminal elements in return for royal pardon; but in one way or another levies were provided for the Low Countries, for the war of Granada, and for garrison duty in

---

[47] See below, pp. 357–64.

[48] F. Soldevila, *Història de Catalunya* (Barcelona, 1934), ii. 226–27; Reglà, *Felip II i Catalunya*, pp. 41–63. See also J. Vicens Vives, *Notícia de Catalunya* (Barcelona, 1954).

Italy. In Barcelona galleys were constructed, equipped, and manned, and they operated in the defence of the Mediterranean against the Turk and of the coasts against the corsairs. And money was available on occasion: in the first general cortes of the reign in 1563 Catalonia granted Philip 300,000 pounds, and 500,000 in the cortes of 1585. But all this co-operation was qualified by two things. It was given more willingly when Philip's imperial needs coincided with the local interests of Catalonia, and more reservedly when they were regarded as the special interests of Castile; for this reason the Catalans had a large contingent at Lepanto, but were poorly represented in the Spanish Armada. Moreover, it was restricted by the resources of the country. The economic limitations of Catalonia were demonstrated to Philip in 1561 when he required his viceroy, García de Toledo, to procure him a loan of 100,000 ducats. The viceroy was obliged to reply that there was little credit to be obtained in Barcelona, for merchants had little money, and to raise even a small and occasional loan he himself had had to mortgage his property and pay an interest of 9–10 per cent.[49]

The loyalty of Catalonia, within its means, was never seriously in doubt. Yet Philip II found Catalonia a difficult country to govern. The trouble lay not in the *fueros*—local offices were limited to Catalans, but unlike Aragon, they accepted Castilian viceroys—but in social and economic conditions.[50] He had little trouble with Barcelona or any other urban centre, for the merchant classes were weakened by the decline of trade and by the universal aspiration to aristocratic status. But in the highlands of Catalonia his writ was probably less effective than in any other part of Spain. In the mountain cantons brigandage was endemic and kept the whole area in constant state of semi-revolt. Private feuds, often sparked off by an assassination, were openly fought by the highland gentry and the brigands they patronised, while local officials were either sympathetic, or fearful, or short of troops, and certainly handicapped by the remoteness of the mountain districts and their proximity to France, where criminals could take refuge.

At the root of the trouble was a problem of subsistence; the area was poorly endowed by nature, weak in crops, periodically short of foodstuffs, and life there was a fight for survival. Poverty bred lawlessness. The area lay along one of the vital routes from Castile, via Barcelona, to Italy, a route which was used not only for communications but also for the transit

[49] Braudel, *op. cit.*, p. 418.
[50] See above, p. 117, and references to Braudel there; also Reglà, *Felip II i Catalunya*, pp. 109–66, and the same author's 'La cuestión de los Pirineos a comienzos de la Edad Moderna. El intento imperialista de Gastón de Foix', *Estudios de Historia Moderna*, i. (1950), 1–32, and 'El envio de metales preciosos americanos de España a Italia a través de la Corona de Aragón durante los Austrias', *ibid.*, iv. (1954), 189–203.

Elizabeth of Valois, third wife of Philip II by A. Sánchez Coello

of treasure. The temptation was irresistible: official couriers were often robbed and the treasure convoys ran the risk of capture by bands of brigands who made their first big haul in 1587. But the problem was also related to the predicament of the Catalan nobility. Seigneurial jurisdiction of a feudal kind, lay and ecclesiastical, abounded in Catalonia. More than half the country was covered by semi-independent franchises, which not only prevented the king's writ from reaching his subjects directly but also gave rise to conflicts of jurisdiction between neighbouring lords, mutual encroachments, and subsequent friction, with retainers mobilised in their lord's cause. And the country contained more nobles than it could support. There was only one grandee in Catalonia—the Duke of Cardona—but a horde of nobility and gentry; and the prospects for younger sons were bleak indeed. As there were not enough offices to go round in Catalonia itself and those in Castile and the empire were monopolised by Castilians, there was passionate rivalry between families for the few vacancies that did exist, or in default of these for honours, privileges and pensions.[51] Unless a younger son could marry into Castilian society he was often faced with economic ruin. Again, poverty bred lawlessness. Deprived of political and military careers, large numbers of Catalan gentry turned to brigandage, fighting their rivals with large bands of armed retainers. And brigandage was expanding in Philip II's reign. In 1564 he ordered his administrators to scour the country for malefactors, 'because I understand that in this principality there are so many brigands and men of evil ways, daily committing murders, assassinations, robberies, and other crimes, that it is impossible to travel there without notorious risk to life'.[52] Much of the time of his viceroys in Catalonia was spent in pursuit of brigands, mobilising search-parties, patrolling the frontier, and whenever possible impressing the malefactors into *tercios* for service in the army. The problem was serious, and rendered even worse by the proximity of France.

Officially France and Spain were at peace after the Treaty of Cateau-Cambrésis, though there was never complete confidence between the two governments. But whatever the political reservations of Philip II, his immediate preoccupation was religion. The growth of Protestantism— Calvinist, organised, and armed—in the neighbouring kingdom struck him as a direct menace to the religious unity of his own, and his anxiety to preserve his own states from contagion became obsessive. Some of his own subjects who were suspect of heresy had taken refuge across the Pyrenees,

[51] See J. Elliott, 'The King and the Catalans, 1621–1640', *Cambridge Historical Journal*, xi. (1953–55), 253–71, and 'The Catalan revolution of 1640. Some suggestions for a historical revision', *Estudios de Historia Moderna*, iv. (1954), 273–300.
[52] Reglà, *Felip II i Catalunya*, p. 125.

and in 1565 his ambassador in France warned him of a propaganda operation organised from Geneva to disseminate heretical books in Spain. On the coasts of Vizcaya and Guipúzcoa the Inquisition increased its vigilance, but the weak point of Spain's defences were the mountains of Catalonia. For many years Catalonia had been a focal point of French immigration, and the source of most of this was the Midi, precisely where the Huguenots were numerous and well organised. Then there was contraband, a way of life in the Catalan Pyrenees, like brigandage to which it was allied. A popular item of contraband was horses, an article of war, whose export from Spain was forbidden; and it was suspected that many horses were going to Huguenot rebels.

The coincidence of the two factors, brigandage within Catalonia and Calvinism beyond the Pyrenees, made this Philip II's weakest frontier, and in his eyes created a problem of security. He saw a possible point of contact between the two groups of rebels, especially as the brigands were defying ecclesiastical censure. As he wrote to his viceroy in June 1566, 'the usual habitat of these people (brigands) is on the French frontier, where the danger of sowing this evil (resistance to ecclesiastical authority) is all the greater, and the means of kindling the fire so much easier'.[53] The year 1568 was a crucial year for Philip II, as has been seen. The rising of the moriscos of Granada, and the rebellion in the Low Countries, where Calvinism had penetrated into his own states, all increased the pressure on his resources. Compared with these problems the danger in Catalonia was insignificant and never a comparable threat to security. But in the context of the foreign situation it alarmed the Spanish authorities. The wars of religion had begun in France in 1562; from then on the Huguenots began to defy not only the French monarchy but also Philip II, attacking his shipping and threatening his communications with the Low Countries, where from 1566 the pressure of his own Calvinist subjects was becoming more insistent. In the circumstances it was difficult to keep a sense of proportion, especially as he was vulnerable in the Pyrenees—a kind of no-man's-land where Huguenots and brigands mixed. The frontier monasteries and bishoprics, notably the rich see of Urgel, were the targets of both: Huguenot bands penetrated the frontier in search of booty for their cause and also, it was alleged, to proselytise, while Catalan brigands plundered church wealth with the backing of a penurious gentry who had a reputation for anti-clericalism and designs on ecclesiastical property.[54] Far away in Madrid, Philip II magnified the whole situation.

[53] Philip II to Hurtado de Mendoza, 21 June 1566, *ibid.*, p. 91.
[54] *Ibid.*, pp. 85–97.

As early as May 1560 he ordered the viceroy of Catalonia, García de Toledo, to maintain the strictest vigilance on the frontier and to assist the Inquisition in its investigations there, while in the following year he ordered the religious beliefs and practices of Gascon immigrants to be examined, and even their entry to be restricted if it could be done without giving offence to the French government.[55] From 1564, when he appointed a new viceroy, Diego Hurtado de Mendoza, father of the Princess of Eboli, Philip II gave repeated instructions to improve frontier fortifications, search out Huguenots, suppress brigandage, and much of the viceroy's administration was directed to these tasks. In 1568, the crisis year for Spain, Hurtado de Mendoza ordered the local authorities of the Pyrenean zone to raise all available forces in readiness for a possible attack from the 'Lutherans (sic) who have risen in France and revolted against Our Lord God and against their lord, the Most Christian King of France, and as they have such a powerful army'. In May of the same year Philip II issued an edict prohibiting the subjects of the crown of Aragon from studying in foreign universities, thus specially reinforcing in the eastern kingdoms the order which had been applied to the whole of Spain in 1559. And in July Hurtado de Mendoza relayed to all the bishops of Catalonia yet another order of the king, which stated that 'For the preservation of the Catholic faith we prohibit any French subjects of whatever condition (i.e. including priests) from teaching children in any subjects in the principality and counties'.[56] This prohibition coincided with a period of increasing French immigration; on some days, it was reported, 400 immigrants entered through the pass of Carol alone. Some of these were believed to be Protestants, the advance guard of a large-scale invasion, and anxiety was such that the viceroy himself patrolled the frontier, personally supervising defences.

By this time the government was convinced that the situation was critical, though the crisis existed largely in its own imagination. It only needed the Inquisition to distort matters further and add an element of absurdity to the whole situation. The Inquisition, like Philip himself, was alarmed by Huguenot activities on the frontier and civil disturbances in the highlands, for it was employed to combat both. It was also provoked by the knowledge that its activities had long been unpopular in Catalonia where they were regarded as an unwarranted intrusion on regional prerogatives, and met with the passive resistance of local officials and inhabitants alike. Soon it had conjured up an illusion of religious dissent in Catalonia allied to the Huguenots. Evidence was seen on all sides, but particularly in the refusal of

[55] *Ibid.*, pp. 76–77.
[56] *Ibid.*, pp. 184–87; see the same author's 'Felipe II y el bandolerismo catalan', *Hispania*, xv. (1955), 544–58.

the Catalans, voiced by the *Diputación General*, the standing committee of the cortes, to pay the *excusado*, or tax on temporalities of parishes, conceded by the pope to Philip II. In this way, with characteristic inaccuracy, the Inquisition was led to confound a constitutional issue with a religious one, and to brand as heresy the Catalans' defence of their prerogatives. They reported the matter to Rome and Madrid. In Catalonia the charge was received with a mixture of disbelief and indignation, but the local authorities were soon aware of its nature, for the municipal council of Barcelona took notice of the fact that on 29 November 1569 there arrived in Barcelona from Rome some memorials 'which had been presented in the court of Rome to His Holiness by the procurator fiscal of the Holy Office, accusing the Catalans of heresy'. But the accusation was taken seriously in Rome and Madrid, and Philip II in particular fell for the story. Conscious of his weakness in the Pyrenees, and lacking confidence in the semi-autonomous authorities in Catalonia, where the Inquisition was the only tribunal of the central government, he actually seems to have believed that Catalonia was inclining to the Protestant cause. The judgement was erroneous and ill-informed, but he acted upon it. He ordered the Deputies corporatively to ask pardon of the Inquisition, and their refusal only confirmed his suspicion. On 19 July 1569 Hurtado de Mendoza, acting under instructions, though he himself considered the charge of heresy among the Catalans to be 'very far from the truth', ordered the imprisonment of the Deputies as well as some other officials.[57] Shortly after this sensation, and when Philip II imagined that heresy had taken root in Catalonia, there was a minor Huguenot invasion in the county of Roussillon. When the viceroy called on the local nobility to raise forces to meet the attack the latter refused to acknowledge any obligation to do so, but voluntarily offered to serve the king in defence of the country.

Philip II's judgement had been warped by the religious tensions of these years and by an excess of confidence in his Inquisition. He soon realised his mistake and took measures to correct it. To clear Catalonia of the heresy charge, the city of Barcelona sent an emissary to the king, who was then in Córdoba on the occasion of the morisco rebellion—which was overcome with the help of the levies recruited in Catalonia. The mission was not difficult. On 5 March 1570 Philip wrote to the councillors of Barcelona, recognising the falsehood of the charge, and claiming, with some disingenuousness, that he had not been deceived. And the prisoners were freed.

The entire episode, for all its fantasy, was a lesson in how to govern

---

[57] On this incident see Reglà, *Felipe II i Catalunya*, pp. 188–96; Soldevila, *Història de Catalunya*, ii. 240.

Catalonia. The trust which Philip II placed in the Inquisition was often misplaced but usually understandable, given the conditions of his government. Any institution which operated in the whole of Spain, regardless of local restrictive rights, was valuable to the crown, and in the interests of efficiency Philip II had to take his agencies where he could find them. For both these reasons the Inquisition was an essential instrument of his government, and he expanded its authority whenever and wherever he could, especially in the eastern kingdoms and often at the expense of his secular officials. But reliance on the Inquisition had its drawbacks, for the tribunal took a partial view of affairs. In 1569, in particular, it had confused a special situation in the highlands with the question of security in Catalonia as a whole. Philip II himself never repeated the mistake. Brigandage, of course, was a permanent condition, and Huguenot pressure revived from time to time. In 1570 a large Catalan force under Hurtado de Mendoza threw back a Huguenot attack on Perpignon, and in the 1580's Philip II was ever watchful of the activities of Henry of Navarre and his Calvinist supporters.[58] But he understood that Catalonia itself was loyal and would co-operate with his government within the limits of its resources and in return for observance of its local prerogatives. As his viceroy, Manrique de Lara, reported in 1587: 'These people are obviously most loyal to Your Majesty, and deserve all credit for it; but occasionally I find them more slippery and changeable than any other nation I have seen.'[59] The view was typically Castilian; but the fact that the viceroy who made it had been sent from Castile and was accepted by the Catalans bespoke the basic harmony between Philip II and his eastern subjects. There was no reason for him to hold a trial of strength with Catalonia, as he was eventually forced to do with Aragon.

The relation between Philip II and Catalonia was vital to his international as well as his domestic interests, for Catalonia was a Mediterranean state, strategically situated between Castile and her Italian dependencies and an important base for operations against Spain's Moslem enemies. Defence of the Mediterranean was particularly urgent in the 1560's. Indeed, for the first fifteen years of his reign Philip II had to give priority to the Mediterranean. In spite of the preoccupation of his diplomacy with France and of his growing estrangement from England, the major concern of his foreign policy and the greater part of his resources were directed to defence and counter-attack against the Turk.

---

[58] Reglà, *Felip II i Catalunya*, p. 89.
[59] Manrique de Lara to Philip II, 11 September 1587, in Riba, *El Consejo Supremo de Aragón*, p. 126. On viceregal administration in Catalonia see Reglà, *Els segles XVI i XVII: els virreis de Catalunya* (Barcelona, 1956).

CHAPTER VII

THE WAR WITH ISLAM

1. The Morisco Problem

Two world religions faced each other in the Mediterranean, and the claims of each to dominion were absolute. Yet in Spain Christians and Moors had lived together for centuries: immediately after the reconquest Spaniards had tolerated the Moslem religion, and the church had tempered its hostility with some understanding. This attitude changed not because of the increasing intransigence of the Habsburg monarchs and their spiritual advisers but because of the growing power of Islam. During most of the sixteenth century Spain was never given the opportunity to tolerate Mohammedanism or even to accept terms of co-existence. After the rapid expansion of Ottoman power in the fifteenth century, the Christian conflict with Islam was a fight not for supremacy but for survival. In America and the Far East the driving missionary enterprise of the Counter-Reformation pushed Christianity to new frontiers. In the eastern Mediterranean, however, the frontiers of Christendom were contracting, and the impact was felt even in the west. Spain in particular was on the defensive against the encompassing surge of Islam from the Levant and North Africa. The Ottoman Turks and their allies, accurately identifying the greatest obstacle to their supremacy, waged a relentless war on the rival empire, which gave it no choice but to arm.

In the subsequent conflict it was inevitable that the first to suffer should be the partisans of Islam within Spain itself. As an isolated minority they had been tolerated; as potential allies of the national enemy they were regarded as an intolerable risk to security—a reflection of official fear rather than of oppression. The new policy was initiated in 1502, when the Moslems of Castile were given the alternative of conversion to Christianity or expulsion; in 1525 the same choice was offered to those of Aragon. In the mass conversions which followed, Mohammedanism was nominally excised from Spain, but in fact it remained to torment her for the rest of the century. For the moriscos, as the new converts were called, had accepted baptism under duress, without conviction and without instruction. They continued to form a community apart, stubbornly attached to their old religion, language, dress, and traditions. An exasperated government tried every policy it knew for over a hundred years. Abused, indoctrinated, and favoured in turn, for ever suspect—and taxed—the moriscos were finally expelled in the dramatic decision of 1609.

The policy of repression was due essentially to repeated failures of attempts at conversion and assimilation, and as this was fundamentally a conflict of religions it was difficult to resolve. But the difficulty was aggravated by political conditions. It was taken for granted that the moriscos were in contact with national enemies. Such suspicions may have been exaggerated, but it is important to understand why they were held. For the moriscos undoubtedly presented a problem of security. Although there was no communication between the two enemy religions, the frontier separating Spain from Islam was not an iron curtain. The moriscos were a restless people and produced a constant stream of emigrants—across the Pyrenees through France and Italy to Constantinople, where they might serve the Turks as soldiers, interpreters or spies, and by sea from southern Spain to North Africa. As the Spanish authorities could not provide a continuous patrol of the entire southern and eastern coasts, they could not prevent a two-way traffic between their own territory and North Africa, nor halt the flow of refugees outwards and the smuggling of arms and ammunition inwards. Commando-type raids occurred, in which deserters returned, freed their relatives and friends, and at the same time captured Christians to sell in the Algiers market. In August 1565 raids, prepared with the help of morisco collaborators, penetrated as far as Órgiba in the kingdom of Granada.[1] Collaboration with the Barbary corsairs was also on the increase. At times there was even fraternisation between Christians and Moslems in a way that the state could hardly be expected to condone. In 1540, on the occasion of an abortive Algerian attack on Gibraltar, some eighty Christians found themselves temporarily in the hands of the corsairs; a kind of armistice was concluded and parleys were held; Algerian ships entered the port, sailors disembarked and walked in the town, looking up acquaintances among former captives or employers, and eating in the taverns; and amidst the exchange of goods and familiarities, the civilian population helped to transport fresh water needed for the enemy fleet.[2] The government's helplessness bred further fear and repression. To prevent the escape of moriscos and the raids of their allies, it tried to forbid morisco access to maritime districts, those of Andalucía in 1579 and those of Valencia in 1586. But edicts of this kind were impossible to administer along deserted coasts and without adequate guards. Illegal entrants continued to help their friends, and escape was an almost daily occurrence; and the refugees, filled with a fierce hatred

[1] Braudel, *La Méditerranée et le monde méditerranéen à l'époque de Philippe II*, p. 583.
[2] Ibid., 554.

of Spain and of Christianity, were powerful recruits for the Moslem
cause.

Such a challenge to its authority would have taxed the resources, and the
patience, of any state in the sixteenth century. But the problem was even
more complex than it appears at first sight. It involved not one, but many,
morisco communities, corresponding to the different regions where Moors
had survived during the reconquest—in Valencia, where the moriscos formed
a large peasant population subject for the past three hundred years to a
land-owning nobility who became their defenders against popular resentment and state suspicion; in Castile, where they were a small minority
dispersed among a large Christian population; and in Granada, where they
were a conquered people who retained their own leaders and the memory
of a recently lost independence.

In Valencia the towns were predominantly Christian and the moriscos
were concentrated in the rural areas, especially in the highlands, where they
formed an absolute majority of the population.[3] Their withdrawal to remote
mountain districts was attributed by Spaniards to a desire to avoid the
company of Christians, and it is true that here they were far removed
from political and ecclesiastical authorities. But they had no choice, for
the Christians had already appropriated the best land. The fertile *huertas* of
Valencia were not, as is often imagined, morisco preserves but a virtual
Christian monopoly. The inferiority of the moriscos was further emphasised
by their servile condition, for they belonged to the nobility. In this part of
Spain the reconquest of the thirteenth century had taken the form of surrender by the Moors, who consequently survived in large numbers with
their religion tolerated. They also continued to occupy and work the land,
but as this was granted by the kings of Aragon to their noble followers, the
Moslem peasants became the property of the new landowners, and were
then gradually pushed into the less fertile regions by incoming Christian
tenants. But their ability to work even inferior land made them a fruitful
source of revenue and services to their lords, who thus had a compelling
reason for supporting a policy of toleration. This was ended not by the
state but by the rebels of the *Germanía*, who rose against aristocratic and
royal power in 1519 and began to attack the noble protectors of Moorish
peasants.[4] The Moors themselves were suddenly faced with a worse dilemma
than royal policy was ever to impose on them—baptism or death. In this
way they were hounded into mass conversions, and it was now (1521) that
they came to be called New Christians or moriscos. It was debatable, of

---

[3] See T. Halperin Donghi, 'Les Morisques du Royaume de Valence au XVI siècle',
Annales. Économies. Sociétés. Civilisations, xi. (1956), 154–82.

[4] See above, pp. 46–47.

course, whether such baptisms were valid, and doubts were raised in Rome as well as in Spain; but the matter was settled to the satisfaction of the Spanish authorities in 1526 when Charles V officially recognised the conversions and sanctioned the policy which underlay them. A minority of Moors still refused to conform, and of these some were expelled. Others revolted in the wild mountains of Espadán in 1526. It was a bitter struggle, rendered worse for the authorities by the reluctance of the aristocracy to commit their forces against their own vassals. Resistance was eventually crushed, but only with the help of 3,000 German troops sent by the emperor.[5]

The rebellion showed the latent strength of the moriscos, and they managed to secure relatively moderate conditions: although the obligation to accept Christianity remained, they were allowed to retain their own customs and were exempt from the Inquisition for forty years.[6] This was a partial return towards a more tolerant policy, but it still gave no meaning to conversions which were merely official. The moriscos were Christians by force and Moors by inclination. Meanwhile, official policy became increasingly bereft of ideas. Wavering between indulgence and repression, the state seemed motivated by little more than financial considerations, for co-operative moriscos made good taxpayers. The ecclesiastical authorities, refusing to preach in Arabic and, with few exceptions, failing to sustain any programme of education, reached neither the minds nor the hearts of their new converts.[7] In spirit morisco Valencia remained part of Islam, attentive to every change in the balance of power in the Mediterranean, a nation within a nation, with its own leaders who represented its interests before the crown and frequently arranged corsair transport for those who wished to emigrate to Algiers. In the second half of the century they increased their numbers much faster than the Old Christians, a fact which did not go unnoticed and was attributed by Spaniards to the absence of ecclesiastical celibacy in the Moslem religion.[8] As a growing community they were the object of even greater suspicion. The state saw them as a risk to security,

[5] P. Boronat, *Los moriscos españoles y su expulsión* (2 vols., Valencia, 1901), i. 160.

[6] *Ibid.*, pp. 160–62.

[7] Halperin Donghi, 'Les Morisques du Royaume de Valence au XVI siècle', *op. cit.*, pp. 171–74.

[8] Within a general rise of population in Valencia, the moriscos increased by 69 per cent., from 18,683 families in 1563 to 31,715 in 1609, compared with the Old Christian increase of 44·7 per cent., from 44,894 families to 65,016; in 1609 the morisco population of Valencia was about 135,000. See H. Lapeyre, *Géographie de l'Espagne Morisque* (Paris, 1959), pp. 29–32, 203–04. According to a more recent estimate, the moriscos of Valencia may have increased from 85,500 in 1572, when they were 29 per cent. of the total population of the kingdom, to 143,000 in 1609, or 30.3 per cent. of the total. See Antonio Domínguez Ortiz and Bernard Vincent, *Historia de los moriscos* (Madrid, 1978), p. 76.

the church as a menace to religion, while the mass of poor Christians viewed them with a hatred born of jealousy and resentment. Only the nobles were satisfied, as their labourers—and their rents—increased. The very size of this alien community was one of the causes of its final ruin—the expulsion of 1609, a measure which had already been advocated in the Council of State in 1582.[9]

In Aragon the morisco community reproduced some of the features of that of Valencia, forming a substantial minority concentrated in one part of the country, in this case the fertile Ebro Valley, particularly around Zaragoza.[10] Here too the reconquest had followed the same lines as in Valencia, the majority of Moors remaining and working for the incoming Christians. Small groups survived in the towns as artisans and petty traders—in Zaragoza they were leatherworkers and makers of arms and gunpowder—but the greater number were to be found in the rural areas where they formed active agricultural and pastoral communities and earned the protection of their Christian lords. Many of the valleys of this region were entirely Moorish, and the conversions to Christianity at the beginning of the sixteenth century were for the most part superficial: in some villages it was said there were only three Christians—the priest, the notary, and the innkeeper. As in Valencia, the moriscos here were regarded as a security risk, but in this case it was because of their proximity to France and their alleged communications with Huguenots as well as the old suspicion of collusion with Islam. For this reason the spasmodic campaigns of the Inquisition to reconcile them to the church usually included a demand that they surrender their arms, while the feudal nobility of Aragon were anxious to preserve their bands of armed retainers. Their refusal to disarm caused alarmist rumours to circulate in 1575–76 that the moriscos were collaborating not only with the North Africans but also with French Huguenots poised on the Catalan frontier. In this way the religious problem became confounded with the problem of security in the Pyrenees, and the Inquisition tightened its frontier control in an attempt to prevent the passage of arms and emigrants. Much of the panic of these years was, of course, self-induced. Reporting to Philip II in 1575 the vice-chancellor of Aragon expressed his scepticism of alleged morisco collusion with North Africans and Huguenots, which he regarded as impracticable in both cases; in his view the Aragonese nobility kept their morisco retainers armed for the purpose of their own private feuds. In turn

[9] Boronat, *op. cit.*, i. 291–94.
[10] On the moriscos of Aragon see Braudel, *op. cit.*, pp. 576–79. Their number increased from 48,713 in 1575 to 61,000 in 1609, about 21 per cent. of the total population of Aragon; see Domínguez Ortiz and Vincent, *op. cit.*, pp. 77, 83.

the nobility might give their support to the moriscos in the latter's conflicts with rival agricultural communities, such as the mountain shepherds, as happened in 1585. But the problem of the moriscos must also be seen in its international context.[11] The collusion of some of them with French Huguenots—and they certainly traded in arms and gunpowder—though of little significance in itself, was alarming in existing circumstances. During the 1570's and 1580's Spanish naval and military forces were occupied on many fronts and Spanish interests exposed to many enemies; any communication, however nebulous, between the moriscos and national enemies was fearfully construed as treasonable.[12] In the quest for security, however, the Inquisition was more concerned to repress than to educate.

In Castile there was yet another morisco community, but one with features of its own. Here the problem was acute from the very beginning of the sixteenth century, as a result of the new policy of intolerance adopted by the Catholic Monarchs. In 1492 the Moorish Kingdom of Granada came to an end with the capture of the city by Ferdinand and Isabella. By the terms of the capitulation the Moors were to be allowed the free exercise of their religion, their laws, and their customs. Boabdil, the Moorish king, was given the Alpujarras as a fief for himself and his heirs in perpetuity. But the Spaniards had second thoughts, for they were unable to bring themselves to tolerate an alien religion or risk their security by permitting a bridgehead for Islam within Spain itself. Within a year, therefore, Boabdil was shipped off to Africa, and, ignoring the advice of local authorities, Cardinal Ximénez de Cisneros initiated a policy of forcible conversion. The campaign was needlessly provocative and included the burning of numerous copies of the Koran and Arabic manuscripts. The consequence was that the Moors in the Albaicín quarter of Granada rose in rebellion, and when this was crushed they were forced to accept conversion (1499). Meanwhile, the revolt had spread to the neighbouring mountains, and here resistance continued for another two years. At this point a decree was issued (11 February 1502) offering all the Moors in the Kingdom of Castile the choice between conversion and expulsion. Most of them chose the first, but, as in Valencia and Aragon, their Christianity remained purely nominal and once again the church failed to overcome the persistence of Moorish ways.

The decision taken in 1502 was applied not only to the recently conquered inhabitants of Granada, but also to the older *mudéjares*, those Moors of Castile who had long lived in the midst of Christians, freely practising their

[11] J. Reglá, 'La cuestión morisca y la coyuntura internacional en tiempos de Felipe II', *Estudios de Historia Moderna*, iii. (1953), 217–34.
[12] Boyd, *Cardinal Quiroga, Inquisitor General of Spain*, pp. 49–54.

religion. These were not important numerically, and therefore hardly a threat to security. For the reconquest in Castile had been ruthless and total: whereas Aragon had subjugated and exploited its Moors, Castile had driven them off and repopulated the land with Christian settlers. Consequently only a small Moorish minority survived, scattered over a vast area and assuming significant proportions only in Murcia and Andalucía; and they tended to concentrate in the towns, where they lived a ghetto-like existence in their ancient *morerías*. In 1575 they numbered some 30,000.

2. The War of Granada

In Granada, on the other hand, the moriscos were a more compact and a more prosperous society, and it was they who formed the most intractable element in the whole morisco problem. In the town of Granada and the eastern half of the kingdom a native Moorish society survived, powerful—and growing—in numbers, and with a governing class of its own. This recently independent people was bound to resent any attack on its basic conditions of living. Politically, the kingdom of Granada was simply annexed to Castile in 1492 and preserved no autonomous rights. It obtained a voice in the cortes, but this meant very little. The intention of Castile, in fact, was to absorb and assimilate Granada as quickly as possible. After the reconquest Christian lords were installed in its rich and highly developed lands. Officials and clergy followed, some less honest than others but all enjoying the advantages of the country. Here was a 'colonialism' within Spain itself—a new settler class, a subject population, civil and military oppression.[13] Not all of this was done in the name of religion: much of it was clearly the result of a 'rush' to a new acquisition which was economically attractive. Indeed, like the Indians in the New World, the moriscos had their protectors, such as the saintly Hernando de Talavera, first archbishop of Granada, who devoted his life to converting the Moors through sympathy and understanding, and the Mondéjar family, hereditary captains-general of Granada, who frequently risked office and reputation defending moriscos.[14] But official policy was not consistent, and the moriscos were alternately persecuted out of frustration and ignored in return for heavy subsidies.

The economy of the moriscos of Granada, like that of their Moorish predecessors, lay chiefly in the silk trade with Italy. Granada, as well as Almería and Málaga, had factories which turned out fine silks, and there were looms in most of the villages. Silk was almost the sole cash crop in

---

[13] Braudel, *op. cit.*, pp. 580–81.
[14] H. C. Lea, *The Moriscos of Spain* (Philadelphia, 1901), p. 212.

the Alpujarras; since cocoons weighed little, they could be transported at small expense on mule-back, and the mountains had long been thickly planted with mulberry trees. Silk production and manufacture, therefore, were fruitful sources of taxation and ones which the crown exploited to the full; in addition, subsidy was added to subsidy as the moriscos desperately bought off royal attentions.[15] Pressure on morisco land was also increasing. From 1559 agents of the crown were checking on all title deeds in order to reclaim crown lands; those who could not produce legal evidence of ownership had to pay a composition fee to the crown or have their land confiscated and resold. Consequently, the moriscos needed their Arabic title-deeds more than ever at the very time when the campaign against their language and culture was reaching its peak.

Yet the crisis in relations between the state and the moriscos of Granada which grew to a climax in the 1560's was not exclusively a Spanish responsibility. Across the Mediterranean, in North Africa, Algiers waged religious and economic war on Spain, and threatened not only her shipping but her coastal security. The source of Turkish pressure was more distant but more powerful, and the combined forces of Islam seemed to engulf the entire Mediterranean. The danger became more acute than ever in the 1560's. The Turks began to penetrate into the western Mediterranean, and in 1565 they besieged Malta. This was accompanied by a growth in the frequency and scope of corsair attacks on the Granadine coastline, from their bases in Tetuán, Cherchell, and Algiers. In 1558, a force of 4,000 attacked Berja; in 1559, 150 Algerian Turks attacked the castle of Fuengirola; in 1560, morisco corsairs disembarked at Castil de Ferro and evacuated the inhabitants of the village of Notaes. But the most spectacular raid was that made on Órgiba in the winter of 1565, when corsairs from Tetuán beat Spanish regular troops in a running fight, marched 20 miles inland, carried off several hundred moriscos, and re-embarked in safety.[16]

The moriscos themselves gave cause for anxiety on grounds of security, internal and external.[17] Banditry and piracy were endemic among them. In the 1560's bandits variously called *bandoleros*, *salteadores* and *monfíes*, according to region, were active in all morisco Spain, in Aragon, where they

---

[15] Two of the leaders of the 1569 rebellion were connected with the dyeing trade: Aben Aboo was a dyer, and Aben Farax, the leader of the Christmas night raid on the Albaicín, a dyer's journeyman. See K. Garrad. 'The Original Memorial of Don Francisco Núñez Muley', *Atlante*, ii. (1954), p. 223 n. 4.

[16] Braudel, *op. cit.*, p. 583; Garrad, 'The Original Memorial of Don Francisco Núñez Muley', *op. cit.*, p. 203.

[17] Domínguez Ortiz and Vincent, *op. cit.*, pp. 29–31, 39, 78–80; Andrew C. Hess, 'The Moriscos: An Ottoman Fifth Column in Sixteenth-century Spain', *American Historical Review*, 74, 1 (1968), 1–25; Garrad, *op. cit.*, p. 203 n. 6.

operated in collusion with French Huguenots, in Valencia, where nobles organised their morisco vassals into private armies, and in Andalucía, where *monfíes* openly fought Christians. Morisco pirates haunted the coasts of Valencia and Andalucia, with almost total impunity. And all this time the moriscos kept arms, openly or in secret, in spite of the surveillance of the authorities. As the Moslem campaign grew in intensity, the moriscos entered into subversive communication with the Cherifs of Morocco, the pirates of Tetuán, and the Sultan of Constantinople. The Ottomans sought to use moriscos as a fifth column and, while diverting Spanish efforts to internal security, to take some of their major objectives such as Cyprus and Tunis. A morisco tortured by the Inquisition in 1565 revealed that morisco spies sent information to the Turk via Lyons, and that the moriscos were ready to seize ports along the coast of Granada if the Turk captured Malta. Morisco spies were sent to Malta from Constantinople to collect information about Spanish naval strength. In isolation these were petty incidents, but in view of the known strength of the enemy and the inadequacy of their own defences, it was natural that the Spanish authorities should believe a collusive action was building up, in which Granada was designed as a bridgehead for a Moslem invasion of Spain. There were 150,000 moriscos in the kingdom of Granada in the 1560's, compared with 125,000 Christians. No one doubted that the morisco majority was a power in the land.

The crisis in Granada, therefore, had wider roots than the growth of the morisco population and its oppression at the hands of officials and Old Christians. The hatred and suspicion directed towards the moriscos increased in proportion to the danger from Turkey, real or imagined, and became overpowering once the siege of Malta had begun.[18] Hatred was fed from other sources, it is true—from a popular resentment of the successful morisco artisan and trader, and from knowledge among Christians that the Koran and not the Bible was the principal sacred text in Granada. But these were old scores. The issue was brought to a head in the 1560's primarily because of official concern for security. The very success of Islam outside of Spain brought heavy retribution on its partisans within.

Tension was already acute even before the government took action, and its own ineptitude was merely the last straw. In November 1566 Inquisitor general Diego de Espinosa prepared with Philip II an edict imposing various prohibitions on the moriscos. On New Year's Day of 1567, the eve of the anniversary of the Catholic Monarchs' triumphal entry into Granada in 1492, Pedro de Deza, who had been appointed President of the Audiencia of Granada precisely for the purpose, proclaimed the edict and began to

---

[18] Braudel, *op. cit.*, 586–87.

enforce its provisions. By the new law the moriscos of Granada were required to learn Spanish within three years, and from then onwards it would be a crime to speak, read, or write Arabic, in public or in private; they were also required to abandon their native costumes, their Moorish surnames, their customs and their ceremonies; and they were forbidden the use of their baths, on the ground that they provided opportunity for practising the ritual ablutions prescribed in the Koran—indeed the campaign was begun by Deza's removing the beautiful Alhambra baths. The intention behind these measures was to denationalise the moriscos and make them Spanish Catholics, and the folly of it was that the authorities believed this could be done by government decree. Nor had they even prepared for opposition. For the moment, certainly, the moriscos seemed content to negotiate, as they had done in the past, in the belief that a reprieve could be bought as usual. Their procurator, Jorge de Baeza, went to Madrid to remonstrate with Philip II, while their elder statesman, Francisco Núñez Muley, presented a memorandum to Deza, in which he protested their past and present loyalty in face of bitter persecution, and argued that from the religious point of view the morisco usages and traditions condemned by the edict were of a purely regional nature not incompatible with Christian doctrine, while economically trade would be disrupted and royal revenue would suffer if the edict were enforced. These arguments had proved successful in the past, especially with the more tolerant—or more penurious—administration of Charles V. But they had little effect on Philip II, who, as Deza informed Núñez Muley, 'valued religion more than revenue'.[19] He might have added that the political situation in the Mediterranean was no longer propitious for toleration.

Negotiations lasted for a year, and when the moriscos realised their futility, all the pent-up resentment they nurtured suddenly exploded, and they decided once more to revolt. The date they chose was Christmas Eve, 1568, and although the insurgents failed to raise the Albaicín they quickly spread the revolt in the mountains of the Alpujarras, between the Sierra Nevada and the coast. Indeed the revolt had its true base in the mountains. From there it spread to the plains, but not to all parts. It was essentially a rural movement and the towns were less committed, more integrated perhaps with Christian Spain. The leader of the moriscos, Fernando de Valor, was of old Arab stock, a descendant of the Caliphs of Córdoba;

[19] The memorial of Núñez Muley is printed by Garrad, *op. cit.*, pp. 204–26. For the reply of Deza see Luís del Marmol Carvajal, *Rebelión y Castigo de los Moriscos de Granada* (1606) (Biblioteca de Autores Españoles, Madrid, 1852), p. 166; this and Diego Hurtado de Mendoza, *Guerra de Granada* (B.A.E., Madrid, 1852) are the classical narrative sources of the rebellion and war.

reverting to his Arab name of Aben Omeyya, he was proclaimed king under an olive tree. A year later he was assassinated, and his cousin Aben Aboo became king in his place. Leaders such as Aben Daud, Aben Farax, and Aben Aboo were Granadine moriscos, but most of the others and especially the commanders in the field were from the mountains. The mountain chiefs came from the traditional social hierarchy of the moriscos and identified more easily with their cause, in contrast to the urban upper class which had become more integrated with the conquerers and less close to the morisco masses. In the social structure of the movement family solidarity counted for as much as economic or political calculation, and whole clans held together in support of the rebellion, or in loyalty to the crown. Beyond the economic and social motives, this was a minority fighting for its identity in an alien Spain. Families previously enemies came together in a common cause. The movement began with 4,000 insurgents in January 1569, rose to 30,000 at the height of mobilisation, and numbered 25,000 in the spring of 1570, of whom 4,000 were Turks and Berbers. These numbers, compared to a Christian force of 20,000 at its peak, testify to great participation among the morisco masses.[20]

The moriscos of Granada soon established contact with their allies in Valencia. And a number of missions were sent to North African countries, to Algiers and Tetuán, and also to Constantinople, seeking help and military support. From Algiers they received volunteers, munitions, and food supplies, Christian captives serving as payment. Algiers had a religious interest in the war of Granada, and the numerous arms gathered for the rebels were assembled in an Algerian mosque. But it also profited from it; while Spain was thus immobilised, Euldj Ali took Tunis in 1570. The Turks seized their opportunity too. The Sultan Selim II regarded the moriscos as allies within the enemy lines and he would have sent more arms and men if he had not had commitments elsewhere; his intervention was certainly envisaged in Madrid. But the Sultan preferred to use the occasion to pursue his immediate interests in the eastern Mediterranean, and although his fleet left port it was to attack Cyprus, not to help the moriscos.

Even without Turkish intervention, however, these were critical years for Spain. The government was caught unprepared in Granada. Although it had sanctioned the policy of its officials and the campaigns of the Inquisition, the last thing it seems to have considered was military preparedness. Indeed, the south of Spain had recently been stripped of regular troops in order to swell the *tercios* of the Duke of Alba in the Low Countries, where Philip II had an even greater rebellion on his hands. Consequently, Spain entered

---

[20] Domínguez Ortiz and Vincent, *op. cit.*, pp. 39–50.

the war of Granada at a time when her resources were stretched to the limit and her interests widely exposed. Then, during the first year of hostilities, she was paralysed by indecision over methods of campaigning. It was difficult to reach the rebels in their mountain fastnesses, and to cut off their allies along the coast; for although the Spanish galleys were alerted it was impossible to blockade the long coast-line of rebel territory with its innumerable coves and its accessibility to the ships of Algiers. In these circumstances the war became a long and confused process of patrols and ambushes, fought with a mutual savagery which was born of desperation among the moriscos and of weakness among the Spaniards. The *monfíes*—morisco brigands who roamed the Sierra Nevada in bands and terrorised whole districts even in peacetime—were fanatical Moslems who killed and tortured every priest they could catch. When the moriscos conquered Serón they killed 150 men and reduced 80 women to slavery. The Spaniards retaliated indiscriminately. On 3 February 1569 Francisco de Córdoba led 800 men in the assault of the rocky promontory of Inox, near Almería. The Christians made their way against a deluge of projectiles, and eventually broke the resistance of the moriscos, killing 400, taking 50 prisoners for the galleys, and reducing 2,700 women and children to slavery. A few days later the marquis of Mondéjar captured the fort of Guajar after a firece struggle and put to the sword everyone there, men and women. Morisco property was invariably taken as booty. It was only from January 1570 that the Spanish commander, Don John of Austria, impelled by fear of Moorish intervention from abroad, decided on a full-scale campaign with regular troops from Italy and eastern Spain in place of the Andalusian militia. This was combined with a policy of expulsion in the lowlands in order to cut off the mountain rebels from their supplies and accomplices. Following a decree of June 1569, 3,500 moriscos from the town of Granada were herded out of their homeland and dispersed throughout La Mancha. Starved of support, ruthlessly pursued, and in the final stages smoked out of their caves to a brutal death, the rebels in the mountains were crushed into submission in the course of 1570. The closing scene took place in a cave at Berchules, where Aben Aboo was stabbed to death by his own followers.

The revolt had lasted two years and strained the resources of the country to the utmost. The settlement, therefore, was bound to be hard. It was decided to deport all the moriscos of the kingdom of Granada, whether they had risen or not, inland to other parts of Spain. On 28 October 1570 orders were issued for the evacuation, and Don John fixed 1 November as the date of assembly; chained and fettered the moriscos were led in long convoys towards the towns and villages of Extremadura, Galicia, La Mancha, and Old Castile. Of the 80,000 deportees in 1569–71 not all reached their destination; the arduous winter journey took a heavy toll of life, and their ranks were depleted by at least 20 per cent. and perhaps 30 per cent. before the resettlement was completed.[21] A further 3–4,000 were deported in 1584–85. Even so, the expulsion was not total, and in 1587 about 10,000 moriscos were still living in Granada.

The problem of Granada seemed to be solved at last. To fill the vacuum caused by this immense migration, the empty lands were confiscated by the crown and offered on favourable terms, together with cattle and tools, to colonists recruited in Galicia, Asturias, and the regions of León and Burgos. Within a few years about 12,500 families came to find their New World in Granada and occupied 270 of the 400 villages and hamlets which had been abandoned. Yet the results were not completely successful. The crown itself made some profit out of the transaction: from confiscations and sales—to poor settlers, to magnates, to monasteries and churches—it received a substantial income.[22] But in Granada itself new problems were created and old ones revived. Among the lands offered, many were of poor quality, situated in the Alpujarras and other mountain districts, for the Old Christians already occupied the best *vegas* in the plains. Disappointed in their expectations, many of the new settlers were discouraged and left.[23] Of the villages still abandoned some were very small or had been burned during the fighting, but others lay in coastal districts which remained empty and uninhabited owing to the fear of corsairs. Consequently, although the Christian population of Granada was substantial and increasing, the Alpujarras and the neighbouring coastal district were much less peopled than they had been and thus continued to provide a problem of internal security. Moreover, many of the new immigrants, coming as they did from remote mountain villages in a region which had never been occupied by the Moors, were often scarcely more Christian than their morisco predecessors. An ecclesiastical historian of the seventeenth century notes that

> it is not surprising that the inhabitants of the Alpujarras have abandoned their ancient faith. Those who live in these mountains are Old Christians; they have not a drop of impure blood in their veins; they are subjects of a Catholic king; and yet, for want of teachers, and as a result of the oppressions to which they are subject, they are so ignorant of what they ought

---

[21] J. Caro Baroja, *Los moriscos del reino de Granada* (Madrid, 1957), pp. 57–85; Lapeyre, *Géographie de l'Espagne Morisque*, pp. 124–25; Domínguez Ortiz and Vincent, *op. cit.*, pp. 50–56.

[22] Merriman, *The Rise of the Spanish Empire*, iv. 95.

[23] See F. Oriol Catena, 'La repoblación del reino de Granada después de la expulsión de los moriscos', *Boletín de la Universidad de Granada*, vii. (1935), 305–31, 499–528.

to know to obtain eternal salvation, that they hardly retain a few vestiges of the Christian religion. Do you think that if today, which God forbid, the Infidels made themselves masters of their country, these people would long delay in abandoning their faith and embracing the beliefs of the conquerors?[24]

Without really solving anything in Granada, the policy of deportation only aggravated the morisco problem by extending it to the whole of Castile. Prolific, active, and resourceful, the Granadine moriscos were not welcome among their neighbours, and the task of assimilating them and making them Catholics and Spaniards was insuperable. Spanish opinion became increasingly hostile as it became more aware of their existence. One of Philip II's officials declared in 1588: 'We must count all the moriscos avowed enemies, both those originally in Castile and those recently dispersed from Granada . . . who are as Moorish as those in Africa.'[25] Later official opinion, after the reign of Philip II, considered the entire policy of dispersion an error of judgement: 'It was a great mistake to expel the moriscos of Castile from the Alpujarras; it would have been better to have kept them there under guard, at their own expense, rather than distribute them throughout the kingdom.'[26] For the next forty years they were a constant preoccupation of the government, as can be seen from the regular reports of their numbers and location demanded of *corregidores* and religious authorities. The intention had been to spread them thinly over a wide area. But they tended to leave their allotted districts, and their wandering urges made it difficult to keep track of them. Not all of the designated areas received their true quota: few reached Galicia and Old Castile, but New Castile, La Mancha and Andalucía had heavy intakes. Within these areas they gravitated towards the towns, where there were greater opportunities and perhaps less obvious restrictions. Many of them even made their way back to Granada, and there had to be a further minor expulsion in 1584. Hounded by the authorities and remembering their harsh treatment in 1570, the embittered Granadine moriscos became more recalcitrant as the years passed. Out of the frustration of their new life came criminal tendencies, and some of them joined outlaw gangs to live by robbery and violence. And ironically they still played on the nerves of the government, this time in a new context: from 1589 there were chronic, if irrational, fears of a rising in Andalucía in liaison with English invaders.

[24] Francisco Bermúdez de Pedraza, *Historia eclesiástica de Granada* (1637), quoted in A. Dozy, *Histoire des Musulmans d'Espagne* (4 vols., Leyde, 1861), ii. 45 n. 1.

[25] Boronat, *op. cit.*, i. 635.

[26] Duke of Lerma, 1608, *ibid.*, ii. 469.

And yet in the whole of Castile there were only about 80,000 moriscos out of a total population of about seven millions.[27] Why should an oppressed minority cause so much panic and resentment? The official reasons were not necessarily the most compelling ones. Churchmen, it is true, denounced their indifference to Christianity and their secret attachment to the ways of Islam; soldiers and officials were still preoccupied with possible insurrection and treason with external enemies. But public opinion was inflamed by more prosaic reasons than these. What most Spaniards resented in the moriscos was their sobriety, enterprise, avarice—and their increasing numbers. Cervantes, as usual, accurately reflected popular sentiments:

It would be a miracle to find among so many people even one who believes sincerely in the sacred Christian faith. Their sole aim is to coin money and then keep it, and in order to gain they work and do not eat. When a *real* enters into their possession, provided it be not a worthless one, they condemn it to perpetual imprisonment and eternal obscurity; so that always gaining and never spending, they accumulate the greater part of the money that there is in Spain. They are its money-bags, its moth, its magpies, and its weasels. They gather everything, they hide everything, and they swallow everything . . . There is no chastity among them, and neither men nor women enter the religious life. They all of them marry, they all multiply, because sober living augments the causes of generation. War does not consume them, nor any occupation overtask them. They rob us quietly and easily, and with the fruits of our inheritance which they resell to us they wax rich.[28]

To the mass of the population moriscos were odious because they evaded national responsibilities in religion and war, and quietly increased their numbers. Above all, they earned too much and spent too little. These allegations were not necessarily true; at least there is no statistical evidence that population growth among the moriscos was due to their evasion of national responsibilities. Moreover, their economic situation varied from region to region, and from group to group among themselves, for they too had their social structure. In Valencia and Aragon the moriscos were rural workers, many of them subject to seigneurial exactions, and most of them poor. The moriscos of Castile and those who managed to stay in Granada were better off and a few were affluent. Most of the moriscos of Castile were occupied not on the land but as small traders, artisans, and muleteers. These jobs were not highly regarded in Spain and not necessarily very remunerative.

[27] Lapeyre, *Géographie de l'Espagne Morisque*, p. 130.
[28] *Coloquio de los perros*, in *Novelas ejemplares*.

But the moriscos made them more profitable than they usually were; some of them acquired substantial fortunes and provoked a jealousy which was then extended to their entire community. They were also thought to corner vital supplies and charge high prices. Finally, they were content with a lower standard of living than the majority of Spaniards; as a report of the Inquisitor of Valencia noted in 1582, 'it is known from experience that a family of old Christians needs as much for its sustenance as two families of moriscos'.[29] Consequently, although the industry of the moriscos has been exaggerated and they were by no means the only workers in Spain, their resourcefulness was beyond doubt, and their survival was an affront to Spanish sensibilities.

And yet, in the final analysis, what made moriscos different from the rest of Spaniards was their religion. As the archbishop of Toledo declared, 'they are true Mohammedans, like those of Algiers'.[30] The accusation may have been intolerant, but it was also true. The moriscos remained unadapted and unadaptable. Spain, which began the modern period of its history by tolerating a large heterodox minority—a unique, though brief, record in the sixteenth century—ended by trying to force it into submission and finally admitted defeat. The policy of expulsion adopted in 1609 was a reflection of impotence.

3. THE DEFENCE OF THE MEDITERRANEAN

The morisco problem was only one aspect of the Spanish struggle with Islam. In the Mediterranean Spain was on the defensive against the combined power of the Ottoman empire and its allies in North Africa. Hence she had to maintain her scattered possessions in North Africa, to defend her own coasts and those of her Mediterranean dominions, to protect her commerce and shipping, and to contain the westward expansion of the Ottoman Turks. From his improvident father Philip II had inherited all these problems unresolved, together with a naval force unequal to its commitments.[31] At the time this was still the area where Spanish interests were most dangerously exposed. Consequently, for the first twenty years of his reign the main concern of Spanish foreign policy was not the problem of Protestantism nor relations with northern Europe, but defence and counter-attack against Islam in the Mediterranean.

The source of Moslem power was Turkey, and its leader Suleiman the

---

[29] Boronat, op. cit., i. 596.
[30] Quoted in Braudel, op. cit., p. 593. On the religion of the moriscos see P. Longás, Vida religiosa de los moriscos (Madrid, 1915).
[31] See above, pp. 79–80, 92–98.

Magnificent. The triple content of its policy—religious, imperial and economic expansion—was sustained by a powerful navy and the distinguished corps of Janissaries. Ideologically there was no hope of compromise, nor did Spain or Turkey wish for any. Indeed the Sultan was surrounded by extremists who wished to push his policy beyond the limits of realism: a group of Moslem fanatics in Constantinople led by Mohammed Sokoli was urging him to attack Spain itself, and in 1569 the revolutionaries of Granada were in contact with this group. But there were other pressures and influences in the Turkish capital. French, and later English, policy was represented there, as the European enemies of Spain sought political and commercial alliances. On Constantinople converged most of the elements hostile to Spain in the Mediterranean. Through the medium of international commerce, which found a meeting place there, quite a few merchants of Oriental origin but lately resident in the Iberian peninsula succeeded in gaining influence among the Turks. Fiercely anti-Spanish, they were usually animated by bitter hatred of Christendom. One of the most important of these was a wealthy Jewish merchant, Joseph Miques-Mendes, variously known as 'Leader of Israel' and Duke of Naxos, who had arrived in Constantinople via Venice about 1550. Friend and confidant of the Sultan—and his supplier of fine wines—he also tried to exert a political influence, evidence of which could be found in most of the Turkish plans of aggression, including that against Cyprus in 1570.[32]

Closer to Spain, Algiers formed in effect another Turkish state and one which was a direct threat to the Peninsula, as has already been seen. But although Algiers was the strongest of the Barbary states it was not the only one. East of the Maghreb, the 'kingdom' of Tripoli developed in the image of Algiers. As its interior was desperately poor, Tripoli had to live off the sea; therefore its struggle with Spain was a struggle for material survival in which the food supplies of the entire western Mediterranean were at stake. Spain had to fight to protect her shipping routes and her grain supplies from Sicily against a resourceful—and hungry—pirate state. From 1560 Barbary corsairs infested the whole of the western Mediterranean, operating in powerful squadrons which launched sudden and massive attacks.[33] In the summer of 1561 Dragut blockaded Naples with thirty-five vessels; on one occasion corsairs captured eight galleys in a single raid; in 1566 they seized twenty-eight Biscayan ships off Málaga; in one season alone they carried off fifty vessels in the straits of Gibraltar and on the Atlantic coasts of Andalucía and the Algarve; a raid into the interior of Granada yielded 4,000 captives. Between 1570 and 1620 the corsairs enjoyed a heyday. From bases in Algiers,

[32] Braudel, op. cit., p. 537.   [33] Ibid., 693–715.

Bizerta, Tripoli, Tetuán, and Larache, they intercepted galleons and carracks from the East and West Indies, raided the Canaries, played havoc round Barcelona, and struck repeatedly at vital Spanish communications in the Mediterranean, all in search of booty and the ransom money paid by rich captives or by Christian charitable agencies.

The Turks and the Barbary states were each a danger on their own, but combined they were almost irresistible. Fortunately for Spain the winter season kept them apart and broke up their concerted striking power, but during the summer they reinforced and supplemented each other and were capable of launching a massive offensive. In these circumstances it was urgent for Spain to rethink her defence policy. The resources of Charles V had been diverted to his interests in central Europe and elsewhere: in the Mediterranean his policy had been bankrupt of ideas; neglecting permanent naval power, he had used improvised forces in occasional and largely fruitless expeditions against the bases of Islam in North Africa. Lacking the continuity which naval power demands, Philip II had to begin almost from scratch. He thus started at a disadvantage, and the initiative remained for some years in the hands of the enemy. But under his direction and with a more far-seeing programme, Spanish policy acquired a new sense of urgency and much greater force. He began by giving priority to the Mediterranean, once he was free of the war with France. He then undertook to change traditional strategy. Dropping the policy of flamboyant and adventurous expeditions, he substituted a long-term programme of military and naval reform.[34] A bricks and mortar policy was applied to existing fortresses, such as Oran, in order to make them impregnable and thus render relief expeditions unnecessary. Above all, he began to lay the foundations of Spanish naval power by scouring the western Mediterranean for existing vessels and priming his own shipyards. But all this he had to learn by bitter experience in the early years of his reign.

Indeed, he made a false start and simply began where his father left off, by committing his forces to a premature offensive before his reform programme was really under way. On the ground that his newly won peace with France deprived the Turk of an ally and a port in the western Mediterranean, and anxious to strike at one of the chief bases of the corsairs, in June 1559 Philip authorised the use of his Italian galleys in an expedition against Tripoli. The latter had been captured for Islam by Dragut in 1551 and was regarded as important for the security of Spanish rule in Sicily and of her economic life-line in the Mediterranean. But to attack Tripoli was to

---

run the risk of provoking the Turk to hit back; Philip II took the risk because
he counted on the Turkish fleet being immobilised for distant operations
by loss of its ally, France; in doing so he made a serious miscalculation.
Worse still, and against his better judgement, he allowed the operation to
outgrow his original objective. His own intention had been to launch a
light and rapid raid while the season was good—the kind of operation the
corsairs themselves performed so adroitly. But the Duke of Medina Celi,
viceroy of Sicily, wished to lead a glorious expedition against the infidel,
.nd envisaged an old-fashioned operation on a larger and more ponderous
scale. Between the two, it took six months to assemble all the ships, troops,
and stores from Spain's various dominions—a classical example of the
difficulties of communications in the Spanish empire—and concentrate them
at Messina and Syracuse. By then the element of surprise had gone: Dragut
was ready, and so was the Turkish fleet. And as the unwieldy force, inexpertly
commanded on its naval side by Gian Andrea Doria, a shadow of his distinguished uncle, slowly made its long publicised way to Tripoli, they were
given yet further time to prepare their reply. For it was folly to sail in
December, and the weather forced the fleet to halt at Malta. Then, having
given Dragut the opportunity to escape from Djerba to Tripoli, the Spaniards
decided it would be easier to attack the former and thus take the island
instead of the town, gaining a base for further operations. The expeditionary
force disembarked on 7 March 1560 without incident. It thus placed itself
in an impossible position and revealed the error of judgement on which the
entire enterprise was based. It immediately became dependent on the sea
for supplies—at a time when Turkish naval supremacy was undisputed.
Piali Pasha proceeded to give Spain a lesson in naval warfare. With astonishing
speed he took the Turkish fleet out of Constantinople in April and attacked
on 12 May. Paralysed by indecision and handicapped by their inferior forces,
the Spanish commanders sacrificed everything to escape. In the ensuing
panic they lost forty-two out of their eighty vessels. Though Doria and
Medina Celi were among those who managed to slip away, thousands of
troops remained in the fort, besieged by the Turkish fleet. Philip II decided
to abandon them, arguing that they had longer supplies than the enemy.
But in fact they were at the mercy of the Turk, and water shortage forced
them to capitulate on 31 July. Spain thus lost 18,000 men, and the Turkish
fleet returned in triumph to Constantinople with its haul of ships and
prisoners.

Djerba was an utter disaster from which little was retrieved, an immense
blow to Spanish prestige and power, and a major victory to Islam in the
fight for control of the central Mediterranean. But it was also a lesson. It
was now clear to Philip II that he could not contain the Turk, or even hold

the coasts of his Mediterranean states, without a powerful naval force. From 1560 he began his programme of naval rearmament in the ports and docks of Sicily, Italy, and Catalonia.[35] Just after the peace of Cateau-Cambrésis Spain's Mediterranean fleet consisted of about ninety vessels, divided mainly between four squadrons of galleys—those of Spain, Naples, Sicily and the hired Genoese unit. Many of these were lost at Djerba, but between 1560 and 1564 the squadrons were remobilised and remanned. Italian shipyards responded quickly to the new demand, but this had to be paid for; in 1560 Philip II received a subsidy from the pope in the form of a tax on the Spanish clergy, in addition to the *cruzada*. As the defence of Christendom was also involved Philip II expected aid from his Italian allies—Savoy, Florence, and Genoa—as well as from Portugal, but they preferred to hire out their vessels, so these too had to be paid for. Consequently, he initiated a renewed effort by Spain herself. From 1561 production was revived in the shipyards of Barcelona, with the help of Genoese and Basque technicians. In December 1562 the cortes of Castile were specially convoked for an extraordinary subsidy to finance the naval programme.[36] The result of these efforts was that by September 1564 García de Toledo, commander-in-chief of the Mediterranean fleet, disposed of about 100 galleys between the coasts of Spain and Africa.

The inexplicable respite provided by the Turk in these years enabled Philip II to try out his new forces against the corsairs. The great Algerian offensive against Oran, one of the most important Spanish possessions, was repulsed after a siege which lasted two months (April–June 1563). The garrison was relieved and the squadron of Hassan Barbarossa decisively beaten. But more important than the victory was the way in which it was won. Profiting again from the lesson of Djerba, Philip II organised his relief action promptly and effectively. Co-ordinating his various resources, ordering the galleys from Italy, assembling them in Cartagena, dispatching them quickly, he overcame the tremendous obstacles of communication with an efficiency which belies the traditional picture of his slowness and caution. Thanks to his initiative, by 1564 Spain was able to take the offensive in the western Mediterranean, which he regarded as a minimum requirement, especially after the defeat of Djerba. For he had still not decided to measure himself with the Turk or hasten the great struggle into which he was later drawn.[37] In any case there were still defence gaps to be filled and defects of organisation to improve. In May 1565 the Turkish fleet suddenly arrived off Malta, the island of the Knights of St. John whom Suleiman had already

---

[35] Braudel, *op. cit.*, pp. 813–28.   [36] Duro, *Armada española*, ii. 49.
[37] Braudel, *op. cit.*, pp. 841–43.

expelled from Rhodes and Tripoli. It had been suspected for some time that his fleet would move westward, but its destination was uncertain; yet in spite of repeated warnings, those responsible for the defence of the island —the Spanish authorities and the Grand Master of the Knights—were taken unawares by the rapidity of the attack. The Knights defended their charge with spirit but could not prevent the Turk landing 25,000 troops and over-running the island. Confined to a few forts, the defenders resisted fierce Turkish onslaughts for almost four months, but by September they were near the end of their resources. Yet where was the relief force all this time? Philip II has been criticised for typical vacillation in an emergency. The Spanish response was certainly slow, but this must be measured against the obstacles of distance and organisation. García de Toledo was unwilling to improvise and commit his forces piecemeal against the Turk; he preferred to employ a single and powerful fleet in one blow. But this took time to assemble, and in these conditions Spanish machinery and the collaboration of Philip II and his commander stood the test remarkably well. This was proved by the result. García de Toledo took his relief force of Spanish infantry from Naples and Sicily and struck the Turks decisively: in a brief campaign they were routed from the island.

The years 1559 to 1565 were the last period of undisputed Turkish supremacy. The victory of Malta gave a new impetus to the Spanish revival. From 1565 the programme of naval reconstruction in Barcelona, Naples, and Sicily was intensified. Having temporarily blocked the Turkish route westward, Spain could now deal with the corsairs in isolation and assure some freedom of navigation. In 1566 Suleiman the Magnificent died, and the Ottoman empire passed into the weaker hands of Selim II. But if this was the beginning of the end for Turkey, Philip II showed no inclination to hasten the process. With rare discrimination he kept his policy to the strictest limits of defence and refused to anticipate his prospects. It must be said, also, that circumstances in the second half of the 1560's prevented him from giving his undivided attention to the Mediterranean, or from taking immediate advantage of his more favourable position there. From 1566 the Low Countries began to impinge more urgently on Spanish policy and to pull it towards the north. And once Philip II decided that the challenge to his authority there could only be met by force he put the full weight of Spanish military power behind his decision. But this involved stripping his Mediterranean defences of their best troops as well as diverting his financial resources, for the veteran *tercios* of Naples, Lombardy and Sicily formed the core of the Duke of Alba's army and were posted to Ghent, Liége and Brussels.[38] After this he had no alternative but to proceed with caution in

[38] *Ibid.*, p. 873.

the Mediterranean. It was the double charge on Spanish policy, and not the defects of personality which historians are so anxious to find in Philip II, that accounts for his apparent hesitancy. He did not have sufficient resources to perform both tasks thoroughly and quickly, or fulfil all the demands made on him. The pope was urging a league against the Turk, but distracted by the Low Countries and anxious not to provoke Protestant susceptibilities by a spectacular alliance at the very time he was moving a huge expeditionary force to northern Europe, Philip could not co-operate. At the same time he did not have a choice of alternatives—the Mediterranean or the Low Countries. Spain always had to fight the Turk, for she always had to defend herself. But an outright offensive against the infidel was a different matter —this was precluded by Spain's commitments in the Low Countries and the opportunity which these gave her enemies in northern Europe.

During 1567 and 1568, therefore, the Mediterranean became temporarily a secondary theatre of war, partly because of the new diversion and partly because the Sultan himself provided a brief respite. Selim II suffered heavy losses in the Hungary campaign of 1566, and in 1568 he signed an eight years' truce with the Emperor; perhaps he himself wanted to be free in order to prepare his impending attack on Venice and Cyprus. Spain was thankful for another breathing-space, especially as from 1569 she had a second revolt on her hands—in Granada. The Low Countries were already consuming troops and money, and this left Italy and Spain wide open to a Turkish fleet, which had an additional temptation—and bridge-head—in Granada. The years 1569–70, therefore, were years of crisis for Spain, perhaps her greatest crisis in the sixteenth century. The prospect of a crusade against Islam was remote indeed.

4. LEPANTO AND AFTER

In July 1570 a Turkish force landed on Cyprus, and on 9 September Nicosia fell. Cyprus was a Venetian possession, and with its sugar plantations and its salt mines, its cotton and wine production, it was a valuable one. So Venice was forced to rearm and start looking for allies. With his forces tied down in Granada and the Low Countries, Philip II's first thoughts were nearer home, and he began to improve his defences in Italy and North Africa. Then, pressed by the papacy as well as by Venice, he reluctantly ordered his fleet east in an attempt to save Cyprus. The Spanish vessels joined a hastily improvised force consisting of Venetian, Genoese, and papal units, which sailed in September 1570. It never reached its destination. Torn by distrust among the various nationalities, shaken by severe weather, and paralysed by news of further Turkish success in Cyprus, the fleet returned demoralised to its base.[39] The projected Christian alliance had received a serious setback.

Alone, Venice was helpless. She was a naval power to be reckoned with —though her reserve fleet was in dry dock—but she did not have the men or the provisions to fight a large-scale war with the Turk. Her interest, therefore, was to align with the west and make her local war a general one in which Christendom itself had a stake. On the other hand, Venice had more reason to come to terms with the Turk than to fight him, for she preferred to keep her trade routes open by commercial treaties with the Sultan. Her trading interests included not only the distribution of the silks, cottons, and spices of the Far East, which she picked up in Alexandria and the ports of Syria and Asia Minor, but also the provision of her own vital grain supplies. For her national territory was insufficient to feed her large population, and rather than rely on rival states in Italy she procured her cereals from southern Russia or the Balkans; the Turk was thus in a position to cut her commercial life-line and threaten her with famine. For these reasons Venice traditionally avoided anti-Turkish coalitions and naturally fought shy of Spain. Indeed, she usually wanted the best of both worlds—an understanding with the Turk in good times, and the protection of the west, which meant Spain, in times of emergency. And from any alliance she usually defected as quickly as possible. In 1570, however, she could hardly remain aloof, sheltering under the cover of the two great rivals, when one of them had begun to attack her.

Now that she wanted a Spanish alliance, Venice found it difficult to get. The realism and absence of crusading spirit in Philip II's policy has already been noticed. He had never officially withdrawn from the endless war with the Turk, for he continued to receive the precious subsidies from Rome, but he had shown his readiness to accept a tacit *détente* and his unwillingness to indulge in speculative offensives. In this he was supported by his ministers; when news from Cyprus first arrived Cardinal Granvelle, who represented Philip II in Rome, advised the king against giving any assistance to Venice. In fact there would have been a stalemate, with each party looking to its own interest, had not the pope brought them together and persuaded them into commitment.

Pius V was an enigma to Philip II and his ministers. Political popes they understood, but a saint confounded them. Various features mingled in the vigorous personality of the seventy-three-year-old Dominican.[41] A deeply

---

[39] L. Serrano, *La Liga de Lepanto entre España, Venecia y la Santa Sede, 1570–1573* (2 vols., Madrid, 1918–20), i. 68–84.

[40] Braudel, *op. cit.*, pp. 916–32.

[41] For an estimate of Pius V see Serrano, *op. cit.*, i. 31–33.

spiritual man, a theologian, simple and politically inexperienced, he refused to admit that 'reasons of state' should decide political and religious affairs. Having fought heresy in Italy as Grand Inquisitor and reformed the church in Rome itself, he then projected his religious feelings into plans of crusade against Protestantism and Islam, to be sanctioned by armed force wielded by a Christian league. The pope who excommunicated Elizabeth I was unlikely to be deterred, or impressed, by the national interests of Spain and Venice. He refused to consider the commercial calculations with which Venice was preoccupied, and the diverse commitments of Philip II meant nothing to him. But although he fought the Spanish king bitterly over ecclesiastical jurisdiction, he had long admitted that he was the only ruler on whom he could rely for a league against Islam. Neither the king of France, who had pro-Turkish ties, nor the emperor Maximilian II, who had an uneasy truce with the Sultan, would listen to his pleas. He therefore concentrated on Spain, offering renewed subsidies to Philip II, and sending his representative, Luís de Torres, to open negotiations. Meanwhile, he himself began to organise a papal fleet.

The negotiations were slow, for Pius V was demanding not mere assistance for the immediate occasion but a general league against the Turk with massive striking power. 'It is clear', said the instructions of Torres, to be repeated to Philip II, 'that one of the principal reasons which has driven the Turk to break with the Venetians is that he believes he will find them alone, without hope of allying themselves with Your Majesty, occupied as he is with the Moors of Granada and unable to cope with both.'[42]

Certainly the Sultan had counted on the diversion in Granada to protect him from Philip II. But here he had miscalculated: one of the reasons why Spain finally accepted the project of a league was because her passions had been roused by the revival of the old struggle with Islam in the Peninsula itself. Political and financial considerations, of course, also played their part. As the pope himself argued, the frontier defences of Venice in the Mediterranean were ultimately those of Spain herself, and a league would give Philip II the services of the fleet, the men, and the arms of his ally. Moreover, the unrenewed *cruzada*—a loss of 400,000 ducats a year to the Spanish king— was now conceded by the pope, and this was the kind of argument which Philip II appreciated. For all these reasons he gave his agreement in principle eight days after Torres had rehearsed his lengthy arguments. The decision was one of the most difficult he ever made, but he himself was not unaware of the favourable circumstances in the years 1570–71 which suddenly—and

---

[42] *Ibid.*, i. 53; on the mission of Torres see also L. Pastor, *History of the Popes from the close of the Middle Ages*, xviii. 369–73.

exceptionally—enabled him to engage Spain up to the hilt in a single objective. At last the Low Countries seemed firmly held under the iron rule of the Duke of Alba; England had internal distractions of her own in the northern rebellion of 1569, followed shortly by the Ridolfi plot. Philip II quickly seized this momentary respite in the west to strike a blow at his enemy in the east.

Even so there were many setbacks before the final alliance was signed on 20 May 1571.[43] The negotiations were so complicated by mutual distrust among the various parties that it seemed unlikely they would ever be concluded. Venice as usual proved difficult: in spite of her official denials she twice tried to come to an understanding with the Turk, and only gave her consent to the league when she was convinced that there was nothing to be hoped for from Constantinople.[44] The conclusion of the treaty, therefore, and its solemn proclamation in St. Peter's on 25 May were a personal triumph of the pope. Its sanction, on the other hand, depended mainly on the power of Spain. For this was not simply a temporary arrangement for Cyprus but a military alliance for three years against Islam itself; and although it was directed in the first instance against the Levant, it did not exclude eventual expeditions against the North African states of Algiers, Tunis, and Tripoli. By the terms of the agreement, the three allies—Spain, Venice, and the papacy—engaged to assemble by the 1 April each year a force of 200 galleys, 100 sailing ships, 50,000 troops and 4,500 light cavalry, the expenses of which were to be shared in the proportion of three parts by Spain, two by Venice, and one by the papacy. Spain thus bore the greater burden, but her contribution was decisive in more than military supplies. For these vast forces had to be fed, and Venice herself to be sustained while her supply lines from the east were cut. Philip II undertook to open his Italian markets to Venice and to protect her against a price rise by selling at cut rates and without heavy export taxes. This was one of the most vital provisions of the treaty: without Spanish grain supplies the future campaign would have been impossible.

The commander-in-chief of the forces of the league was the Spanish captain-general, Don John of Austria, fresh from his recent victory over Islam in Granada. Sensitive to the condition of his birth and embittered by his inferior status, Don John had long resented an imagined victimisation at the hands of his royal brother. Now, at the age of twenty-four, his passion for action and a supreme command seemed about to be satisfied. Yet in spite of desiring his appointment, Philip II could not overcome a permanent

---

[43] On the protracted and frustrating negotiations see Serrano, *op. cit.*, i. 85–101, and Pastor, *op. cit.*, xviii. 385–406.

[44] Braudel, *op. cit.*, 924–25. Even after signing the league Venice was ready at least to listen to French offers of mediation with the Turk, *ibid.*, p. 931.

suspicion of his half-brother's youth and judgement. Ever since he had given him his first public office as commander-in-chief of the Spanish navy on the retirement of García de Toledo in 1568, and throughout the war of Granada, he had kept him under the tutelage of the Catalan magnate Luis de Requesens, his former ambassador in Rome and future governor in the Low Countries. Requesens, intelligent and broad-minded, was one of the most distinguished Spanish administrators in the sixteenth century, but he was a thorn in the side of Don John. And so he continued even in 1571. By the terms of his instructions from Philip II, Don John was assigned a large council with powers too absolute for his liking; within this, a smaller council consisting of Requesens, Gian Andrea Doria, the Marquis of Santa Cruz and Juan de Cardona, had the right to guide him in all his actions.[45] Moreover, Requesens was posted permanently to his galley as a kind of censor, and through his hands all orders and correspondence had to pass before they were signed by the younger man. Frustrated by these restrictions, Don John was soon beset by disagreements over strategy among the allied advisers. According to his instructions he was to lead the forces of the league to the Levant as quickly as possible in order to give battle to the enemy on every occasion that offered; but he was not to expose the fleet without near certainty of victory, and he was to return from the Levant at the beginning of autumn. Here different interpretations were possible: Don John's own instinct was for immediate action, but some of his advisers, including Doria, favoured a cautious and defensive policy on the grounds that the season was too late; while the Venetian and papal commanders, furious at the delay, were blaming the Spaniards for it.

Don John left Madrid on 6 June for the assembly point at Messina, collecting on the way the various units of the Spanish contingent and calling at Naples for the papal blessing and the consecrated banner of the league. In spite of allied criticism, he and the Spanish galleys did in fact arrive on time—23 August—and even before the arrival of the full Venetian complement. And their presence immediately raised the morale of the allied forces and gave them some unity. Don John himself made a good impression from the start, and his relations with his immediate subordinates, the commanders of the Venetian and papal fleets, Veneiro and Colonna, were excellent. His drive and personality forged the collection of disparate and squabbling units into a homogeneous whole. Seeing the Venetian galleys short of troops, he had the initiative—and the courage—to make them take 4,000 Spanish and

---

[45] Instructions of 26 June 1571, Serrano, *op. cit.*, i. 107–8; for additional instructions and an example of conflict between Don John and Requesens see M. Fernández de Navarrete, etc., eds., *Colección de documentos inéditos para la historia de España*, iii. 187–91, 194.

Italian veterans from Philip II's forces.[46] By distributing his resources in this way he improved the quality of the entire fleet, and made its units more mobile and interchangeable. Finally, he imposed his own decision—to search out the enemy and destroy him.

The Turkish fleet, commanded by Ali Pasha, had been at action stations since the beginning of the season, when almost 200 galleys were distributed between Negrepont, their supply base, and Cyprus. Reinforced with thirty vessels of Euldj Ali of Algiers, it proceeded west, and now it made its first mistake. Unable to resist the temptation of looting in the Adriatic, it dissipated the months from June to August in petty actions which tired its forces and did not even prevent the Venetian fleet from making a break and joining the allies. So the Turks entered battle after a weary summer and past the peak of their form. The lateness of the season thus became an asset to the league and one which Don John was wise to seize. The Christian fleet left Messina on 16 September and made first for Corfu. There it learnt that Famagusta, the last Venetian stronghold in Cyprus, had fallen, and that the Turkish fleet was in the Gulf of Lepanto. Don John decided the time had come to risk all.

The two fleets, searching for each other, suddenly met at sunrise on 7 October 1571 at the entrance to the Gulf of Lepanto, where the Christian fleet managed to contain the enemy.[47] Face to face over some five miles of sea, Christians and Moslems could count at last the other's forces: 230 Turkish galleys confronted 208 Christian, though the latter were equipped with greater firing power and contained the well-armed Spanish infantry.[48] Don John, following contemporary tactics, advanced his six Venetian galleons to form a vanguard of heavy firing power; behind it he divided his galley fleet into four squadrons in line of battle, the left under the Venetian admiral Barbarigo, the right under Doria, and the centre under the commander-in-chief himself, with the fourth squadron under Santa Cruz forming a rearguard. The Turkish galleys were similarly disposed. About noon the wind dropped, and under a burning sun and cloudless sky, with a mutual hoisting of sacred banners, battle was joined. The Turks tried to outflank the enemy at both ends of the line. On the right Doria was outmanoeuvred and lured into extending his line to the extreme wing; he thus left a gap in the centre and was drawn further and further

[46] Serrano, *op. cit.*, i. 114–15.

[47] On the battle of Lepanto see Serrano, *op. cit.*, i. 124–42; the same author's *España en Lepanto* (Madrid, 1935); Anderson, *op. cit.*, 36–46; Sir William Stirling-Maxwell *Don John of Austria* (2 vols., London, 1883), i. 402–27, ii. App. 6; and a series of contemporary accounts in *Colección de documentos inéditos para la historia de España*, iii. 184–360.

[48] Serrano, *La Liga de Lepanto*, i. 119–20.

away from the main action, to which he contributed little. On the left the Venetians kept their position and stood up to superior forces more successfully, in spite of the loss of their leader Barbarigo. In the centre Don John's galley with its 300 Spanish veterans made straight for the flagship of Ali Pasha and its 400 Janissaries. As other galleys closed and grappled with the enemy, the battle became a series of fierce and bloody struggles between small groups of infantry, and the carnage mounted. The death of Ali Pasha, whose galley the soldiers of Don John and Colonna carried by storm, decided the conflict about 4 o'clock in the afternoon. The allied victory was overwhelming. Only thirty-five Turkish galleys escaped; the rest were captured or sunk, with losses of 30,000 killed or wounded and 3,000 prisoners; 117 Turkish galleys and six galiots were shared among the victors. But the victory was dearly bought, for the allies lost twelve galleys, 9,000 dead and 21,000 wounded. It was probably true that the sea suddenly appeared to the combatants to flow red with human blood.

Lepanto was an outstanding feat of technique and courage. The leadership of Don John, the counsel of Requesens, the powerful fire of the Venetian galleons, the excellence of the Spanish infantry, the skilful manoeuvring of the Spanish galleys, all combined to crush the Turk and give joy to Christendom. But what had the battle decided? Because of its own losses and the lateness of the season the allied fleet had to return to Italy. The Ottoman empire, with its powerful military machine and its long tentacles by land, was untouched. Cyprus remained under Turkish rule. The Sultan replaced his losses with astonishing rapidity, so that within a year he had a fleet of 220 vessels at sea again. And the North African pirates were still at large. Nevertheless, Lepanto was not a victory without a result.[49] The spell of Turkish power was broken. Christendom had won at last a moral breakthrough, and freed itself of an old sense of inferiority. Cervantes, who was wounded in the battle, spoke in Don Quixote of 'that day, which was so happy for Christendom, because all the world then learned how mistaken it had been in believing that the Turks were invincible at sea'. Lepanto marked the end of a period, the end of Turkish supremacy. More immediately, the Christian galleys received an immense reinforcement of manpower in the form of prisoners-of-war, while the Turkish fleet was stopped from rampaging with impunity in the central Mediterranean, where Italy itself could have been attacked. This shock to their confidence, among other reasons, made the Turks less ready to commit themselves westwards, and the subsequent disengagement was the worst possible disaster for their fleet—it began to rot in the ports from inactivity.

[49] For a discussion of the consequences of Lepanto see Braudel, *op. cit.*, 922–44.

But these developments were in the future. Fot the moment the allies had their troubles too. National interests, and the mutual distrust to which they gave rise, precluded any possibility of a crusade against Islam. It soon became clear that the allies would only co-operate when their own interests happened to coincide; both Venice and Spain wanted to use the league for their own purposes, Venice in the Levant and Spain in North Africa, and only the pope continued to speak of the interests of Christendom. Under his inspiration another and bigger fleet was assembled at Messina in the spring of 1572 to take further action against the Turk in the Levant. But after the death of Pius V (1 May 1572), Philip II made a complete *volte-face* and ordered Don John to suspend the departure of his galleys.[50] In the ensuing uproar he tried to argue his way out of the charges of treachery hurled at him by his allies. The official reasons he gave for his action were the death of the pope and fear of an imminent rupture with France. But the real reason was his unwillingness to divert the resources of Spain to serve Venetian interests in the eastern Mediterranean. He preferred to strike at Islam where the blow would be most useful to Spain—at Algiers, an enemy outpost, its western base for war and piracy, the point of departure for attacks on Spain and her dependencies. As he explained to his ambassador in Rome, he wanted 'to gain some benefit for my own subjects and states from this league and all its expenses, rather than employ them in so risky an undertaking as a distant expedition in the Levant'.[51] For the pope's benefit his ambassador was to mention his commitments in the Netherlands and his fear of French and English intervention, but not to breathe a word of Algiers.

Yet no one was deceived: the allies saw through his excuses and Spanish concern for Algiers was so well known that his officials dared not mention it. From the entire allied camp, not only from the Venetians and Gregory XIII, but also from Granvelle, Requesens, and Don John, who had taken the cause of the league to heart, came a barrage of protests. He was told that his action would immediately drive Venice to treat with the Turk, and that the new pope had at his disposal the major portion of the Spanish war budget in the Mediterranean, the *excusado* and the *subsidio*.[52] Philip II bowed before the storm and returned to his initial position in the league. He agreed to an expedition to the Morea in 1572, with a reluctance which was soon justified. The operation took the form of a campaign along the wide stretch of coast between the Gulf of Corinth and Cape Matapan on the western side of the Morea, a strange theatre of war with few convenient bases for

---

[50] Instructions of 17 May 1572, Serrano, *op. cit.*, i. 213–31, 194–95.
[51] Philip II to Juan de Zúñiga, 2 June 1572, *ibid.*, i. 305–09.
[52] *Ibid.*, ii. 7–58; for the Navarino campaign see *ibid.*, ii. 90–150.

the allies.[50] They had counted on a rising of the local population, without, however, doing anything to prepare it; when they arrived there was not even a sign of revolt. They then began another search for the Turkish navy. The latter had been replaced with an immense effort, but it had no intention of risking another Lepanto. Consequently, as the enemy kept aloof and refused combat, the forces of the league had no alternative but to return to Italy, with nothing to show for a costly campaign.

The root of the league's trouble lay in the fact that the distances of the Mediterranean were too vast to allow it to sustain a naval war in the Levant. And out of frustration came dissension. Venice in particular was beginning to feel the strain, as her commerce was crippled and her finances were exhausted. With nothing to show for her efforts—Cyprus was unrecovered —and convinced that she was being exploited by Spain, she opened negotiations with the Turk and abandoned the league on 7 March 1573.[53] The news was received with some bitterness in Spain, but Philip II kept his head and behaved with his usual calmness. Indeed, the defection of Venice was a blessing in disguise. Spain still possessed a powerful fleet which could be usefully employed on more limited, and more national, objectives. Reverting to an African policy, Philip II decided to attack Tunis. It was his last big mistake in the Mediterranean. Don John took Tunis without difficulty on 11 October 1573, appointed a native governor, left a garrison, and returned to Naples. But it was hardly a victory: the operation did not touch the interior of the country and the base itself was difficult and expensive to hold and supply. While the Spaniards were still making up their minds what to do with it, and were torn between the expansive ideas of Don John and the prudence of his king, the Turkish fleet attacked in July 1574. The Spanish garrison capitulated (13 September), while Don John, waiting for instructions from Spain and disillusioned to the point of lethargy, was too late to do anything except return to Spain to consult with his brother.

Only three years after Lepanto the Turks had demonstrated once again the strength of their fleet and the quickness of their striking power, and Philip II had to look once more to his defences in the Mediterranean. Yet Tunis was the last great Turkish victory before decline. It was followed by a period in which both powers were glad to disengage. Distracted by his interests in Persia and finding the Moors of North Africa no longer the enthusiastic collaborators they had been in the past, the Sultan was forced to restrict his ambitions. For his part Philip II had too much on his hands in the Low Countries and too little money in his treasury to take advantage of his enemy's difficulties and continue the offensive. Indeed, the Mediterranean

[53] *Ibid.*, ii. 285–312.

was too big a battlefield, and exceeded the resources of both powers; consequently the withdrawal was mutual and eventually brought a halt to the
old conflict. To this extent Philip II's policy of disengagement had more
justification than the ambitious policy of Don John. The restraint that he
exercised on his brother was not a question of jealousy, suspicion, and
excessive caution: unlike Don John, who was obsessed by his own projects,
the king could see the whole picture, and he realised that the momentary
respite which had made Lepanto possible could not last indefinitely. Philip II
was never in a position to strike more than one blow at a time or to give
himself and his resources to a single task. He accepted these limitations and
his realism was an asset to Spain; he did not lose his head in the wild schemes
which were projected after Lepanto, and unlike his father and his brother
he was not disturbed by dreams of crusades. Moreover, the policy of peace
was the most ruinous one possible for the Turk; for the resultant inaction
killed the Turkish navy by ruining its ships and depriving its seamen of
experience. What Lepanto had failed to complete, peace achieved in a few
years.

Spain already had its spies and its intelligence service penetrating the
Ottoman empire, and the Spanish authorities were constantly importuned
by suitors of one kind or another—renegades trying to win their way
back to grace, former captives posing as specialists in the Levant, Knights
of Malta, imperial envoys. After 1573 these informants increased their efforts,
hoping for returns from a policy of peace.[54] It was 1577, however, before
authentic contact was made, when Martín de Acuña—another adventurer
—brought back the first truce from Constantinople. In the following year
Giovanni Margliani, a Milanese who had been ransomed after his capture
at Tunis in 1574, took over the negotiations and raised them from their
picaresque beginnings to a more serious, though still discreet, level. But the
Spaniards would never treat with what they called 'those Turkish dogs' in
formal diplomacy, for the scandal, loss of face, and possible humiliation
were too much to endure. The Turks on the other hand were reluctant to
negotiate with anything less than an embassy, but they agreed to a year's
truce in 1578, then another in 1580, and finally to one of three years in 1581.
This marked a new stage in Spain's external relations with Islam: since the
advent of Philip II she had never been crusading, now she was clearly
opportunist. After the mission of Margliani a recognised peace was in
operation, for the truce of 1581 seems to have been renewed in 1584 and
again in 1587. And when hostilities broke out again in the 1590's it was
largely a question of bluff and counter-bluff. To interpret the *détente* with

[54] On the truces and their negotiation see Braudel, *op. cit.*, pp. 984–1008, 1074–84.

the Turk as the end of the religious spirit in Spanish policy is to miss the point of the latter. Political as well as religious interests had infused the foreign policy of Philip II from the earliest years of his reign, as they had that of his predecessors. After 1580 his political—and religious—objectives were turned elsewhere, and the power which had been directed against the Turk now had to confront more dangerous enemies in northern Europe.

Meanwhile, the face of the Mediterranean was changing. From the 1580's the northern maritime countries began to penetrate the Straits of Gibraltar in increasing numbers and to make a challenge for a share of eastern commerce. The periodic shortages of grain suffered by Spain and other Mediterranean countries—particularly acute from 1586 to 1590—gave them their card of entry and opened the area to Dutch and English shipping. But England was interested in more than the grain trade with Christendom. From about 1578, and especially from 1581 when the Levant Company was formed, her agents were negotiating commercial 'capitulations' with the Turk and establishing a trade in Mediterranean and eastern products in exchange for textiles, tin, and lead.[55] Bernardino de Mendoza, the Spanish ambassador in London, was particularly interested in this trade, and in November 1579 he reported his observations to Philip II:

> The Turks are also desirous of friendship with the English on account of the tin which has been sent there for the last few years, and which is of the greatest value to them, as they cannot cast their guns without it, while the English make a tremendous profit on the article, by means of which alone they maintain their trade with the Levant. . . . As this sending tin to the infidel is against the apostolic communion, and your Majesty has ordered that no such voyage shall be allowed to pass the Messina light to the prejudice of God and Christianity, I advise the viceroy of Sicily of the sailing of these ships. . . .[56]

Spain hotly disputed English trade because it was a means of supplying war materials to the national enemy and the enemy of Christendom. But Elizabeth I was not averse from a political understanding with the Turk, especially in 1580, the year of the first English 'capitulation', when the question of the Portuguese succession was imminent and began to threaten the balance of power in the Atlantic. An understanding with the Turk

---

[55] Ibid., 165–67, 469–502; on English shipping in the Mediterranean and Levant see also Sir Godfrey Fisher, *Barbary Legend. War, Trade and Piracy in North Africa, 1415–1830* (Oxford, 1957), pp. 111–36.

[56] Mendoza to Philip II, 28 November 1579, *Colección de documentos inéditos para la historia de España*, xci. 439–40.

would be a means of striking at Spain without actually declaring war.[57] In November 1582 Elizabeth signed the commission of her first ambassador to the Sultan, William Harborne, who was to be an assiduous advocate of the English cause, commercial and political. Commercially, the prospects of England were good, owing to the excellence of her ships, the low price of her textiles, and the quality of her organisation, which was perfected by a system of convoys from 1591 as protection against Spanish patrols. But there was a political objective too, and an intelligence service, and this became increasingly active throughout the 1580's when the Spanish Armada was being prepared. Elizabeth sought an alliance with the Turk, using the argument that Protestants and Moslems were alike haters of the 'idolatries' practised by the king of Spain; in particular she wanted the Sultan to send a fleet to attack Spain in the Mediterranean, as a diversionary blow at the impending Spanish offensive on England. Politically, however, England had come to the Mediterranean too late. Elizabeth's approach to the Ottoman empire coincided not with the period of its greatest power and aggression but with that of its retreat and decline, when its reasons for attacking Spain were less urgent and its truces more frequent. For this reason the English overtures were unsuccessful, both before and after the Armada. Politically, the Mediterranean had been neutralised; Spain's battlefield was now the Atlantic.

[57] See E. Pears, 'The Spanish Armada and the Ottoman Porte', *English Historical Review*, viii. (1893), 439–66; H. G. Rawlinson, 'The Embassy of William Harborne to Constantinople, 1583–8', *Transactions of the Royal Historical Society*, 4th series, v. (1922), pp. 1–27; *C.S.P. Venetian* (London, 1894–97), viii.; Braudel, *op. cit.*, pp. 489, 1075.

CHAPTER VIII

SPAIN AND THE COUNTER-REFORMATION

1. The Campaign for Uniformity

THE liquidation of the war with Islam was a response to mounting pressure from northern Europe. Here, too, religious passions were roused: the rebellion in the Low Countries and the hostility of England were an affront to the Catholic sensibilities of Spaniards as well as a blow to their political and economic interests. Yet Spain, 'the scourge of heretics, the light of Trent, the sword of Rome, the cradle of St. Ignatius', was no more a crusader against Protestantism than she was against Islam.[1] To view her as the champion of the Counter-Reformation is to ignore the secular content of her foreign policy, her adverse relations with the papacy, and her own religious development in the sixteenth century. It is also to distort the character of the Counter-Reformation itself. Spain, as has been seen, had led the way in church reform even before the advent of Luther, and had subsequently embraced the cause of Erasmus with enthusiasm.[2] By the 1540's, however, the Erasmists had been scattered, the Inquisition was increasing its vigilance, and the conciliatory approach to religious problems was becoming more difficult to maintain.

Between 1556, the year of Charles V's retirement to Yuste, and 1563, when the Council of Trent finally ended its deliberations, the climate of religious opinion in Spain underwent yet a further change. The Spanish Inquisition was now in different and harsher hands: Hernando de Valdés, archbishop of Seville and Inquisitor general from 1547 to 1566, reinforced his implacable hatred of heresy with a personal ambition to make himself indispensable to the crown by successful campaigns in defence of orthodoxy. His theological adviser was the Dominican, Melchor Cano, whose profound scholarship and elegance of style made him one of the most distinguished theologians of his time, but whose reaction to heresy was so sensitive that he could hardly distinguish mysticism from Illuminism, and when in doubt was guided by his own relentless formula: 'There are propositions which, without overturning the edifice of the faith, shake it.'[3] The ecclesiastical authorities were now working more closely with the state, and this was

[1] The description is that of Menéndez Pelayo.
[2] See above, pp. 64–73.   [3] Bataillon, *Erasme et l'Espagne*, p. 768.

under the direction of Philip II, who returned to the peninsula from the Low Countries in 1559. Yet the growing tension was caused not by personalities in Spain itself, much less by the policy of Philip II, the so-called champion of the Counter-Reformation. Conditions themselves had changed. The old generation of Spanish humanists had gone. After the peace of Augsburg Charles V had renounced his efforts to arbitrate between Rome and the German Protestants, while in Rome itself the dreams of reconciliation held by humanist reformers had yielded to the firmer—and more realistic—policy of the papacy. For the facts were now against conciliation. Protestantism had advanced to unassailable positions: in Germany and England it was organising itself into national churches, and in France it was growing in power. While attitudes were hardening all over Europe, a new and more intransigent element had entered the situation. Militant Calvinism, efficiently organised and operating from its headquarters in Geneva, was sending out its missionaries and its propaganda. And Calvinism could hardly be approached with an olive branch. The Spanish authorities were soon aware of its existence, not only because of its penetration into the Low Countries but also because its presses were turning out literature for Spain itself. For the first time heterodoxy in the peninsula seemed closely related to international Protestantism, at the very time when the latter was organising its churches; as Spanish dissenters made their way to Geneva, Paris, and the Low Countries, the Inquisition began more searching inquiries into the possible contacts they had left behind.

In these circumstances, Philip II could not renew the initiative taken by his father, even if he had wanted to. The only possible policy seemed to be to strengthen his religious defences. A law of censorship had existed since 1502; by decree of 7 September 1558 this was given more ruthless sanction when the importation of books without royal licence was made a crime punishable by death and confiscation of property.[4] Meanwhile, the list of prohibited books had been growing steadily longer. The University of Louvain prepared the first Index of prohibited books in 1546, and on the basis of this the Spanish Inquisition published its own in 1551–52, to be distinguished from the Roman Index which was first published by Paul IV in 1558 and which was not accepted as binding in Spain. The Index was periodically revised, and extended, so that by 1583 it not only proscribed the works of all known heretics but also included the names of many who had distinguished themselves in the service of the Catholic church, such as Thomas More and John Fisher, Fray Luis de Granada and Juan de Avila, on the grounds that some of their works had been so written that they could

---

[4] On the Spanish censorship see A. Rumeu de Armas, *Historia de la censura literaria gubernativa en España* (Madrid, 1940).

be misused and misinterpreted. The Prohibitory Index of 1583, prepared by Inquisitor general Quiroga, was followed by an Expurgatory one in 1584, the first of its kind in Spain, giving the expurgations necessary to make acceptable the books enumerated, rather than condemn them outright; here Erasmus outstripped all other entries.[5] According to the rules of the Inquisition all manuscripts and books needed a licence from its secretary before they could be published, and all bookshops and libraries were subject to search. The gradual extension of censorship was accompanied by other measures designed to strengthen the intellectual barriers between Spain and Protestantism. When Philip II decided to return to Spain in July 1559 he was reluctant to leave any of his Spanish subjects behind in the Low Countries exposed to contamination; he therefore notified all Spaniards studying at the University of Louvain to return to Spain within four months and to check with the Inquisition for clearance when they did return.[6] Then, by decree of 22 November 1559, he forbade all Spaniards to study in foreign universities.

In the eyes of the authorities these measures were justified not only by the potential danger of Protestantism in Spain but by its actual existence; religious peace had been shattered by the new religion itself. In the 1550's a group of Lutherans was discovered at Valladolid and another in Seville. It would be inaccurate to describe these as 'Protestant communities', as is sometimes done, for they were hardly organised churches and looked more like conventicles of Illuminists such as had alarmed the Inquisition in 1525. Nevertheless, their doctrines had close affinities with those of Protestantism —justification by faith alone, denial of purgatory and of the value of the sacraments and good works, rejection of confession and of papal authority. And it is conceivable that without the investigations of the Inquisition they might have become authentic Protestant sects, especially as their leaders were not obscure enthusiasts like those of the Illuminists but men of some standing in civil and ecclesiastical society. The inspirer of the Valladolid group was probably Carlos de Seso, a layman who had absorbed some of the new doctrines in his native Italy and brought them with him to Spain about 1550. But its most distinguished member was Dr. Agustín de Cazalla, a canon of Salamanca, who had been appointed court chaplain in 1542 and had spent nine years in Germany and the Low Countries in the emperor's household, afterwards returning to Spain.[7] Cazalla's travels in northern Europe and subsequent contact with Seso were probably less important in

---

[5] Boyd, *Cardinal Quiroga*, pp. 72–74; see also M. de la Pinta Llorente, 'Historia interna de los índices expurgatorios españoles', *Hispania* xiv. (1954), 411–61.

[6] Bataillon, *op. cit.*, p. 764.

[7] See Menéndez Pelayo, *Heterodoxos*, iii. 395–418; Bataillon, *op. cit.*, pp. 750–54.

his religious development than his own process of thought; in any case he was a celebrated preacher and one not given to hiding his reforming views, and soon he was denounced to the Inquisition for alleged heretical doctrines not only on Justification but also on Purgatory and other matters. With him were compromised his whole family, Fray Domingo de Rojas, member of the Dominican community of San Esteban and son of the Marquis of Poza, Antonio de Herrezuela, a lawyer of Toro, the religious of the monastery of Belen, and a number of aristocratic adherents. By the time the Inquisition began to act the movement had offshoots in Zamora, Palencia, Toro, and Logroño.

When the news from Valladolid became known, Charles V was already in retirement at Yuste and Philip II was in the Low Countries. Charles immediately wrote to the Regent, his daughter Joanna, urging a policy of quick and ruthless repression: 'It must be seen whether they can be prosecuted for sedition and disturbance of the republic, thus incurring the penalty of rebellion without mercy.'[8] Meanwhile, for reasons of his own, Inquisitor general Valdés was equally anxious for a policy of repression, using the ecclesiastical process he commanded. For Valdés felt the insecurity of his own position on two accounts: as archbishop of Seville he was in disgrace for a recent failure to co-operate financially with the crown; as Inquisitor general it was his duty to ensure that situations like that in Valladolid did not arise. To save his own face, a successful heresy hunt, with victims at all costs, was urgently called for. But to effect this the Inquisition needed powers even more absolute than it already possessed, for, as it was then constituted, it lacked jurisdiction over bishops—and Valdés had his eye on a victim more highly placed than any in the Valladolid group—and it was customary to reconcile those who begged for mercy and confessed their errors, which enabled repentant heretics to escape the ultimate penalty. Writing to the papacy in September 1558 he argued that the Spanish Inquisition needed all the support and power it could get, as before his own appointment it had become a run-down machine, crippled by poverty and staffed by judges 'who were not experienced in detecting Lutheran errors'; the recent outbreak occurred among people of importance and it would be dangerous not to make an example of them; for Lutheranism promised relief from church burdens, which might make it welcome to the common people, while the tribunals of the Inquisition might be reluctant to condemn people of quality.[9] On these grounds he requested a papal brief authorising him to go beyond existing ecclesiastical law and to condemn the guilty no matter what the circumstances. His request was successful: papal briefs of

[8] Lea, *History of the Inquisition in Spain*, iii. 434–35.
[9] Valdés to Pius IV, 9 September 1558, in Lea, *op. cit.*, iii. 566–72.

1559 granted the Spanish Inquisition a limited jurisdiction even over bishops and authorised it to condemn penitents even though they begged for mercy, when it was believed that their conversion was not sincere.[10] Armed with these powers, it then struck at the Valladolid group in two sensational *autos de fe* in May and October 1559. At the first Melchor Cano preached for an hour; at the second Philip II himself was present.[11] Cazalla, Rojas, Seso, and twelve others were relaxed to the secular arm and executed; of these only Herrezuela died for his beliefs, and he was burnt alive; the rest had recanted, and so were strangled first then burnt. In calmer times, and before the determination of Valdés to have his victims, these recantations would have been accepted; after his detailed and abject confessions, Cazalla himself expected to escape the death penalty and was shocked to learn that the time of clemency had passed. The minor victims, who escaped with sentences varying from life confinement to light penance, were fortunate indeed.

Meanwhile, another substantial Lutheran group had been discovered in Seville. Its inspirers were Juan Gil—usually known as Dr. Egidio in the Latinised form of his name—and Dr. Constantino Ponce de la Fuente, canons of the Cathedral of Seville.[12] Neither of these were clearly Protestants. Egidio was pursued by the Inquisition from about 1550 but escaped with relatively mild treatment. Constantino had been court chaplain and preacher and as such had accompanied Prince Philip in the Low Countries and Germany during the years 1549 to 1551. Soon after taking up residence as canon of Seville in 1556 he was attacked for both Lutheran doctrines and his Jewish descent. Thrown into prison in 1558, there he died, to be subsequently burnt in effigy as a Lutheran, as was Egidio, after his death. Meanwhile the Seville group had been growing in numbers, with two focal points—the Hieronymite monastery of San Isidro and the house of Juan Ponce de León, a son of the count of Bailén. The Inquisition began to act when it discovered two loads of heretical books conveyed from Geneva by Julian Hernández, whose career as a muleteer was probably a cloak for this kind of operation. Over 800 persons were tried by the Inquisition, many of them women of upper-class families. In two *autos de fe* in 1559 and 1560 over thirty victims were relaxed to the secular arm for the death penalty, including two Englishmen, and as recantations were rarer than at Valladolid, so more died at the stake.

The policy of repression put an end to any chance of organised Lutheranism in Spain, if it ever existed.[13] But Valdés had still to claim his greatest

[10] *Ibid.*, iii. 436.
[11] See Menéndez Pelayo, *op. cit.*, iii. 418–30, 431–39.
[12] *Ibid.*, iv. 75–122; Bataillon, *op. cit.*, 561–79.
[13] The number of 'Protestants' in Spain tried by the Inquisition was not over 400 in all; Schafer; *op. cit.*, ii. 208–32.

victim—the archbishop of Toledo and primate of all Spain. Bartolomé de Carranza was a Dominican friar who for many years had taught theology at Valladolid.[14] Charles V had sent him to the Council of Trent where he stood out determinedly against Protestantism and in favour of improving ecclesiastical discipline. Appointed confessor to Prince Philip in 1550, he accompanied him to England in 1554, and spent three years there, frequently preaching in the Chapel Royal; at first he seems to have advocated moderation in dealing with English Protestants, but afterwards when he himself was accused of Protestantism he naturally wished to avoid any ambiguity and claimed that he had been far more anti-Protestant than the rest of Philip's clerical entourage and to have used his influence to send Cranmer to the stake. In 1557 he was appointed archbishop of Toledo, and almost immediately his enemies accused him to the Inquisition of heresy, citing his famous *Commentaries on the Christian Catechism*. The purpose of the Inquisitor general's application to the papacy for permission to try even bishops was now clear. Valdés had long envied Carranza his successful career, and the elevation of his rival to the see of Toledo, a prize which he himself had hoped for, only increased his hatred. In Melchor Cano, Carranza had another personal enemy; the two had been academic rivals since their student days, and as professors at Valladolid; from Cano he could expect little mercy. Consequently, his arrest on 22 August 1559 was not an impartial act of justice but reflected in some degree motives of personal resentment on the part of his detractors. Unfortunately for Carranza, his theological language was neither incisive nor accurate; although he was by no means a heretic, he was given to exaggerated expressions, which could be misinterpreted if anyone were malicious enough to seek heresy where none were intended.[15] The malice of Valdés and the Spanish Inquisition kept Carranza in jail at Valladolid for over over seven years. During this time the case became a struggle over jurisdiction between Philip II and the Spanish Inquisition on the one hand, and the papacy on the other, while the alleged heresy involved was reduced to almost secondary significance.[16]

In the sixteenth century persecution of dissenters was not exclusive to Spain; it has been aptly remarked that 'Spanish repression is distinguished less for its cruelty than for the power of the bureaucratic, police and judicial machine at its disposal'.[17] Where Spain differed from its neighbours was in

---

[14] On the Carranza case see Menéndez Pelayo, *op. cit.*, iv. 7–73; G. Marañon, 'El proceso del arzobispo Carranza', *Boletín de la Real Academia de Historia*, cxxxvii. (1950), 135–78.

[15] On the weakness of Carranza's theological language see Beltrán de Heredia, *Historia de la reforma de la Provincia de España, 1450–1550*, p. 182.

[16] For the sequel see below, pp. 276–77.   [17] Bataillon, *op. cit.*, p. 530.

possessing an agency which specialised in the pursuit of heresy. But the Spanish Inquisition, like any other institution, must be studied with an awareness of chronology: it did not behave in exactly the same way in every period of its history. Moreover, an institution is comprised of men, who modify old policies or form new ones: Valdés was succeeded by Inquisitors like Espinosa and Quiroga, who had their prejudices but did not see a heretic in every devout priest. The Inquisition had certainly not fired its last shot in the campaign for uniformity, as will be seen, but once the immediate tension of the 1550's had passed, the reign of terror initiated by Valdés did not last long beyond his term of office. At the same time it is useful to remember that the Spanish Inquisition was not a creation of the Counter-Reformation, for it had existed since the previous century, before Protestantism was born. And in unleashing it against heresy at the beginning of his reign Philip II was not acting in collusion with Rome. Relations between Spain and the papacy during the pontificate of Paul IV (1555–59) were worse than they had ever been and precluded any chance of concerted action. Yet in one exceptional case Spain had already co-operated effectively with the papacy to produce a more positive response to Protestantism than mere repression. Spanish representatives had distinguished themselves in the first two assemblies of the Council of Trent and were to do so in the third and most decisive one.

2. THE COUNTER-REFORMATION IN SPAIN

To define and defend Catholicism by means of a Council was as vital a part of Philip II's policy as it had been of his father's.[18] But conciliar action was in abeyance at the time of his accession. Repudiated by France, the second assembly of the Council of Trent had been scattered in 1552 by the defeat of Charles V and the threat of a Lutheran invasion over the Brenner Pass. Its recall was delayed not only by the international situation but also by the election of a violently anti-Spanish pope in 1555. Paul IV was pre-occupied with other interests than a Council, among them the expulsion from Italy of 'that breed of Moors and Jews, those dregs of the earth', as he described his Spanish enemies. His hostility revived the Franco-papal alliance and resulted in war with Spain. It was not until 1559, when a new pope was elected and France and Spain came to terms in the Peace of Cateau-Cambrésis, that the work of reform begun in the earlier sessions of the Council of Trent could be resumed. But now there was a new complication, for the question was debated whether the Council of Trent should

[18] See above, pp. 81–82, 90–96, 98–104.

be continued or whether a fresh start should be made.[19] In Germany a religious settlement had been already reached by the Peace of Augsburg, and the new Emperor, Ferdinand I, feared that this would be upset by the revival of the Council of Trent; he wanted a new Council favourable to radical changes in the discipline of the Church and conciliatory towards Protestants. The French government, preoccupied with the progress of Calvinism among its own subjects, also demanded a new Council, to be held in France, to include Protestant representatives, and to be ready to discuss Protestant doctrine. Pius V was rescued from these difficulties largely by the support of Spain. A junta of Spanish theologians called by Philip II came out unmistakably on the side of continuing the old Council, partly in order to preserve its condemnation of the Lutheran doctrine of Justification, and this decision was seconded by the king himself. Support of the powerful Spanish interest thus enabled the pope to recall the Council of Trent, which held its final assembly from 1562 to 1563, almost fifty years after the appearance of Luther's Wittenberg theses.

To attribute to Spain the success of the Council of Trent—'as Spanish as it was ecumenical'—hardly does justice to the leadership of the papacy and the contribution of the Italian and French delegations.[20] But Spain undoubtedly played a major rôle, not only numerically—there were 130 Spaniards in the final assembly—but also in the quality of her representatives.[21] These included Cardinal Pacheco, bishop of Jaén; the Dominican theologians, Melchor Cano and Domingo de Soto; the eminent canonist, Diego de Covarrubias; and an able group of Jesuits. The papacy itself showed a predilection for Spaniards. Of the fourteen theologians whom the pope sent to the Council during the three assemblies as his own delegates, eleven were Spaniards, a choice which reflected their learning as well as their impeccable orthodoxy. Among the special theologians of the Holy See were the Spanish Jesuits Laínez and Salmerón, who, together with the Frenchman Favre, had been recommended by Loyola himself. Laínez was probably the most influential theologian at Trent, and his views on Justification were included in the official Acts of the Council.[22] The Spanish party at Trent, of course, were just as sensitive to the interests of their own country and the directions of their own ruler as any other delegation there. But the Spanish king, unlike the king of France, was not embarrassed by

[19] See H. Jedin, *Ecumenical Councils of the Catholic Church* (Eng. trans., London, 1960), pp. 142–86.
[20] The description is that of Menéndez Pelayo, *op. cit.*, iv. 406.
[21] C. Gutiérrez, *Españoles en Trento* (Valladolid, 1951), pp. 1038–43; see also R. Burgos, *España en Trento* (Madrid, 1941).
[22] See F. Cereceda, *Diego Laínez en la Europa religiosa de su tiempo, 1512–1565* (2 vols., Madrid, 1945–46).

Protestant subjects, and consequently he was never tempted to urge concessions to Protestant opinion. For this reason, as well as because of its own
orthodoxy, the Spanish party supported the adoption of a specifically
Catholic position by the Council of Trent, and the principles of doctrine
and discipline which this entailed. The condemnation of the Lutheran view
of Original Sin and Justification, the definition of Catholic doctrine, the
adherence to the tradition of the church as well as the Bible as the basis
of authority, the acceptance of the Latin Vulgate text as the official version
of Scripture, the special position granted to Thomist philosophy, the
insistence on clerical celibacy, the reform of the clergy and the provision
for their better education, the strengthening of episcopal power—all these
measures, embodied in the most vital decrees of the Council, were supported
and promoted by the Spanish theologians.

Yet Spanish opinion did not coincide entirely with the views of the
papacy; on two issues—episcopal jurisdiction and the prerogatives of the
crown—it expressed a national point of view. The final assembly of the
Council was almost wrecked by the disputes over the derivation of episcopal
jurisdiction. The question of whether bishops exercised authority as delegates
of the pope or received it directly from God affected the interests both of
the papacy and of the national episcopates. If bishops had an independent
power, what became of papal supremacy? And did not the Spanish crown
regard its bishops as a national rather than a papal body? Without drawing
extreme inferences, or questioning papal authority, the Spanish bishops at
Trent defended the divine right of episcopacy; in this they followed the
Spanish tradition of limiting the scope of papal intervention in Spain, and
also emphasised their old conviction that ecclesiastical reform was more
likely to be promoted by native bishops than by the policy or the agents
of the Roman Curia. But episcopalism was defeated at a theoretical level,
for the decision of Trent strengthened the hands of the bishops by giving
them extensive powers of visitation and of summoning diocesan synods,
but as delegates of the papacy, which remained the head of the hierarchy
and the supreme court of appeal. In practice, however, the Spanish bishops
had a powerful advocate in their own king, who was extremely sensitive
about his rights of patronage. Philip II had his own reservations about
some of the decisions of the Council. He suspected those decrees which
seemed to threaten the supremacy of the crown over the Spanish clergy,
including the provision that 'the appropriate provincial synod and in the
final instance the pope should examine the character and orthodoxy of all
new prelates'.[23] This reform was not acceptable to Philip, because it would
give the pope some influence in ecclesiastical appointments. On the question

[23] Pastor, *History of the Popes*, xv. 358; xvi. 364–66.

of the Spanish Inquisition the king was equally adamant: there should be
no diminution of its jurisdiction, as some bishops at Trent would have
liked.[24] He instructed his ambassadors, Diego de Vargas in Rome and the
Count of Luna at Trent, to make sure that the pope and the council did
not interfere in any way with the Spanish Inquisition, or with anything
that touched his authority. He believed he had the right to direct the
Roman Curia and the Council, and when Pius IV protested, the Spanish
ambassador expressed surprise and reprimanded him.[25] Therefore, after
Pius IV had ratified the decrees of Trent by a papal bull of 26 January
1564, Philip II spent many months vacillating between publishing and not
publishing them. Eventually he decided in favour of publication, but only
with the proviso that they did not encroach on the rights and privileges of
the Spanish crown, especially in appointments to benefices. This virtually
invalidated those canons of the Council which would reduce the influence
of the Spanish king in ecclesiastical jurisdiction and in the provision of
bishops in his dominions.[26]

The reluctance of Philip II to publish the decrees of Trent illustrates one
of the basic weaknesses of the Council. It was not an executive body: it
could lay down principles but it could not apply them. The papacy was
the only executive body it contained, but the papacy's power of intervention
was limited even in Catholic countries, and it depended on the co-operation
of secular rulers. Philip II was sincere in his desire for ecclesiastical reform;
he devoted an immense amount of his time to church affairs, and it is clear
from his correspondence that in filling episcopal sees his concern for
religious standards survived the most intense obsession with the political
and financial details of each appointment. But he insisted that reform should
develop under his authority and take account of Spanish conditions. For
this reason, while he supported the holding of provincial councils to
implement the Tridentine decrees, he also insisted on the attendance of his
own deputies. In November 1565 Pius IV objected to the presence of
laymen in ecclesiastical councils, which he regarded as a usurpation of papal
jurisdiction and a cause of the scandalous saying that he was not pope in
Spain.[27] Remembering the aspirations of the Spanish episcopate at Trent he
believed that the independence it had failed to secure in the Council was
now being promoted indirectly in Spain itself. He was also critical of
Spanish bishops for opposing appeals of litigants to Rome, which he

[24] M. Philippson, 'Felipe II y el Pontificado', Estudios sobre Felipe II, ed. R. de Hinojosa
(Madrid, 1887), pp. 121–22.
[25] V. de Lafuente, Historia eclesiástica de España (Madrid, 1879), vii. 80.
[26] Pastor, op. cit., xvi. 106–07.
[27] L. Serrano, ed., Correspondencia diplomática entre España y la Santa Sede durante el
Pontificado de S. Pio V (Madrid, 1914), i. 30–32.

regarded as another infringement of the conciliar decrees.[28] But these complaints had little effect in Spain: in 1582 the papacy was still objecting to Philip II's sending royal delegates to the synod of Toledo, and the objections were still in vain.[29]

The work of reform advocated by the Council of Trent, therefore, was promoted in Spain under the control of the crown and its ecclesiastical advisers, and developed at the pace set by them. It was a cautious process, its intellectual standards were marked by scholarship rather than speculation, and it owed more to the private enterprise of reformers like St. Teresa than to official initiative. In its formative years its character was established by Gaspar de Quiroga, whose rule was that of an ecclesiastical statesman rather than of a pioneer in the mould of Ximénez. The appointment of Quiroga, in fact, was characteristic of the religious policy of Philip II. A canon-lawyer by training at Salamanca and Valladolid, canon of Toledo under Archbishop Tavera and Auditor of the Roman Rota from 1554 to 1556, he soon brought himself to the notice of the crown by his uncompromising support for the royal prerogative in ecclesiastical affairs and by his ability to deal with the papacy. It was his regalism, as well as his integrity and judgement, which earned him preferment. In 1558 Philip II employed him as inspector of monasteries in Naples and Sicily, a post which he held concurrently with membership of the Council of Castile; the success of his mission in Italy led to his appointment to the presidency of the Council of Italy in 1567 and to the bishopric of Cuenca in 1572. Quiroga's career, which was typical of the Spanish tradition of combining civil and ecclesiastical office, each bolstering the other, was crowned by his appointment as Inquisitor general in 1573, archbishop of Toledo and primate of Spain in 1577, and cardinal in 1578. The instruments of religious reform and security were now in his hands.

At Cuenca Quiroga introduced the religious policies which he was to employ on a larger scale when he became archbishop of Toledo. He was a resident bishop, who set an example by his own frugal living and was conscious of his pastoral mission. His religious programme was subsidised from the revenue of his see, and included church reform by diocesan synod, the promotion of education and social services, and patronage of the arts in the service of religion; to implement his plans he developed a close working agreement with two orders, Augustinians and Jesuits, which were the agencies through which he employed his funds for welfare and education.[30] At Toledo he had even greater scope for action, and from here he virtually directed the work of the Counter-Reformation in Spain. He

[28] *Ibid.*, i. 37–38.   [29] Boyd, *op. cit.*, p. 30; Pastor, *op. cit.*, xix. 364.
[30] Boyd, *op. cit.*, pp. 20–22.

began with a reforming operation in his own archdiocese, urging the clergy to improve their standards of piety and worship, insisting on stricter control of religious processions, and once again making provision for the extension of Christian education.[31] Negatively an important theme of his reforms was to prevent the indiscriminate mingling of the sacred and the profane, by excluding secular celebrations and bullfights from religious occasions and limiting the number of *fiestas*. More positively he organised the preparation, discussion, and publication in 1581 of a new *Manual of the Sacraments*, in order to regulate the administration of the sacraments in Spain. To extend his programme and impose it at the highest level he called a special synod in Toledo in 1582, which bishops from various dioceses attended; many of the topics on the agenda were abandoned because of the usual lack of agreement among the representatives of different districts and orders, but an agreed plan of reform was eventually adopted, in general conformity with the decrees of Trent. Seminaries for the training of priests were projected; rules for the celebration of Mass, clerical dress, and the minimum qualifications in candidates for ordination were agreed upon; a campaign to enforce clerics to reside in their benefices was decided, and provisions were made to exercise jurisdiction over those who failed to perform their priestly duties. Quiroga spent the rest of his life administering this programme, guided by the twin principles of uniformity and centralisation; and by the time of his death in 1594 he was also known as a munificent patron of the arts for the glory of religion; it was no coincidence that El Greco lived and worked in Toledo, the headquarters of the second wealthiest see in Christendom and the home of his most distinguished ecclesiastical patron. Nevertheless, the action of Quiroga was strangely deficient in what is usually regarded as one of the most characteristic reforms of the Counter-Reformation. In accordance with a decree of Trent and with one of the decisions of the Council of Toledo concerning the foundation of seminaries, Quiroga formed a commission to consider the possibility of erecting a seminary in Toledo. After many meetings the commission reported unfavourably, and in spite of the promptings of Gregory XIII Quiroga agreed with the commission, on the grounds that while it was desirous to carry out the decrees of Trent other factors such as crop failures and poor economic conditions made it impossible for benefice holders to increase their contributions beyond their regular commitments. Thus, twenty years after the conclusion of Trent, the primate of Spain and the holder of one of the wealthiest sees in the church, who gave generously to the state and to patronage of the arts, pleaded penury for failure to establish a seminary.[32]

[31] *Ibid.*, pp. 27–32.   [32] *Ibid.*, p. 37.

Intellectually Quiroga lacked vision rather than good will, and he was incurably cautious. Indeed it was his duty to be cautious, for he was also Inquisitor general. The old question of papal jurisdiction over the Spanish Inquisition had already been resolved in favour of the crown before the régime of Quiroga. He himself never questioned papal supremacy in spiritual matters, and as he saw it the Inquisition came under the pope's delegated power; but he did as much as he could to diminish this power in practice and to preserve the *de facto* independence of the Spanish tribunal. He also extended the jurisdiction of the Inquisition as an instrument of civil administration in the service of the state, often at the expense of royal officials. As the power of the latter could be limited by local laws and immunities, Philip II approved the extension of Inquisition authority in every case; but while this gave his administration an efficient agency, it also made the Inquisition more liable to abuse as an instrument of political repression.[33] Yet here its touch was light indeed compared to its ponderous approach to intellectual developments.

3. Scholarship and Regalism

A characteristic feature of the renaissance in Spain had been a revival of biblical and theological studies. Yet the Spanish church of the Counter-Reformation proved incapable of assimilating creative speculation in these fields and could only tolerate a barren and lengthy repetition of old knowledge, with the result that original thought was sacrificed to security and the Counter-Reformation lost one of its most promising assets. For the intellectual controversies in Castile in the second half of the sixteenth century were not a question of orthodoxy versus dissent, but represented rather two ways of approaching theological studies. On the one hand a group of conservative scholastics endlessly repeated the doctrines and the methods of the medieval schoolmen, and often spoke as though it were heresy to dispute the views of Aristotle and St. Thomas Aquinas. Another group, the true heirs of the Spanish renaissance, endeavoured to assimilate the new acquisitions of sixteenth-century science and scholarship, and apply them to sacred studies; in the works of scholars like Fray Luis de León and Alonso Gudiel an attempt was made to integrate the best of scholasticism with more recent knowledge and so to effect a restoration of the biblical sciences. Yet these men, orthodox though they were, aroused suspicion almost before they opened their mouths. As the distinguished exegete, Diego de Zúñiga, remarked in 1584, any interpretation of the Bible that differed from the currently accepted one was regarded as Jewish subversion:

[33] See above, pp. 215–17.

'The stupid clamour of those people (the reactionaries) has produced such a panic in many learned exegetes that they have ended up by retiring from their noble and holy task, because they believe that it is impossible for a person of culture to devote himself safely to the study of sacred letters.'[34] The tension was aggravated by the conditions of academic life in Spain. In the 1570's the various religious orders were divided uncompromisingly into rival camps and competed ruthlessly for university and ecclesiastical vacancies. Appointments to university chairs, which were decided by vote of students, were the occasion of intense campaigning by rival orders on behalf of their candidates. The conflict between the Dominicans and the Jesuits was fought with no holds barred, but perhaps the bitterest rivalry of all was that between the Dominicans and the Augustinians, and this coincided to some extent with the dispute between the old learning and the new.

The opening rounds were fired by a group of conservative scholastics led by the malevolent León de Castro, a theologian of Salamanca, who denounced a number of distinguished Augustinian scholars to the Valladolid Inquisition.[35] Among others, Luis de León, Professor of Theology at Salamanca, and Alonso Gudiel, Professor of Scripture at the University of Osuna, were arrested in March 1572. Behind the personal animosity of the accusers for the accused lay the more fundamental issue of scriptural exegesis. Gudiel was accused of giving a literal meaning to the texts on the subject of Christ which precluded any prophetic and allegorical meanings. His defence was that a literal historical interpretation was not incompatible with a prophetic one, since it was derived from the acts and words of Christ, and was thus perfectly orthodox. But in June 1572 the Inquisition's theological consultant, Hernando del Castillo, condemned as heretical the doctrine attributed to Gudiel concerning the literal meaning of various texts.[36] Before the case was settled, Gudiel died in prison in April 1573, and the Valladolid tribunal notified the various Augustinian houses that he was in error and died outside the faith. Over ten years later, Inquisitor general Quiroga, unsatisfied with the case, reopened it, and this time Castillo cleared Gudiel of heresy, saying that statements of St. Thomas were open to discussion and could be questioned without committing heresy, though extreme caution should be observed. The implications of Castillo's own *volte-face* were not considered.

In the trial of Luis de León the issues involved were more diverse. Poet

[34] Quoted in M. de la Pinta Llorente, *Causa criminal contra el biblista Alonso Gudiel* (Madrid, 1942), p. 27.
[35] For a useful summary of these cases, see Boyd, *op. cit.*, pp. 65–74.
[36] On the case of Gudiel see Pinta Llorente, *Causa criminal contra el biblista Alonso Gudiel*, passim.

as well as theologian, he was brought to account for his translation of the *Song of Songs* into Spanish, for his alleged deprecation of the Latin Vulgate text of the Bible, and for his views on predestination and grace.[37] But in his case, too, the most heated controversies developed over the interpretation of the Vulgate edition approved by the Council of Trent. Luis de León drew a scholar's distinction between the Vulgate as written by St. Jerome and the various printed texts of this version, which often differed from one another in detail. However, he preferred the Hebrew original above all. The case against him was not strong, especially as some of the evidence came from Dominicans, against whose competition he had won his Chair at Salamanca in 1561, and from Fray Gabriel Montoya, prior of the Augustinian monastery at Toledo, who bore him a personal grudge. But meanwhile the interminable processes of the Inquisition deprived him of his Chair and kept him in prison for year after year. In spite of promptings from Inquisitor general Quiroga to hasten with the case, the Valladolid tribunal allowed its machinery to grind on regardless of human considerations. Eventually Quiroga himself intervened. Making a distinction between a dogmatic and an undefined proposition, he acknowledged that the latter was susceptible to rational argument for or against. And he ordered his deputies at Valladolid to acquit Luis de León with a warning to be more careful in future, and to withdraw from circulation the manuscript copy of his Spanish version of the *Song of Songs*. By this time, however, Luis de León had been in the jails of the Inquisition for over five years. On returning to his Chair at Salamanca he is reported to have begun his first lecture with the words, 'As I was saying last time . . .'. If the anecdote is true, it was an expression of bitterness not of resignation.

The Inquisition, however, had not yet finished with the intellectuals: within a few years it turned its attention to Francisco Sánchez de las Brozas, 'el Brocense', a humanist scholar who specialised in philology but was also interested in cosmography and astronomy and often discussed the Ptolemaic and Copernican systems of the universe. Copernicus was not proscribed by the Spanish Inquisition, but Aristotle was another matter. When Sánchez questioned Aristotle's definition of logic, declaring that it was based on ignorance, Fray Mancio of Corpus Christi College, Salamanca, challenged him on the grounds that the doctrines of St. Thomas Aquinas were founded on Aristotle, and the Catholic faith on St. Thomas. To this Sánchez replied that he considered Mancio's statement to be heresy; moreover, if it could be shown that his faith was founded on St. Thomas then he would look for another faith. As a result of this statement, the Valladolid tribunal

---

[37] A. F. Bell, *Luis de León. A study of the Spanish Renaissance* (Oxford, 1926), pp. 101–61.

began to move against 'el Brocense' in January 1584. He defended himself with vigour, arguing that he did not question what had been decreed by the church, but merely considered that in matters of history and philosophy, sacred and profane, some theologians were most ignorant and needed instruction. His defence was foolproof, and the Inquisition could do no more than reprimand and release him.[38]

Together with the proceedings against the biblicists Martín Martínez de Cantalapiedra and Gaspar de Grajal, these were the only important cases in which the Inquisition prosecuted scholars, and even here, with the intervention of Quiroga, a rough though belated justice was eventually done; and such cases were a reflection not only on the Inquisition but also on conditions in Spanish universities, where rival groups of scholars vented their envy and competed for power by denouncing others to the dreaded tribunal. This had a pernicious effect on scholarship and creative work in Spain and affected the climate of opinion in which they could flourish. Moreover, the fear among writers engendered by the Inquisition cannot be measured in terms of the number of prosecutions: its hostile gaze circumscribed intellectual activity and encouraged the adoption of conventional and conformist attitudes, even outside of faith and morals. Contemporaries were not unaware of the damage that was being done, and some of them were sensitive to the larger implications of this deterrent to speculation. Juan de Mariana, the distinguished Jesuit theologian and political philosopher, who had himself on occasion worked for the Inquisition in an advisory capacity, was highly critical of the tribunal's methods of investigation and voiced his disquiet at their effect on scholarship in Spain. Commenting on the experience of Fray Luis de León, he wrote:

> The case made many people anxious, as they awaited its result. For men of learning and reputation were forced to defend themselves while in prison against something that was quite dangerous to their lives and good name. What a miserable situation is that of the virtuous man! As reward for his achievements he has to endure the hatred and accusations of the very people who should be his defenders. With such an example, the ambitions of many gifted men were bound to decline and their energies to weaken and perish. The case in question disheartened many, as they saw the danger to others and the torment which threatened those who freely stated what they thought. In this way many changed over to the other side or decided to bow before the storm. Indeed, what could be done? Is it not madness to exert oneself in vain and to exhaust oneself

[38] See A. F. Bell, *Francisco Sánchez El Brocense* (Oxford, 1925); A. Tovar and M. de la Pinta Llorente, *Procesos inquisitoriales contra Francisco Sánchez de las Brozas* (Madrid, 1941).

only to achieve hatred? Those who shared the popular opinions went on doing so with greater gratification and they encouraged ideas that were acceptable, ideas in which there was less danger but no greater concern for truth.[39]

Mariana was one of those who remained true to his convictions; thirty years after the case of Luis de León the hand of the Inquisition descended on him too.

Hostile to speculation, the ecclesiastical authorities looked with more indulgence on those whose interests lay in reform and in reviving and extending religious belief and practice. The greatest impetus to religious revival, however, came not from the hierarchy but from the private endeavours of individual reformers. In the first half of the sixteenth century the most outstanding figure in the reform movement was St. Peter of Alcántara (1499–1562), who, having studied at Salamanca, joined the recently instituted Discalced Franciscan Reform and lived a life of extreme austerity. It was he who provided a link with later reformers. He first met St. Teresa at Avila in 1558; besides counselling her in spiritual matters, he took an interest in her initial foundation in 1562 and was instrumental in obtaining the sanction of the bishop of Avila for it. St. Teresa of Jesus and St. John of the Cross, authors of masterpieces of Christian mysticism, were also founders of the Discalced Carmelite Reform, and between 1562 and 1576 founded numerous reformed convents and monasteries.[40] The obstacles of inertia, vested interests, and outright resistance which beset their pro-gramme were immense; St. John of the Cross was kidnapped by unreformed Carmelites in 1577 and kept for eight months in solitary confinement in Toledo, during which time he was periodically flogged by his enemies. But the Discalced Carmelite Reform triumphed in the years 1579–82 when its promoters managed to enlist some support from church and state. St. Teresa, who was grateful to Quiroga for his approval of her *Life*, also found him 'very favourable to the Discalced', though occasionally she felt frustrated by his intransigence over details. Philip II himself was interested

---

[39] *Pro Editione Vulgata* (1609) in J.-P. Migne, ed., *Scripturae sacrae cursus completus* (Paris, 1839), i. 589. Mariana's essay was a modified version of his report on the Polyglot Bible of Arias Montano made for the Inquisition twenty-five years previously; it was published in 1609 in Cologne as part of a collection of smaller works under the title *Tractatus VII*, and is printed in Migne, *op. cit.*, i. 587–698. One of these works dealt with the debasement of the Spanish currency, and it was largely for this reason that Mariana was arrested by the Inquisition and charged with lèse-majesté for having criticised the fiscal policies of the king before a foreign audience. He was released after one year but the treatise on currency was placed on the Spanish Index and the *Pro Editione Vulgata* was expurgated.

[40] See E. Allison Peers, *Handbook to the life and times of St. Teresa and St. John of the Cross* (London, 1954).

Foundation of Convent of Pastrana by St Teresa of Jesus

in the movement and did something to further its progress, especially during the critical years of the conflict with the Observance between 1576 and 1580; St. Teresa often wrote to him on its behalf, and although she considered his support did not go far enough, it was with royal assistance that a separate province for the Discalced was authorised by Gregory XIII in 1580, a vital stage in the process of reform.

Much of the caution of the Spanish authorities in religious affairs stemmed from an unwillingness to provide any occasion for papal intervention and a hostility to foreign influences, and was a reflection of a religious nationalism which, while it never reached the positions adopted by Protestant states, fell far short of the ideals of the papacy. Philip II and the Spanish Inquisition were always anxious to reduce Italian influence in the Spanish church; for the Italian clergy were suspect in Spain, and Philip II, confident of his own orthodoxy, described them as 'prone to licentiousness and liberty', and compared their 'dissolute' ways unfavourably with the 'holy principles of the Spanish religious'. Similar sentiments can be seen in the instructions given to the Spanish ambassador in Rome in 1562, when he was ordered to ask the pope to concede the segregation of the Franciscans of Sardinia from their Italian obedience and their incorporation in the province of Aragon. In the same year the Spanish king also requested that the Cistercians of Aragon be freed from French religious jurisdiction, because, as he explained to the pope, 'heresies have penetrated France and are increasing there, and it would be most dangerous and harmful to our Christian religion, which, praise God, is preserved in my kingdoms, to suffer such coming and going between Spain and France, where the Cistercian Order has its government'.[41] But the bitterest conflict of all raged around and within the Society of Jesus; it was the new order of St. Ignatius, Spanish in its origins, international in its development, that was the greatest challenge to national susceptibilities.

By the middle of the sixteenth century the Society of Jesus had come to play a leading rôle in the Counter-Reformation. Led by a general with virtually unlimited power and animated by a spirit of utter obedience, the Jesuits occupied advance positions in the struggle against heresy and in the promotion of the Catholic faith. Yet the order did not originate simply as a reaction to Protestantism.[42] In the years of his apprenticeship in religion Protestantism did not preoccupy Ignatius Loyola; in his first organised

[41] Quoted in Reglà, *Felip II i Catalunya*, p. 175.
[42] On the origin of the Jesuits see J. Brodrick, S.J., *The Origin of the Jesuits* (London, 1948); P. Casanovas, *San Ignacio de Loyola, fundador de la Compañía de Jesus* (Barcelona, 1954); P. Leturia, *Estudios Ignacianos* (Rome, 1957); on the Society in Spain see A. Astraín, *Historia de la Compañía de Jesus en la Asistencia de España* (7 vols., Madrid, 1902–25).

enterprise he and his companions tried to reach the Near East, not Germany, and when this attempt failed he offered himself and his followers to the pope, willing to do whatever work the pope appointed them to; and they were appointed in fact not to countries where Protestantism was spreading but to Italian towns and villages, which always remained in name at least Catholic. Of his first companions only one worked directly among the Reformers, and he was sent at the pope's express request, and for a limited time. It was not until the mission of Canisius that the Jesuit Counter-Reformation began in earnest, and that was a decade after the death of Ignatius. The first Jesuits for the most part confined themselves to Catholic countries, and when Ignatius sent the greatest of them, St. Francis Xavier, to do missionary work he sent him not to central Europe but to the Far East. In its most primitive form, therefore, the Jesuit order was intended exclusively for men bound by solemn vow to go at a 'moment's notice wherever the pope might direct them. This precluded what later became one of the most characteristic features of the society and one of its most important contributions to the Counter-Reformation, namely its educational system, which involved regular work in a fixed place of residence. And it was only gradually that Ignatius accepted the idea of providing schools for Catholic youth. And this was a Spanish idea. One of the aristocratic recruits of the society, Francis Borgia, Duke of Gandia and Viceroy of Catalonia in 1541, founded the little University of Gandia in 1547; although the foundation had little significance from a cultural point of view, it first directed the activities of the order into educational channels, and for the first time provided education for lay pupils side by side with its own members. In 1550 Borgia gave Ignatius money to found a college in Rome, and it was from this that the Gregorian University grew. But the founder of the order was still unwilling to provide education for others than his own members. Then, under pressure of the Spanish viceroy in Sicily, the Spanish ambassador in Rome, and the pope himself, he authorised the opening of a mixed college at Messina for the education of Jesuits and non-Jesuits, and it was from this experiment that Jesuit education, with its mixture of scholasticism and humanism, sprang and developed.[43]

While the society was widening its objectives, it was also developing its organisation. In its original form there were few signs of that autocracy and militarism with which it was later credited. When Ignatius gathered together his first six companions in Paris, there was no paternalism and he was not in command; his vote in their consultations was no weightier than theirs. And in debating the organisation of the movement in Rome in

[43] On Jesuit education in Spain see J. S. Diaz, *Historia del Colegio Imperial de Madrid* (Madrid, 1952).

1539, when they decided to take a vow of obedience to one of their own number, the discussion was conducted and votes were taken with scrupulous regard for free speech. The constitution of the order cost Ignatius years of study and writing; he then submitted it in 1551 to those of the Fathers whom he could summon to Rome, revised it in accordance with their suggestions, and sent it to be tested experimentally for a long period in Spain, Portugal, and other countries. And it was two years after he died before it became the actual law of the society.[44] This gave the order its distinctive organisation, the most novel features of which were its intimate dependence on the papacy, to which its members took a special vow of obedience and offered themselves for the propagation of the faith, and concentration of power in a central executive—a general in Rome—which contrasted with the more federal constitutions of the older religious orders. The general was elected for life by the General Congregation of the order, which was made up of provincials and two other representatives.

The centralisation of power and policy, with the centre outside of Spain, together with the society's special relation with the papacy was an affront to the absolutist susceptibilities of the Spanish crown and to the spirit of Spanish nationalism. Ideally the society was a supra-national body. Although it was Spanish in origin, it quickly recruited members from all nations, and its internationalism is usually seen as one of the strongest forces by means of which the papacy fought the idea of religious nationalism. It is true that the Jesuits drew much of their effectiveness from the fact that they were an international order. But early in its history national rivalries appeared within it, and it was to counter the nationalist sentiments of the Portuguese province that Ignatius wrote his famous letter on obedience. In some ways the activities of the order itself lent themselves to this tendency. For the Jesuits were anxious to win for their spiritual mission the support of powerful people, and in an age of *cuius regio eius religio* they were not averse from gaining influence over kings and princes; while their own training and ability, and the fact that many of their members were recruited from the aristocratic classes, enabled them to win some successes in this direction. From this it was not a big step to their allowing themselves to be used to perform political services, often against the true spirit of the order. This, too, tended to foster national antagonisms within the society, especially if the Jesuits in a particular country were prepared to follow the policy of their sovereign rather than of their spiritual head. This is precisely what happened in Spain, where a group of Spanish Jesuits, for nationalist reasons and with the support of Philip II, violently opposed the centralisation of the order's executive.

[44] Brodrick, *op. cit.*, p. 102.

As long as Spaniards monopolised control of the order, opposition was dormant. For the society was Spanish not only in its origin but also in its personnel. Four of the first six followers of Ignatius were Spaniards; of the twenty-five members of the first General Congregation in 1558 eighteen were Spaniards; the first three generals of the society were all Spaniards. In 1573, however, a Belgian was elected general, followed in 1581 by a second non-Spaniard, the Neapolitan, Claudio Aquaviva. A group of Spanish malcontents now organised a movement within the society to reduce the authority of the general in Rome and to make the four provinces of the society in Spain more independent of his control.[45] The position they adopted appealed to Philip II, for it promised to give him the oppor-tunity to control the Jesuits and diminish their dependence on the papacy. After various minor conflicts between the Spanish Inquisition and the society, the real trial of strength came in 1587 when Philip II ordered his ambassador in Rome to secure papal approval for an inquisitor or bishop to inspect all the religious orders in Spain. Under cloak of a general permit, the visitation of the Jesuits was begun by the Bishop of Cartagena in 1588, when he was ordered to discover, among other things, why the superiors were not chosen by vote, why the governor of the order was dependent on Rome, and what was the purpose of the peculiar nature of their vows. The inquiry, in fact, was directed not at reform of the order but at the very nature of its constitution. In the first house visited the Jesuits did all in their power to hinder the visitation, and in September 1588 Aquaviva persuaded the pope to suspend the inspection. Philip II replied by replacing the episcopal inspector by a compliant Jesuit one, José de Acosta, a distin-guished missionary recently returned from the Indies, and through him working for the summons of a General Congregation which would change the constitution of the society. A Congregation did, in fact, meet in 1593, but thanks to a desperate campaign waged by Aquaviva, the functions of the central executive and the unity of the Jesuit system remained unrestricted. In his struggle to get these principles acknowledged, Aquaviva preserved one of the essential characteristics of the order, while Philip II failed in his attempt to nationalise it and bring it under Inquisition control. The entire episode was yet another example of the Spanish crown's anxiety to acquire greater control over the institutions subordinated to papal jurisdiction which were operating in Spain, and was part of the more general problem of Philip II's relations with the papacy.

[45] See Astraín, op. cit., iii; Boyd, op. cit., pp. 82–87; M. de la Pinta Llorente, Actividades diplomáticas del P. José de Acosta (Madrid, 1952).

4. PHILIP II AND THE PAPACY

The view that Philip II was the secular arm of the Counter-Reformation is based on the assumption that his own claims must be taken at their face value, and on the fallacy that because the religious motive was sometimes present in Spanish policy, therefore it was always present and was the most important motive.[46] The popes he had to deal with took a different view. They considered that Philip II, like his predecessors, used his prestige as a Catholic sovereign to pursue objectives that were essentially political. A characteristic summary of the papal view of Philip II's foreign policy was given in 1589 with reference to his ambitions in France: 'The King of Spain, as a temporal sovereign, is anxious above all to safeguard and to increase his dominions. . . . The preservation of the Catholic religion which is the principal aim of the Pope is only a pretext for His Majesty whose principal aim is the security and aggrandisement of his dominions.'[47] Sixtus V, it is true, had a deep and personal aversion to Spain and a low estimate of its king, but these opinions were not peculiar to one pope. There were conflicts between Philip II and almost every pope with whom he dealt, which makes it impossible to explain those conflicts in terms of personalities and points to some deeper and more permanent cause. It also makes it impossible to speak of 'the forces of the Counter-Reformation' as though there were a crusading alliance between Spain and the papacy. Protestantism had very little to fear from co-operation between Spain and Rome. In the experience of both powers there was more conflict than co-operation, and it was conflict over two main issues, ecclesiastical jurisdiction and foreign policy.

Even in ecclesiastical affairs the pope's writ hardly ran in Spain.[48] The domination of the church by the crown was probably more complete in Spain in the sixteenth century than in any other part of Europe, including Protestant countries with an Erastian system. The power of the crown had developed not simply in the interests of absolutism but also in the interests of reform. Beginning with Ferdinand and Isabella, the Spanish church was reformed with the active encouragement of the crown, which succeeded in eliminating the practical applications of papal supremacy not only because they competed with royal sovereignty, but also because they were

[46] Much of the following material has already appeared in J. Lynch 'Philip II and the Papacy', *Transactions of the Royal Historical Society*, 5th Series, ii. (1961), 23–42.

[47] Instructions addressed to Cardinal Caetani, legate of Sixtus V in France, regarding the settlement of the dynastic question in 1589, in M. de Boüard, *La légation du Cardinal Caetani en France, 1589-1590* (Bordeaux, 1932), p. 62. For further evidence of papal suspicion of Philip II, at different times, see Pastor, *History of the Popes*, xxi. 262–73; xxii. 47–64; xxiii. 195 ff.

[48] See Philippson, 'Felipe II y el Pontificado', *op. cit.*, pp. 91–160.

regarded as obstacles to reform. The crown's right to provide to bishoprics and abbacies was originally sought in part as a protective measure against the abuses of the papacy whose nepotism in Spain was notorious. Disputed from 1479, the right was definitely won by Charles V in 1523, when his former tutor, Adrian VI, granted him in perpetuity the right to appoint to bishoprics; by the end of the reign most of the other important and lucrative benefices in the Spanish church had also accrued to the crown. Consequently Philip II disposed of ecclesiastical benefices whose revenues amounted to vast sums of money, and was able to exercise a stranglehold on the personnel of the church. The Spanish clergy looked to the crown rather than to Rome, and Philip II, in spite of his devotion to the church and concern for reform, could not resist the temptation to exploit this power for political or economic ends. Appointments were preceded by financial arrangements whereby the grateful appointee engaged to pay the crown a percentage of his revenues.

Spain did not have an Act in Restraint of Appeals, but in fact appeals were restrained and a Spaniard had almost as little chance of appealing a case to Rome as an Englishman had. Based on the argument that the king was the protector of his subjects, including the clergy, and that they had a right of appeal to him, while Rome was too far away, the crown controlled ecclesiastical tribunals through the Council of Castile, which regarded itself as an ecclesiastical court of appeal and, supported by the Spanish hierarchy, consistently opposed appeals to Rome. The papacy considered this contrary to the decrees of the Council of Trent and complained about it. By a decree of 27 October 1572, however, the Council of Castile declared null and void papal briefs which cited Spaniards before foreign courts in ecclesiastical cases.[49] This made it impossible for the ecclesiastical tribunals of Rome to exercise any jurisdiction in Spain. From the Council of the Inquisition, which was appointed by the crown as has been seen, there was no appeal; in principle it was admitted that the pope, as supreme head of the church, had delegated power to the Spanish Inquisition, but once the authority had been delegated it was regarded as beyond recall.

There still remained the possibility that the pope might counter-attack with spiritual sanctions. Therefore these important prerogatives of the Spanish crown were protected by the right it claimed to scrutinise papal bulls and briefs and to prohibit their publication if they contradicted the laws and customs of the country. If the pope replied by excommunication, this was considered void in Spain and those who attempted to apply such bulls were punished by law.

[49] Serrano, ed., *Correspondencia diplomática entre España y la Santa Sede durante el Pontificado de S. Pío V*, i. 37–38; Philippson, *op. cit.*, pp. 151–52.

To preserve and extend his ecclesiastical prerogatives Philip II waged a relentless war with the papacy which formed a permanent background to their political relations. In this struggle with Rome he had the consistent support of the Spanish church. When Philip consulted his theologians and bishops, as he frequently did, they usually agreed with him. His bishops, of course, were appointed by him and he appointed men of strongly regalist views. Nevertheless, Spanish churchmen were in a dilemma; they owed their appointments to the crown but they could not, nor did they wish to, disavow the pope. Even when they were worried about this, however, they were less concerned about principles than about the practical difficulties that Philip could bring upon himself by the way he was behaving. As Inquisitor general, Cardinal Quiroga was careful to consult the papacy as well as the crown on all questions dealing with jurisdictional rights, and his advice to Philip was that the pope should be kept as content as possible.[50] The Dominican theologian, Melchor Cano, wrote a memorandum to Philip II on the subject, but he was clearly concerned with the practical effects of papal hostility. He reminded Philip that dealing with the pope required the greatest prudence, for even though he were personally weak he was still the vicar of Christ. If Philip challenged the authority of Rome, he might be damaging his own authority by breaking Catholic unity and weakening the traditional Christian authority in the minds of his own subjects. The pope could be very useful to Spain, especially in times of war, to rally public opinion in a religious way to the government's policies.[51]

Cano was referring to crusades against infidels and protestants. There was, however, a more urgent way in which the pope could be useful to Spain, and this was one of the reasons why Philip II never quite overstepped the mark. He needed the material as well as the moral support of the pope: the Spanish crown's financial interests were tied to the papacy. As supreme head of the church the pope disposed indirectly of ecclesiastical revenues without which Philip II would have been helpless in many of his undertakings. To a king whose resources were never equal to his commitments, this was not simply a minor or extraordinary income but, as has been seen, a permanent and major item in his budget,[52] and he could not get it without papal co-operation. For this reason, although his ambassadors might occasionally threaten the pope with schism, the papacy was too important to Philip II ever to be relinquished.

Before Spain and the papacy began to diverge on foreign policy,

[50] Quiroga to Philip II, 16 March 1574, British Museum, Egerton MS. 1506, fo. 18v.
[51] Melchor Cano to Philip II, B.M. Egerton MS. 444, fos. 19–52.
[52] See above, pp. 137–38.

constant tension was engendered by jurisdictional disputes. After his disastrous experience with the violently anti-Spanish Paul IV, with whom he was at war for the first two years of his reign, Philip II exerted his utmost influence in the conclave of 1559, where his efforts seemed to be rewarded with the election of Pius IV whose early policy, particularly in financial affairs, was accommodating. Philip, however, pressed the friendship too far, and on two outstanding matters he came into conflict with the papacy on a question of principle, the decrees of the Council of Trent and the case of Archbishop Carranza.[53] Not surprisingly even the docile Pius IV began to kick: Philip withdrew his ambassador in 1563 and the pope refused to renew the subsidy, which expired in 1564. The king and his agents soon discovered that they had even less chance of bullying Pius V, who was convinced that the supreme authority of the church should be real and not merely nominal. Indeed, they were at a loss as to how to deal with a pope who was a saint and not a politician. His ambassador, Requesens, warned Philip that he needed different treatment from other popes, because he did not recognise considerations of human prudence or reasons of state and would serve God regardless of practical and political consequences.[54] He was not prepared to yield to Spanish pressure and in particular he was not prepared to recognise the jurisdiction of the crown over the clergy and the practice of retaining bulls, both of which he regarded as violations of the rights of the church. At first he refused to concede the *subsidio* and the *cruzada*; among other things he was scandalised at the way the latter was preached and traded in Spain. Above all, however, Pius V was determined to take the Carranza case to Rome.

Carranza, as has been seen, had been imprisoned by the Spanish Inquisition as a Protestant heretic, despite the protests of the Council of Trent and the pope. By 1566 the case had become a struggle for ecclesiastical power between pope and king: the pope demanded that Carranza be tried in Rome, while the Spanish Inquisition, backed by the king, refused to hand him over. Pius V was more resolute than his predecessor, and on the grounds that the councils of the church reserved to the pope cognisance of episcopal cases and that Carranza could not get a fair trial in Spain, he was determined to bring the case and the person of the archbishop to his tribunal in spite of frequent requests of Requesens and the repeated letters of Philip himself that he should be tried in Spain.[55] The pope told Requesens that 'the day you see that I have changed my mind in this matter you will

---

[53] See above, pp. 257–62, for the Council of Trent, and pp. 255–56 for the Carranza case.

[54] Requesens to Philip II, 4 July 1566, *Corr. Dip.*, i. 287.

[55] *Corr. Dip.*, i. 174, 329, 337.

know that I have gone mad'.[56] He never did change his mind. Philip II, however, had equally strong reasons for his position. The claim of the Spanish Inquisition to judge so important a case in the interests of its own power and prestige, and in order to demonstrate that not even the primate of all Spain was exempt from its jurisdiction, was one that Philip could not ignore. He believed that he needed the Inquisition to govern Spain, and Requesens told the pope that the king considered he could not preserve religion in his dominions without defending the Inquisition against every thing.[57] There was also another point, and Pius V put his finger on it when he remarked that Philip wished to prolong the matter eternally because in the meantime he was enjoying the considerable revenues of the see of Toledo.[58] In the end Philip II yielded, and after more than seven years' imprisonment in Valladolid Carranza left for Rome in December 1566. How did Pius V overcome the obstinacy of the king and the tenacity of the Spanish Inquisition against all expectations? Some historians have argued that he feared the threats of the pope.[59] But the papal brief containing the said threats, and sent so secretly that even the papal secretary knew nothing of it, did not reach the nuncio who had to execute it in case of disobedience until some days after the king had resolved to submit.[60] It has also been claimed that Philip was genuinely influenced by the sanctity, disinterestedness and religious zeal of Pius V. There was no doubt, of course, that Philip II sincerely recognised the spiritual supremacy of the pope. But perhaps we can find another clue in the report of Requesens: 'There is no *cruzada* yet, but no doubt there will be when he gets satisfaction over Carranza.'[61] In any case it was done in such a way that the Spanish Inquisition managed to save its face: the pope allowed as many inquisitors as Philip cared to send to join the tribunal in Rome. And the tactics of the Spanish government and Inquisition still caused interminable delays, so that it was nine years later and after three successive popes had come into the case before a decision was reached in Rome. Carranza was found not guilty of heresy but made to abjure as 'highly suspect' sixteen propositions taken from his books, sentenced to five years' reclusion and suspended from exercise of his arch-episcopal functions during this period. Two months after sentence was passed he died.

Meanwhile, although conflict over jurisdiction continued, Pius V was not

---

[56] Requesens to Philip II, 23 February 1566, *Colección de documentos inéditos para la historia de España*, lxviii. 455–56.
[57] *Corr. Dip.*, i. 49, 256, 271.
[58] Requesens to Philip II, 3 May 1566, *ibid.*, i. 224.
[59] Menéndez Pelayo, *Heterodoxos*, iv. 62; Lea, *History of the Inquisition of Spain*, ii. 79.
[60] *Corr. Dip.*, i. 298, 330.
[61] Serrano, *ibid.*, p. lxiii; Requesens to Philip II, 27 Dec. 1566, *ibid.*, i. 432.

in a position to hold himself aloof from Spain. His anxiety to organise a Christian league against the Turk, for which he knew he could only rely on Spain, forced him to seek an alliance with Philip II, which resulted in the organisation of the Holy League and the destruction of the Turkish fleet at Lepanto in October 1571. In these circumstances the pope had to bend to Philip II as the only monarch who would help him against the infidel and who was already pressed financially by the rebellions in the Low Countries and the Alpujarras. Religious objectives caused Pius V to come to the assistance of his ally, and by the beginning of 1571 he had not only renewed the *cruzada* but also the subsidy on the Spanish clergy for five years. The condition for the latter was that the king should maintain sixty galleys to fight the enemies of the church. In fact they were soon used for other purposes. For a moment Spanish political interests in the Mediterranean had coincided with papal religious objectives. But it was not Philip's intention to engage in a long-term campaign against the Turk. After Lepanto Spain no less than Venice began to withdraw from the alliance, and in spite of papal pressure Philip II began a policy of disengagement with regard to the Turk.[62] There was, therefore, no crusade in the Mediterranean.

The possibility of divergent policies had also shown itself in the Low Countries. In the final analysis papal and Spanish policy coincided in the Low Countries. Philip II regarded religious unity as the indispensable condition for political unity and consequently he never intended to tolerate heresy. Rome, unable to act by itself, considered that the only hope for Catholicism in the Low Countries lay in the success of the Spanish cause there. Whether Philip II tried negotiation or force the papacy supported him, and supported him financially, as has been seen. It had no alternative. That is not to say, however, that Philip II was serving the church. In the Low Countries he was fighting for his own political inheritance. While supporting the church, he refused to be guided by it. On the contrary, he continually imposed his own will on it and regarded it as a subordinate ally: he went so far as to say that he had not been sufficiently supported by the papacy in his policy towards the rebels.[63] In fact it took some time for Spanish and papal policy to settle down together in the Low Countries. At first Philip II had the pope as well as the rebels to contend with. From early in 1566 Pius V was urging him to go in person to the Low Countries and arguing that his presence there was the only safeguard for the church. He also sent his own nuncio to investigate. Philip II ignored the advice and

[62] See above, pp. 239–49.

[63] B. de Meester, *Le Saint-Siège et les troubles des Pays-Bas, 1566–1579* (Louvain, 1934), p. 159. See below, pp. 288–308.

objected to the nuncio. Month after month the pope continued to blame the unfortunate Philip for Catholic losses in the Low Countries, because he was not there in person, and the king's only reply was evasion.[64] When the news from the Low Countries became worse and Philip could no longer maintain an optimistic front to the pope, he protested his zeal for religion in words that have since been regarded as his political philosophy: 'You can assure His Holiness that rather than suffer the slightest prejudice to religion and the service of God I will lose all my states and a hundred lives if I had them, because I do not wish nor do I intend to be lord over heretics.'[65] But this was written to his ambassador in Rome for papal consumption and because he was not in fact doing what the pope wanted him to do, going to the Low Countries in person.

In another matter too he was out of step with the pope. Pius V wanted a peaceful remedy, a negotiated settlement, whereas Philip was coming to the conclusion that force was going to be necessary. Eventually he convinced the pope that only an army would solve the problem, though Pius thought that it would merely be necessary to frighten the rebels with a show of force.[66] Philip decided to send in the Duke of Alba and his Spanish *tercios*. But how was the king going to describe the war? Would he call it a war against heretics, a sort of holy war, or would he call it a war against rebels? The pope would have preferred that the accent be placed on its religious character, that it be called a war against heretics rather than the suppression of a rebellion. The Spanish view was different.[67] In an interview with the papal nuncio in Madrid, Alba insisted that the pope had nothing to do with this affair and that the war would be waged according to the same form as that used not long since by Charles V in his struggle against the German Lutherans; that is as a war governed by reasons of state against rebels. To present the situation like this, argued Alba, would better avoid the intervention of England or other Protestant powers in northern Europe to help their co-religionists, while it was in the interest of no ruler to condone rebellion even in the subjects of another. Moreover, to put the accent on the political aspect of the enterprise would enable Alba to recruit German Lutheran troops for his army. This advice prevailed. In the view of Spaniards they were fighting a punitive war against rebel subjects who were resisting their legitimate sovereign. The fact that Philip II was concerned to gloss over the religious aspect, of course, does not

[64] *Corr. Dip.*, i. 131, 156–57, 237–39, 299, 308–12.

[65] Philip II to Requesens, 12 August 1566, *ibid.*, i. 316.

[66] *Ibid.*, i. 399–403, 431.

[67] Meester, *op. cit.*, pp. 82–85; L. van der Essen, 'Croisade contre les hérétiques ou guerre contre des rebelles. La psychologie des soldats et des officiers espagnols de l'armée de Flandre au XVIe siècle', *Revue d'Histoire Ecclésiastique*, li. (1956), 55–57.

mean that he did not think he had good religious motives. These he took for granted. He was arguing in fact that he was fighting the rebellion on political and religious grounds, but that it was wiser to be discreet about the religious ones in case Protestant powers were provoked by the presence of a huge crusading army in northern Europe. Gradually, however, Philip II came to worry less about discretion. In his correspondence with his governors in Brussels he spoke of 'rebels and heretics'. When in 1586, two years before the dispatch of the Armada against England, the king of Denmark tried to serve as mediator between Philip II and Elizabeth I, the Spanish king disavowed all responsibility for the war, and in reply to the suggestion that he should grant liberty of conscience to the rebels he wrote to the Danish king: 'One should not ask me a thing like that. For if it is clear that other sovereigns do not allow their subjects to have a religion other than the one they themselves profess, for reasons of state as well as for religious motives, why then should this attitude be denied to me?'[68] After the death of Don John, Farnese continued to speak always of 'heretics and rebels', thus assimilating the political and the religious character of the struggle. And in the letters of soldiers and officers, as well as in the Spanish chroniclers of the sixteenth century, the royal army is always called 'the Catholic army', and the war is waged, according to them, 'to defend the Catholic religion'.[69]

In Philip II's policy towards England, however, there was no ambiguity: he refused to align himself with the papacy and he was guided by political and not religious considerations. It is well known that he long repudiated aggressive Catholic plans against England and sought to protect Elizabeth against the hostility of the papacy, because he had no wish to further the interests of Mary Queen of Scots and of France. Twice he stopped Elizabeth's excommunications: in 1561, after the queen had refused to receive the papal nuncio, and again in 1563, when he blocked the excommunication debated in the Council of Trent. As late as 1570, when the papal bull of excommunication was finally issued, without consultation with the Spanish king, he forbade its publication in his own states and did all he could to prevent its reaching England. He protested to the papal nuncio and wrote to his ambassador in London that the bull 'will embitter feelings in England and drive the Queen and her friends to oppress and persecute the few good Catholics who still remain there'.[70] To Elizabeth herself he wrote that no act of the pope had caused him such displeasure. Nevertheless, in 1569 Philip

[68] L. van der Essen, *Alexandre Farnèse, prince de Parme, gouverneur général des Pays-Bas* (5 vols., Brussels, 1933–39), v. 78.

[69] Van der Essen, 'Croisade contre les hérétiques ou guerre contre des rebelles', *op. cit.*, p. 58.

[70] Philip II to D'Espés, 30 June 1570, *C.S.P. Spanish, Eliz.* (London, 1892–99), ii. 254.

II had been tempted to do something about England, but this had nothing to do with papal or religious objectives. It was the result of a number of provocations of a naval and commercial nature—the English pirates, Hawkins in the Caribbean, the seizure of the Duke of Alba's pay ships. He toyed with the idea of supporting the movement of rebellion in the north of England in 1569 and told Alba to hold himself at the ready.[71] After the rebellion had started—and failed—he authorised Alba to prepare an armed attack against Elizabeth, arguing that the way of force seemed the only way left to him.[72] But the decision to move had to come from Alba who regarded himself as the arbiter of Spanish policy in northern Europe and who was wise enough to see the folly of attempting any expedition; in his view more could be gained by negotiation.[73] In 1571 Philip reacted in a similar manner to the Ridolfi plot. Ridolfi had no credit with the Duke of Alba but he got the blessing of the pope, who for some time had been pressing Philip to do something for English Catholics. In July the king urged Alba to prepare an expedition against England in order to co-operate in the dethronement of Elizabeth and the substitution of Mary Queen of Scots.[74] But this order need not be taken seriously, for once again the initiative was left to Alba. He tersely advised the king that the conspirators were not to be trusted, and once again Philip concurred. After the failure of the Ridolfi plot Philip II remained indifferent to the fate of English Catholics, whose numbers and weakness did not serve his policy.

Consequently there was no co-operation between Philip II and Gregory XIII for an enterprise of England. Throughout the 1570's Philip consistently ignored papal proposals for an attack on England. The defence of his interests in the Low Countries, in Portugal and in America were more pressing problems than the launching of a crusade against Elizabeth. And when he finally decided to organise an expedition for the invasion of England, it was for a series of political and economic reasons rather than religious ones, and its objective was to strike at the source of the English attack on Spain and the empire. Philip II wanted the co-operation of the papacy for financial reasons and for moral support in his claim to dispose of the crown of England. He might have procured this from Gregory XIII, but Sixtus V was much more difficult.

[71] L. P. Gachard, ed., *Correspondance de Philippe II sur les affaires des Pays-Bas* (5 vols., Brussels, 1848–79), ii. 63; *Documentos inéditos*, xc. 186–87; see also P. O. de Törne, *Don Juan d'Autriche et les projets de conquête de l'Angleterre, 1568–1578* (Helsingfors, 1915–28), i. 42 ff.

[72] Philip II to Alba, 16 December 1569, *Documentos inéditos*, xxxviii. 258; Philip II to Alba, 24 December 1569, *ibid.*, p. 273.

[73] Gachard, *op. cit.*, ii. 70.

[74] Philip II to Alba, 14 July 1571, Gachard, *op. cit.*, ii. 185–88; see also Törne, *op. cit.*, i. 112–13.

The election of Sixtus V in April 1585 was a blow to Philip's hopes. Both men personally disliked each other. Moreover, the energetic and independent character of the new pope soon showed itself in a series of disputes over jurisdiction and protocol, so that when the Armada was being prepared, both sovereigns were squabbling over whether the papal nuncio in Spain should be styled 'monsignor' or 'monsignor reverendissimo'. It is true that both king and pope had an interest in England, but it was not the same interest. Moved by his suspicion of Philip II and Spanish power, Sixtus at first preferred a peaceful approach to Elizabeth. This policy was based on a serious miscalculation—that the queen could be converted to Catholicism—and naturally earned the contempt of Philip. 'It would seem', he remarked in the margin of his ambassador's letter, 'that the war in Flanders does not appear to him a great undertaking, nor that he knows what it costs. He is deceived about England and labours under a delusion.'[75] After the execution of Mary Stuart, the pope himself ceased to be deceived, yet he never ceased to admire Elizabeth, constantly comparing her favourably with Philip and contrasting her successes with his failures. In the final analysis, however, the pope could not oppose Philip's attack on England. He had not the means of doing so and in any case he could not ignore the interests of Catholicism, however low these might be in Philip's list of priorities. Therefore, while he regretted the necessity of the Armada and deplored Spanish slowness, he gave it his financial as well as his moral support in the treaty of July 1587.[76] In addition he made great efforts to extract from Henry III at least a promise of French neutrality.[77] Yet it was an uneasy alliance. At the level of jurisdiction the running fight between pope and king continued with its usual acrimony, and a series of minor disputes over titles, precedence, protocol and jurisdiction were raised into major issues and ran concurrently with the preparation of the Armada, so that the two allies presented no united front and the pope was openly speaking of excommunicating the king of Spain.[78] Philip ceased writing to the pope and only communicated with him through his ambassador. The Venetian ambassador in Rome reported Sixtus as saying: 'The king and his Armada are becoming ridiculous, while Queen Elizabeth knows how to manage her affairs. If that woman were only a Catholic, she would be loved by us more than any other sovereign, for she has great qualities. . . . That Spanish Armada gives us anxiety. We have strong

[75] J. A. von Hübner, Sixte-Quinte (Paris, 1870), i. 329, 364–71, 372; ii. 476, 495, 500–504; iii. 4–5.

[76] Text of the Treaty of 29 July 1587 in A. O. Meyer, England and the Catholic Church under Queen Elizabeth (Eng. trans., London, 1916), pp. 520–23.

[77] Hübner, op. cit., i. 392–94.

[78] Pastor, op. cit., xxi. 269.

presentiments that it will not succeed.'[79] In the spring of 1588 the pope was full of pessimism and confided to the French ambassador that everything was going from bad to worse, that Philip was constantly asking for the subsidy which he had promised, but which he had promised only when success had attended their efforts and the expedition had landed.[80] From Philip's point of view, therefore, the alliance was not even bringing the money he hoped for and needed.

After the defeat of the Armada there was even less chance of persuading Sixtus to pay the subsidy. The Spanish ambassador in Rome, the count of Olivares, on hearing of the disaster from the Duke of Parma, was the first to tell the pope of it, and a series of stormy audiences followed. According to the terms of the treaty for the subsidies the pope owed the king a million *escudos*, which the ambassador now claimed. The pope refused to pay on the grounds that the provisions of the treaty did not apply to this payment, which was only due in the event of a landing being made in England, and he told Olivares to drop the subject. 'I find him', reported the ambassador, 'very lukewarm in his tokens of satisfaction whenever good news comes from Spain and not much affected by bad news from that quarter. Envy of Your Majesty's greatness and his horror at parting with money act more powerfully upon his nature than do the welfare of the church and zeal to see the annihilation of heresy in the world.'[81] The failure of the Armada, in fact, ruined the already tenuous relations between the two allies. Irritated in the extreme, Sixtus V began to doubt the power and capacity of Philip II and to reproach himself for having wasted his time and money. Unimpressed by Philip's difficulties and urgent demands, he never payed the million *escudos*. He now argued that he had never advised the sending of the Armada; the king had only been interested in subduing England and adding to his empire, while the last thing he had thought of was the restoration of Catholicism, which was the essential condition for the pope. It was more than simply want of faith, however, that made Sixtus V reserved towards his ally. He admitted that he was like a fly compared to an elephant before the king on whose dominions the sun never set.[82] The failure of the Armada, therefore, had its compensations. No more than any other sovereign in Europe did he want a universal monarchy under Philip II. He never disguised his opinion on the subject. To the Venetian envoy he more than once expressed his wish for a balance of power in Europe: 'Great Christian princes require a counterpoise; for if one prevails the others run the risk of giving in on many things which he

[79] Hübner, *op. cit.*, i. 389–91.   [80] *Ibid.*, p. 396.
[81] Olivares to Philip II, 26 Sept. 1588, *ibid.*, iii. 257–61.
[82] Pastor, *op. cit.*, xxi. 273.

may ask for.'[83] This was one of the reasons why he was anxious for the security of France. It was over the French problem, the final issue between Philip II and the papacy, that relations between the two completely collapsed and that their religious as well as their political interests most clearly diverged.

In September 1585 Henry of Navarre and Henry of Bourbon were declared heretics and pronounced incapable of succeeding to the throne of France.[84] Sixtus V soon regretted this mistake, which was due partly to his inexperience and partly to Spanish influence, and began to favour a policy of conciliation towards Henry of Navarre in the hope of his conversion. If Philip II, exploiting religious conflicts, succeeded in getting the crown of France, how could the pope then resist his power, which would dominate almost the entire Catholic world? And would he not then increase his pressure in Italy? The interests of religion as well as of politics caused the pope to work in France against the Spanish party and the League. In the mind of the king of Spain the question of the succession was the essential issue, while it was only secondary in the eyes of Sixtus V. To become eligible in the eyes of the papacy Henry of Navarre had only to return to Catholicism. Philip foresaw this and therefore he had to argue that his conversion could only be a pretence, for he refused to countenance the candidature of Henry on any account. Consequently in the years 1587–88 he made it clear in Rome that if the pope accepted Henry's conversion and candidature, then he would oppose it and fight, even if it meant the dismemberment of France. It was 1590 before the pope forced the issue with Spain, when he received in audience the Duke of Luxembourg who, as official representative of the Catholic supporters of Henry of Navarre but in reality sent by the king himself, had instructions to improve relations between Henry and the Roman Curia. Sixtus began to favour a reconciliation with the French monarchy on grounds of personal sympathy and of policy. Spanish opinion was outraged. Philip II and his ministers tried everything they knew to get the pope to dismiss Luxembourg, which provoked Sixtus into replying that he would listen 'to the devil himself if he came here'. Eventually Philip instructed his ambassador, Olivares, to force the pope to ratify the promises made in his favour and in particular to dismiss the Duke of Luxembourg, to excommunicate all French prelates who were supporters of Henry of Navarre, and to declare that as a relapsed heretic the latter could not be admitted to the bosom of the church and was incapable of succeeding to the throne of France. The pope was unwilling

[83] Hübner, *op. cit.*, ii. 516.
[84] For the following see Hübner, *op. cit.*, ii. 168, 172–76, 288, 298, 307, 351–52; iii. 477–91.

to do any of these things, and after Olivares had had recourse to intimi-
dation, threatening schism and coercive measures, there took place between
them that violent interview in which Olivares in the name of his king
threatened the pope with a public protest against his conduct, while Sixtus
called the count a 'criminal, scandalous creature, the cause of all these
troubles', and threatened to expel him from Rome. Philip tried another
ambassador and maintained the pressure, with some apparent success. He
received the promise that Rome would never recognise as king of France
anyone who did not have the approval of Philip II; Luxembourg ceased to
receive audience; and on 19 July 1590 an offensive and defensive alliance
was concerted between the pope and the Spanish ambassador. But this was
merely a draft of a convention and not a signed treaty. Moreover, the pope
always found new pretexts for modifying the fulfilment of this agreement
and he successfully refused to commit himself to Spain. Consequently the
news of his death in August 1590 was received with relief in Spain in the
conviction that there could not possibly be another pope who was a greater
enemy of Spaniards. Clement VIII, however, was equally reluctant to
serve Spanish policy. Unwilling to oppose the victorious and converted
Henry IV simply to satisfy Spanish interests, or to provoke a schism between
France and Rome for purely political reasons that had little to do with the
papacy, in September 1595 the pope absolved and recognised the monarch
whom Philip II still considered simply as the prince of Béarn and a relapsed
heretic and with whom he had been at war since January of the same year.

The conflict between Philip II and the papacy over France summarises
the essential issues between the two. Philip II believed that he had the
right to tell the pope what was best for the church. The pope believed
that Philip was confusing what was best for the church with what was
best for Spanish interests. In the midst of the stormy interviews with
Olivares, Sixtus V wrote to Philip II reminding him of the obligation
under which the pope was to listen to heretics, protesting against the threats
of councils and schisms, and declaring that he could not admit that secular
princes should constitute themselves judges of the vicar of Christ. Philip II's
view of papal obligations and his own rights was quite different. In his
answer to the pope he wrote:

Nothing has surprised me more than to see your Holiness, after an act
inspired by God (the bull against Henry of Navarre) leaving time to the
heretics to take root in France, without even ordering that the Catholic
partisans of 'the Béarnais' should separate from his cause. The church is
on the eve of losing one of its members; Christendom is on the point
of being set on fire by the united heretics; Italy runs the greatest danger,

and in the presence of the enemy we look on and we temporise! And
the blame is put upon me because, looking at those interests as if they
were my own, I hasten to your Holiness as to a father whom I love and
respect and as a good son remind him of the duties of the Holy See! By
God's mercy, where have you found in the whole course of my life
reasons for thinking of me as you tell me men think of me, and by what
right do you tell it me? God and the whole world know my love for
the Holy See, and nothing will ever make me deviate from it, not even
your Holiness by the great injustice you do me in writing such things to
me. But the greater my devotion the less I shall consent to your failing
in your duty towards God and towards the Church, who have given
you the means of acting; and, at the risk of being importunate to your
Holiness and displeasing you, I shall insist on your setting to the task.[85]

In the pope's eyes the task in question was one of serving Spanish political
interests in France. But Philip II was not the first ruler, nor the last, to
believe that his own interests and those of religion were identical.

[85] *Ibid.*, ii. 304; iii. 451.

CHAPTER IX

THE TURNING POINT:
TO THE ATLANTIC AND THE NORTH

SIR FRANCIS WALSINGHAM, that constant advocate of an English-led Protestant league against Spain, wrote to the Earl of Leicester from his embassy in France in 1571: 'I conclude that we rest on evil terms with Spain, whereof there must grow redress either by composition or by sword. Redress by composition may seem scarce sure, as that which will serve their turn for a while, they can disguise their malice for a time. Redress by the sword, comparing our forces with theirs may appear at first sight void of all possibility. But if you consider the opportunity that this present time offereth. . . .'[1] The advice, inverting the terms, might equally have been given to Philip II by any of his more militant advisers, for Spain too had its Walsinghams and England its weaknesses. But Spain's greatest general was not one of the war-mongers. If the Duke of Alba, archetype of the Castilian warrior, whose whole life was dedicated to the sword, preferred redress by composition and sought accommodation with England, the reason must have been compelling indeed. The reason was the Netherlands, Walsingham's 'opportunity' but for the Duke of Alba and his sovereign a trap from which there was no escape. Here Alba's reputation was torn to shreds: sent by Philip II in 1567 to reduce his rebellious subjects to obedience, six years later he was caught in the rising tide of revolution, 'not only', as he himself put it, 'up to my neck but over my head'.[2] Philip II's tiny dominion in the north became a gigantic battlefield, the weakest sector of his defences, consuming his men and money voraciously. Here his political, religious, and economic interests were starkly exposed, his policies resisted by his own subjects, and his difficulties exploited by his foreign enemies. In these conditions Elizabeth I did not need to attack Spain, and Philip II could not afford to attack England. From 1567 Spain was pinned down on two fronts, in the Mediterranean and in the Low Countries. For the following ten years, until he could disengage from the Turk, Philip II's double commitments

---

[1] Quoted in Conyers Read, *Mr. Secretary Walsingham and the Policy of Queen Elizabeth* (3 vols., Oxford, 1925), i. 153.
[2] Alba to Philip II, 24 Feb. 1573, *Epistolario del III Duque de Alba, Don Fernando Alvarez de Toledo*, ed. Duke of Alba (3 vols., Madrid, 1952), iii. 294.

overlapped in time and stretched his resources to breaking point, so that in 1575 he was forced to declare the second state bankruptcy of the reign. These were reasons enough to prevent his seeking redress from England by the sword and from indulging in anything beyond defence and diplomacy. Like Elizabeth he preferred to wait and see.

I. THE REVOLT OF THE NETHERLANDS

After Charles V abdicated the sovereignty of the Netherlands to Philip II in 1555 the people of the seventeen provinces found themselves ruled, not by an emperor, but by a foreign king. This in itself was a loss of status. To be part of an empire, equal to the other parts, was one thing, to be a dominion of Spain was another. Philip II's attempt to rule his dominion by the absolutist methods with which he was familiar in Castile made the situation doubly intolerable and created opposition—opposition to the king of a foreign country and its system of government. To Spain the Netherlands were equally foreign. Unlike Castile and Aragon, they were not an integral part of the crown's inheritance but an appendage recently acquired. Why, then, was Philip II determined to hold them at all costs? What were they worth to Spain?

Materially their worth was immense. After the Indies they were Castile's most important economic life-line, a market for her wool and a source of vital goods and services. By the middle of the sixteenth century Antwerp was the greatest commercial centre in Europe, an entrepôt between north and south, trading not only in the manufactures of the Netherlands themselves but also in agricultural and industrial goods from the rest of Europe and in a growing volume of colonial products. The large reserves of capital thus accumulated made it a centre of international finance, where governments as well as private merchants sought loans. On both accounts, commercial and financial, Antwerp had clients all over Europe, but especially in Spain. Every year large fleets sailed from Bilbao and Laredo to the Low Countries, and an even larger volume of Netherlands shipping sought the ports of the peninsula. The Spanish and Portuguese merchant colonies in Antwerp were larger than those of any other nation: an estimate covering the years 1553–54 accounted for 200 Spanish merchants, and by 1560 the Spanish colony numbered 300.[3] In the same period exports to the Iberian countries accounted for two-thirds of the total exports of the Netherlands.

[3] L. van der Essen, 'Contribution à l'histoire du port d'Anvers et du commerce des Pays-Bas vers l'Espagne et le Portugal à l'époque de Charles Quint (1553-1554)',Bulletin de l'Académie royale d'Archéologie de Belgique, iii. (1920), 39–64; see also J.-A. Goris, Étude sur les colonies marchandes méridionales (Portugais, Espagnols, Italiens), à Anvers de 1488 à 1567 (Louvain, 1925), p. 70.

The Spanish market, in fact, was vital to the Netherlands, for it helped to restore their adverse balance of trade with England, Italy, Germany, and France, and this was one reason why some kind of political link with Spain was not necessarily inimical to them.

But whatever the value of Spain to the Netherlands, the Netherlands had greater value to Spain. From them or through them Spain received textiles (accounting for 30 per cent. of the exports from Antwerp to the peninsula), metal and metallurgical products needed for equipping domestic and colonial agriculture and industry, arms for her military forces, and mercury for her silver mines. Above all, she received two vital commodities—cereals and naval stores. English and Baltic grain supplemented Spain's imports from France and the Mediterranean countries, and helped to make good the chronic shortages of cereals from which she suffered, while timber and other naval stores from the Baltic were an urgent necessity to a sea power whose demands outstripped domestic resources.[4] These goods, of course, were not produced by the Netherlands themselves, but their merchants specialised in buying them cheaply and they possessed the shipping to transport them to Spain. Against these imports Spain sent to the Low Countries colonial products such as spices, sugar, cochineal, and hides, and important supplies of salt, oil, wine, fruits, and saffron. But her greatest export was wool, for which the Low Countries were her most important market, absorbing about 60 per cent. of the total Spanish product.[5] By the sixteenth century the wool of Castile had largely replaced the English product in the textile centres of the Netherlands, partly because of the decline of English exports and partly because the political link with the Low Countries provided favourable conditions of competition for Spanish merchants.[6]

Spain, then, had a considerable stake in the Low Countries. She did not profit directly, of course, from all their commercial activities, but she had a share in their wealth, her merchants were deeply involved in their trade, and they were an important and protected market for her few, and therefore vital, exports.[7] Moreover, they supplied indispensable commodities which the state as well as its subjects needed and which relieved it of the necessity of depending entirely on foreign suppliers or on foreign shipping. In the final analysis, perhaps, most of these assets could have been preserved under a different relationship than direct possession exercised by absolute government. But Philip II knew no other relationship. Even if the Low Countries had been devoid of economic value to him, he would still have regarded

[4] V. Vázquez de Prada, *Lettres Marchandes d'Anvers* (4 vols., Paris, 1960–61), i. 67–87.
[5] Carande, *Carlos V y sus banqueros. i. La vida económica de España*, 57–59.
[6] C. Viñas y Mey, *Los Paises Bajos en la política y en la economía mundial de España* (Madrid, 1944), p. 330.
[7] On Spain's balance of payments problem see above, pp. 150–52.

them as his rightful inheritance, as indeed they were. And in his eyes there was only one way of governing them—by the absolute methods he used in the rest of his dominions. Anything less he could not trust; short of absolutism he believed he could not impose his will, least of all in religion. He refused to tolerate Protestantism; apart from the question of conscience, which was probably decisive in his case, experience showed that Protestants did not tolerate Catholics, and it was inconceivable to him that he should allow his Catholic subjects to be persecuted by heretics. The logic was inexorable. But it was also incomplete, for the majority of his subjects in the Low Countries were Catholics and remained so for many years to come.

Religion, in fact, was only part of the complex of Philip II's policy in the Low Countries, as it was of that of his opponents there. Absolutism had yet another end in view—revenue. Philip II was not indifferent to the opinions and the interests of his merchants, if only because he wanted to tax them. For the same reason he was interested in the wealth of the Low Countries, an irresistible target for a government at its wits' end to finance the war with which his reign began. It was not easy to tax the Low Countries, but he never gave up hope of making them contribute to the expenses of his policy in northern Europe. As long as the war continued, until 1559, the day of reckoning was postponed, for Philip was forced to conciliate the Estates (the provincial and general assemblies with whom he had to negotiate taxation), while they were prepared to concede at least a portion of his financial demands. The crisis was deferred to the post-war years when the king was not so ready to compromise and his subjects saw less reason to contribute. But in Philip's view the reason was just as urgent, for he had to meet the onerous debt left by the wars and rescue his finances from impending disaster. To tap the wealth of the Netherlands effectively he had to use methods of government more absolute than those of his predecessors in order to break through the constitutional restraints on his authority. In this way the political and financial problems merged: absolutism and taxation went hand in hand. This procedure was perfectly consistent with his principles of government. He ruled the component parts of his empire by a combination of central authority and regional devolution, allowing such local autonomy as was compatible with his sovereignty. But what was possible to overlook in Aragon and Catalonia, where, as has been seen, there was little at stake and where the central authority was close enough to intervene if necessary, could not be ignored in the Low Countries, where there were vital issues at stake—religion and revenue—and where central authority was already attenuated by the factor of distance.

The obstacles in the way of taxation were real. The grants of subsidies, whether in general or provincial assemblies, were subject to allotment by the provincial Estates, and they were never permanent. Moreover, if the tax yielded any surplus over the absolute total agreed upon, then the surplus remained not in the royal treasury but with the separate Estates. These conditions had long been experienced by Charles V. In 1542 he tried to improve the crown's position: he asked the various Estates to agree to the innovation of direct taxes at fixed rates. Most of the Estates were induced to accept an income tax set at 10 per cent. on real and at lower rates on personal property and salaries. But the emperor did not attempt to deprive the Estates of their political rôle in the allotment and collection of the tax, both of which remained in their hands.[8] It was a compromise, and for this reason the Estates were persuaded to co-operate. But Philip II was not prepared to compromise; debate over allotment and delay in collection were inimical to his sovereignty and inadequate for his needs. Yet he began his reign more dependent on the Estates than his father had been. In 1556 he proposed an income tax, but he was refused by the Estates then and again in 1558, and he had to be content with antiquated extraordinary grants, subject to allotment and collection by the Estates. Their greatest concession was the Nine Years' Aid of 1558, which yielded 800,000 Flemish pounds a year; but officers of the Estates assessed the taxes, and collected them, and it was before them that the troops paraded to receive their pay. Granvelle observed that the system was perfectly devised to place royal finances in the hands of merchants. And worse was to come. In 1559 the Estates drew up a list of political grievances, and increasingly they became the vehicle of resistance to Philip's methods of government. He instructed his regent secretly never to convoke them again.

His regent was his half-sister, Margaret of Parma, whom he left in charge of the Low Countries when he returned to Spain in 1559. Margaret was the illegitimate daughter of Charles V, her mother was Flemish, and she had been brought up in the Low Countries. But she was clearly a 'Spanish' governor, and she was bound by her instructions. These enjoined her in matters of policy to take the advice of three members of the Council of State, of whom the most important was Antoine Perrenot, Lord of Granvelle, the son of Charles V's principal minister, a Burgundian, but as devoted to the Spanish crown as any Spaniard. This inner committee thus usurped the functions of the Council of State and thereby deprived the higher nobility of the Netherlands of any responsibility for government. Native councillors, like William of Orange and Lamoral of Egmont, who had expected Philip II to govern through them, the natural leaders of the country and the traditional advisers of the king, soon discovered that the Council was a mere mask

[8] G. Griffiths, 'Representative Institutions in the Spanish Empire in the sixteenth century. II. The Low Countries', *The Americas*, xii. (1956), 233-45.

behind which Philip governed through Cardinal Granvelle. Aware of their resentment, the regent advised Philip to exercise restraint, with some effect: in 1561 he withdrew his *tercios*—a concession to his financial advisers in Spain rather than to his political opponents in the Netherlands—and in 1564 he removed the hated Granvelle. But concessions only led to further demands, and as resistance to royal authority became more general so it grew in content. A deputation representing the lesser nobility presented a demand to the regent (April 1566) to moderate the enforcement of the decrees against heretics and reduce the operations of the Inquisition. In the course of the summer of 1566 she was forced to accede to their demands. Thus the alienation of the nobility assisted the progress of militant Calvinism.

The fact was that the Netherlands were only one of a number of problems which pressed themselves upon Philip II and had to take their place in his order of priorities. In the period 1559–66 his hands were tied by more urgent commitments in the Mediterranean. The maritime offensive of the Ottoman Turk and his ally in the west, Algiers, forced Spain to fight a long and costly war of defence and counter-attack in which the first respite did not occur until the death of Suleiman the Magnificent in late 1566. These immediate dangers prevented Philip from assigning sufficient men and money to the Netherlands to stifle the growth of opposition there. The Netherlands nobles were fully aware of the link between the two fronts and exploited it, while the best Philip could do was to buy time. Thus he had to watch the development of a concerted opposition, reduce Spanish troops, recall Granvelle, allow his central government to be eroded by noble power, and even moderate the heresy laws in 1566. But concessions only gave heart to his enemies and finally led to religious disorder and outrage.[9]

Protestantism had come to the Netherlands in three forms. By 1519 Lutheranism had already made considerable progress in Antwerp among the Augustinian friars and the resident Hanseatic merchants, while converted Spanish and Portuguese Jews actively promoted the new faith.[10] It soon spread throughout the south, but its penetration remained sporadic, and organised Lutheran communities survived only in Antwerp and perhaps in Bruges. Then Anabaptism, with its apocalyptic vision of the kingdom

---

[9] On the revolt of the Netherlands see P. Geyl, *The Revolt of the Netherlands* (London, 1932); E. H. Kossmann and A. F. Mellink, *Texts Concerning the Revolt of the Netherlands* (Cambridge, 1975); Geoffrey Parker, *The Dutch Revolt* (London, 1977); Geoffrey Parker also studies the wider context of the revolt, including the link with the Mediterranean, in *Spain and the Netherlands, 1559–1659: Ten Studies* (London, 1979), pp. 28–29. On Granvelle see M. Van Durme, *El Cardenal Granvela (1517–1586)* (Barcelona, 1957), pp. 199–271. See also above, pp. 104–7.

[10] L. E. Halkin, *La Réforme en Belgique sous Charles-Quint* (Brussels, 1957).

of God on earth, and its revolutionary appeal to the socially oppressed, began to stir the urban masses in the late 1520's, and provided the majority of the Protestant martyrs in the southern Netherlands, perhaps 1,000 out of 1,600 victims of repression under Charles V. Finally Calvinism, propagated from Geneva and Strasbourg, penetrated the Walloon regions in the period 1540–45, and from towns like Tournai and Valenciennes gradually extended its base into Flanders, to reach Antwerp by the mid-1550's. Antwerp, with its foreign merchants, its clandestine printing presses, its semi-autonomous government, a stronghold of the Lutherans and a haven for the Anabaptists, now became a bulwark of the Calvinist community of the southern Netherlands. And the central government, the provincial council of justice, and the papal Inquisition all failed to quell its newest dissenters.

This was the situation which Philip II inherited and to deal with it he continued the policy of his father, issuing 'placards', or edicts against heresy, and pursuing it with the Inquisition. Yet within a few years he was faced with a revolutionary opposition beyond anything his father had experienced. The difference cannot be explained entirely in terms of the personality and policy of the new king. It is true that Philip II was more inflexible than the emperor, who had allowed the Inquisition to be excluded from certain provinces, had mitigated the 'placards' of 1550 in their application to Antwerp, and had applied them in general with a moderation which was alien to Philip II and which he was determined to end. On the other hand, contrary to the rumour which circulated in the Netherlands and which played some part in exciting the opposition of Catholics as well as Protestants, he never intended to introduce the Spanish Inquisition. The reason was simple, and he gave it himself: 'The story they invent that we wish to introduce the Spanish Inquisition there is false and without foundation, because the Inquisition of the Low Countries is more merciless than the one here.'[11] He was referring to the fact that the Inquisition in the Netherlands, canonically papal but with appointments in fact controlled by the crown, followed a procedure which allowed no pardon even to repentant heretics. So Philip II was content with the institution he inherited from the emperor and urged it to greater efforts. Yet even this was not sufficient to account for the greater resistance to royal authority. The decisive difference was in conditions. Most of the heretics executed under Charles V were Anabaptists, whom everyone hated and in whose repression Charles received the co-operation

[11] Philip II to Margaret of Parma, 17 July 1562, quoted in M. Dierickx, S.J., 'La politique religieuse de Philippe II dans les anciens Pays-Bas', *Hispania*, xvi. (1956), 130–43, especially p. 137.

of the ruling classes of the Netherlands. But by 1559 there was a change; the peace of Cateau-Cambrésis opened the southern frontier to increasing numbers of Calvinists who now penetrated more deeply than they had done in the previous reign. Calvinism was more successful than Lutheranism or Anabaptism because it was organised efficiently, possessed a propaganda machine, and was part of an international movement with directing and recruiting bases outside the Netherlands. Its leaders preached and prompted active resistance to the authorities, and made Calvinism the focus of organised opposition, which, as it lacked the social overtones of Anabaptism, drew adherents from the lower nobility and the burghers.[12] After the departure of Granvelle, the tolerance, or indifference, of magnates like Orange and Egmont, allowed it to spread in all the southern provinces, and the Netherlands officials, affected by Erasmist ideas of toleration and hostile to the Inquisition, were reluctant to execute the 'placards' against heresy. In June 1565 a commission of three bishops, three professors of Louvain, and three high officials, advised Philip to exercise moderation, but advice like this only convinced the king—probably rightly—that he could not rely on local officials and that moderation would allow Calvinism to win further successes. Consequently, in October 1565 he again insisted on a rigorous application of the anti-heresy laws by the Inquisition, and he refused to regard himself bound by the concessions that Margaret of Parma was forced to make in the summer of 1566. Instead, he began to prepare a new policy and new instruments.

By this time he had already given the opposition further cause for resentment. For Philip II had a policy of reform as well as repression. In the spirit of the Counter-Reformation he introduced the Jesuits into the Netherlands, founded the University of Douai, and—more significantly—in 1559 created fourteen new bishoprics in which he incorporated some abbacies. To both bishoprics and abbacies he had rights of presentation, with an understanding that his candidates would be appointed by the pope. The measure was needed in the interests of ecclesiastical reform, but it also had political repercussions, for in one move Philip increased the number of his supporters in the Estates General, where the prelates would have seats, and extended his rights of patronage at the expense of the local nobility. Thus his policy was interpreted even by his Catholic opponents as another example of Spanish intervention.

By 1566, therefore, the interaction of Philip II's policy and local conditions had created a revolutionary situation. His absolutist methods stimulated an

---

[12] See H. G. Koenigsberger, 'The Organization of Revolutionary Parties in France and the Netherlands during the Sixteenth Century', *Journal of Modern History*, xxvii. (1955), 335-51.

SPAIN AND THE
NETHERLANDS

NORTH
SEA

ENGLAND

FRIESLAND

GRONINGEN

DRENTH

London
R. Thames

Margate

Dover

Calais

Gravelines

Dunkirk

Nieuport

Ostend

Sluys

Flushing

Middleburg

ZEELAND

Bruges

Ghent

FLANDERS

Lille

Tournais

HAINAULT

Arras

Valenciennes

ARTOIS

Cambrai

Amiens

St. Quentin

Vervins

Rocroi

PICARDY

Rouen

R. Oise

R. Aisne

FRANCE

R. Seine

Paris

Amsterdam

Leyden

Delft

Brill

Rotterdam

UTRECHT

Utrecht

Deventer

Zutphen

R. Yssel

Nymegen

R. Waal

Breda

GELDERLAND

Antwerp

BRABANT

Brussels

Namur

R. Meuse

LIEGE

LIMBURG

R. Rhine

LUXEMBURG

English Channel

0   25   50   75 Miles

.... Frontier between the Spanish Netherlands
in the south and the United Provinces in
the north, after the latter had established
their independence.

295

already latent opposition, but this opposition was not homogeneous, for it represented the interests of different political, religious, and economic groups. The higher nobility objected to the removal of political opportunities which the introduction of bureaucratic government entailed, and their resentment was increased by the parlous state of their private finances, hit by inflation and by their own heavy expenditure.[13] As their economic position was being undermined, they were all the more dependent on political or administrative careers; once they lost their monopoly of civil and ecclesiastical preferment they would lose the opportunity of compensating for the decline of income from their estates. This is precisely what Philip II's method of government threatened to do. The lower nobility were even more heavily in debt; dependent on fixed incomes from land, they were particularly hit by rising prices from about 1550 and desperately searching for opportunities to extricate themselves from their predicament.[14] And their opportunities were even less than those of the higher nobility. Yet the aristocracy were not revolutionaries: they wanted to capture the machinery of state without subverting the social and religious order. But, under cover of their estrangement from the crown and of the universal resentment of Philip II's ecclesiastical policies, the Calvinists were able to come out into the open and defy the authorities. In spite of their converts among burghers and lower nobility, the majority of the population was still nominally Catholic; but there was much religious indifference and many 'politiques' who were prepared to work with any religious group that opposed the Spanish administration. Calvinism, however, was not a proletarian movement, as Anabaptism had been. There are reasons for believing, moreover, that working-class conditions in the Netherlands under Philip II were less oppressive than in the reign of his father; conditions of industry and trade were good until at least 1580, in spite of political conditions, and from about 1556 wages began to catch up with prices.[15] The political and religious opposition of the privileged classes would only receive mass support when economic conditions were oppressive and people sought release from their misery and hunger. This was rare in Philip II's reign, when the ratio between incomes and prices was generally favourable to wage-earners. But a crisis of subsistence did occur in 1566, and for a brief period the different elements of political,

---

[13] G. Griffiths, *William of Hornes, Lord of Hèze, and the Revolt of the Netherlands (1576–1580)* (Berkeley, Calif., 1954), pp. 9–15.

[14] H. G. Koenigsberger, 'Property and the Price Revolution (Hainault, 1474–1573)', *Economic History Review*, Second Series, ix. (1956), 1–15.

[15] C. Verlinden, J. Craeybeckx, and E. Scholliers, 'Mouvements des prix et des salaires en Belgique au XVIe siècle', *Annales. Économies. Sociétés. Civilisations*, x. (1955), 173–98; Verlinden, 'Crises économiques et sociales en Belgique à l'époque de Charles-Quint', *Charles-Quint et son temps*, pp. 177–90; and see below, pp. 308–13.

religious, and social protest coincided. When the resistance of the nobles to Philip II's methods of government brought about a moderation in the enforcement of the anti-heresy laws, Calvinists moved into action, and hunger added working-class violence to what was momentarily a collective opposition. The result was a great outburst of riots in the towns in August 1566, accompanied by looting of churches and monasteries and wholesale destruction of Catholic religious iconography.

Violence against his own religion in his own dominions shocked Philip II profoundly. He determined to suppress the opposition by force before it was too late. The task was formidable, for the opposition was no longer in its infancy and it was difficult to identify it accurately, dispersed as it was among different groups and interests. Whom should he strike—the Catholic nobles or the Calvinists? The former were themselves alarmed by the explosive results of even partial toleration, and after the events of August there was a reaction in favour of authority and Catholicism, which Margaret of Parma skilfully exploited to restore order. If not pressed too far, the nobles might possibly be won back to allegiance. At the same time, once the economic crisis of 1565–66 had passed, there was no longer mass support for the opposition from the politically inert. This left only the Calvinists. Now was the moment, Margaret of Parma advised Philip in the spring of 1567, to make concessions, this time from a position of strength. Philip II ignored the advice, and his reasons are not far to seek. Moderation had been tried and had failed: it compromised his own authority and allowed Protestants to terrorise Catholics. It was the dual nature of his objectives, political as well as religious, which drove him to adopt a policy of total repression. He had no desire to isolate the religious opposition by making bargains with his political opponents, for he was convinced the time had come to bring the latter to heel. To make his sovereignty effective he was prepared to use its ultimate sanction—the army. A pause in the conflict with the Ottoman Turk enabled him to send to the Netherlands all the Spanish troops who had served in the Mediterranean theatre of war; together with German and Netherlands units, these briefly gave him an army of 60,000 for the northern front.

2. FROM ALBA TO FARNESE

In December 1566 Philip II had already commissioned the Duke of Alba to proceed to Italy and assemble an army out of the veteran Spanish forces stationed there.[16] Slowly but, given the difficulties of distance and the king's

[16] L. P. Gachard, ed., *Correspondance de Philippe II sur les affaires des Pays-Bas*, ii. 600–602, 619–22.

other commitments, with a superb effort of organisation, the *tercios* of
Lombardy, Naples, and Sicily were moved northwards, and on 9 August
1567 their vanguard entered Brussels. With it came its general and Philip's
new governor, the Duke of Alba. His mission was to crush the political
and religious opposition, and at the same time to complete the process of
centralisation and absolutism, or, as his secret instructions told him, 'to
make all the states into one kingdom, with Brussels its capital'.[17] He moved
quickly into action. Side-stepping the Council of State and other local
institutions, he struck at the opposition with a new instrument, the Council
of Troubles, or Council of Blood, as it came to be called. This was a tribunal
of seven, three of whom were Spaniards, operating with virtually absolute
powers under the presidency of the governor himself. Its purpose was to
root out heresy, but it was equally concerned with destroying the political
opposition. Anticipating the danger, William of Orange escaped across the
German frontier but others were slower. The counts of Egmont and Hornes
were lured to Alba's headquarters in Brussels and there arrested in September
1567. The new governor was also equal to military threats. Orange recruited
an army in Germany, and in the spring of 1568 launched the first attack on
the Spanish occupation forces, hoping this would attract noble and popular
support; but the reaction against the religious riots of 1566 had gone too far
to permit an alliance of the political and religious oppositions. As a further
deterrent to any who were wavering in their allegiance, Alba executed
Egmont and Hornes in the main square of Brussels on 5 June. Having
terrorised the nobility and isolated Orange, he then overwhelmed the
invading troops with his own superior forces.

Confident of his strength, Alba proceeded with his programme of political
repression and pursuit of heresy, with a ruthlessness that has earned him
universal condemnation. He himself, of course, was a soldier, and his
political philosophy was simple: 'Kings are born to give orders, subjects to
obey them.'[18] He had long been advocating a policy of repression, and his
views were known to Philip II; he was also acting under instructions.
Responsibility for what followed, therefore, must be shared between him
and his sovereign. Alba himself did not consider his methods particularly
cruel. Referring to the imprisonment of Egmont and Hornes, he wrote:
'It would have been easy to arrest more, but the intention of the king was
not to spill blood, nor am I partial to that; if it is possible to remedy the
situation here by any other means, those means will be taken, for it is not
intended to uproot this vineyard, only to prune it.' To Philip II himself he

---

[17] In A. L. E. Verheyden, *Le Conseil des Troubles. Liste des condamnés (1566–1573)*
(Brussels, 1961), p. 508.
[18] *Epistolario del III Duque de Alba*, i. 58.

wrote: 'The tranquillity of these states is not to be gained by beheading men who are moved by the persuasion of others.'[19] He seems, in fact, to have intended to instil terror by example, and to crush the opposition by eliminating its leaders. But he cast his net widely, and what was to him a 'pruning' operation, to the people of the Netherlands was a widespread attack on their lives and property. Could the thousands of victims of the Council of Troubles, drawn as they were from all social classes, be regarded as leaders? Between 1567 and 1573 the tribunal condemned 12,302 people, of whom 1,105 were executed or banished.[20] Superficially it was accomplishing the objects for which it had been established, but beneath the surface it was stirring up yet greater resentment. Its policy of political repression helped to revive resistance to the Spanish monarchy and its agents. Anyone with political or administrative responsibility lived in fear of its dread hand, and its heavy confiscation of property hit heirs as well as victims. The question of property was important: this was to be seen unmistakably in the reaction to the second stage of Alba's programme.

Alba was expected to raise money as well as restore order—money to finance his army and administration, so that the Netherlands could be ruled without subsidies from Spain. And he was expected to do this by methods which did not compromise royal authority or involve any concessions to the Estates. By March 1569 he was ready to meet the Estates—and to extinguish them. He proposed a 1 per cent. non-recurrent income tax on property, together with sales taxes of 10 per cent. on personal and 5 per cent. on real property. The Estates were deprived of any rôle in administering these taxes, and the sales taxes were intended to relieve the crown of the need ever to consult them again.[21] The Estates objected on two grounds. Politically the permanent nature of the sales tax—which looked suspiciously like the Spanish *alcabala*—threatened their very existence, while its social implications augured ill for their traditional privileges. For the new taxes were designed to tap the national income rationally, irrespective of privilege and exemption, and they were intended to fall on those best able to pay, simply according to the value of property or the price of its sale. Under the old system, however, whereby the Estates themselves assessed taxation within an agreed total, those represented in them passed the burden elsewhere, the nobles and clergy to the third estate, the third estate to unrepresented towns and the rural population, with the result that those whose interests were powerfully

[19] Alba to Requesens, 14 Sept. 1567, *ibid.*, i. 675; Alba to Philip II, 14 Sept. 1567, *ibid.*, i. 672-73.

[20] Verheyden, *op. cit.*, pp. 22-477.

[21] Griffiths, 'Representative Institutions in the Spanish Empire in the sixteenth century. II. The Low Countries', *op. cit.*, pp. 240-42.

represented—Antwerp, for example—escaped comparatively lightly. This was the whole point of their debating and administering the rates of assessment. Alba, of course, was not a precursor of modern principles of taxation: he was interested in revenue not welfare. But there were elements of equity and efficiency in his proposals, and if they were a threat to political freedom they were also incidentally an attack on social injustice. Certainly the Estates saw them as an attack on the privileged classes, as well as on the institution in which they were represented. And the attack came in the form of absolutism, for although Alba 'convoked' the Estates he did so in a peculiar way: he met them not as a corporate or general body but in separate interviews with the representatives of each province, forbidding them to have any conference with deputies of other provinces.

It was one thing to order, another to execute. Revenue was raised from the income tax, but not to the required amount. Then, after a two-year compromise subsidy, the sales tax came into operation in 1571.[22] With his usual contempt for commoners, Alba believed that resistance would be impossible, because the main burden would fall not on the clergy or nobility but on merchants and tradesmen. But the formula which worked in Spain could not be applied to the Netherlands, though Alba's miscalculation was political not economic. Indeed the economic effects of his fiscal policy have been traditionally exaggerated: industry and trade were not brought to a standstill, nor were their promoters abruptly ruined.[23] But the political effects went deep. Even if property owners in the Netherlands had wealth enough to contribute to the cost of government, they objected to financing a foreign government and a foreign administration. By these measures Alba built up further stores of resentment against his régime, and ultimately drew into opposition many who had been unmoved by the agitation for political or religious autonomy.

For the moment, however, there was still no sign of rebellion from the mass of the people. In any case Alba's overwhelming military strength gave him control of the situation by land. But this did not last long. In 1570 the Mediterranean front became active again when the Turk resumed the offensive; for the next two years, during and after Lepanto, Philip II was pinned down in the Mediterranean and could spare little for Alba in the Netherlands. The rebels attacked again, and from 1572 to 1576 Spain had to fight on two fronts, unable to win yet determined not to lose. Moreover even the military position of Alba had its Achilles heel: it was extremely vulnerable by sea, for Philip II had sent his magnificent army to the Nether-

---

[22] H. Pirenne, *Histoire de Belgique* (3rd edn., 7 vols., Brussels, 1909–32), iv. 21–4; see also *Epistolario del III Duque de Alba*, ii. 768–71, 780–83.
[23] See below, pp. 308–9.

lands without adequate naval cover. Effective resistance, therefore, had to come from outside, and it came in 1572. The pirates of the maritime provinces in the north of the Low Countries, operating from bases in England, had long been harrying Alba's lines of communication with Spain. Expelled from England, the 'Sea Beggars' seized the Zeeland town of Brill on 1 April 1572; from there they proceeded to capture other towns, including Flushing, which commanded the Scheldt, and within a few weeks occupied all Zeeland and Holland except Middelburg and Amsterdam. Yet even now it was hardly a popular revolt: it was a conquest, supported by a minority within the towns acting as a fifth-column; Calvinists replaced Catholics in the municipalities, often imposing themselves—and their religion—by violence and terror. The stirrings of resistance in the south, however, were too faint to undermine Alba's position there. For four more years the southern provinces remained obedient to Philip II, and the rebellion was confined to Holland and Zeeland, where it was protected from the Spanish infantry by the natural lines of defence provided by the great rivers, and, in the absence of Spanish naval power, was unmolested by sea. In spite of his last despairing efforts, Alba never overcame the rebellion in the north. Chronically short of money, and with the discipline of his unpaid *tercios* disintegrating before his eyes, he was no longer even a successful general. In October 1574, the 'decrepit old bird' as he called himself—he had another major campaign in front of him ten years later—was recalled and replaced by Requesens.

The appointment of Luis de Requesens was an admission by Philip II that Alba's methods had failed. The new governor brought a spirit of moderation to his office, as he had done to previous assignments, in Rome, Milan, and as counsellor of Don John in Granada and at Lepanto. Philip II knew his views and he respected them: Requesens advised a general pardon, the suppression of the Council of Troubles, and the abolition of the sales tax; he also wished to call the Estates General and through them negotiate with the rebels. But these terms were hardly more acceptable to the rebels in the north than those of Alba, for they contributed nothing to the basic debate between royal sovereignty and local autonomy; Philip II's methods may have changed, but his objectives remained the same—the restoration of his imprescriptible sovereign rights. Therefore, although Requesens published a general pardon (5 June 1574) and offered to abolish the sales tax in return for a subsidy, his approach made little impression in the south and was ignored in the north. Like Alba, he had to fall back on the army, at first with more success than the great general. True, the Spaniards lost Middelburg, their last stronghold in Zeeland in February 1574, but elsewhere the royal forces made some striking recoveries and steadily reduced the area of resistance. And in April the legendary Sancho Dávila inflicted a heavy defeat on an army of German mercenaries under Luis of Nassau at Mook, in the valley of the Meuse. But the victory was superficial and heralded a more profound defeat. The Spanish troops mutinied and occupied Antwerp, and Requesens was forced to negotiate with them in order to save the town from a sacking. This reacted unfavourably on his own policy of conciliation, and exposed a new weakness in Philip II's position. Once he could no longer rely on his own troops, he lost the ultimate sanction of his rule, and once he could no longer control them, he lost the confidence of the very subjects whom he claimed to be protecting.

Philip II's Army of Flanders consisted at its peak of 70,000 men drawn from Germany, the Netherlands, Italy and Spain. The elite units were Spanish and Italian, and one of the problems facing the king and his planners was to get these to Flanders quickly and securely. After 1568 the journey by sea was too hazardous. Only the land route remained. The first stage was from Spain to Lombardy via Genoa; the troops then travelled through Piedmont and Savoy, Franche Comté and Lorraine, countries which were possessions or allies of the king of Spain, and so into the Netherlands. This was the Spanish Road, a vital military corridor, which supplied the northern front and conditioned Spain's foreign policy for many decades to come.[24] To place an army on this distant front was a great feat of organisation. To control it was more difficult. The root of the trouble was Philip II's inability to pay his troops. The Netherlands were the largest and longest drain on his already strained resources. Lack of money for the war against the rebels constantly harassed his governors and immobilised their policies. Time after time projected campaigns had to be abandoned and the final blow delayed, simply because the money to finance them had not arrived. And penury finally struck at the heart of his power, in the very districts where he was obeyed. Mutinous troops drove off their officers, organised themselves with an unwonted discipline, and sought to occupy a wealthy town in order to get supplies and live off the inhabitants. Between 1572 and 1607 there were 46 mutinies, some of them major revolts lasting a year or more and involving thousands of men, including Spanish troops, whom Philip II regarded as 'the sinews and security' of his rule in the Netherlands. Their chief object was to secure payment of overdue wages, sometimes running into months or years, and normally they did not end until the claim was settled. While

[24] See Geoffrey Parker, *The Army of Flanders and the Spanish Road, 1567-1659* (Cambridge, 1972), pp. 59–79, 290–2, for details on both logistics and mutinies. See also L. van der Essen, 'Croisade contre les hérétiques ou guerre contre des rebelles', *op. cit.*, p. 43, and the same author's *Alexandre Farnèse, prince de Parme, gouverneur général des Pays-Bas*, ii. 7–24.

the mutinies did not have a political aim, they had political consequences, halting campaigns, subverting Spanish authority, and diverting large amounts of money into pay settlements. They also taught a fatal lesson, that the Spanish authorities were incapable of protecting civilians. In 1575 Philip II went bankrupt for a second time, repudiating his debts, and regaining control of the revenues on which his debts had been secured. The bankers then refused to lend him money or to transfer it abroad. For the next two years the Netherlands were starved of supplies. Shortly after the death of Requesens in March 1576 the troops mutinied again. In a great 'Spanish Fury' they terrorised Antwerp, killed 8,000 civilians, and gravely impaired Philip II's authority in the Netherlands. Brussels itself, the seat of the royal government, was momentarily at risk.

In the absence of a governor general, the immediate representative of Philip II was the Council of State. Already divided between supporters and opponents of Spanish absolutism, it was now incapable of guaranteeing order in the capital. The gaps in royal authority so quickly exposed were as quickly exploited. As the government of Philip II was incapable of providing security, the provincial Estates undertook to provide it for themselves. The Estates of Brabant began to raise militia forces of their own, thus exercising power independently of the crown and its agents. On 4 September 1576 they arrested the 'royalist' members of the Council of State, reconstituted it without Spaniards, and induced it to invite representatives from Holland and Zeeland to meet at Ghent with those of the southern Estates. The resistance movement of these months was not popular in origin, nor even directed by local magistrates; its leaders were a group of nobles, including the heirs of Hornes and Egmont, who were avenging the executions of 1568 and seeking the restoration of their confiscated estates.[25] It was also predominantly Catholic. Would it be able to work with the rebels in the north? The answer to this question was reached with the assistance of the Spaniards themselves. On 4 November, after a brush with nationalist forces, the Spanish troops hurled themselves on Antwerp; the bloody massacre that followed was worse than any of its predecessors, and, by showing that no one's life or property were safe, helped to sink the differences between the Catholic south-west and the Protestant north-east. On 8 November the Pacification of Ghent was proclaimed, uniting the Netherlands against foreign absolutism with a programme of expelling the Spanish troops, calling the Estates General to settle the religious question with moderation, and restoring confiscated property. Here at last was a *general* rebellion. The Estates General were now exercising sovereignty and conducting day-to-day

[25] Griffiths, *William of Hornes*, p. 30.

administration. Yet the rebellion was not as strong as it looked. In the first place, there was still no solution to the religious problem. Calvinism was dominant in Holland and Zeeland, but Catholicism was the exclusive faith in the other provinces, and neither religion tolerated the other; soon there was a revolution within the revolution, as Calvinists revolted in Antwerp, Brussels, and Ghent, overthrew the Catholic magistrates and installed their own dictatorships. This raised a second issue. What reception should be accorded to the new governor general whom Philip II was planning to send? Should he be recognised or resisted? Those who feared that Calvinism was monopolising the revolution preferred to negotiate with the king and his representative, while those who distrusted the king looked to Orange and the partisans of outright resistance. Here was a chance for Philip, if only he could take it. Unfortunately he chose the wrong man and the wrong policy. If he was to exploit the political and religious divisions among the rebels, he would have to do so from a position of strength. For this he needed a statesman with a strong army. Instead he sent a soldier and deprived him of his troops.

Don John of Austria was reluctant to go to the Netherlands, the graveyard of so many careers. He was still dreaming of a kingdom for himself within the Spanish empire and the title of 'Highness' which his half-brother denied him. But he believed he might use his new command as a stepping-stone to greater things—the conquest of England, marriage with Mary Stuart, and the throne seized from Elizabeth.[26] Philip II humoured these romantic illusions, for he had a pathetic trust in the value of prestige and hoped that the man who beat the Turk would also cow the heretic, but in the Low Countries not in England. To restrain his ardour he gave him precise instructions, and these were conciliatory; saving royal authority and the Catholic religion, Don John was to go to almost any length to bring peace to the Low Countries, even to the point of removing the Spanish troops and dehispanising the administration; with his usual eye to detail, Philip even instructed him to avoid taking his mistresses from among the leading families of the country.[27] Don John, who arrived in the Netherlands in November 1576, was convinced that his real need was more troops and more money, but pacification was not inimical to his ideas, provided it split the enemy and enabled him to deploy the troops evacuated from the Low Countries in an invasion of England. By the short-lived Perpetual Edict (12 February 1577) he accepted most of the rebel demands, including the departure of the Spanish troops within twenty days. On these terms the Estates, without

---

[26] Törne, *Don Juan d'Autriche et les projets de conquête de l'Angleterre, 1568–1578*, i. 151–88; ii. 6–12, 46, 60–109.

[27] Gachard, *Correspondance de Philippe II sur les affaires des Pays-Bas*, iv. 450–64.

reference to William of Orange, agreed to receive him as their governor general and maintain the Catholic religion. Don John, of course, wanted to remove the troops by sea, pursuing still his own private 'enterprise' of England. For once Philip II and the northern rebels were in agreement. The king disliked his servants executing independent policies and had no wish to break the peace with England, least of all by means which were bound to fail. Holland and Zeeland, commanding the maritime exits from the country, refused to allow the army to cross their territory. Therefore, in April the *tercios* filed southwards by land for Italy, and Don John was left without access to England and without power in the Netherlands. His position in Brussels was now untenable. So in July he seized Namur; from there he issued more uncompromising demands against the Estates General and requested Philip II to restore his troops, an admission that he had failed to pacify the opposition and was going to revert to military force. In December the *tercios* began to arrive back in Luxembourg, and in January 1578 they routed the rebels at Gembloux, near Namur. It was a striking victory, but a local one. Starved of money, Don John did not have the resources to take Brussels or to prevent William of Orange from reconstituting the rebel party. His last months were spent in a torment of frustration and the growing belief that for him, as for so many others, the Netherlands were a death-trap. He was right. On 1 October 1578, at the age of thirty-three, he died of typhus.

While royal policy was floundering, torn between conciliation and force, the rebels had troubles of their own. The government of the Estates and the unity it represented were disrupted by the social and religious revolution which accompanied the political rebellion. The rift between the aristocratic and plebeian elements in the revolt, between the Duke of Aerschot and his associates on the one hand and William of Orange and the commons on the other, led to a parting of the ways. In their desire to counter the influence of Orange and his Calvinist and burgher allies, the southern nobility became estranged from the cause they had once led. In 1578 they began to withdraw their support from the government of the Estates General and to consolidate their control of the provincial Estates in the south, while a group of malcontent younger nobles organised a military movement of their own which attempted to pursue a course independent of king and Calvinists alike.[28] As this was essentially a Catholic reaction against the growing power of Calvinism, and an aristocratic reaction against the claims of the burghers, it presented an even greater opportunity to Philip II than the one he had missed in 1576. This time he made no mistake: he appointed as his governor general a

[28] Griffiths, *William of Hornes*, pp. 46–54.

superb statesman, and gave him the financial and military backing he had denied Don John.

Alexander Farnese, Duke of Parma, was one of the few of his foreign subjects whom Philip II trusted with high office. Educated at Alcalá with Don John, he had also served with him at Lepanto, and his dashing action at Gembloux helped to win Don John's solitary victory over the Estates. As a soldier he was outstanding. Few of his contemporaries commanded such confidence from their troops; his magnificent appearance and entourage, his courage, his insistence on discipline and refusal to condone excesses, his readiness to mix with his men, above all his success, gave him the personal prestige which no amount of royal support could supply. But he was more than a great general: his intellectual qualities raised him far above the rest of Philip II's commanders and made him the best possible choice for salvaging his sovereign's authority from the wreckage of insurrection. It must also be added that, in a period when receipts of American treasure were reaching unprecedented proportions, he possessed greater financial, and therefore military, power than his predecessors. And he was already briefed to take over from Don John, so there was no repetition of the fatal interregnum that had followed the death of Requesens. This time conciliation could be offered from a position of strength. On matters other than allegiance to the crown and the maintenance of Catholicism, Farnese was free to manoeuvre.

In April 1579 he reached an agreement with the malcontent nobles, who promised to return to their allegiance in exchange for the payment of their troops and a promise to withdraw the *tercios*. This formed the basis of the Treaty of Arras (17 May 1579) between Farnese and the Walloon Estates, which in January had already agreed in the Union of Arras to negotiate a reconciliation; the treaty reconciled Hainault and Artois to Philip II and maintained the exclusive position of Catholicism, in return for recognition of their autonomous privileges and the exclusion of foreigners from the government.[29] But the heart of the matter was the location of military power. Farnese agreed to withdraw the Spanish and foreign troops from those provinces adhering to the Treaty of Arras, but this left him free to employ them where resistance to Spain continued, as in Brabant and Flanders —another way of exploiting disunity and a further inducement to those who still held aloof. As he proceeded to reduce the centres of resistance in the south-west, Farnese won growing allegiance by his consummate diplomacy. Death sentences for treason were few and were never retrospective, being confined to the period after the Treaty of Arras; those, like William of Hornes (heir of the executed count), who defected to the camp of Orange or his ally, the Duke of Anjou, were executed as a deterrent to others. At the

[29] Van der Essen, *Alexandre Farnèse*, ii. 95–149, 196–225.

same time he rewarded those, like Philip of Egmont (son of Alba's victim), who gave their loyalty and service to the king, by showing them that their property and titles were secure under the crown and could be extended at the expense of the crown's enemies.[30] Thus from 1579 the royal government avoided the mistakes of 1568 when it had alienated a whole network of aristocratic families by executing their leading members. The new solution, similar to the one which was already successful in Spain itself, was to deprive the nobility of its feudal liberty by compensating it with economic and social privilege. Farnese's success in recovering the southern provinces for Spain, therefore, owed much to local conditions in the Netherlands—to aristocratic disquiet at the social implications of revolution. Caught between the crown and the militant revolutionaries, the nobles decided that their privileges could best be saved from attack by the latter through alliance with the former. His success also owed much to the persistence of Catholicism in the south even in areas where Calvinism was politically dominant; in Antwerp, for example, after seven years of Protestant rule, Catholics were still in a majority in 1585.[31] Nevertheless, the boundaries of separation between the northern and southern Netherlands were determined not only by religion and politics. Ultimately they were determined by military power: it was the military successes of Farnese, and their limits, that decided which part of the Netherlands returned to the Spanish allegiance.

In January 1579, shortly after the Union of Arras, the north-eastern provinces bound themselves in a counter-union, that of Utrecht, to maintain Protestantism and independence; and the Protestant towns of Flanders and Brabant soon associated themselves with this resistance. The only answer to the Union of Utrecht was military force, and this Farnese deployed in a double-barrelled offensive consisting of sieges and economic warfare; first he isolated each centre of resistance, then he starved it out. Having mopped up the last remnants of rebel outposts in the Walloon south-west, he then advanced north into Brabant and Flanders, systematically reducing Ypres, Bruges, Ghent, Brussels, and finally, on 17 August 1585, Antwerp.[32] His magnanimity in victory consolidated his gains; all the conquered towns received liberal terms, and Protestants were given periods of grace to turn Catholic or leave. But with the occupation of Brabant and Flanders, Spanish power reached its limit. Protected by their great rivers and their incomparable sea power, the north-eastern provinces, whose core was Holland, Zeeland, and Utrecht, remained impregnable. There, although Philip II might

[30] Griffiths, *William of Hornes*, pp. 78–80.
[31] Smit, 'The present position of studies regarding the Revolt of the Netherlands', in J. S. Bromley and E. H. Kossmann, *Britain and the Netherlands* (London, 1960), p. 25.
[32] Van der Essen, *Alexandre Farnèse*, iii. 120–49; iv. 134–48.

maintain the legal fiction that he was reducing rebel subjects, in fact he was fighting a losing war with an independent power. And the war his enemies chose to fight was a maritime one.

3. THE BATTLE OF THE ATLANTIC

The economic value of the Netherlands to Spain had been a concomitant of their political subordination, as has been seen. But what were they worth once Spanish sovereignty was challenged? The Duke of Alba had professed to be indifferent to economic considerations: 'It is far better to preserve by war for God and the king a kingdom that is impoverished and even ruined than, without war, preserve it entire for the benefit of the devil and his disciples, the heretics.'[33] Philip II was not so insensitive. He ordered Alba to extend 'great privileges and liberties to foreign merchants in order to increase trade', and to maintain thirty ships to guard commercial communications in the Channel.[34] For some years Spain preserved the Netherlands without impoverishing them and without reducing them to the ruin threatened by the Duke of Alba and depicted by later historians, who have tended to exaggerate and pre-date the economic disasters of the time.[35] Local industry survived the fiscal measures of Alba and the blockade of the Scheldt by the rebels and their allies from 1568. The years 1570–80 were ones of reasonable prosperity for the production of linen fabrics at Oudenard, and crisis did not begin before 1580 when the town was badly damaged by the royal army. The textile production of Hondschoote was hardly affected by the action of the rebels or the policy of Alba; production and export were maintained in some quantity from 1562 to 1570, fell a little from 1568 to 1575, but rose again after the 'general pardon' of 1574, and reached a record figure in 1578, falling from 1579; in 1580 the town was badly pillaged by royal troops, and suffered further destruction at the hands of the Duke of Anjou's army in 1582. The incidence of emigration tells the same story: the movement from the south to the north was not really significant in the 1560's and 1570's; it only reached substantial proportions between 1585 and 1590, naturally beginning rather later than the economic crisis; in this case the south's losses were the north's gains—the revival of the textile industry in Leyden, for example, owed something to the arrival of immigrants from the south.[36] The economic crisis in the Low Countries under

---

[33] Pirenne, *op. cit.*, iv. 7.

[34] Secret Instructions, in Verheyden, *op. cit.*, 508.

[35] See the traditional account by Pirenne, *op. cit.*, iii. 218; iv. 411–25, and the comments of C. Verlinden, 'En Flandres sous Philippe II: durée de la crise économique', *Annales*, i. (1952), 21–30.

[36] Verlinden, 'En Flandres sous Philippe II', *op. cit.*, pp. 24–26, 27–28.

Philip II, therefore, was of much shorter duration than is usually supposed, and ought to be dated mainly between 1580 and 1590. Its causes were not the closure of the Scheldt, nor the exaction of new taxes, nor the immigrations. The real causes are to be sought in the operations of reconquest of the southern provinces undertaken from 1579. The success of Farnese was gained at a price; the devastation wrought by his army and his methods of cutting off supplies adversely affected the economy of the country, while the restoration of Spanish rule resulted in the flight of many Protestants. But the subsequent crisis was relatively brief, and this accounts for the rapid recovery of the country in the first half of the seventeenth century.

Antwerp, of course, was more exposed to the impact of war, for its prosperity depended largely on the maintenance of maritime communications. But allowing for this, its progress and decline followed roughly the same pattern. Its mid-century prosperity gave way to years of difficulty but not disaster, between 1568 and 1573 when collaboration between the Dutch rebels and English and French pirates closed the Scheldt to navigation, at a time when the fiscal policy of the Duke of Alba was already making trade more expensive. But Antwerp had considerable powers of resistance, even to the excesses committed by mutinous troops.[37] After the victory of Dávila at Mook in 1574, 4,000 unpaid troops took over Antwerp for six weeks, threatening and negotiating in turn, and only withdrew when they were paid. During this period no exchange business was conducted and many merchants quit the town. But by the beginning of 1575 business had picked up again, though it was soon struck by further disasters. The suspension of payments by Philip II in September 1575 paralysed credit on the Antwerp exchange and halted business. This was followed by the terrible sack of the town in November 1576, when many commercial buildings and stocks of merchandise were burnt and the citizens once again had to buy off the royal troops. The English had already sought another market for their textiles in Hamburg; now many other businessmen left and took their trade elsewhere. But these were mainly foreigners; most of the Spanish and Portuguese merchants remained and gradually reorganised their affairs. Then in the summer of 1577 Antwerp surrendered to William of Orange, and the Estates General proclaimed its sovereignty there. Again, some Spanish merchants remained and continued to trade with Spain via Holland and Zeeland. But gradually political and religious difficulties forced many of them to emigrate to Cologne, and after this exodus the economic life of Antwerp declined, especially from 1578; in 1582 only three Spanish firms remained, while on the eve of the capture of the town by Farnese in 1585 there were less than ten merchants left altogether. Antwerp was now under

[37] Vázquez de Prada, *Lettres marchandes d'Anvers*, pp. 27–34.

Spanish domination. When Farnese entered most of the Spanish merchants returned; exchange and commercial business revived again, especially dealings with the government. But Protestant merchants left and took their business to Amsterdam and Middelburg, while normal trade was broken by the Anglo–Dutch blockade of the Scheldt. From now on Antwerp had to trade with the outside world via Dutch ports, especially Amsterdam, paying transit dues, losing its international status, and forfeiting its position of entrepôt of spices and precious metals. In this period maritime warfare made direct commerce with Spain extremely hazardous, and more was done from Hamburg, Nantes, and Rouen, than from the Netherlands themselves.

Communications between Spain and the Netherlands had long been under attack by the rebels and their maritime allies. The difficulties of distance and transport operated against Spain from the very beginning. Moreover, the revolt of the Netherlands was an international question, for Spain's possession of a base in the north naturally aroused the susceptibilities of England and France, while her difficulties there enabled them to strike at the weak point in her defences. Direct intervention would have caused war, but France and England could strike at Spain through the freebooting operations of their subjects, who could be officially disavowed. Piracy became the normal form of cold-war, a source of great profit to the maritime populations of France, England, and Holland, and a glaring exposure of Spain's weakness in northern waters. The pressure became more relentless when the wars of religion began in France. From 1562 Huguenots and their English allies, operating from privateering bases in Le Havre and the Isle of Wight and with licences obtained from the French governor of Le Havre, attacked not only the ships of their French enemies but, much more frequently, Spanish and Flemish vessels plying between Spain and the Netherlands.[38] To the protests of Philip II's ambassador, De Quadra, Elizabeth replied that she had no legal power over Le Havre, but even had she been sincere in her disavowal of piracy she could not have restrained her subjects, least of all men like Thomas Cobham and Martin Frobisher who regarded all Spanish ships as legitimate prey. In July 1563 Granvelle advised Philip that the most effective reply was not diplomatic protest or negotiation, but retaliation in kind. But even if the king had possessed the means to do this, he did not wish to risk alienating England, and he could not afford protective convoys from Spain to the Low Countries. Even Philip II's patience, however, had its limits. Exasperated by the piracies committed during the first French war of religion, and at the attack in 1564 on two vessels sailing from the Netherlands when English pirates killed the crews and robbed to the extent

[38] M. Fernández Alvarez, 'Orígenes de la rivalidad naval hispano–inglesa en el siglo XVI', *Revista de Indias*, viii. (1947), 311–69.

of 40,000 ducats, he ordered a general embargo on English ships in Spanish ports, confiscated goods of 30 vessels, and detained many English seamen. So with the arrival in London of a new Spanish ambassador, Guzmán de Silva, in July 1564, the main question at issue was piracy and a solution to the consequent interruption of trade between the Netherlands and England. But this was purely diplomatic pressure, and Philip seems to have been taken in by the assurances of Elizabeth, at least to the extent of not retaliating or arming his vessels, though Spanish merchants were asking him to do so. Meanwhile piracy continued. Philip II's prolonged mistake in these years was to rely on diplomacy instead of taking strong defensive measures. Obsessed by the fear of a Franco-Scottish pincer movement on England and the formation of a new block of enemies in the north, he was over-sensitive to English feelings and too anxious to avoid offending Elizabeth. He received his reward in 1568.

The massive movement of Spanish troops from Italy to the Netherlands in 1567 deeply disturbed France and England. Here was Spain poised with incomparable force in the heart of northern Europe. Where would the Duke of Alba lead this army once it had crushed the rebels? Had it really come simply to restore order, or was this a mask and were the Netherlands a base for a Catholic crusade? On every possible occasion Philip II repeated that this was purely a political matter within his own states, and sought to reduce the religious issues with the argument that he was merely exercising sovereign rights over his own subjects. But he did not allay French suspicions, much less those of England. The operation was too provocative to be ignored and too exposed not to be attacked. And the simplest method of attacking it was to cut its maritime communications with Spain. In December 1569 a squadron of Biscayan vessels carrying money for the pay of the Duke of Alba's troops sought refuge from Huguenot raiders in English ports. On Cecil's advice, and with a mixture of political and economic motives, Elizabeth seized the cargo.[39] Theoretically the money still belonged to the Genoese bankers who had contracted with Philip II to pay his representatives in the Netherlands, and Elizabeth offered to indemnify the bankers. But more important than the legal aspects of the case were the economic and strategic consequences. The Duke of Alba retaliated by seizing the goods of English subjects in the Low Countries, while in Spain itself English fleets were detained in Biscay and Andalucía. Elizabeth replied with a general embargo on Spanish and Netherlands goods in England. From these mutual seizures, England gained much more than Spain, both in money and in property, so Elizabeth had less inducement than Alba to reach an agreement. Her action

[39] Conyers Read, 'Queen Elizabeth's seizure of the Duke of Alba's pay ships', *Journal of Modern History*, v. (1933), 443–64.

also gave unmistakable notice to Spain that the Channel route to the Netherlands could be closed at her discretion. In fact it was closed to Spanish shipping for more than eighteen months; English seamen, sheltering under the policy of their government, unleashed a new campaign against Spanish vessels in combination with a vicious offensive from the Huguenot seamen of La Rochelle who sold most of their booty in England, and with the mounting assault of the Dutch raiders who operated from English bases. For Spain the crisis of 1568–70 was the worst for many years, and the economic consequences were felt in the complete disorganisation of her maritime communications with the Netherlands. Piracy without remission, embittered on the English side by the treatment of Hawkins at San Juan de Ulúa, cut the great imperial route of Spanish money for the Low Countries and crippled the trade of Spanish merchants. This was the first serious defeat for Spain in the battle of the Atlantic.

The Duke of Alba was not completely insensitive to commercial interests, and he was also aware of the danger to his communications. So he prudently avoided a complete rupture with England, though the situation was inflammable. The maritime conflict in the Atlantic and the Caribbean, the meddling of the Spanish ambassador, D'Espés, in Elizabeth's difficulties with Mary Stuart and the northern rebels, the papal bull of excommunication of 1570, all increased the tension of these years. Even the cautious Philip almost reached the point of risking a military trial of strength with England.[40] But Alba kept his head. Arguing shortage of money, lack of opportunity in England, and the difficulty of the European situation, he restrained his sovereign. And he was right: there was no alternative but to negotiate. The Low Countries were already eating up money and troops; in 1569, with the outbreak of the war of Granada, Philip had a second rebellion on his hands and his Mediterranean front to consider. To attempt more in these circumstances would have been suicidal. By March 1573 Alba's negotiations bore fruit in the Convention of Nimwegen which included mutual agreement on the property seizures, and provided for the restoration of trade between England and the Low Countries for a period of two years.[41]

By this time, however, the Sea Beggars had captured Brill and spread revolution in Holland and Zeeland. Possession of Flushing enabled them to command the Scheldt, and from 1572 a new blockade of Antwerp began and a new stage in the maritime war. The Spaniards could not even hold Middelburg, which was taken by the rebels in February 1574. From then on the rebels were in a position to control all navigation with Spain, raiding the shipping that tried to get through, selling their prizes, and making trade themselves at the expense of Antwerp. Spain's lack of sea power in the north

[40] See above, pp. 280–81.　　　　　[41] Conyers Read, *Walsingham*, i. 308.

had never been more ruthlessly exposed. Searching wildly for the answer to their predicament, Philip II's counsellors advised an economic counter-blockade as the only effective form of fighting the rebels: by stopping their trade with Spain it was thought they would be cut off from their main source of subsistence.[42] But the advice was unreal. It was impossible to prohibit the rebels from trading with Spain, because Spain could not subsist without the goods and services the rebels provided. Inevitably, one of these was grain; this they bought cheaply every summer in Baltic ports (for there was a surplus in Poland and few competitors), stored in their warehouses during the winter, and sold in the Iberian peninsula the following spring. In exchange they procured precious bullion. Thus the Netherlands were doubly voracious of American treasure: as fast as Spain poured money into their defence, the rebels earned some of what remained by trading with Spain. Philip II could not escape from this dilemma, for he lacked the shipping to supply his own needs, and what he had could not break the Dutch stranglehold on his northern communications. For both objects, to supplement his merchant marine and fight Dutch sea power, he needed additional fleets. In his desperation he even turned to Sweden. From the Baltic he sought ships and naval stores, and this was the purpose of the strange mission of Francisco de Eraso to John III of Sweden in 1578—to sound the possibility of engaging a Swedish fleet to reduce the Netherlands rebels and strike their international accomplices.[43] Nothing came of this approach and eventually Philip II was forced to admit that a policy of blockade against the Low Countries—and against England—was beyond the means of Spain, for she had neither the economic power, nor the seamen, nor the ships necessary for such drastic measures. In commerce the Dutch had more to fear from their own leaders than from Philip II. From 1577, when Orange took Antwerp, the authorities there tried to prohibit trade with Spain, and in 1582 the Estates General renewed the prohibition on the export of grain to the peninsula. But political objectives foundered on economic realities, as Philip II had already learnt. The maritime populations of Holland and Zeeland lived almost exclusively from commerce and shipping, and they preferred to profit from their enemies by trade as well as fight them by privateering.

4. WARNINGS FROM ENGLAND

The gap in Spain's imperial defences opened by the revolt of the Netherlands was soon widened, as the maritime war spread into the Atlantic and

---

[42] Vázquez de Prada, *op. cit.*, pp. 59–60; Braudel, *La Méditerranée*, p. 490; see also above, p. 154.

[43] F. Ruiz Martín, 'La etapa marítima de las guerras de religión, Bloqueos y contra-bloqueos', *Estudios de Historia Moderna*, iii. (1954), 195–214.

beyond. Here the prize at stake was even more valuable than Spain's dominion and trade in northern Europe. It was her greatest and wealthiest overseas possession—her empire in America. And here, in Philip II's reign, the supreme threat to security came not from the French, whose sea power was unequal to Spain's, nor yet from the Dutch, whose greatest assault was still to come, but from the English. Philip II's policy towards England was conditioned primarily by political and economic considerations and not by the objectives of the Counter-Reformation.[44] Furthermore, it was focused essentially on English action in the two parts of his empire where his defences could be pierced—the Netherlands and America. In both cases his policy was animated by national, not religious, objectives. He himself, of course, did not necessarily distinguish between the two, and seems to have believed that Spain's interests were also those of Catholicism. Nevertheless, there was a distinction. In the interests of power, and its defence, he was ultimately prepared to go to war; in the interests of religion he preferred other means.

Religious hostility between Spain and England went deep on both sides, but, in spite of Cardinal Quiroga in Spain and of Sir Francis Walsingham in England, it was a conflict of ideas, not of arms, and it embittered relations but did not break them. Superficially it might have seemed that Philip II possessed a potential fifth-column among English Catholics, but he himself understood that the situation was not what it appeared to be. In the early 1560's, before the English Catholic population began to decline, he refrained from giving it a political lead, for that might have served the interests of Mary Queen of Scots and produced a Guise empire in the north. Later, he seems to have appreciated that English émigrés did not necessarily speak for their co-religionists at home, and that they exaggerated the strength of Catholic opposition to Elizabeth. Therefore, although he allowed his ambassadors in London considerable latitude in intriguing with any opposition that existed, this was essentially a pressure device of the kind used by most rulers, including Elizabeth, to exploit the weaknesses of their rivals, and did not commit him to armed intervention. The actual assistance English Catholics received from Philip II was of a different kind. The English seminary at Douai in the Netherlands was founded with his permission and assistance for the purpose of training priests for the English mission. By the close of the sixteenth century there were also seminaries at Valladolid, Lisbon, Madrid, and Seville, all subsidised by the Spanish crown. Beyond this Philip II was not prepared to go.[45]

[44] See above, pp. 280–84.
[45] See J. H. Pollen, S.J., *The English Catholics in the reign of Queen Elizabeth* (London, 1920); A. O. Meyer, *England and the Catholic Church under Elizabeth* (London, 1916); P. Hughes, *Rome and the Counter-Reformation* (London, 1942).

Political rivalry and economic warfare, however, were another matter. Spain's weakness in the Netherlands gave Elizabeth an opportunity far greater than anything Philip possessed in England. William of Orange may have received some financial assistance from Elizabeth as early as 1568, and in 1572 to counteract French influence she allowed companies of English volunteers to cross the Channel. For the moment, however, Philip was saved from direct intervention by England because England feared intervention by France; if Spain were forced to quit the Netherlands and the subsequent vacuum were filled by France, the strategic implications for England would be even more alarming. Philip II's sovereignty in the Low Countries, therefore, had little to fear from Elizabeth; throughout the 1570's her primary objective was to force him to withdraw his army, and her means were diplomacy, traffic with the rebels, and the attack on his communications which she had already initiated.[46] But it was obvious to Philip II that England was in a position to do more than this if necessary and that the queen was reserving her freedom of action. Meanwhile, in America English policy was less inhibited.

The colonial monopoly claimed by Spain had already been disputed by her rivals.[47] The legal justification for the monopoly—the papal bull of demarcation of 1493 granting lands towards the west and the south to the crown of Spain—was not accepted by other nations, nor could the Treaty of Tordesillas of 1494 between Spain and Portugal ratifying the agreed demarcation have any legal validity for third parties. Neither France nor England considered themselves bound by it. In 1534 Francis I of France formally informed the Spanish ambassador in Paris that he did not renounce his rights in America. For Elizabeth and her government the fact that the grant of monopoly had been made by the pope was only another reason why it should be rejected, and from at least 1561 they argued that occupation must be effective to constitute possession. As neither side would retreat from its claims, international treaties were usually silent about America. At least as early as the Treaty of Cateau-Cambrésis of 1559 between Spain and France, however, an oral agreement seems to have set up the famous 'lines of amity'—the meridian of the Canaries and the Tropic of Cancer—beyond which might would make right and ships sailed at their own peril, and from which evolved the principle of 'no peace beyond the line'.[48] But beneath the legal and diplomatic arguments the basic question was one of power.

[46] See R. B. Wernham, 'English Policy and the Revolt of the Netherlands', in Bromley and Kossmann, *Britain and the Netherlands*, 29–40.

[47] Modern research on the challenge to the Spanish Indies is seen to best advantage in K. R. Andrews, *The Spanish Caribbean. Trade and Plunder 1530–1630* (New Haven, 1978).

[48] F. G. Davenport, *European Treaties bearing on the history of the United States and its Dependencies* (Washington, 1917), pp. 219–21.

Spain was in the New World by right of conquest and settlement, and by virtue of her superior power; against this, other nations would have to fight their way in. The French attempted to do so by piracy on the high seas and colonisation in North America. Spain replied by tightening her maritime defences and sending an expedition to wipe out the short-lived Huguenot settlement in Florida in 1565. English enterprise began more modestly, but was more persistent.

Before England began to attack the Spanish colonial monopoly by piracy and privateering, her merchants and seamen made various attempts to share in it by peaceful means. These had already begun before the reign of Elizabeth, but from the early 1560's they acquired a new urgency and greater organisation, and the search for markets and metals now received the encouragement of the state itself. The example of French piracy had shown that Spain's imperial defences were not impregnable, and it was known that the Spanish West Indies were short of vital commodities—especially labour. Against this background, John Hawkins made his first slaving expedition to the Caribbean in 1562-63, selling in Hispaniola negroes he had bought in West Africa. He was breaking the Spanish law on two accounts: no foreigner might go to the Indies without licence, and no goods might be sold there unless they had been registered at Seville. The licence he procured from a local official—caught, as colonial officials usually were, between the policy of the crown and the pressure of the settlers—allowing him trading facilities 'so far as I am authorised and by law may so do' was worthless, for the formula was not recognised in colonial law.[49] In Spain the authorities confiscated those of Hawkins' returns which he had sent experimentally to Seville for declaration, and dispatched orders to the West Indies forbidding the colonists to trade with him. But in spite of the confiscations the profits of the expedition were sufficient to justify another in 1564-65, and this was made with the queen's sanction, with the participation of one of her ships, and with the help of money invested by her ministers, so that Hawkins could truthfully say to Spanish officials on the mainland of South America that he had sailed 'by order of Elizabeth, Queen of England, whose fleet this is'.[50] Again, in view of the needs of the settlers the local officials could not apply the legal prohibitions against trading with foreigners, but even so Hawkins had to extort 'licences' by threatening to use force. By this time the Spanish authorities realised that Hawkins was making a real—though small—break in their monopoly, and doing so with the support of powerful interests in the English government. As diplomatic complaints

---

[49] I. A. Wright, ed., *Spanish Documents concerning English voyages to the Caribbean, 1527-1568* (London, Hakluyt Society, 1929), p. 60.
[50] *Ibid.*, pp. 82-3.

were useless, the only effective answer Spain could make was force greater than that which Hawkins himself threatened to use—if the transgressor could be caught.

In 1567 Hawkins prepared his third expedition, another state under-taking, with government supervision and the queen's participation. He attempted to lay a false trail in advance, and the Spanish ambassador in London was told that the fleet was destined for the African coast and had no intention of intruding in Spain's colonies. In fact it was another slaving expedition to the Spanish Main. The governor of Venezuela refused Hawkins permission to trade, and while the prohibition was hardly more effective than previous ones it was difficult to resist it peacefully. At Río de la Hacha Francis Drake, whose second voyage to the Caribbean this was, opened fire on the Treasurer's House and captured a caravel, while Hawkins himself, whose nature was less tempestuous than that of his subordinate, had to force trade upon the settlement against the will of the local authorities. On his way home, however, he put in at San Juan de Ulúa in New Spain for repairs; there in September 1568 he was trapped by the annual Spanish fleet arriving with the new viceroy of Mexico, Martín Enríquez. The English version of what followed alleged Spanish treachery, and the Spanish docu-ments themselves seem to confirm it; from a fortified sand-bank Hawkins commanded the entrance to the harbour, and he allowed the Spanish fleet to enter in return for a promise that he might retain his position. Having been lulled into a false sense of security, he was then viciously attacked, his flotilla was shattered, and he and Drake managed to escape with only two vessels.[51] Hawkins, of course, had not been in a position to make conditions with a superior force, and in Spanish eyes he was a corsair with no rights. In any case he had been told by Guzmán de Silva, the Spanish ambassador in London, what to expect if he were caught in the Indies, and Drake's aggressive conduct at Río de la Hacha belied the peaceful nature of the expedition.

The trading voyages of Hawkins were only a pin-prick in the vast economic structure between Spain and the Indies, and the returns he gained were insignificant compared with the wealth which flowed to Seville.[52] But he was a danger to the Spanish monopoly and the notion that he should earn a licence by patrolling the Caribbean for Spain, if it was ever seriously intended by Elizabeth and Hawkins, could hardly be taken seriously by Philip II. There had never been any possibility that Spain would concede a

[51] *Ibid.*, pp. 128–62; see also J. A. Williamson, *Hawkins of Plymouth* (London, 1949); and for a Spanish view, A. Rumeu de Armas, *Viajes de John Hawkins a América* (Seville, 1947).
[52] See above, pp. 171–72, and references to Chaunu there.

legal English trade in America. Now the English themselves understood the position, and it was in this sense that the incident at San Juan de Ulúa marked a turning point in Anglo-Spanish relations. It coincided with that tension in Europe from 1568 which drove Spain and England further apart and unleashed a concerted Protestant attack on Spanish shipping and communications. And in the Indies, what England could not gain by trade she now tried to take by force. From 1571 Drake began his campaign of piracy in the Caribbean, capturing booty and prisoners in an unlimited attack which extended to the West Indies the maritime assault already countenanced by the English government in home waters. Legally Drake was a pirate—there was no official war and he himself had no commission—but indirectly he was an agent of the queen's policy. In 1572 he went in search of treasure, not at sea, but on land, at the key point of the silver route from Peru on the Isthmus of Panama. There the Spaniards only held Panama itself on the Pacific coast and Nombre de Dios on the Caribbean, with a wayside station between them; and security in the interior was weakened by the hostility of a tribe of *cimarrones*, runaway negro slaves, with whom foreign raiders could league to strike at the common enemy. Drake first attacked Nombre de Dios, but failed to capture any treasure; six months later he tried to ambush the mule trains, and again he failed; the third attempt, another ambush, was successful, and Drake got back to Plymouth with a vast load of precious metals. He had also revealed a weak link in the process by which treasure was relayed to Spain. If Englishmen could hold the Isthmus and penetrate the Pacific, the ships that brought the treasure from Peru could be attacked and plundered. John Oxenham, who had been with Drake in 1572–73, tried to do precisely this in 1576 as a private venture, crossing the Isthmus by river to the Pacific coast, introducing an element of religious warfare by mocking Catholic beliefs and practices on the way, and finally intercepting some treasure ships. The Spanish authorities, however, replied energetically; the English were routed, the treasure was recaptured, and Oxenham, having been tried by the Inquisition, was hanged in Lima.[53]

This ended attempts to reach the heart of the Spanish empire by striking across the Isthmus of Panama. But there was another way into the Pacific, via the Straits of Magellan, and Drake took it when he circumnavigated the world between 1577 and 1580. As one gap in Spain's imperial defences was closed, another was prised open. The objective of Drake's latest expedition was to discover, not new lands, but new trades, and it was directed to the Moluccas and perhaps China; but to this official programme was added Drake's own scheme of attacking Spanish commerce on the west coast of

[53] I. A. Wright, *Documents concerning English Voyages to the Spanish Main, 1579–1580* (London, Hakluyt Society, 1932), pp. 108–234.

America.[54] The authorities in the empire were not warned in time of this expedition and there was no general alert. Once he had navigated the Straits of Magellan and was making his way up the Pacific coast his presence was known in Panama, but Spanish defences were weak on this coast, and the distances were so vast that it was difficult to keep track of his movements. Consequently he raided the Peruvian coast with impunity and in March 1579 captured a valuable cargo of silver, after which he drew away northwards and then westwards. When he returned to England he was received with national acclaim, and, no longer caring what Philip II thought, the queen knighted him.

The exploits of Drake stirred the patriotism and imagination of Englishmen, but were naturally less impressive to Spaniards. Piracy was a sign of weakness, not of strength. The actions of the English sea-dogs were a tribute to the superior power of Spain, who actually possessed the colonies that England could only raid. These colonies were not adequately defended, it is true. Since neither sovereignty nor revenue were endangered by the sacking of minor towns and the seizure of coastal shipping, Spain spared little effort for the protection of America, and resistance in the Caribbean was slight until about 1586.[55] The inhabitants were left mainly to provide for their own defence with local militia forces and without sufficient arms or artillery; there were few important forts or garrisons in American ports before 1585. The use of fleets against sea raiders was hardly more advanced than military defences, though the English menace led to some improvement. After long debate the crown decided that the convoy warships of the trade fleets, which patrolled against corsairs while awaiting the return of their merchantmen, were insufficient, and by 1582 permanent patrols of the Caribbean coasts were provided and operated with growing efficiency against lesser corsairs, so that only strong squadrons had much chance of success.[56] But the Chilean and Peruvian coasts were still highly vulnerable, as Drake demonstrated in 1579.

The weakness of imperial defences, however, was the result of factors far more powerful than lack of organisation or of resources.[57] Spain had experience of conditions in America, and knew what was possible there. The distances involved were too vast to be adequately embraced by any defence system. A coastguard fleet would have been of little use on the great expanse of the Pacific coast. Fleets could escort treasure convoys, as the flotilla escorted

[54] H. R. Wagner, *Sir Francis Drake's Voyage round the World. Its Aims and Achievements* (San Francisco, 1926), pp. 15–27.

[55] R. D. Hussey, 'Spanish reaction to foreign aggression in the Caribbean to about 1680', *Hispanic American Historical Review*, ix. (1929), 286–302.

[56] See above, pp. 167–68, and references to Chaunu there.

[57] Chaunu, *Séville et l'Atlantique*, iii. 267–68.

the annual convoy from Callao to Panama, and they could provide local defence, as the Armada of Tierra Firme protected Cartagena and other points along the Spanish Main. But further than this it was impossible to plan. It was beyond the means of any power to patrol the whole of the South American coast-line from the Antilles to the Straits of Magellan and from there to Panama. It was only possible to provide guards for the fleets, especially on the Atlantic crossing, and it was a piece of calculated and successful planning for Spain to concentrate her efforts and resources here, even at the expense of general imperial defence. The same factors, of course, made Drake's exploits less impressive. His penetration of the Pacific was a great feat of navigation rather than of strategy. It was not difficult to appear at virtually any point in the Spanish empire, as long as it was merely a question of navigating and looting. But it was less easy to found a colony or capture a treasure fleet, for colonies had to be sustained and the fleets were adequately guarded. Drake's operations, therefore, annoyed Philip II, but they did not deprive him of a single colony or enable England to gain any. Even the prizes taken were minute compared with the treasure which continued to reach Spain and the trade which she still controlled.[58]

Nevertheless, Drake was still at large, and it was difficult to know where he would strike next. The feeling of insecurity which filled Spanish merchants and shippers was more important than the actual losses they sustained, for it made them hesitate to invest further in the Indies trade and caused them to lose confidence in the ability of their own government to protect them. Moreover, it was becoming increasingly obvious to Philip II that, by probing his defences and exploiting his weaknesses, Elizabeth was waging war on him without actually declaring it, and that the initiative was in her hands. But what could he do? Diplomacy was useless; the Low Countries were exposed to foreign intervention; and it was almost impossible to catch pirates once they had left their base, for they were lost to view in the immense spaces which enveloped his empire. Was there any other solution? If the rebels in the Low Countries were shielded by his enemies, could he isolate them from external help? Above all, if his colonies were too vast to be defended in America, could they be defended in Europe? Could he eliminate the bases of the enemy in England itself? Before he could answer these questions Philip II had another enterprise to complete, and Spanish policy had a further process of re-orientation to undergo. Gradually after Lepanto, and more urgently from 1578, when truces with the Turk became regular, he began to withdraw from the war in the Mediterranean and to reduce

[58] See above, pp. 172–73; see also Wagner, *op. cit.*, pp. 194–212, who describes Drake as a 'captain of industry' rather than an explorer or statesman.

his commitments there to the minimum of defence.[59] From 1579 he initiated a new policy in the Netherlands, and Farnese began to win back some of the ground which had been lost since 1566. Philip II was now turning Spain unreservedly from the Mediterranean to the Atlantic, in order to face the greatest danger which threatened him and to prepare for the day of reckoning with his enemies in the north. The first stage in this change of direction was the annexation of Portugal.

[59] See above, pp. 248–50.

CHAPTER X

WAR AND RECESSION

1. THE ANNEXATION OF PORTUGAL

IN 1578 King Sebastian of Portugal led a suicidal expedition to Morocco with the object of conquering and converting its Moors. The Portuguese army, badly supplied, exhausted by heat and marches, and ineptly commanded by the irresponsible king, was overwhelmed at the battle of Alcazar-Kebir on 4 August, and Sebastian himself was killed. He left no direct heir. The next five years were critical ones for Portugal, and for Spain. Spanish policy had already been pulled more insistently towards the Atlantic, first by the revolt of the Netherlands and then by the hostility of England. Now, with Portugal leaderless and drifting, Philip II could vindicate his own claims to her throne; if he were successful he would be able not only to close a vulnerable sector of his peninsular defences but also to increase his power in the Atlantic by acquiring a new kingdom, another empire, a larger seaboard, and an additional fleet. He accepted the challenge, and the struggle for supremacy in the Atlantic was now joined as he turned Spain ponderously towards the ocean and the north. At the same time his financial position began to improve, after the state bankruptcy of 1575; the influx of American treasure grew to unprecedented proportions in the 1580's and augmented the Spanish war potential. In these circumstances Spain passed from defence to attack, from the caution characteristic of the first half of Philip II's reign to the imperialism of its last two decades. But first Philip had to prepare his domestic front.

Since 1573 the most influential voice in the administration had been that of the secretary of state, Antonio Pérez, the new leader of the old 'peace' faction. But Perez's influence was not decisive. During the governorship of Don John in the Netherlands the secretary and his associates, the Marquis of los Vélez and Cardinal Quiroga, advocated a settlement with the rebels and an invasion of England. The advice was premature; the king wanted peace in the Low Countries, but he was not yet ready for war with England. But Philip II did not strike down people who disagreed with his policy; he simply ignored them. Pérez's transgression went much deeper. For reasons which are still obscure, with the intention perhaps of making himself indispensable to both Philip II and Don John, he played upon the already tense relations between the king and his half-brother. Philip knew that Don John had ambitions in England; he also learnt that from the Low Countries he was negotiating with the pope and the Catholic party in France in order to gain allies for a cross-Channel invasion.[1] But Don John's policy, though independent, was not subversive. It was Pérez who made it appear more dangerous than it was and who produced a scapegoat, Juan de Escobedo, Don John's secretary, a man ambitious for himself as well as for his master. Corresponding secretly with the governor and his secretary, Pérez showed the king the minutes of his dispatches and the confidential letters he received in return; he thus encouraged Don John and at the same time fed Philip's suspicion of his half-brother. But in 1578 Escobedo arrived at court to represent the views and needs of Don John before the king. Pérez now ran the risk of having his intrigues and his disclosure of state secrets exposed. So he struck first; blaming Don John's ambitions on Escobedo, he incited the king against him and ended by persuading Philip that he must be eliminated.[2] The king seems to have consented to the proposal, believing as usual that he had emergency powers of execution without trial. Pérez first tried to get rid of his rival by poison, and when this failed he had him run through by hired assassins in the streets of Madrid on 31 March 1578.

The matter, of course, could not rest there. In spite of his precautions, Pérez had not been able to cover his tracks completely; soon public rumour was attributing the crime to him, and Escobedo's family were demanding justice. Mateo Vázquez, Pérez's rival in the secretariat, took note of the accusations and began to denounce him to the king. Philip, tortured now in his own conscience, moved uneasily between two courses of action. He was careful not to admit that the assassination took place with his consent, but at the same time he refrained from pursuing Pérez, partly because of his own feeling of guilt, partly because of what Pérez could reveal. But when Don John died and his papers arrived in Spain, Philip was convinced that his half-brother had been innocent and that Pérez had deceived him. He was also becoming increasingly irritated by the political association between Pérez and the Princess of Eboli, and suspected that there was a leakage of state information. The king's attitude now changed. By this time his greatest political problem was the Portuguese succession. The negotiations for this were in the hands of Pérez himself, an official whom he could no longer trust and whose record in the handling of state secrets was suspect. He decided to remove him. But first he must assemble a new administration. Alba was still in disgrace; Los Vélez had recently died, also out of favour; Quiroga was not in complete agreement with the king's

[1] Marañón, *Antonio Pérez*, i. 226–51.   [2] *Ibid.*, i. 253–73, 345–72.

Portuguese policy. So Philip looked for men who were not closely associated with his previous advisers. His first choice was Cardinal Granvelle.

Granvelle was a hard and skilful diplomatist who had begun his career as secretary of Charles V by specialising in northern affairs; since his removal from the Low Countries in the 1560's, however, he had served the crown in Italy, first in negotiating the Holy League, then as viceroy of Naples from 1571 to 1575, and finally as counsellor of the Spanish embassy in Rome.[3] In every office he had proved himself utterly loyal and dependable, an incisive thinker, and a constant advocate of Spanish power, especially in the Atlantic and the north. In March 1579 Philip II summoned him from Rome with the words: 'I have special need of your person and your help in the tasks and cares of government . . . the sooner you come the happier I shall be.'[4] With him was recalled Juan de Idiáquez, Spanish ambassador in Venice. Only when the new team was virtually in position did Philip move against his former favourite. On the evening of 28 July 1579 Pérez worked with the king on some papers until ten o' clock; an hour after he left he was arrested. Shortly afterwards the Princess of Eboli, who had been threatening those who maligned her associate, especially Mateo Vázquez, and whose growing insubordination Philip found intolerable, was also taken into custody. For the rest of her life she was confined to an apartment in her palace at Pastrana. The case of Pérez himself was left for longer investigation.[5] On 1 August Granvelle arrived at court and received his instructions; in the same month Idiáquez was appointed secretary of state in place of Pérez. With a new—and harder—administration, Philip II was ready to complete his reorientation of Spanish policy and to extend his power in the Atlantic. Granvelle's official appointment was to the presidency of the Council of Italy, but he was also Philip's chief adviser in northern affairs and, until about a year before his death in 1586, the leader of the entire administration.[6] And his first mission was the enterprise of Portugal.

Since the end of the fifteenth century relations between Spain and Portugal had hung on a delicate balance of rivalry and collaboration. After their early competition for empire the two countries had found a *modus vivendi*, Spain gravitating towards America, Portugal towards the Indian Ocean. Their imperial economies thus became complementary: Portugal, whose empire was essentially a commercial one, needed Spanish American gold and silver for exchange purposes, while Spain had to buy the pepper,

---

[3] See above, pp. 291–92.
[4] See Merriman, *The Rise of the Spanish Empire*, iv. 350; van Durme, *El Cardenal Granvela*, p. 343.
[5] See below, pp. 360–61.   [6] van Durme, *op. cit.*, pp. 343–49.

spices, and silks from the Portuguese East Indies which her own empire lacked. From then onwards they had a common interest in preserving their colonial monopoly against incursions from the powers of northern Europe, and Portugal collaborated with her neighbour in protecting the Atlantic crossing. But Spain was the more powerful of the two partners, in manpower, territory, and revenue. And Philip II, like most of his contemporaries, felt greater security in sovereignty than in alliances: as long as Portugal was independent, a vital part of the Iberian peninsula and a rich overseas empire might escape his influence and fall under that of a rival power. For this reason he had his eyes fixed on Portugal long before his nephew Sebastian died in 1578, and he was ready to assert his claims to the Portuguese crown as soon as the opportunity occurred. The opportunity came sooner than he expected; Sebastian did not leave a direct heir. He was succeeded by his great-uncle, the Cardinal Henry, the last surviving legitimate son of Manoel I; and the reign of this epileptic old man could be no more than an interlude, with the problem of succession still to be solved. Portugal herself was hardly in a position to withstand the crisis, for the disaster of Alcazar-Kebir reduced her power and disrupted her economy. A large part of the Portuguese nobility was captured by the infidel; to pay the enormous ransoms the country had to empty itself of specie needed in its commercial relations with the Far East, as well as of jewels and precious stones. The many prisoners taken drained the tiny kingdom of manpower it could ill afford to lose and weakened it militarily. To crown all, the succession fell into the incompetent hands of an old man; irresolute and vindictive, Cardinal Henry dismissed the old administration but failed to provide the country with the leadership it required. For all these reasons Portugal was now extremely vulnerable to foreign intervention.

As son of the Empress Isabella, eldest daughter of Manoel I, Philip II had strong claims to the Portuguese crown after Cardinal Henry.[7] True, there were also rival claimants, among them the Duchess of Braganza, Catherine de Medici, queen mother of France, and Antonio, the Prior of Crato, who was an illegitimate descendant of Manoel I. But none of their claims were as strong as those of the Spanish king. Philip II was convinced that his hereditary rights were incontestable, and to get them recognised in Portugal he began a campaign of propaganda and diplomacy. Spanish jurists and theologians were recruited to demonstrate the justice of his cause. Through his agents in Lisbon and his aristocracy on the Luso-Spanish border he addressed to the Portuguese public, especially the nobility and the procurators of the cortes, a series of messages which contained a mixture

[7] See A. Dánvila, *Felipe II y el rey Don Sebastián de Portugal* (Madrid, 1954), and *Felipe II y la sucesión de Portugal* (Madrid, 1956).

of flattery, promises, and threats, and usually a reference to Spanish military power.[8] To Lisbon he sent his Portuguese expert, Christóvão de Moura, whose judicious use of money—but especially promises of money—recruited a Spanish party. Philip also received the collaboration of the Jesuits, who had great influence in Portugal not least with Cardinal Henry. Above all, he began to reconnoitre Portuguese frontier defences and to make ready for action. Yet in spite of this pressure he could not procure a Portuguese declaration in his favour, or hurry Cardinal Henry into organising one. And when the cardinal died in February 1580 he had still not solved the succession problem. On the other hand he had rendered one useful service to Philip.

To save Portuguese independence it would have been necessary to arm the country in support of a national candidate. The mass of the people, especially the urban population and the lower ranks of the secular clergy, abhorred the prospect of Spanish domination. But they were given no lead. The cardinal had neglected the problem of defence, preferring to spend money on ransoming the nobles in Morocco. In any case, were the propertied classes in Portugal, the nobles and the merchants, ready to make the sacrifices necessary to equip a national army? If the Portuguese people were betrayed, they were betrayed by their own ruling class. And the latter had compelling reasons not to resist. Anyone with a stake in colonial trade would be tempted to seek the support of Spain rather than resist her. They needed American treasure, many of their ships were already profitably employed in the service of Spain and the Spanish Indies, and they could hope for further protection against corsairs and foreign rivals on the immense ocean routes which separated them from their sources of wealth. Moreover, as neighbour of a greater state, Portugal could only have maintained its position as the last independent unit in the peninsula by alliance with the enemies of Spain, the Protestant English or Dutch, or the Calvinist-ridden French, and such an alliance—as the Prior of Crato was to discover—was incapable of rousing a national rally. But the Spaniards were aware of the possibility of foreign intervention, and they had it in mind when they moved into Portugal.

Cardinal Henry had left a council of regents to govern until his successor should be chosen. Of these, two or three were won to Philip II's cause and were useful to him in helping to immobilise Portuguese defences. But he had no intention of allowing them—or the cortes, or the pope—to regulate the succession; for he considered his rights were imprescriptible and not to be submitted to arbitration. And he was now in a position to enforce them,

[8] Duque de Maura, *El designio de Felipe II y el episodio de la Armada Invencible* (Madrid, 1957) pp. 42–62, 65–66; J. Reglá, Contribución al estudio de la anexión de Portugal a la Corona de España en 1580', *Hispania*, xxi. (1961), 22–48.

thanks to the preparations made by Granvelle.[9] In the early months of 1580, with government encouragement, the Castilian nobles began to raise forces at their own expense, while the towns contributed troops, ships, and funds in a national effort which underlined the inertia of the Portuguese. And with Granvelle's insistence, Philip overcame his aversion from the Duke of Alba and recalled him to service in February 1580 as commander-in-chief of the invading army. By the middle of June all was ready; the Spanish army crossed the frontier near Badajoz, watched by the king himself, and advanced rapidly on Lisbon, while the fleet under the Marquis of Santa Cruz stationed itself at the mouth of the Tagus. Between the two Don Antonio and his nationalist supporters were helpless. Lisbon surrendered at the end of August. Don Antonio, wounded in battle, escaped to the north pursued by a cavalry force under Sancho Dávila, and eventually took ship abroad. The southern part of the country was occupied by the supporting forces of the Spanish grandees. It took only four months to occupy the whole of Portugal. Philip II boasted: 'I inherited it, I bought it, I conquered it.' In fact Portugal was practically handed over to him.

Already before the occupation Philip II had promised to respect the constitutional rights of the Portuguese. Now he came to Portugal to implement his promises. At the cortes of Thomar in April 1581 he was formally recognised as king of Portugal and arranged the terms of annexation, which were published the following year in a *carta patente*.[10] He undertook never to hold the Portuguese cortes outside the kingdom and never to legislate on Portuguese affairs in a foreign assembly; the office of viceroy was to be conferred only on Portuguese or members of the royal family; administrative, military, naval, and ecclesiastical appointments were to be reserved exclusively to Portuguese; the country was to be garrisoned only by Portuguese forces; for consultation on Portuguese affairs the king was to retain a group of specified advisers and officials, all of Portuguese birth, who would compose a Council of Portugal; colonial trade was to remain unchanged, administered by Portuguese officials, conducted by Portuguese merchants, and carried in Portuguese ships; finally, all frontier customs between Castile and Portugal were to be abolished, and there were provisions against the introduction of Castilian taxation. A sixteenth-century monarch could hardly have conceded more to a conquered country. Portugal was not incorporated in the crown of Castile or treated as a subject nation; it preserved its administration and its identity, even more effectively than the other kingdoms of the Spanish crown. The concessions made by Philip II reflected not only his anxiety to avoid opposition but also his permanent principles of government and his conviction that regional

[9] van Durme, *op. cit.*, pp. 349–52.   [10] Merriman, *op. cit.*, iv. 372–78.

devolution was the best way of ruling his many kingdoms. And on the whole Philip II kept his promises. Naturally he chose Portuguese advisers and officials who were most Castilianised, like Moura, and made a member of his own family, the Archduke Albert of Austria, his viceroy; and in 1593 he seems to have restored the frontier customs between Portugal and Castile. But apart from this there was no direct violation of the pledge of 1582 until the reign of Philip IV.[11]

On receipt of the news from the metropolis the Portuguese empire rallied to Philip II without a fight. In Goa, the East Indies, and Brazil the new régime brought little immediate change, and the king continued to appoint Portuguese officials. As this was a union of crowns, not of states or of nations, the economic effects were also limited; in itself the union could not overcome the vast distances which separated the Spanish and Portuguese empires or alter their different structures. Indeed, Portugal gained something. Her colonial economy had always rested on collaboration with Spain, as has been seen; now her association with the great power could be closer, and their mutual interests in preserving their monopoly more effectively promoted. The long-term prospects for Portugal, however, were not so promising, and collaboration ultimately reverted to rivalry. For Portugal now acquired the enemies of Spain as well as its king. The Dutch in particular found it more difficult to procure the spices which they had traditionally bought in Lisbon and were drawn to seek them directly in the Far East; in the 1590's they began their invasion of the Portuguese monopoly which was to end in its outright destruction, and in the following century they extended their offensive to Brazil.[12] And in the event, as Spain was fully extended defending her own empire, Portuguese interests were neglected.

In the Azores, however, Spanish intervention was decisive, for these were a strategic point in imperial communications, a rendezvous for incoming fleets from the Indies. As Don Antonio had adherents there, he sought to make the islands a base for the recovery of Portugal. Having failed to interest Elizabeth I in his project, he enlisted the assistance of a French expedition which left for the Azores in June 1582. But Philip II was ready for it. He sent the Marquis of Santa Cruz with a powerful Spanish-Portuguese force which destroyed the French contingent. Don Antonio escaped to England, and the French tried again the following year. Again they were pursued by Santa Cruz, and again they were beaten off. And this time Spain completed the conquest of the Azores.

---

[11] On Portugal under Spanish rule see D. Peres, ed. *Historia de Portugal* (8 vols., Barcelos, 1928–37), v. 289–474.
[12] See C. R. Boxer, *The Dutch in Brazil, 1624–1654* (Oxford, 1957).

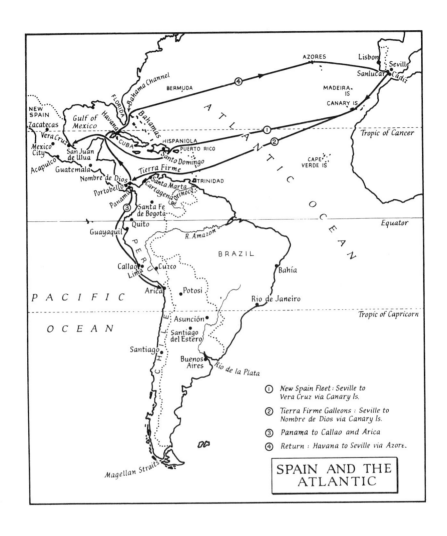

New Spain

Zacatecas

Vera Cruz
Mexico City
Acapulco
Guatemala
Nombre de Dios
Portobello
Panama
San Juan de Ulua
Gulf of Mexico
Havana
Bahama Channel
FLORIDA
CUBA
Bahamas
BERMUDA
AZORES
Lisbon
Seville
Sanlucar
Cadiz
MADEIRA IS
CANARY IS
HISPANIOLA
PUERTO RICO
Santo Domingo
CAPE VERDE IS
Tropic of Cancer
Tierra Firme
Santa Marta
Cartagena
Orinoco
TRINIDAD
Santa Fe de Bogota
Quito
Guayaquil
PERU
R. Amazon
BRAZIL
Bahia
Callao
Lima
Cuzco
Arica
Potosi
Rio de Janeiro
Equator
Tropic of Capricorn
PACIFIC OCEAN
ATLANTIC OCEAN
Asunción
Santiago del Estero
Santiago
Buenos Aires
Rio de la Plata
Magellan Straits

① New Spain Fleet: Seville to Vera Cruz via Canary Is.
② Tierra Firme Galleons: Seville to Nombre de Dios via Canary Is.
③ Panama to Callao and Arica
④ Return: Havana to Seville via Azores.

SPAIN AND THE ATLANTIC

Philip II was now ruler of a unified peninsula, with greater territorial and naval power in the Atlantic. He was also the possessor of the two largest colonial empires of the sixteenth century, the defences of which were improved by his acquisition of the Azores. This sudden aggrandisement naturally provoked his enemies, especially England. In a sense, of course, Spain needed Portugal as security against foreign intervention in the weakest part of the peninsula, in much the same way as England needed Ireland. But Portugal also gave Philip II greater striking power. The face of Spain was now turned unmistakably towards the west and the north. From the time Philip II took up residence in Lisbon—he stayed there from 1581 to 1583—he placed the centre of his composite empire on the edge of the ocean and gave notice to his enemies that he occupied a new and advanced position in the battle of the Atlantic. His great naval victories in the Azores in 1582–83 were a sign of the times; greater battles for greater stakes were to follow. In 1586 Granvelle advised Philip to reside permanently in Lisbon, where he could better organise an expedition against England: 'While France is devastated by civil war, and the Turk is seriously weakened by the attacks of Persia, the government will find it advantageous to transfer itself to Portugal, for from there it can draw on the resources of the Mediterranean and the Atlantic in order to launch the attack on England and continue the pacification of the Netherlands.'[13] Even without the presence of the king, Portugal was a strategic asset. And Philip II's naval advisers, frustrated by defensive warfare, were anxious to exploit it.

2. THE ENTERPRISE OF ENGLAND

The Marquis of Santa Cruz, whose great naval career from the battle of Lepanto to that of the Azores reflected the progress of Philip II's policy, could barely contain his excitement at the prospect of Spain's new-found strength in the Atlantic. In his brilliant action against the French squadron in 1583 he believed he had fought English ships, too, and that he had defeated two enemies at once. Now was the time, he urged, to take the offensive against England. From the Azores on 9 August 1583 he advised Philip to prepare an expedition for the following year to overthrow the 'heretic woman', make himself king of England, and thence subdue the Netherlands. He envisaged a direct sea-borne invasion, sailing from Spain, with himself in command. The king's reply was vague but not disheartening: 'The situation is such that it is not possible to speak with certainty at the moment . . . but I am ordering provisions of biscuit from Italy, and expediting the construction of galleons and the hire of ships in Vizcaya,

[13] van Durme, *op. cit.*, p. 370.

and everything else which seems necessary in preparation for a favourable opportunity; and I am also ordering Flanders to be ready for what you suggest.'[14]

In fact he had already sounded Farnese in words which showed that the idea of Santa Cruz had found a response in his own sentiments: 'We must stop the help which the rebels receive from England, and restore the latter to Catholicism'; if necessary, force would have to be considered; but he admitted that 'to launch the expedition in the sole expectation of assistance from the Catholics would be hazardous'. Farnese replied with characteristic realism. In his view little could be expected from the Catholic population in England which was too weak to organise a rising, while 'the English Catholic exiles speak more from a desire to return home than with a sense of reality'; Spain must operate alone, without allies, and would therefore have to provide a large invasion force, at least 34,000 troops; absolute secrecy was necessary, otherwise England would take alarm and organise her defences and alliances; therefore, the expedition should be launched from the Netherlands where troop movements were a daily occurrence, and in any case the Channel crossing was infinitely easier than the voyage from Spain; if the operation were successful, of course, it would hasten the reduction of the Low Countries, but it was Farnese's own view that it would be better by far 'to complete the conquest of the Low Countries first—the possession of Flushing would facilitate the operation against England'.[15] By the end of 1583, therefore, Philip II had on his desk a naval and a military plan for the invasion of England, one seeking to launch it directly from Spain, the other, though with more diffidence, suggesting a cross-Channel expedition from the Low Countries. The idea of the Spanish Armada was born. All the prudent king now needed was an opportunity and, still more perhaps, a final push from his enemies.

Throughout 1584 the project remained in cold storage. Two things prevented it from dying—English action in the Low Countries and in the Indies. On all fronts the cold war was becoming warmer. In January 1584 formal diplomatic relations between Spain and England ended when the Spanish ambassador in London, Bernardino de Mendoza, was expelled on a charge of complicity in the Throckmorton plot for the liberation of

[14] Santa Cruz to Philip II, 9 Aug. 1583, in C. Fernández Duro, *La Armada Invencible* (2 vols., Madrid, 1885), i. 241–43; Philip II to Santa Cruz, 23 September 1583, *ibid.*, p. 243, and Maura, *op. cit.*, 162–63. The outstanding modern work on the Spanish Armada is G. Mattingly, *The Defeat of the Spanish Armada* (London, 1959); on the planning of the operation, though no precise dates are given, see pp. 80–85.

[15] Philip II to Farnese, 12 September 1583, in J. Lefèvre, *Correspondance de Philipe II sur les affaires des Pays-Bas*. Deuxième partie. (4 vols., Brussels, 1940–60), ii. 405–6; Farnese to Philip II, 30 November 1583, *ibid.*, ii. 428–29, and van der Essen, *Alexandre Farnèse*, iii. 160–63.

Mary Queen of Scots and the deposition of Elizabeth. In the Netherlands William of Orange was assassinated in July 1584 by the Burgundian Balthazar Gérard, 'whose heroic action', remarked Farnese, 'is an example to the whole world'. Farnese himself, crowning the recovery of the southern provinces with the capture of Antwerp in August 1585, was now poised to move on Holland and Zeeland. This double blow to the rebel cause, together with the immobilisation of France by the outbreak of civil war in the spring of 1585, persuaded Elizabeth to intervene directly in the Netherlands. In August 1585 she signed a treaty with the United Provinces by which she pledged military aid in return for the right to put English garrisons into Brill and Flushing, the likeliest invasion ports; at the end of the year the Earl of Leicester led an expeditionary force 7,000 strong across the Channel. The new alliance was not a complete success, but it was sufficient to thwart Farnese's programme in the north, and it forced Philip II to ask himself again whether the best place to defend the Netherlands was in England. Meanwhile, English maritime hostility had forced him to consider whether England was also the best place to defend the Indies.

In May 1585 Philip II ordered the seizure of all English ships in Spanish ports. In September Elizabeth released Drake and his fleet, nominally to make reprisals for the Spanish action, in fact to wage outright—though undeclared—warfare on Spain and her empire by raiding colonies and, if possible, intercepting returning treasure fleets. After calling on Vigo, and a costly diversion to Cape Verde, Drake made for the Caribbean where he swooped on the unprepared and undefended town of Santo Domingo in Hispaniola, occupied it for a month, subjected it to organised pillage, and left with a ransom of 25,000 ducats and a haul of miscellaneous booty. From there he sailed to Cartagena on the Main, a more important centre protected by a strong natural position and already warned of Drake's approach. Again, however, the fortifications were weak and there was no garrison, so Drake had little difficulty in capturing it; again he burnt and demolished buildings until he got the required ransom (107,000 ducats). Then, as he had not the resources to sustain a base in the heart of the Spanish empire, he withdrew, outraged that he should be considered a mere pirate.[16] The expedition was not a spectacular success: it had done considerable damage to public and private buildings but not to fortifications, for there were few of these in the Indies; and even counting the ransom money the promoters were out of pocket, for Drake had missed two

[16] According to a Spanish report, Drake found at Cartagena some dispatches warning of his coming, 'and because in them it read "Francis Drake, corsair" he was much offended, as though he were not a corsair'; see I. A. Wright, ed., *Further English Voyages to Spanish America, 1583-1594* (London, Hakluyt Society, 1951), p. 134.

treasure fleets with their vast cargoes. Indeed, the treasure supply to Spain —the fuel for the offensive she was preparing—continued to flow undisturbed: the Mexican fleet reached Spain with its bullion in 1586 and the Main fleet in the following year.[17] Nevertheless, Drake's expedition was an act of war which no self-respecting monarch could ignore, least of all when so much wealth and power was at stake. Philip II had been given another demonstration that his imperial defences were vulnerable, his own subjects unprotected, and English privateers virtually immune. The danger to Spain's life-line was growing, and it was now clear that unless she asserted herself in the Atlantic her prospects as an imperial power were doomed. The Spanish king did not harbour these sentiments in isolation, remote from the desires of his subjects. They, too, wanted the issue with England settled; the merchant and maritime classes in particular pressed for a crushing blow against the national enemy, whose sea-marauders struck at their vital interests.[18] And Philip II was now prepared to fight for command of the sea.

On 17 August 1585, the same day as the capitulation of Antwerp, Philip II again brought up the subject of the enterprise of England, requesting Farnese to consider what form an invasion should take and what could be done from the Low Countries when the moment was propitious.[19] The project was on the move again, and it was now clear that in Philip's mind at least it was a question of a double operation, a military expedition from the Low Countries as well as a maritime one from Spain. And it was precisely Drake's appearance on the Spanish coast in September 1585, and his subsequent offensive in the Indies, which revived the Spanish side of the operation and brought the idea of a sea enterprise out of cold storage. In collaboration with his admiral, Santa Cruz, and his governor general in Andalucía, the Duke of Medina Sidonia, the king began to prepare a sea-going fleet to pursue Drake to the Indies and challenge him at sea; throughout the spring of 1586 the equipping and manning of the fleet were given priority in Seville, and Philip urged Santa Cruz to sail as soon as possible, pointing out that to take a squadron to the Indies did not mean abandoning the enterprise of England—on the contrary it would facilitate it.[20] But preparations were slow and eventually it proved to be too late to catch Drake at sea. Even so the effort was not wasted: Santa Cruz's fleet was now made the basis for a great Armada to search out the sea-raiders in their home base. And as the machinery went into motion the link between the Indies and the Armada became closer, embracing not only objectives but also resources. Early in 1587 Medina Sidonia, who was the king's chief agent on the commissariat side of naval preparations in Andalucía, requested

[17] Ibid., p. lxvi.
[18] See above, pp. 153–54.
[19] van der Essen, op. cit., v. 160.
[20] Duro, La Armada Invencible, i. 329–30.

advice on whether there should be a trading fleet to New Spain that year in view of the needs of the Armada being assembled in Lisbon; his own view was that it was essential to maintain yearly fleet sailings to the Indies 'since on communications between these two worlds depends our wealth and power in this one'. The king's opinion, transmitted through his secretary, Idiáquez, underlined the dual motive of the enterprise and the fact that the interests of the Indies and those of the Armada were not incompatible:

> The intervention of the English in Holland and Zeeland, together with their infestation of the Indies and the Ocean, is of such a nature that defensive methods are not enough to cover everything, but forces us to apply the fire in their homeland, and so fiercely that they will have to rush back and retire from elsewhere. . . . They are powerful at sea, and that is their great asset; therefore His Majesty's Armada should not sail under-strength but should be the largest and most powerful one possible. On this assumption His Majesty requires your opinion on whether the New Spain fleet had better be detached from its normal duties this year in order to reinforce the Armada with its full complement of troops, seamen, ships, artillery, and the rest. For the objective of this Armada is no less the security of the Indies than the recovery of the Netherlands.[21]

After the king's initiative in reviving the enterprise of England in the second half of 1585, Santa Cruz himself returned to the theme, and this time, in view of Drake's expedition to the Caribbean, he too linked it unmistakably with imperial defence. On 13 January 1586 he again urged Philip II to attack England, arguing that the queen of England, lacking resources to defend her kingdom at home, operated by sending fleets to make war on Spain at sea and in the Indies; to this the king had still made no effective reply, yet his subjects were losing heavily in trade and property, and the crown itself was losing much more in revenue than an invasion of England would cost; 'these', he concluded, 'are the defects of defensive wars'. Philip II then asked Santa Cruz for a plan of campaign, and within two months the admiral had prepared his famous 'Relation'.[22] In it he asked for 150 sail, not counting freighters, and over 60,000 troops, estimated the cost of an eight months' campaign at nearly four million ducats, and showed that he still conceived the expedition as a unified one from Spain. The king, however, had already been forming his own views on this point, and on 7 February he again requested information and advice from Farnese.

---

[21] Medina Sidonia to Idiáquez, 22 Feb. 1587, Maura, *op. cit.*, pp. 163–67; Idiáquez to Medina Sidonia, 28 Feb. 1587, *ibid.*, pp. 167–68.

[22] Duro, *La Armada Invencible*, i. 244–47, 150–319.

The latter's dispatch of 20 April outlined a programme more akin to the ideas of the king than to those of Santa Cruz.[23] 'The substance of the England operation', argued Farnese, 'consists in three elements: the first and principal one is secrecy; the second is security against France; the third is security in the Low Countries.' From principles he passed to technical requirements. He would need a striking-force of 30,500 troops; this could be concentrated at Dunkirk, Nieuport, and Gravelines in readiness for a quick crossing in barges escorted by a fighting squadron to a point between Dover and Margate. But the essential condition for this kind of operation was secrecy, for it was extremely vulnerable to naval attack. Therefore, in case the English fleet were alerted, Farnese formulated an alternative plan. This required 'mastery of the sea'; the king should equip a powerful fleet in Spain, capable of destroying or containing the English squadrons, and thus guaranteeing the crossing of Farnese's troops. In his view, therefore, an Armada was only necessary if the element of surprise were lost in the cross-Channel operation from the Low Countries; in that case an Armada would have to force a passage through to the invasion point. But he admitted his fear that the enterprise was now common knowledge.

Considering the two plans, that of his admiral and that of his general, Philip II gradually integrated them into one of his own. Farnese would assemble an expeditionary force on the Flemish coast, ready to embark in barges. Santa Cruz would prepare a fighting fleet at Lisbon which would cope with the English navy and carry a strong force of Spanish infantry. The Armada would rendezvous with Farnese's army and escort it to an invasion point somewhere near the mouth of the Thames, preferably 'the cape of Margate'. Once the invasion force had landed, Santa Cruz would secure its communications by sea; he could also engage the English fleet if necessary or possible, though the main function of the Armada was to convoy a landing-force.[24] In this way the king made use of the nucleus of a fleet which Santa Cruz had already assembled; he availed himself of the incomparable skill of Farnese in land warfare, and employed his Flanders veterans rather than carry the whole army from Spain; and he kept the way open for retreat. To this extent the plan was plausible. On the other hand it contained some serious flaws.

The dual command was dangerous: it presupposed perfect liaison between the admiral and the general, and liaison between Philip II's subordinates was never perfect, least of all when the distance separating them was that

[23] Farnese to Philip II, 20 April 1586, Lefèvre, *Correspondance*, iii. 105–107; van der Essen, *op. cit.*, v. 164–68.

[24] E. Herrera Oría, S.J., *La Armada Invencible, 1587–89. Documentos procedentes del Archivo General de Simancas* (Valladolid, 1929), pp. 130–34.

between Lisbon and the Low Countries. Philip II directed the operation personally; he was the sole co-ordinator, holding all the strings and nego-tiating with each commander separately. And Philip II was a long way from the field of action. The result was that his commanders could never keep up with his frequent changes of mind—as late as December 1587 he was ordering Santa Cruz to prepare two armadas, and urging Farnese to cross the Channel before any armada arrived—and neither the general nor the admiral ever really understood each other's objectives. As communi-cations between the two forces were so faulty, it was almost impossible to synchronise their junction in advance, especially as the Spaniards did not command a suitable port in the Low Countries. This, indeed, was the basic defect in the operation: lack of a deep-water port, capable of taking the Spanish galleons, exposed the Armada to operating far from home without a base, and left Farnese's army without an escort from the point of em-barkation. Farnese referred frequently to this gap in the plan, and Philip II himself understood it, for as early as December 1585 he had admitted to Farnese that 'without a port we can do nothing'.[25] Yet the two commanders never discussed it between themselves, and the king seems to have persuaded himself that a junction could be effected in mid-Channel or at 'the cape of Margate'. But it was folly to assume that the Dutch and English blockading squadrons would allow Farnese's barges to emerge unscathed, and that Margate Roads afforded any refuge. And there still remained the most insuperable obstacle of all, the invasion and occupation of England. Behind Elizabeth's apparent inertia, her retention of Drake, and her refusal to sanction Hawkins's plan for a blockade of the Spanish coast, lay a readiness to move into action quickly once danger approached. The English fleet was a powerful fighting force, composed of swift, weatherly and well-armed galleons, designed to sink ships rather than kill men. Moreover, in spite of the record of the army of Flanders and its commander, the conquest and occupation of a foreign country by an invading army, unsure of a rising in its support once it got there, was a highly speculative operation, especially as English land defences were not negligible. To question ultimate objectives, however, would be to lose faith in the entire enterprise, and even the realist Farnese was not yet reduced to that extreme. The fruits of success were too tempting.

In any case Spain had immense reserves of power, and on these Philip II now began to draw. From mid-1586 his commissariat was moving, slowly

---

[25] van der Essen, *op. cit.*, v. 162; again in February 1587 Philip admitted that they only disposed of one sure port—Dunkirk—and it could not take large vessels, a problem on which he wanted Farnese's advice, Philip II to Farnese, 28 Feb. 1587, Lefèvre, *Correspondance*, iii. 185.

but with purpose. In these years the crown's income from the Indies was enormous;[26] to it was joined the revenue from Castile and from the church —in spite of his scepticism about the king of Spain's motives, Pope Sixtus V renewed the *cruzada* for seven years at the end of 1585. With money, it seemed, everything was possible. Contracts were made for naval stores and provisions, the search was begun for Baltic timber, for ships and seamen; the Spanish naval yards increased their efforts; and in spite of English vigilance in the Channel convoys from the Hanse towns reached Spain with vital supplies of food, naval stores, and ordnance and some of their vessels were bought to augment the Spanish fleet. All this, of course, took time and the cost was appalling. Farnese had stipulated an invasion date in October 1586; apart from the element of surprise, speed was cheaper. But Philip II never underrated English power and believed that overwhelming force would be necessary to overcome it; in July 1586 he informed Farnese that there was no hope of the expedition being ready before the spring of 1587. By that time an event had occurred which gave him a greater sense of urgency. The execution of Mary Stuart in England on 18 February 1587 had a double significance for Philip II: it removed the risk of France benefiting from the substitution of Mary for Elizabeth on the English throne, and it enabled Philip to assert his own claims to the English throne, if not for himself then for his daughter. His hereditary claims were not strong, but they were improved at least in papal eyes by the Protestantism of Mary's son, James VI of Scotland. In July 1587 Philip reached an agreement with Sixtus V in a formal treaty by which the pope promised him a subsidy of one million ducats on condition that the expedition sailed before the end of the year and that Spanish troops actually landed in England; and if it were successful then Philip would nominate, with papal approval, a king pledged to Catholicism.[27] Since the execution of Mary Stuart, Philip had convinced even the pope that his preparations were serious, as indeed they were, both inside and outside Spain.

Farnese had underlined the need for 'security against France'. The object was to immobilise France and thus prevent her from assisting England and from intervening in the Netherlands during the absence of the Spanish army. The means were already at hand—civil dissension. Since the death of the Duke of Anjou in June 1584 the legal heir to the throne then occupied by Henry III was the Protestant Henry of Navarre. The prospect of the latter's succession was as abhorrent to Philip II as it was to the Catholic party in France, and on 31 December 1584 Philip concluded with the Guises the secret treaty of Joinville which revived the Holy League in France by giving it the support of Spanish subsidies, with a programme of

[26] See above, pp. 172–73.   [27] See above, pp. 284–85.

stamping out Protestantism and preventing Henry of Navarre from succeeding to the throne. In the following months Philip II's ambassador,
now Bernardino de Mendoza, who found greater scope for his talents in
France than he had done in England, established close contact with the
Catholic revolutionaries, and acted as Philip's paymaster to the League.
Thanks to Mendoza's skilful diplomacy, playing on the political and
religious divisions within the country, France was indeed gradually immobilised. In July 1585 Henry III, cornered by the League and its Spanish
ally, outlawed the Huguenots; in September Sixtus V issued a bull denouncing Henry of Navarre as a lapsed Catholic and incapable of succeeding to the throne of France. For the next two years the Huguenots were
fighting for survival, while Mendoza conspired with his allies to reduce the
French crown to complete dependence on the Guise and the Catholic
party. But timing was important, for the ambassador had to synchronise
his operation with the actual departure of the Armada. Throughout 1587 he
kept his preparations simmering and brought them to boiling point just at the
right moment. By a *coup d'état* on 12 May 1588 Henry of Guise completed
his control of Paris, and the king fled to Chartres. On the eve of the invasion
of England France was neutralised and Farnese's western flank secured.[28]

Security in the Low Countries, the third of Farnese's stipulations, was more
difficult to attain. Farnese aimed at leaving a large army, equal to that already
there and capable of containing an offensive by the rebels during his absence.
This he could do if he were given enough money. But there was still the
problem of improving his position on the coast, where he still did not hold
a deep-water port in which his army could join the Spanish fleet. In the
summer of 1587 he moved quickly on Sluys on the Flemish coast, a strategic
point not so much because of its harbour facilities as because of its position
on the network of waterways between Bruges and the east Flanders coast
across which he had to get his troops and barges from inland. In appalling
conditions, with his usual superb technique, he laid siege to Sluys with
a small flotilla at sea and his veteran infantry on land. After one of the
most difficult actions he had ever fought he took it on 5 August, aided
as much by English and Dutch ineptitude as by his own skill. He then
began constructing canals linking Sluys and Nieuport, to enable his barges
to pass from the Scheldt above Antwerp to Dunkirk, the embarkation
point, without risking destruction in open water at the hands of the
Dutch.[29] But Sluys was not the deep-water port Farnese was seeking. He
himself wanted to take Flushing, and was increasingly of the opinion that
defeat of the rebels was necessary to conquer England rather than the reverse.

[28] Mattingly, *The Defeat of the Spanish Armada*, pp. 45–53, 136–56, 193–213.
[29] van der Essen, *op. cit.*, v. 127–40, 220–21; Lefèvre, *Correspondance*, iii. 237, 334.

But Philip II, anxious to save his resources, had decided to run down his military machine in the Netherlands before restarting it for the invasion of England. Yet the invasion was taking longer and longer to prepare; the greater the delay the greater the deterioration suffered by existing forces, and the more costly the whole enterprise became. Farnese now expected the invasion to take place in 1587 at the latest. With 30,000 troops and the money he had received from Spain his resources were at their peak in September 1587. By March 1588 sickness and death had reduced his army to 17,000, his provisions were consumed, his money was spent, and he was as far away from England as ever. In between he complained bitterly to Philip II: immobilised by the ruinous delay, he was even prevented from making progress in the Low Countries; his troops were in poor condition, and above all the Armada would not be able to co-operate directly with him because he still had no port capable of taking vessels of heavy draught; therefore its rôle would have to be diversionary, to keep the English fleet occupied and prevent it from attacking his barges; even so the Dutch squadrons would be able to blockade his exit from the Flemish coast; to crown all the whole enterprise was now the talk of Europe, and the only way of laying a false trail lay in peace negotiations.[30] In the autumn of 1587 the king himself had instructed Farnese that while the invasion of England was to go forward without fail, with no peace on any terms, the English were to be lured into negotiations as a diversion. Elizabeth, in fact, was ready to talk peace, but not to close her eyes to the obvious military planning that accompanied the negotiations.

The cause of the delay was the difficulty of getting the Armada to sea. In 1587 Drake struck it a heavy, though not fatal, blow. Raiding Cadiz at the end of April he caught, among other units, the New Spain fleet, on which Philip intended to draw to reinforce the Armada; altogether he sank, burnt or captured about 24 vessels, and thus reduced the stock of ships at Philip's disposal.[31] Then, from a temporary base at Sagres, he captured some supply ships carrying barrel-staves needed for making water-butts and casks; if the Armada was subsequently deficient in provisions it was due to the initiative of Drake rather than the fraudulence of its contractors.[32] After the departure of the raiders Spanish preparations were resumed, but the search for over-whelming striking power made Santa Cruz more prudent than his master. From September 1587, with mounting impatience, Philip sent letter after letter to his admiral, urging him to sail and giving him a few weeks' grace at a time in

[30] Farnese to Philip II, 12 Sept. 1587, 21, Dec. 1587, 30 Mar. 1588, van der Essen, *op. cit.*, v. 188–90, 198–200; Lefèvre, *Correspondance*, iii. 257–58, 285–86.
[31] Chaunu, *Séville et l'Atlantique*, viii, 2, 1, pp. 726–28, 769.
[32] Mattingly, *The Defeat of the Spanish Armada*, pp. 116–17.

order to complete his preparations, add to his ships and improve his stores. The king's frustration led him to issue conflicting orders which only increased the confusion and underlined the failure of liaison long in advance of the Armada's sailing. In December he was trying to get Santa Cruz to form two armadas, one to go straight to Farnese with troops, return, and join the other to form a single unit. But there was still no movement from Santa Cruz's fleet, and in desperation Philip ordered Farnese to sail without it, thus abandoning one of the essential features of his own plan. Farnese, who had already thrashed this out with Philip and thought they had reached agreement at last, replied that he was ready to cross the Channel on his own in a longboat but he could not send his troops to their death by launching them without an escort.[33] On this occasion at least Philip II was saved from irretrievable disaster by cooler heads than his own. Eventually the expedition was due to sail in February 1588, though Santa Cruz still did not have the fleet he wanted and now he was saying he could not sail until money arrived to pay his men. But for Santa Cruz the moment for sailing never came. He died at Lisbon on 9 February.

Philip II had already decided on his successor—Alonso de Guzmán, the thirty-eight-year-old Duke of Medina Sidonia, son-in-law of the Princess of Eboli, captain-general of Andalucía. Medina Sidonia was a civilian, thoughtful, industrious and honest, but not a seaman. He did not want the appointment, and he tried to argue his way out of it, pleading proclivity to sea-sickness, poverty, inexperience of military and naval affairs, and ignorance of the strategy and tactics of the enterprise.[34] In fact he underrated himself. Philip II wanted an illustrious grandee, powerful in his own right and the possessor of natural rank over the hard-bitten captains in the fleet. For about ten years Philip had used Medina Sidonia as a sort of unpaid viceroy in Andalucía, a key position in imperial strategy, where he had served the king well in civil, military, and naval administration. There he had acquired experience in fitting out fleets, especially the Indies fleets, and had proved himself an intelligent amateur, capable of turning his hands to most assignments and ready to listen to expert advice; for the past few years he had already been used in an administrative capacity in equipping the Armada. And by 1588 the Armada had become increasingly an administrative problem. The last-minute preparations of Santa Cruz for a February sailing had produced chaos, men and supplies thrown haphazardly into ships, captains grabbing what they could by way of stores and ordnance, and everything

---

[33] Herrera Oría, *La Armada Invencible*, pp. 1–11, 98–100, and the same author's *Felipe II y el marqués de Santa Cruz en la empresa de Inglaterra* (Madrid, 1946), pp. 53–61, 138–39; van der Essen, *op. cit.*, v. 201–202.

[34] Medina Sidonia to Idiáquez, 16 February 1588, Maura, *op. cit.*, pp. 241–44; see also, pp. 81 ff., 213 ff.

rapidly deteriorating from inactivity. So Philip II hurried Medina Sidonia to Lisbon before everything disintegrated for lack of a commander, and the admiral's first job was to bring order out of the confusion left by his predecessor. The duke was good at staff work; he established sound relations with his squadron commanders, Juan Martínez de Recalde, Miguel de Oquendo, and Pedro de Valdés, formed them into a council of war, and with them worked out signals, sailing directions and orders, fighting instructions, and a plan of formation against English attacks. Like Santa Cruz and the rest of the Spanish navy he appreciated the importance of guns and realised that he was going to get little opportunity for hand-to-hand combat. He never overcame the shortage of heavy long-range guns capable of destroying ships, or of trained gunners, but he procured more artillery than Santa Cruz had done, as well as more powder and shot, and he did not lead a fleet unarmed for Atlantic warfare. He also got more ships. Philip II had finally decided to detach the eight galleons of the Indies guard under Diego Flores de Valdés from their escort duty with the Main fleet and add them to the Armada, which was also reinforced with the greater part of the Indies fleets themselves.[35] Finally, the duke managed to recruit experienced pilots, some of them Englishmen, familiar with the Channel and the North Sea.

By now the new commander understood the essentials of the operation, which he had in detailed instructions from the king. The central features had survived all the shifts of circumstance and false alarms of royal policy. 'On receiving my order, sail with the whole Armada direct to the English Channel, through there up to the Cape of Margate, to join the Duke of Parma and guard his crossing.' After Farnese's troops had made their landing, Medina Sidonia was to protect his line of supply; at his own discretion he might then give battle to the English fleet, but before that he was not to seek an encounter. 'You should take special note, however, that the enemy's aim will be to fight from a distance, since he has the advantage of superior artillery . . . while we must come to grips at close quarters.'[36] But Philip II did not explain how this was to be done, any more than he explained how the Armada was to overcome the lack of a suitable port in the Channel. He had finished his planning, and now he relied on his faith in divine assistance, a faith shared by the mass of his subjects, somewhat ruefully by his naval officers, and hardly at all by Rome. The Spanish view of the enterprise saw it as the work of God, undertaken with the sanction and support of the church. The king ordered public and private prayers for the expedition's

[35] Chaunu, *op. cit.*, vi., 2, tables 601–668, pp. 861–975; viii., 2, 1, p. 769.

[36] Philip II to Medina Sidonia, 1 April 1588, in G. P. B. Naish, 'Documents illustrating the history of the Spanish Armada', *Naval Miscellany*, vol. IV, ed. C. Lloyd (London, Navy Records Society, 1952), pp. 13–19; Maura, *op. cit.*, pp. 251–52.

success, and advised Medina Sidonia that his men should live as good Christians and 'refrain from swearing and blasphemy and other vices which so offend Our Lord'.[37] Before the fleet sailed all the men confessed and received Holy Communion, and with them went 180 chaplains.

By May 1588 the whole Armada was standing out from Lisbon—two squadrons of galleons in the first line, four squadrons of armed merchantmen in the second, a group of pinnaces for scouting, and a mass of freighters and supply vessels, in all 130 ships, carrying 2,431 pieces of artillery and 22,000 seamen and soldiers, the latter intended both to fight at sea and reinforce Farnese's army. It was less than the minimum estimate of Santa Cruz, and many of the ships were not weatherly, but it was still a formidable array. Its start, however, was not propitious: progress up the Iberian coast was slow, and food and water supplies were already defective. So it had to make for Corunna to take on fresh stores, and there on 19 June it was scattered by a storm. Medina Sidonia, who had been growing more pessimistic the further he got from Lisbon, now wrote a lengthy plea to the king, not so much the cry of a faint heart as an honest attempt to point out the grave risks involved in the operation, requesting him to abandon or defer the expedition because 'with the forces it commands how can it succeed against so powerful a kingdom with so many allies?[38] Philip briefly ordered the duke to reassemble his forces and take on fresh supplies, and to proceed before the weather got worse. With his conscience clear Medina Sidonia accepted the inevitable and from then on his morale improved. A month after the storm the ships were collected, repaired and provisioned, and by 29 July the Armada was off the Lizard. The next day it began to move cautiously up the Channel, and in England the beacons sent their signals across the country.

The main body of the English fleet under the Lord Admiral, Lord Howard of Effingham, and his second-in-command, Sir Francis Drake, was awaiting the Spaniards not, as Philip II supposed, at the eastern end of the Channel in Calais Roads but in the west at Plymouth. And before it even engaged the Armada it won a decisive advantage. As soon as they received word that the enemy was at the mouth of the Channel, Howard and Drake slipped out of Plymouth Sound and managed to get to the windward of the Spaniards; they thus won the weather-gauge and kept it for the rest of the engagement.[39]

[37] Maura, *op. cit.*, pp. 273–74.

[38] Medina Sidonia to Philip II, 24 June 1588, Duro, *La Armada Invencible*, ii. 134–37; Maura, *op. cit.*, pp. 258–61.

[39] See J. S. Corbett, *Drake and the Tudor Navy* (2 vols., London, 1898–99), ii. 208–21; on the Armada campaign see also, J. K. Laughton, ed., *State Papers Relating to the Defeat of the Spanish Armada* (London, Navy Records Society, 2 vols., 1894); D. W. Waters, 'The Elizabethan Navy and the Armada Campaign', *The Mariner's Mirror*, xxxv. (1949), M. Lewis, *The Spanish Armada* (London, 1960), and the same author's 'Armada Guns'; *Mariner's Mirror*, xxviii. (1942), xxix. (1943).

The English could now dictate the terms of battle, relentlessly following the Armada, in ships that were fast and weatherly enough to manoeuvre as they pleased and keep whatever distance they chose as they raked the enemy with their long-range artillery. But Medina Sidonia's captains knew their drill; with great precision the Spanish fleet manoeuvred into its famous crescent formation, presenting a solid defence to the English who followed in their new line-ahead formation and who had to be careful not to be trapped between the two wings. And although the English refused to be tempted in or to allow the Spaniards to grapple, their long-range bombardment, a relatively new technique, was not accurate or heavy enough to pierce galleons. So they failed to break the Armada. The seamanship, discipline, and fighting spirit of the Spaniards were superb; keeping a tight formation, refusing to abandon ships in battle, they moved slowly up the Channel day after day for nine days, while the English spent their shot to no great purpose. After four sharp battles the Armada was still unbroken and full of fight, and still moving on. By 6 August it was at Calais Roads, having lost only two vessels—largely by accident—and suffered relatively light casualties. On the other hand the English fleet was still to windward and was now augmented by the squadron blockading Farnese. And when Medina Sidonia anchored off Calais the crucial moment on which the whole enterprise hung—the meeting between the Armada and the army of Flanders—had arrived at last.

Since the middle of July Farnese had been ready; his troops and barges were assembled at the embarkation points, Nieuport and Dunkirk, awaiting the arrival of the Armada. The news he received confirmed his worst fears. As the Spanish fleet moved up the Channel a series of envoys reached him from Medina Sidonia, asking him to name the rendezvous, come out and join the Armada in the battle with the English, or alternatively to send him forty or fifty flyboats capable of holding the enemy fleet until Farnese made his exit. Flyboats were swift, shallow-draught warships needed for navigation off the Dutch and Flemish coasts. And Farnese did not have enough to break the Dutch blockade unaided. What he did have were canal barges for transporting his troops. These, as he had often insisted to Philip II, could not come out without an escort. As Farnese understood his instructions, it was the Armada's duty to assure *his* passage, not the reverse.[40] But it was equally impossible for Medina Sidonia to close in to the Flemish coast, for Spanish galleons drew water deeper than could be found around Dunkirk; the Armada had to remain in open sea, while the Dutch flyboats, constructed

---

[40] Farnese to Philip II, 22 June 1588, Lefèvre, *Correspondance*, iii. 323–24, van der Essen. *op. cit.*, v. 219–20; Medina Sidonia to Farnese, 6 Aug. 1588, Lefèvre, *op. cit.* iii. 344–45.

precisely for these shallow waters, waited to pounce on the invasion barges as soon as they emerged. There was, therefore, no rendezvous, and the enterprise failed in its most essential point. 'No one regrets this situation more than I do,' reported Farnese, 'from the very beginning I have regretted it.'[41] Philip II knew of these difficulties in advance from Farnese, but Medina Sidonia seems to have learnt them for the first time when he reached Calais. There his position was hopeless: he was exposed without a port, the English fleet had him covered from the windward, and Farnese found it 'humanly impossible' to meet him. But, with grim fatalism, the general went through the drill he had prepared. On 8 August, two days after the Armada's arrival off Calais, he began to embark his troops at Nieuport and Dunkirk; he was still blockaded by Dutch squadrons, and there was a high wind against him. The situation was being bitterly argued between Farnese and the impatient envoys of Medina Sidonia when news arrived which closed the discussion.

In its anchorage off Calais the Armada was a perfect target for fire-ships coming with the wind. Eight of these, launched by the English on the night of 7–8 August, did what guns had so far been unable to do—broke the Armada's formation. The Spaniards slipped their cables and scattered, while the English fleet, now 150 strong, came in for the kill. With a fine display of leadership, helped by skilful squadron commanders and disciplined crews, Medina Sidonia got his big warships into formation again off Gravelines. There, on 8 August, unable to grapple and short of ammunition, they were torn to pieces by the English guns, coming in to close range at last. But the Spaniards were determined to go down fighting; time after time the great galleons came back, and at the end of a day's destruction and slaughter, with their shot exhausted, they were still ready to do battle again, before a north-east squall ended the engagement. At Gravelines, for the first time, the Armada had taken a real beating; only four ships were lost, but the whole fleet was grievously damaged and the human casualties were enormous. It had been driven past the point where it hoped to unite with Farnese and there was no hope of regaining it. From now on it was at the mercy of the weather; driven perilously near the Zeeland sands, it was then blown up the North Sea, and Medina Sidonia had to decide to get his fleet home westwards round the British Isles, defeated and in retreat.

The autumn days were bitter ones for Spain. The great Farnese, helpless on the coast of Flanders, disembarked his troops and returned to Bruges to face a storm of criticism. Medina Sidonia, conscientious in retreat as in attack, led his battered fleet home in a nightmare voyage, losing thousands of his men in Ireland where the English garrison slaughtered those who were

---

[41] Farnese to Philip II, 7 Aug. 1588, Lefèvre, *Correspondance*, iii. 346–47; Farnese to Philip II, 10 Aug. 1588, *ibid.*, iii. 349–50; van der Essen, *op. cit.*, v. 226–27.

not drowned on the savage coasts. He reached Santander on 23 September, semi-delirious from sickness and privation, and protesting feverishly to the king that nothing would get him to sea again.[42] The condition of the survivors who followed him was even more pitiful, and hundreds died in port before they could be got ashore. The leadership of the duke and the skill of his pilots saved a large part of the Armada, perhaps forty-four out of its sixty eight fighting ships. But almost half of the surviving fleet proved to be unfit for further service, and the most grievous blow of all was the heavy mortality among officers and seamen; and in terms of naval power these were more difficult to replace than ships.

Philip II was outwardly unshaken. As years of planning, anxiety and expense collapsed in catastrophe, he continued to administer the affairs of his world empire. A Jesuit priest, Alonso Sánchez, was making his way to the Escorial to seek an interview with the king when one of the dispatches announcing the failure of the invasion of England arrived. Sánchez was seeking aid for the Philippines mission and had a plan for the invasion of China. In the circumstances discretion caused him not to press the latter on this occasion, but on the subject of the Philippines the king received him with his usual courtesy and equanimity, listened to his requests, took his papers, and offered to consider the matter.[43] If the morale of Spaniards did not collapse under the disaster it was partly because of the unshakeable continuity provided by their king. For Medina Sidonia he had not a word of reproach; he gave him permission to return to his estate at Sanlucar, continued to employ him in high office when he had recovered, and never sent him to sea again. The defeat of the Spanish Armada, of course, was not the fault of Medina Sidonia, whose courage and leadership could hardly have been bettered. Nor was it the fault of Farnese, whose tactical and moral sense alike prevented him from sending his army to its destruction. Circumstances were beyond the control of both commanders. If any human being was responsible it was Philip II himself, who failed to co-ordinate the two arms of his attack in the planning stage, and who, knowing he possessed no deep-water port, trusted in the superiority of his forces and decided to risk everything in the hope that somehow, somewhere a junction could be made. But even Philip could be excused in part, pushed as he was to defend his empire, even to the point of sending his fleet on an impossible mission. In any case the disaster was not decisive. England had won a half-success in that she forced Spain back to the starting-point, to begin her naval pro-

---

[42] Medina Sidonia to Idiáquez, 27 Sept. 1588, Maura, op. cit., 265–66.
[43] F. Colín, *Labor Evangélica de la Compañía de Jesus en las Islas Filipinas* (ed. P. Pastells, S.J., 3 vols., Madrid, 1900–02), i. 407–09. I am indebted for this reference to Dr. J. S. Cummins.

gramme all over again. But England had not won the war, or even gained mastery of the sea. The Atlantic was too vast for any single power to dominate in the sixteenth century, and the war continued as before, a kind of stalemate. The English and the Dutch still controlled the Channel, and for his northern supplies Philip had to rely on the readiness of the Dutch to trade even with the enemy, and on the ability of the Hanseatic convoys occasionally to evade English patrols. But Spain still controlled the crossing to the Indies, and here she fought back more successfully.

As Philip II found it impossible for the moment to defend the Indies in England, he had to do what he could to defend them in America itself. Within two years after the defeat of the Armada he had reconstituted his Indies fleets, protecting them with a new force of fighting ships; and to secure his treasure shipments he assigned them to squadrons of *zabras*, fast frigates which could evade enemy raiders.[44] These were vital defence measures, for English privateering took a new lease of life after the defeat of the Armada. Drake's abortive counter-armada against Lisbon in 1589 showed that Spain no less than England was basically immune by land, and that there were greater profits to be found in maritime and colonial warfare. In the summer of 1589 the Earl of Cumberland established a temporary base in the Azores and seized some treasure from the Indies; in 1590 Hawkins and Frobisher made a similar attempt, though they returned home empty-handed; in 1593 Cumberland ravaged Havana and Trinidad. These were the more spectacular, though not the most profitable, expeditions. Every year hundreds of smaller privateering ventures returned a steady profit to their investors: between 1589 and 1591 at least 235 English vessels were at large between the eastern Atlantic and America, picking up what they could from Spanish commerce and colonies.[45] But they no longer raided with impunity: while Philip II was protecting the Atlantic crossing he was also improving his defences in America itself. Drake's great raid on the Caribbean in 1585–86 had really awoken Spain to the danger, and for the next fifteen years there was a consistent plan to defend the colonies by land as well as by sea.[46] In 1586 colonel Juan de Texeda, a military expert, and Juan Bautista Antoneli, the distinguished Italian engineer, were sent to the Caribbean on a tour of inspection, the former to decide what defences were needed, the latter what form they should take.[47] Texeda remained in the

[44] See above, pp. 167–68, 175, and references to Chaunu there.

[45] K. R. Andrews, ed., *English Privateering Voyages to the West Indies, 1588–1595* (Cambridge, Hakluyt Society, 1959), p. 16.

[46] R. D. Hussey, 'Spanish reaction to foreign aggression in the Caribbean to about 1680', *Hispanic American Historical Review*, ix. (1929), 286–302,

[47] Wright, *Further English Voyages to Spanish America, 1583–1594*, pp. 192–93. See also Lope de Vega, *La Dragontea* (2 vols., Madrid, 1935); this edition of Lope de Vega's poem, celebrating—with considerable poetic licence—the death of Drake, also contains

Indies as governor of Havana, while Antoneli returned to Spain in 1587 to draw up a comprehensive plan for fortifying the Caribbean. This was approved by the king, and for the next few years fortifications of major ports like Havana, San Juan de Ulúa, Puerto Rico, and the newly founded Portobello, made rapid progress, while garrisons of regular troops were established or reinforced. In the same years the coast-guard fleets were improved, as local squadrons of galleys were strengthened, renewed or installed. As these were still considered inadequate, the king created for the whole of the Caribbean a new Windward Squadron, which sailed in 1598 and was composed of six frigates and other craft.

The efficiency of the new defences was demonstrated in 1595 at the expense of Spain's most inveterate enemies. Hawkins and Drake, going through the old routine, led another expedition to the Caribbean. It was ten years since Drake had been there, and this time the Spaniards were ready for him. The invaders were beaten off from Puerto Rico and Panama by superior forces, and in the course of the operation the two leaders died from sickness. In one sector at least, therefore, the war went in Spain's favour. Imperial communications and defence were stronger in the last ten years of Philip II's reign than they had ever been, and American treasure continued to swell his resources.

Nevertheless, indirectly Spain was grievously hurt by the English—and increasingly by the Dutch—naval offensive on the ocean and in America. She lost no colonies and little treasure, but the expense of defending them was crippling. To replace or repair ships, to build or renew fortifications, cost money—and the cost was increasing.[48] The increase was related to rising prices in Spanish shipyards from about 1580, a phenomenon noticed and criticised by contemporaries. In the 1580's the Marquis of Santa Cruz, who as well as being a naval officer was also, like his father before him, one of the principal contractors of the Spanish crown for warships, complained bitterly of the price of ships and of the sacrifices which the king demanded of shipowners in providing his armadas, for returns were so meagre. In 1611 Tomé Cano, a former shipper and author of a treatise on naval construction, estimated that the cost of shipbuilding in Spain had tripled since the last decades of the previous century. The main cause of the increase was persistent inflation. Timber and other raw materials for shipbuilding were scarce, and their price rose even higher than the general price increase in Spain.[49] Moreover, between 1580 and 1596, and above all from

a collection of documents on English activity in the Caribbean and on Spanish fortifications; see especially ii. 149–71.

[48] See the superb analysis by Chaunu, *op. cit.*, i. 204–208, and iii. 412, 437, 450, 468.

[49] Hamilton, *American Treasure and the Price Revolution in Spain*, pp. 224, 235.

1600 to 1628, wages in Spain increased much more quickly than the price
of commodities. So the cost of labour as well as of raw materials, the determining elements in shipbuilding costs, advanced beyond the general price
level, and both contributed to raising the cost of imperial defence. Spain
was now feeling the pinch, and her discomfort was rendered more acute by
the difficulty of getting foreign supplies. Spanish ships were unsuitable for
the transport of naval stores, while English tactics were directed to preventing
even neutral countries of northern Europe from trading in war materials
with the Iberian peninsula. To obtain essential supplies the Spanish government was forced to conclude costly contracts with foreign firms, who had
to be compensated for the risks they were running from English patrols,
and sometimes the contracts opened breaches in the colonial monopoly
when the terms included permission for the contractors to trade with
America. The whole process increased the overheads of the Indies trade and
gave Spanish merchants more reason to evade the defence tax; they refused
to participate in the use of frigates for transporting treasure and valuable
goods and the state had to underwrite the entire cost of this expedient.

There was, finally, another factor operating against the Spanish war
effort. As is well known, prices rose more rapidly and more intensely in
Spain than in the rest of Europe; in particular the heavy increase in the cost
of shipbuilding was more peculiar to Spain than to her enemies. This was
appreciated by English as well as by Spanish strategists: in July 1584, when
Hawkins advocated a blockade of Spain, he estimated that even in peace
conditions it was three times more expensive to equip ships in Spain than
in England.[50] As the English and Dutch offensive was based on a less expensive naval economy than that of Spain, the cost of attack was cheaper than
the cost of defence, another advantage to Spain's enemies. The exploits of
Drake and the English privateers, therefore, while they won little from
Spain in territory, trade, and treasure, wounded her deeply in her economy
and war potential. They forced her to spend large sums of money on the
Indies at a time when the cost of prolonged warfare was already inducing
another bankruptcy. This drain on Spain's resources played its part in reducing her strength, and ultimately in hastening her decline.

Philip II was not unaware of what was happening, for he felt it in his
finances. He was still determined, therefore, to destroy the marauders in
their homeland. Since the winter of 1589 he had been planning a second
Armada, hoping to improve on the first by giving it better ships, more
long-range guns, a single command with improved co-ordination, and a
deep-water port. To this extent he had learnt some lessons, though not the
most obvious lesson of all—that England could not be conquered. The fleet

[50] J. A. Williamson, *Sir John Hawkins* (Oxford, 1927), pp. 409–10.

he had assembled by 1596 did not fulfil his expectations, but it was an encouraging sign of his power and resources. His determination to use it was confirmed when in the summer of that year an expedition under Howard and Essex occupied Cadiz for sixteen days, destroyed his New Spain fleet and looted his own territory. For some time he had been thinking of using Ireland as a first stage for an invasion of England, and he had already sent a liaison officer, arms and munitions, to the chiefs of Ulster. The plan was not unrealistic, for Ireland was inadequately garrisoned, contained a disaffected population, and could be approached from Spain by prevailing south-west winds.[51] In October he dispatched his new Armada, this time under the command of Martín de Padilla y Manrique, and destined for Ireland. But the south-west wind became a gale, which scattered the fleet and forced it to take refuge in Ferrol, having lost one-third of its ships and over 2,000 men.

Thereafter Philip was undecided whether to strike England directly or via Ireland; for in April 1596 the Spaniards, now at war with France as well as England, had captured Calais and so at last possessed a Channel port. At the end of the year the king advised the Archduke Albert, his new governor general in the Netherlands, that he was equipping a fleet at Lisbon for the invasion of Ireland; he had 12,300 troops and the vessels which had taken refuge in Ferrol; as the enemies of Spain were assembling it was necessary to destroy one before they all united; this one would be England, for 'the English are the most encumbered and the easiest to strike on their own territory'; the governor general was to give his advice, indicating the possibility of concentrating a great army near Calais; then 'with a good squadron of galleys (sic) to escort it, this army could land in England'.[52] Here was a new edition of the old strategy of 1588! An incredulous archduke, who was already convinced that the only answer to Philip II's problems was peace, went through the merest motions of collaboration, and this side of the operation was eventually dropped for lack of men and ships. But in the autumn of 1597, when the English fleet under Essex was absent in the Azores, Philip sent the reinforced second Armada off again. Almost as big as that of 1588, it was striking evidence of the Spanish naval revival; its commanders had experience of English naval tactics, and a detachment of troops from Spanish-occupied Brittany was to co-operate; the destination was Falmouth. As it approached the Channel, simultaneously with the English fleet returning from the Azores, it was hit by a storm from the

---

[51] See C. Falls, 'España e Irlanda durante el reinado de Isabel de Inglaterra', *Segundo curso superior de metodología y crítica histórica* (Madrid, Estado Mayor Central del Ejército, Servicio Histórico Militar, 1950), pp. 329–54.
[52] Philip II to Archduke Albert, 31 December 1596, Lefèvre, *Correspondance*, iv. 395.

north-east and dispersed. That was the last Armada Philip II sent against England. By this time his resources were stretched to breaking point: for the past two years he had been at war not only with the English and the Dutch but also with France.

3. INTERVENTION IN FRANCE

Philip II had never really reconciled himself to the peace of Cateau-Cambrésis with France. The Huguenot attack on his communications in Europe and America, fear of the spread of Calvinism into his own dominions, French intervention on behalf of the rebels in the Netherlands, each item increased his distrust and his vigilance. In France, however, he had an asset which he had never had in England—civil war. Until 1589, therefore, his weapons were diplomacy and subversion; as long as France was internally divided, her kings hard pressed to maintain themselves against the Guises and the Huguenots, she could be no real danger to Spain; it was sufficient for Philip to support and subsidise the Catholic forces, as he had done on the eve of the Armada. After the defeat of the Armada, however, Henry III summoned up courage to challenge the domination of the League; in December 1588 he had the Duke of Guise and his brother the Cardinal of Lorraine assassinated. His action only stirred the League to greater efforts and plunged France deeper into civil war. Paris and other League towns took to arms; the Duke of Mayenne, the last survivor of the Guise brothers, assumed direction of the movement; and Henry III was forced to throw himself into the arms of the Duke of Navarre and the Huguenots, and with them to besiege Paris; there, on 1 August 1589, he was assassinated by a young Dominican, Jacques Clément. From then onwards it was open war between the Catholics of the League and the man they would not recognise as king of France, Henry of Navarre.

Philip II too was determined to exclude 'the Béarnais' from the throne of France. If France were united under a Protestant sovereign she could be a real danger to the Spanish Netherlands; Farnese would be isolated between the Dutch and the French, and Italy might be open to invasion. But his ambitions went beyond mere defence of his own possessions; he now had the opportunity to claim the throne of France as son-in-law of Henry II and with it to increase his empire. He therefore strengthened his diplomatic mission in Paris, and in September he ordered Farnese to rest on the defensive in the Netherlands and reduce costs, for to prevent the accession of Navarre he might have to send his troops 'openly into France'. To the vigorous objections of Farnese, who saw his programme in the Netherlands once again about to be sacrificed to the foreign policy of the king and money he desperately needed wasted on the League, Philip replied 'the question of France is the principal one at the moment'.[53] The Netherlands were now simply a base for the offensive against France, the war against the Dutch a defensive war. In these decisions Philip II had the unanimous support of his Council of State. And in the ultimate analysis he received the agreement of Farnese, though the latter was uneasy about leaving the Dutch unpacified and would have preferred a compromise settlement in his rear. With these misgivings, Farnese sent a small contingent from Flanders to help the League against Henry of Navarre; the combined Catholic forces were defeated at Ivry (14 March 1590), and Henry laid siege to Paris. Philip II then decided to commit his whole army of Flanders under Farnese in open war on Henry. In these months the king was seized with the same feverish zeal which had possessed him in the enterprise of England; again Farnese was sceptical, and this time his disapproval was shared by Idiáquez in Madrid and by many of the Spanish officers in his own army; and again Farnese obeyed. But he determined to confine his operation to one objective—the relief of Paris.

Farnese crossed the frontier in August; with brilliant economy of effort he evaded the enemy forces, got his troops skilfully across the Marne and took Lagny, the only fort blocking the way to Paris from the east; with both banks of the river under his control he was then able to revictual the capital and force Henry to abandon the siege. To supplement Farnese's invasion from the east Philip sent a flotilla and a force of 3,000 troops to the support of the League in Brittany. Now, as his forces had rescued Paris and he had an army in France, he decided the time was ripe openly to press his claims to the French throne on behalf of his daughter Isabella, or in default of this to dictate an acceptable candidate. Farnese did not agree; his political sense told him that the French would not tolerate this kind of intervention in their affairs; his military sense told him that he could not possibly dominate the country with the forces at his disposal; above all he was anxious for the security of the Netherlands, threatened in his absence by a Dutch offensive and an inevitable mutiny of unpaid Spanish troops, further proof of the impossibility of winning on two fronts at once. Against the wishes of the king he took his army back to the Low Countries in November.[54]

There the situation had deteriorated in his absence. As long as Henry of Navarre continued to divert the attention and the resources of Philip II to France, the United Provinces had their best ally to date. Their leader, Maurice of Nassau, son of William of Orange, had seized the opportunity to prepare his offensive, and when Farnese returned with his army depleted

[53] Parker, *Army of Flanders*, pp. 244–5; van der Essen, *op. cit.*, v. 276–81.
[54] *Ibid.*, v. 293–310.

he struck him hard. By June 1591 he had taken Zutphen and Deventer, which in Spanish hands had cut off the north-east from communication with the heart of the rebel republic; in October he took Nimwegen. While Farnese was struggling to contain the rebel offensive, orders reached him from the king in July to abandon at once all military action in the Netherlands and to go again, as quickly as possible, to the help of the League in France. Again there was a struggle of wills, as Farnese tried to make Philip understand the folly of the course he was pursuing. The prospects for the Netherlands, he argued, were alarming: in the first place the king ran the risk of losing them outright to the rebels unless he maintained a large army; secondly, the condition even of the provinces subject to Spain was deteriorating and the royal cause losing its appeal, because to take the offensive in France meant going on the defensive in the Netherlands, which prolonged the war for the royal provinces, ruined their economy, and exposed them at once to the blows of the Dutch and the mutinies of ill-paid Spanish troops.[55]

But Philip was now blind to rational argument, and his original objective, the security of the Netherlands, seemed to be sacrificed to a policy of imperialism in France. In February 1591 his embassy in Paris, staffed by fanatics who fed his ambitions, had managed to get a permanent Spanish garrison into the French capital. Shortly afterwards he sent a small force to aid the League in Languedoc. His troops in Brittany were still operating. All these, however, were piecemeal efforts, too small to win France. He wanted a major invasion by a powerful army. Ideally Languedoc, accessible from Spain itself and a centre of League resistance, was the best point of penetration; but Philip had his reservations about the League position there, and in any case the army he had in Spain was pinned down from 1590 to 1592 by a rebellion in Aragon.[56] An invasion of France from the east by Farnese's army, therefore, was the only alternative, and to get his general to move he made it a test of his loyalty. In December 1591 Farnese crossed the French frontier a second time to revive the waning fortunes of the League and in particular to relieve Rouen, besieged by Navarre and English auxiliaries. His progress was thwarted by the need to haggle with the League leaders over the terms of the Infanta's succession, the price of Philip II's assistance, but eventually, after a frustrating though brilliantly conducted campaign in which he himself was severely wounded, Farnese forced Navarre and his allies to abandon the siege of Rouen. In mid-June he returned to the Netherlands, his forces again depleted and he himself 'more dead than alive'.[57]

Of all the men who served Philip II in high office, Farnese was probably the most honest, straight-speaking, and realistic. Independence of mind,

[55] Lefèvre, *Correspondance*, iii. 585, 594.   [56] See below, pp. 361–63.
[57] van der Essen, *op. cit.*, v. 325–55; Lefèvre, *Correspondance*, iv. 34–8.

however, even allied to utter loyalty, was not a quality the king admired in his servants. Since the defeat of the Armada Farnese's credit in Madrid had begun to decline; the king's distrust, fed by the vicious slanders of the general's enemies, especially of the Spanish embassy in Paris, was increased when Farnese frankly opposed his policy in France. From the end of 1591 Philip was determined to remove him; though with a duplicity which could hardly be excused as his usual 'dissimulation', he continued to give him apparent signs of his confidence. In October 1592 Farnese was ordered to lead another expedition into France. On his way there he died at Arras on 3 December, in his forty-seventh year, and still unaware that the king had dismissed him.

With his best general gone, his army diminished, and his League allies slow to fulfil the bargain he had struck with them—that they acknowledge the Infanta as queen of France and call the States General to ratify her succession—Philip's prospects in France were worsening. In desperation he sent a third expedition from the Low Countries in March 1593. He was now applying every pressure he could to get the States General to declare for his daughter or for one of his other candidates, while the French sought to evade his intolerable demands, keep the crown out of foreign hands, and preserve their country from satellite status. The only asset Philip had was that Henry of Navarre was a Protestant. This, too, he lost when Henry declared his intention to be converted and in July 1593 was received into the Catholic church. The Spaniards were mortified and refused to accept his conversion as genuine; in Rome their diplomacy worked frantically to prevent the pope from accepting it; but although it took two years, Henry IV received papal recognition. By that time his position in France was secure. He was crowned king in February 1594, ejected the Spanish garrison from Paris, and made himself master of the capital. His conversion was followed by the gradual rallying of the country to his cause, and Philip II could only watch in helpless frustration as one by one his allies defected or were defeated. But there was still a Spanish force in Marseilles and Brittany, and Henry feared that what Philip II could not get by subversion he might try to win by full-scale war. Therefore, to give notice that civil war had ended and that his cause was a national one, on 17 January 1595 he formally declared war on Philip II, because he had 'dared, under the pretext of religion, openly to try and subvert the loyalty of the French towards their natural Princes and sovereign Lords . . . unjustly and publicly pursuing this noble crown for himself and for his own'. He thus underlined that sovereignty in France was the issue at stake.

In a reckless accumulation of commitments, Philip II had brought himself to war with three powers—England, the United Provinces, and France.

And he was no more capable of defeating his new enemy than he was of reducing his old ones. He occupied some positions encircling France, it is true. But the heart of the country was protected by impenetrable barriers of territory and manpower. Even if he found towns to occupy, consciences to buy, and in one case Protestants ready to sell themselves, it was always on the periphery of France. And in spite of his proximity and his fleet he could not even retain his marginal footholds. Toulouse was lost in 1596, Marseilles in the same year; in Brittany his rebel allies had never been on good terms with the Spanish detachment, and although the latter was still there it carried no particular threat for Henry IV; the attempt of the governor of Milan to penetrate from the south-east was frustrated by Henry's victory at Fontaine-Française in June 1595. In fact, Henry's only real problem, and the only hope for Spain, lay on France's north-eastern frontier. There the army of Flanders still had striking power, and its commanders were not without initiative. Spanish victories in Picardy in the first year of the war checked schemes for co-operation between the French and Dutch armies. Then, when Henry expected a push eastwards towards Paris, the Spaniards suddenly went north, taking Calais completely by surprise and capturing it without difficulty in April 1596. Philip II at last had a Channel port. He was not, however, in a position to use it, for his ambitions had overreached his resources. In the first place, he was now faced by an anti-Spanish alliance. His progress in north-eastern France forced Elizabeth I to overcome her distrust of French objectives in the Netherlands, and in May 1596 she signed a treaty with Henry IV, granting him a loan and a force of 2,000 men, in return for his promise not to conclude a separate peace with Spain; the alliance was also joined by the United Provinces. Moreover, Philip's military position in France was basically insecure; this was demonstrated in 1597 when his army took Amiens but lost it within six months. The problem was one of occupying outposts in enemy territory and holding them by force amidst a hostile population; given the forces at his disposal, the problem was insuperable. Finally, he found it impossible to cope with the Low Countries and France at once, especially as he had just gone through a severe financial crisis leading to the bankruptcy of 1596. Philip II's intervention in France had been extremely expensive: the bulk of the 88 million florins sent to the Netherlands in the 1590's was destined for France. It had also distorted political priorities, postponing indefinitely a possible conclusion to the Dutch struggle.[58]

What possible benefit could Spain expect from the war with France? The question was being asked even by Philip's advisers. While Spain was immobilised in vast continental operations, the real profits of war—trade and

[58] Parker, *Army of Flanders*, p. 247.

maritime expansion—were going to England and the United Provinces. The latter had already profited from the ruin of Antwerp and the decline of the southern Netherlands, and they continued to profit by trading with Spain in spite of Philip's efforts to exclude them from his ports. In the Mediterranean a growing volume of Dutch and English shipping was breaking through Spanish patrols in search of trade and winning increasing returns. In the Atlantic Spain's enemies were still disputing her colonial monopoly. Some of the advice Philip II was receiving showed an awareness of the situation which he himself seemed incapable of understanding. From 1595 the papacy had come out unequivocally on the side of French independence; now, to end a war between two Catholic powers which only benefited the Protestant countries of the north, Rome offered itself as a mediator for a Franco-Spanish peace. From the Low Countries Philip had even more urgent advice. Since 1596 his governor there had been his nephew, the Archduke Albert. Although he had spent all his youth at the Spanish court, was more Spanish than Austrian, and was regarded as safe enough to be made viceroy of Portugal, Albert had not surrendered his independence of judgement and, like Farnese, he was free of the megalomania prevalent at court. From the time he arrived in the Low Countries he sought to extricate Spain from a war against three enemies which immobilised his programme in the Netherlands and dissipated the king's resources. He began to put out feelers in France for peace negotiations. If Philip was now impervious to rational advice, even he could see that he had gained virtually nothing from the war with France, and that peace on this front at least was an essential preliminary to dealing with England and the United Provinces. On the initiative of the Archduke, therefore, peace was concluded with France at Vervins on 2 May 1598. Spain gave up Calais and the other places she held in Picardy and Brittany, and gained little in return. For Henry IV believed that France could not be safe if Spain recovered the northern Netherlands, and he continued to give aid to the United Provinces, scarcely bothering to conceal it. From Vervins, therefore, Philip II did not receive quite the breathing-space he had expected. On the other hand he saved a considerable amount of money, and his army could return to the Netherlands.

For the Netherlands Philip had already decided on his solution. He would marry the Archduke Albert to the Infanta Isabella and make them joint sovereigns of the Low Countries, north and south, with semi-independent status. In September 1597 he began to prepare public opinion by official announcements.[59] From the rebel provinces there was silence; they

[59] Lefèvre, *Correspondance*, iv. 426.

had ceased to regard themselves as subjects of the king of Spain or of the Archduke Albert, and they had power enough to continue their resistance. In the southern provinces, on the other hand, the ruling class seemed to welcome the proposal. In any case Philip went ahead. On 6 May 1598, four days after the conclusion of the peace of Vervins, he signed the instrument making over the Low Countries to the Archduke and the Infanta—they were to be married as soon as possible—to be ruled by them as 'sovereign princes', the settlement to apply to the northern as well as to the southern provinces. But what did this 'sovereignty' mean? Albert and Isabella were certainly not puppet rulers. True, their policy remained a Spanish one, but it was Spanish out of conviction and not necessarily proof of their subordination to the king of Spain or to Spanish interests. Far from being blind executors of orders from Madrid, they often resisted the crown's ministers and sometimes took the initiative in policy, as Albert had done in promoting peace with France and was to do again in negotiating peace with England.[60] Nevertheless, although they were something more than governors general, they were something less than independent sovereigns. The Spanish crown did not renounce its hereditary rights. Unless there was issue of the marriage, the Netherlands would revert to Spain on the death of either Albert or Isabella; in fact there was no issue, and the Netherlands did revert to Spain in 1621. But the crucial test, as usual, was the location of military power. Even after the transfer of 'sovereignty' a Spanish army remained in the Low Countries; it was a composite army, including Belgian as well as Spanish troops, and its commander-in-chief was the Archduke; but its officers were appointed by the king of Spain and to him it was responsible. Denied independence of Spain, the Low Countries were also denied equality with her, for they were specifically excluded from trade with the Indies, a stipulation which could hardly appeal to the Dutch. The Low Countries, then, were not independent: they might have their own administration but they were still part of the Spanish imperial system. The southern provinces accepted their status, but the north continued to resist. Philip II, in fact, could not bring himself to liquidate the entire Netherlands problem by the only realistic method possible—by recognising the facts of division and so relieving Spain of a ruinous war which she could never win. Meanwhile the sheer cost of the war remained a burden for several decades to come. Manpower losses to Castile were not easily measured, nor quickly replaced. The great financial drain continued, especially in the years 1586–1607 and 1621–40. Returns from the Indies were immediately devoured by Flanders. The Castilian national debt rose from 36 million ducats in 1557 to 85 million

---

[60] Lefèvre, *Spinola et la Belgique, 1601–1627* (Brussels, 1947), pp. 7–8.

in 1598 and was to reach 112 million by 1667.[61] The Spanish also suffered from the war in the Netherlands. The wool trade from northern Castile diminished considerably by the 1590's, and Iberian colonial interests came under increasing attack from the Dutch enemy.

4. CRISIS IN ARAGON

While Philip II's policy was approaching its nemesis abroad, his rule was also being challenged at home. During the crucial years of his intervention in France, between 1590 and 1592, he had been unable to send an army across the Pyrenees because he needed one in Spain itself. In Castile, of course, his sovereign's writ still ran. With Catalonia he had already reached an understanding. But in Aragon he had experienced mounting resistance, and in 1590 this reached critical proportions. His position there had been weak from the very beginning of the reign, as has been seen. Charles V had warned him that he would find it more difficult to govern Aragon than Castile 'because of the nature of its privileges and constitutions, and because its lawlessness, no less prevalent than elsewhere, is more difficult to investigate and to punish'.[62]

The king ruled in Aragon through his viceroy and with the advice of the Council of Aragon. Both viceroys and councillors were royal nominees, but the king was restricted in choosing them by the rule that all offices in Aragon were reserved exclusively to native Aragonese.[63] The composition of the Council, it is true, was diluted more to royal taste by the fact that Catalans and Valencians had rights of representation there, and the treasurer-general could be a Castilian. Moreover, the right to have a native viceroy was not absolute, though for many years Philip II, with his great respect for regional susceptibilities, behaved as though it was. But in any case while the king had his executive, Aragon had its cortes, and these possessed specific legislative and financial powers and the right to appoint a permanent watch-dog committee. And apart from administration, the king was frustrated by a whole network of local laws and legal practices. The king's justice in Aragon was administered by the Audiencia of Zaragoza, but this was not the only court in Aragon. Royal jurisdiction was challenged by that of another tribunal, the court of the Justicia; this consisted of five members appointed by the crown and sixteen nominated by the Aragonese cortes, and was headed by a magistrate, the Justicia of Aragon, who was nominally appointed

---

[61] Parker, *Spain and the Netherlands*, p. 188.
[62] Quoted in Marañón, *Antonio Pérez*, ii. 481. See above, pp. 209–10.
[63] Riba, *El Consejo Supremo de Aragón en el reinado de Felipe II*, pp. xxx., 90, 116–17.

by the crown for life but whose office was in fact hereditary in a single family, in the sixteenth century the Lanuzas. The Justicia exercised civil and criminal jurisdiction in certain cases, especially those between the crown and the nobility. He also had power to intervene in the proceedings of royal tribunals and officials, either by the process known as *manifestación*, which consisted in taking the person of any accused who claimed to be threatened with violence and putting him in the protective custody of the Justicia's prison while the case was being heard by competent judges, or by issuing *firmas* (letters) to anyone seeking remedy against alleged injustice at the hands of royal officials, the recipient thus obtaining complete immunity from royal power while his allegations were being investigated.[64] These, then, were the *fueros*, or charter rights, of Aragon, and the only tribunal against which they had no validity was the Inquisition.

The 'liberties' of Aragon, however, were not popular or democratic ones. Some of the legal devices were open to serious abuse and tended to make the kingdom a refuge for criminal elements. Above all, they shielded an archaic social structure. Behind these legal barriers lurked a feudalism more primitive than anywhere else in western Europe. For this reason their most fanatical defenders were the nobles of the kingdom, who formed two of the four estates into which the Aragonese cortes were divided, and monopolised land and office.

The independence of the great magnates was tempered by respect for the person of the monarch and regard for the opportunities available if they co-operated with him. But the lower ranks of the nobility, in a country which was not rich, were more extreme in their separatism and more intransigent in their championing of the *fueros*, partly out of resentment of their practical—though not legal—exclusion from the offices and wealth available to Castilians and a consequent desire to keep Aragon for the Aragonese, partly because, as in the case of the great magnates, feudal jurisdiction was at stake. A large part of the peasantry never came into contact with royal officials; their primary obedience was to the lord whose vassals they were and whose feudal power made him their political ruler as well as their economic oppressor; seigneurial officials ruled them and took their feudal dues and services, and seigneurial courts tried them; some Aragonese lords even had the right to strangle their vassals without appeal. The *fueros*, then, worked to the advantage of the ruling class, not of the mass of the people. As the latter did not feel the weight of royal power so they had no reason to oppose it. On the contrary, they sought to escape from the tyranny of their lords by seeking the protection of royal jurisdiction, and

[64] *Ibid.*, pp. xxxiii., 67–71.

in this way the desire of the peasants to see the estates on which they lived incorporated in the crown coincided with the anxiety of the crown to make its sovereignty effective.

Yet for much of his reign, Philip II's preoccupation with other problems, his preference for ruling Aragon from a distance through his representatives there, and his genuine respect for existing law, confined him to encouraging the efforts of the rural populations to transfer themselves from seigneurial to royal jurisdiction and encouraging inter-marriage between the Aragonese nobility and that of Castile in order to further the process of integration. But it was a slow and frustrating process, as Philip knew from one notorious case. The county of Ribagorza, extending north from Monzón to the Pyrenees, and containing seventeen towns, 200 villages and some 4,000 vassals, was too large and too close to France to be allowed to preserve its archaic immunity indefinitely. For over thirty years, and in the face of adverse judgements from the Justicia and the cortes, Philip struggled to wrest it from the jurisdiction of its lord, the Duke of Villahermosa, and incorporate it in the crown.[65] His only assets were the duke's rebellious vassals and the tenacity of the treasurer-general of Aragon, the Count of Chinchón, a Castilian whose hatred of the Aragonese nobility stemmed precisely from a family feud with Villahermosa. Eventually, after tacitly sanctioning outright rebellion by the duke's vassals, Philip forced him to surrender his territories in 1591 in return for a money indemnity. In its mountain remoteness and proximity to France, its anarchy and its family feuds, Ribagorza was a microcosm of Aragon. It was also a lesson to the Aragonese. Observing the treatment of Villahermosa, the nobility and gentry began to fear for their immunities, and raised the usual cry that the *fueros* were in danger.

But Philip was increasing his pressure. At the beginning of 1588, believing the time had come to assert his authority and end the insubordination of the Aragonese, he decided to appoint a viceroy who was not a native of the country, obsessed with *fueros* and tied to local interests.[66] So he sent the Marquis of Almenara, of the great Castilian house of Mendoza, to oust the existing viceroy, the Count of Sástago. The choice was unfortunate, for Almenara, as well as being a tactless and pompous man, was also a friend and relative of Chinchón. Above all, he would be a 'foreign viceroy'. Supporters of the *fueros* claimed that by law all royal officials in Aragon should be Aragonese. Whether the rule extended to viceroys was not clear; even the jurists were divided on the issue, and Philip was probably right in believing that he had the right to appoint a Castilian, as his predecessors

<hr />

[65] *Ibid.*, pp. lii.–lxv.   [66] *Ibid.*, pp. lxxii.–lxxvii., 26–32.

Ferdinand and Charles had certainly done. In any case he himself was a
stickler for the law, and he wanted his right acknowledged in Aragon, not
by force, but in the Justicia's court. The time, however, was inopportune: the
question of the foreign viceroy, topping that of seigneurial jurisdiction,
induced a sense of crisis. Almenara had *fueros* flung at him from every side;
virtually ostracised, his house set on fire, he returned in humiliation to Castile
to report to the king. Philip then removed the Count of Sástago and replaced
him by Andrés Simeno, the bishop of Teruel, an Aragonese but a minor
figure, easy to manipulate and obviously a stop-gap appointment. When
Almenara returned in the spring of 1590, with increased emoluments and
powers, it was clear that the king intended him to exercise authority in
Aragon, with the viceregal title, provided he could have its validity confirmed
in the Justicia's court. As the situation approached a climax, a new factor
entered when Antonio Pérez, in flight from Castile, arrived in Zaragoza
and claimed the protection of the *fueros*.

Since his arrest in July 1579 Pérez had found the net around him closing
more tightly.[67] As the king himself was implicated in the murder of Escobedo
and wanted to get his hands on the compromising documents in Pérez's
possession he had to proceed against his former secretary with caution. First
he was allowed to move around Madrid, while the secret investigation into
his conduct slowly proceeded. Then, when one of the assassins spoke and
the Escobedos and their allies at court pressed their accusations, he was
arrested a second time in January 1585, though to distract public attention
the case against him was confined to charges of trading in offices and state
secrets; on these he was found guilty and sentenced to two years' imprisonment and an enormous fine.[68] On the other hand the judges could not get
him to give up his papers. By this time, however, Philip II was searching for
more than documents; he was also seeking peace of mind over Escobedo's
murder, his own acquiescence in which was now public knowledge. Therefore, to expiate his own guilt and to make it clear that the real responsibility
lay with Pérez, who had misled him about Don John and Escobedo, Philip
put him on trial a second time. In January 1590 the royal prosecutor informed
Pérez that the king admitted knowing that he had had Escobedo killed, but
for his conscience' sake he must know whether the causes given him for the
action were adequate.[69] At first Pérez blandly denied all complicity in the
murder, but under torture he weakened and produced some causes for
Escobedo's death. These, however, were merely vague references to his
bad influence on Don John; they contained nothing of gravity and no proof.
The revelation was fatal to him. As he had no proof of any subversion on

---

[67] See above, pp. 322–24.   [68] Marañón, *op. cit.*, i. 416–48.
[69] *Ibid.*, i. 462–76.

the part of Don John, and therefore nothing to incriminate Escobedo, the king could now believe he had been misled and that the responsibility for the crime was not his but that of Pérez, who had deluded him with false-hoods. Now Pérez could be eliminated in strict justice, and his threat to use state secrets removed once and for all. Pérez himself realised how desperate his situation was. He decided to take to flight. He already had contacts in Aragon who were probably holding his documents for him. In April 1590, with the help of his wife, he escaped from his prison in Madrid and fled eastwards to the land of the *fueros*. As he crossed the frontier, the story goes, he knelt and kissed the ground, crying 'Aragon! Aragon!' Soon he was in the protective custody of the Justicia's prison, 'the prison of liberty' as it was called.

He had chosen his moment well. In Aragon, defence of the *fueros* was then the leading issue and regionalist sentiment was ready for any pretext to resist the crown. There Pérez had supporters, the Duke of Villahermosa and the Count of Aranda among the magnates, and many more in the lower ranks of the nobility, including Diego de Heredia, Martín de Lanuza, and Juan de Luna, all violent feudalists. And in Aragon Pérez was in a country hostile to Castile, close to Béarn and France; with him he had documents which might be damaging, if not to the king's interests, certainly to his reputation. Philip II had to act quickly. In Madrid Pérez was condemned to death in his absence. In Aragon the king entered a formal plea against him before the Justicia's court on charges that the defendant had compassed the murder of Escobedo on false pretences, divulged state secrets, and escaped from prison. But the lengthy judicial proceedings only gave Pérez the opportunity to publicise his views, especially that he had ordered the murder of Escobedo at the king's command, while Philip was thwarted by the slowness and partiality of the Aragonese judges. To stop Pérez from making further capital from the case, and in the conviction that the verdict would be an acquittal, Philip withdrew his charges. He then turned to the one tribunal in Spain against which the *fueros* of Aragon and the authority of the Justicia were of no avail, and whose trials were conducted in secrecy —the Inquisition. Pérez, of course, was no heretic, but on the flimsiest of evidence, furnished obediently and with grotesque distortion by the king's confessor, Diego de Chaves, a case was made on which the Inquisition could act, and in May 1591 Pérez was quietly removed from the prison of the Justicia into that of the Inquisition. His partisans, led by Heredia, then organised a riot in Zaragoza, during the course of which the mob attacked Almenara, who subsequently died of his wounds, rushed the prison of the unpopular Inquisition, and rescued their new idol to deposit him back in the Justicia's prison. From there he conducted his propaganda, attacking the court and the Inquisition, urging the people to defend their liberties even with arms, and showing a rare talent in organising a resistance movement. It was at this time that plans were discussed among the pro-Pérez party to separate Aragon from the Spanish crown and make it into a republic, perhaps under the protection of the Prince of Béarn, Henry of Navarre.[70] In government circles it was feared that 'another Flanders' was being prepared in Aragon.

Among whom did Pérez find his supporters? Not by this time among the magnates, who were alarmed by the turn of events, though the attitude of Villahermosa and Aranda remained ambiguous. Some Aragonese seem to have supported his cause out of a genuine belief in the 'liberties' of Aragon, others understandably because the offices they held—from that of Justicia downwards—depended upon the maintenance of the *fueros*, of which Pérez had become a symbol. But most of his supporters came from the minor nobility and gentry, the so-called 'knights of liberty', who were fighting for their feudal power against royal encroachment or out of frustration at their exclusion from office and prospects in a Spain dominated by Castile.[71] Their leader was Diego de Heredia, who boasted that he had twice availed himself of his right to strangle a vassal, and who was as ready to turn his violent and lawless instincts against the crown as against his own tenants. The feudal nature of the movement, of course, prevented it from having a mass appeal. The peasants had nothing to gain from resisting the king or defending the *fueros*, and Pérez's propaganda found no response in the countryside. Its impact was mainly confined to Zaragoza, the centre of regional government, and a place where a mob could be mobilised. This was seen when the king attempted to have Pérez returned to the Inquisition prison on the 14 September. Again Heredia and his retainers moved into action, scattering the royal guard, and placing Pérez at liberty. The rebels then made themselves masters of the town, persuaded the youthful Justicia, Juan de Lanuza, and the *Diputación del Reyno* to give them formal support, and warned the king that to send a Castilian army into Aragon would be a breach of the *fueros*. Caught between supporting the crown or joining the rebels, magnates and moderates opted for the former. Outside Zaragoza most of the towns also declared for the king. The narrow basis of the movement was now clear for all to see; equally evident was the strength of the king's position.

On the frontier of Aragon Philip II had already assembled an army of 12,000 under Alonso de Vargas, a veteran of the Low Countries; now, as legal negotiations had failed, he decided to use it. At the end of October Vargas led his forces into Aragon without encountering opposition. As they approched Zaragoza resistance within the town disintegrated; Pérez and

[70] *Ibid.*, ii. 551–59.   [71] *Ibid.*, ii. 559–62.

his associates took flight to Béarn, while the Justicia and the 'constitutional' wing of the rebels sought a temporary refuge in Epila. Retribution was rapid and ruthless. The Justicia was taken and executed; many more suffered the same fate; Villahermosa and Aranda were sent to Castile where they died mysteriously in prison; and the Inquisition began to seek out its attackers. From Béarn, Pérez and the émigrés organised a petty invasion which Henry of Navarre sanctioned simply in order to embarrass Philip II in Spain and relieve his pressure on France. But the puny force of rebels and their Protestant allies who crossed the Pyrenees in February 1592 were routed by Vargas and resisted by the local Aragonese, many of whom were vassals of the émigré leaders and all of whom closed their ranks against a Protestant and foreign invasion. The invaders were pursued into France where Heredia was captured and brought back to be executed. As for Pérez, after selling himself, though ineffectually, to France and England, he spent his last years in Paris, an exile without influence and without money; he died in 1611, unpardoned by the Spanish crown.

In contrast to the severity of the repression, the subsequent political settlement was moderate. Aragon could not be expected to preserve its constitution unchanged. In 1588, absolute monarch though he was, Philip had been willing to put his case before the Justicia's court and to seek its sanction for the right to appoint a Castilian viceroy. Now, with an army of occupation in Aragon, he had the country and its institutions at his mercy. He also knew that Aragon was isolated, for the rebels had failed in their attempt to draw Catalonia and Valencia to their cause, and their failure underlined the absence of any feeling of political unity among the eastern kingdoms.[72] The occasion was a perfect test for his principles of government. He had power enough to destroy the *fueros* of Aragon, if he so wished. Yet nothing was further from his thoughts. To give Spain a centralised constitution he would also have had to abolish the immunities of Catalonia and Valencia, and they had given him no reason to do this; even the mass of the Aragonese had eventually rallied to his cause and assisted his army to repel the invasion from Béarn. In any case, Philip II's respect for the traditional structure of Spain and his adherence to a pluralist conception of monarchy prevented him from reducing Aragon to Castile and removing its political identity. And, like his predecessors, he appreciated that he would not add substantially to his power if he did so.

The Aragonese cortes were summoned to Tarazona in June 1592 in order that the changes contemplated should be given legal form. Their agenda was decided in advance by the crown, and the archaic practice requiring

---

[72] On the attitude of Catalonia see Reglá, *Felip II i Catalunya*, pp. 209-10.

absolute unanimity of votes in each of the estates was abolished for the principle of majority vote. None of Aragon's institutions were suppressed, but they were remodelled to meet the requirements of royal power. The king was given the right to nominate a 'foreign viceroy', and Aragon was thus brought into line with the other constituent kingdoms. Those members of the two aristocratic estates of the cortes who had not reached the age of twenty years were deprived of their right to vote, though not of their right to attend. The *Diputación del Reyno*, the permanent committee of the cortes, lost a large measure of its control over the use of Aragonese revenue and over the regional guard, and forfeited its right to call together representatives of the cities of the kingdom. The Justicia now became removable at the crown's pleasure; in this way the king undermined the independence of the office and the family monopoly which had been established over it for so long. The nomination of the members of the Justicia's court was also arranged to put it under the control of the crown, and the Aragonese legal system had many of its anachronisms removed. Finally, to strengthen the hand of the central government, Philip buttressed the power of the institution which projected his authority most effectively outside Castile. He had already used the Inquisition as a political weapon against Pérez and against the rebels; now he used it as a means of royal control afterwards. In December 1593 he removed the army but, against the advice even of the Inquisitor general, Cardinal Quiroga, he placed the Aragonese Inquisition in the newly fortified palace of the Aljafería, and protected it with a royal garrison.[73]

Much of Philip II's programme in Aragon consisted of genuine reform, and was a long overdue attack on the privileges of the feudal nobility. It was also aimed, of course, at removing obstacles to the sovereignty of the crown, though even here it was hardly the action of a tyrant, for the *fueros* had been the privilege of the ruling class, and the tyranny that was felt in Aragon was the tyranny of local lords, not of the central power. As it was, the reform was political, not social, in intent; the nobles still had their estates and their vassals, and to reduce their seigneurial power was a longer and slower process.

5. RECESSION

By 1595 the ravages of age and overwork were telling on Philip. Political blows he regarded as part of his sovereign's condition, and he was inured

---

[73] Boyd, *Cardinal Quiroga*, pp. 92–93, 96–100; on the political settlement see Merriman, *op. cit.*, iv. 595–99.

to them; but now he was afflicted with an increasingly painful blood disease which reduced him to a shadow of his former self. He continued to follow his relentless routine of work, and survived periodic crises in his health, until in June 1598, during a particularly violent illness, he went to the Escorial to prepare for his death. In the Escorial he had spent countless hours alone at his desk, remote from human companionship, but, now that the end approached, carefully and in all sincerity he surrounded himself with his family, his clergy, and his courtiers, as though he wished to demonstrate how a Christian king should die. He continued to transact some business of state, but above all he prepared himself for death, confessing his sins, receiving Communion, and praying with the priests at his bedside. And in the little room from which he could look out on the altar of the great monastic church, he died at daybreak on the morning of 13 September 1598, in his seventy-first year.

The reign had lasted almost half a century, and Spain necessarily bore the impress of Philip's rule for some time to come. He had completed the unity of the peninsula and perfected its constitution, finely balancing the needs of sovereignty and the susceptibilities of the regions in a system of government which combined absolutism and devolution. Whatever else he did for Spaniards he knew how to govern them. And however disastrous his policy was in Europe, he had maintained Spain's military machine, revived her navy, and preserved intact the greatest source of her power, her empire in America; in the last years of his reign the flow of treasure was as secure as it had ever been.

Nevertheless Philip II left Spain on the edge of a crisis, for the economic foundations of her power were even more fragile than they had been at the beginning of the reign, and his government had done nothing to improve them. Life was hard for Spaniards in the 1590's. After the unremitting price rise of the greater part of the century there was an additional spurt of inflation at the end which dealt another blow to living conditions. The price of grain rose by more than 50 per cent. in Castile and Andalucía between 1595 and 1599. Prolonged neglect of agriculture and growing reliance on foreign grain, the supply of which was more precarious during wartime, culminated in a food shortage which left the country on the verge of famine. The situation of the consumer was worsened by the intolerable weight of taxation, as the government sought to compensate for its own difficulties from inflation and to pay for its foreign wars. Producers were also hit by inflation and taxation, and even more businesses were now liquidated, as merchants and industrialists sought to escape from the risks of productive enterprise and from the social stigma of working for a living, to join the ranks of the nobility. Disaster was not complete, and for the moment Spain was saved from the

consequences of her own folly by the money she earned in America. Thanks
to the imperial defences provided by Philip II the colonial revenue continued
to inject some life into the economy of the mother country. But this income
was not invested productively, and therefore it continued to cause inflation.
Moreover, it could not go on for ever; to rely exclusively on colonial
resources was to invite disaster once those resources diminished. But no one
looked to the future, least of all the government. The enormous expenditure
of the state, the luxury spending of the aristocracy and the ruling class, the
anxiety of all Spaniards to live on rents and annuities, pointed unmistakably
to the fact that Spaniards really did believe that wealth lay only in money
and in the interest from money. As the economist González de Cellorigo remarked in 1600, Spain had been reduced to a state where men lived 'outside
the natural order'.[74] The day of reckoning was still to come, though it was
only a decade or two away; once colonial trade declined, the decline of
Spain itself began. Meanwhile, the inertia of the government and the
mentality of the ruling class fostered the two basic conditions which prepared
the way—absence of production, and social stagnation.

As long as Spain fought the kind of wars to which Philip II committed
her, economic revival was impossible. The entire reign was given to warfare
on one front or another, for many years on two fronts at once—the Mediterranean and the Netherlands—and in the 1590's on three fronts at once—the
Netherlands, England, and France. Spain was the only power in sixteenth-
century Europe capable of sustaining such an effort, but what did it gain
her? In the Mediterranean Philip could legitimately claim to be fighting for
survival. In the Low Countries he insisted he was merely defending his rightful inheritance, though against the United Provinces the argument was
unrealistic. In the Atlantic and the Caribbean he was protecting his country's
colonial, and therefore economic, interests. But only in the imagination of
the king himself could his war with France be regarded as a defensive war,
unless it were conceded that he had to appropriate the whole of Europe in
order to defend his interests. In the last fifteen years of his reign Philip proceeded on the assumption that war could gain him any objective he wanted.
Yet there was no order of priorities. The greatest source of Spain's power,
and the greatest field for her religious and political ideals, was her empire
in America. The logical procedure would have been to concentrate her
efforts and resources on this front by cutting them elsewhere. As it was, the
Netherlands were the biggest and most relentless drain on Spanish resources.
Once Philip had placed an army there and committed himself to a campaign

[74] See P. Vilar, 'Le temps du "Quichotte" ', *Europe*, xxxiv. (Paris, 1956), 3–16; and
Larraz, *La época del mercantilismo en Castilla*, pp. 72–75.

by land he could never demobilise; year after year the war devoured his men and money and pinned him down in a conflict which, after the recovery of the southern provinces, he could never win. 'The provisioning of Flanders', remarked a Spanish official two years after the death of Philip II, 'has been and is the ruin of Spain. It provokes the hostility of ministers, and the people cry that an end be put to it.'[75]

The cry had been uttered for some time. As Spain's armies and fleets endlessly consumed the nation's resources for increasingly fewer returns, so the spirit of her people moved from confidence to doubt, and to a growing disillusion with grandeur. In the later cortes of the reign dissenting voices were raised, protesting against the mounting taxation and unnecessary wars, and requesting the king to withdraw his armies from the Netherlands and France in order to concentrate on the military and maritime defence of Spain and her American empire. A demand for a new subsidy in 1593 provoked a memorable debate in which deputy after deputy advised the king to go on the defensive and cut his losses. The deputy for Seville, Pedro Tello, a man who had spent the greater part of his life soldiering, urged the king to consider how in spite of many years of warfare he had been unable to overcome Spain's numerous enemies, and 'in the attempt, God knows, Your Majesty has spent his last strength, and is under no obligation to do more'.[76] The cortes, of course, were impotent, but public opinion found an echo in their deliberations. The king himself had learnt some lessons by the end of the reign; the state of his finances forced him to learn something. He tried to disengage from some of the fronts in northern Europe; from the French front he withdrew successfully in 1598; but from the Netherlands he failed to extricate himself, and with England he saw no alternative to war. In any case, it was difficult to liquidate Spain's imperialist past, just as it was difficult to transform her society. Spaniards continued to live 'outside the natural order', and Spain was still tormented by the old illusions of empire, her resources approaching exhaustion, her weapons growing rustier, yet still launching her expeditions abroad. A few years later Cervantes was to give his fellows and his country an immortal name.

[75] Quoted Braudel, *La Méditerranée*, p. 381.
[76] Larraz, *op. cit.*, 149–53.

APPENDIX I

Note on Spanish Currency

THE basic Spanish money denomination was the *maravedí*. At the beginning of the modern period Spain's standard gold coin was the *excelente de Granada* issued by Ferdinand and Isabella and usually called the ducat (after the Venetian ducat on which it was modelled). The ducat was 23¾ carats fine and was tariffed at 375 maravedís. In 1537 Charles V substituted for it a new unit known as the *escudo*, 22 carats fine and tariffed at 350 maravedís. The ducat, however, continued to serve as a unit of account. In 1566 Philip II increased the tariff of the *escudo* (weight and fineness remaining constant) from 350 to 400 maravedís, a figure at which it remained for more than forty years.

In 1548 Charles V authorised an increased vellon circulation, and in 1552 he reduced the silver content of vellon from 7 to 5½ grains fine. No change occurred in silver money during the reign of Philip II. The standard silver coin in this period was the *real*, which was worth 34 maravedís, the *real de a ocho* being worth 272 maravedís.

Treasure from America was expressed in terms of *pesos*. *Peso* means 450 maravedís' worth of gold and silver. It was equivalent to 42.29 grams of pure silver. For purposes of conversion it is equivalent to 1.2 ducats.

APPENDIX II

TABLE A

TOTAL IMPORTS OF TREASURE IN PESOS (450 MARAVEDIS) BY FIVE-YEAR PERIODS[1]

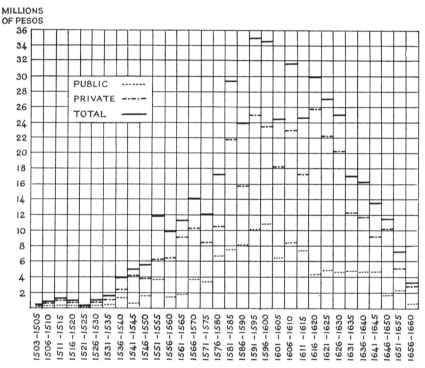

[1] Reprinted from E. J. Hamilton, *The American Treasure and the Price Revolution in Spain 1501-1650* (Harvard University Press, 1934).

TABLE B

TOTAL QUINQUENNIAL TREASURE IMPORTS AND COMPOSITE INDEX NUMBERS OF COMMODITY PRICES[1]

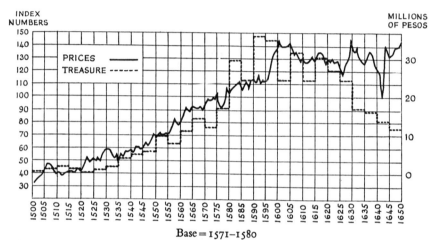

Base = 1571–1580

[1] Reprinted from E. J. Hamilton, *The American Treasure and the Price Revolution in Spain 1501–1650* (Harvard University Press, 1934).

372

TABLE C

COMPOSITE INDEX NUMBERS OF WAGES AND PRICES 1501-1650[1]

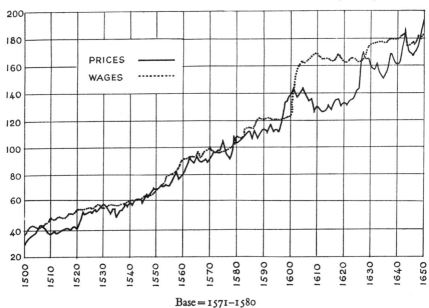

Base = 1571-1580

[1] Reprinted from E. J. Hamilton, *The American Treasure and the Price Revolution in Spain 1501-1650* (Harvard University Press, 1934).

TABLE D

COMPOSITE INDEX NUMBERS OF REAL WAGES[1]

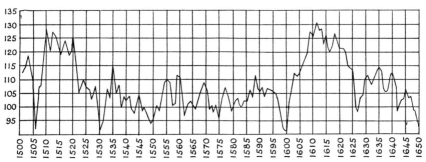

[1] Reprinted from E. J. Hamilton, *The American Treasure and the Price Revolution in Spain 1501-1650* (Harvard University Press, 1934).

Table E

The Indies Trade. Its Expansion and Contraction as shown by the Tonnage of Shipping (Outbound and Inbound Combined) between Spain and America.[1]

1. Trend, established by means of thirteen-year moving average.
2. Annual tonnage figures.

The figures on the left give tonnage in 1,000's of toneladas. Tonelada had different meanings at different dates, but Chaunu has devised a conversion factor for reducing original data into a standard draft tonnage of 2.83 cubic metres. Tonnage statistics—the carrying capacity of the vessels leaving and returning to Seville—furnish the principal data for measuring the trade cycles. Lacking production statistics, Chaunu assumes that the tonnage of shipping measures general economic activity. The average size of ships in the Indies trade increased steadily: it rose from 70 tons in 1504 to 391 tons in 1641–45. Gross tonnage (outbound and inbound) increased from 15,680 tons in 1506–10 to 273,560 tons in 1606–10.

[1] From Chaunu, *Séville et l'Atlantique* (S.E.V.P.E.N., 1957), vii. 54–55.

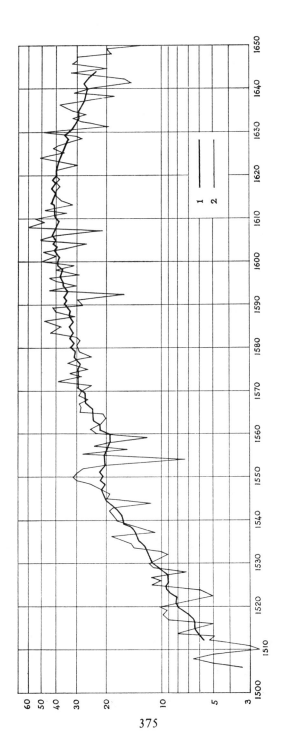

375

BIBLIOGRAPHY OF RECENT WORKS

General

THE study of early modern Spain has advanced in a number of directions in the last fifteen years, not least in the field of social history, and it is fitting that Antonio Domínguez Ortiz, who has given so much to the subject in original research, should also have written distinguished works of synthesis. The first of these, *The Golden Age of Spain 1516–1659* (London, 1971), was a revelation to English readers, and was soon followed by a Spanish version, *Desde Carlos V a la Paz de los Pirineos 1517–1660* (Barcelona, 1974). Yet these have been surpassed by his *El Antiguo Régimen: los Reyes Católicos y los Austrias* (2nd ed., Madrid, 1974), which contains some notable passages on the urban sectors and on the crisis of the seventeenth century, and from which the specialist as well as the general reader will learn. The work of Bartolomé Bennassar, *The Spanish Character. Attitudes and Mentalities from the Sixteenth to the Nineteenth Century* (Berkeley and Los Angeles, 1979), is of a different kind, the reflections of a historian on the life of Spaniards at home, at prayer and at play, in which the archives themselves are made to speak.

From Golden Age to Depression

The reign of Ferdinand and Isabella still awaits its modern Prescott, though our knowledge is increased by the substantial work of L. Suárez Fernández and Juan de Mata Carriazo, *La España de los Reyes Católicos* (*Historia de España*, ed. R. Menéndez Pidal, 2 vols., Madrid, 1969), and that of Miguel Angel Ladero, *Castilla y la conquista del reino de Granada* (Valladolid, 1967).

Pierre Chaunu, *L'Espagne de Charles V* (2 vols., Paris, 1973) is a mine of information and ideas, and ranges well beyond the reign of Charles V. Manuel Fernández Alvarez, *Charles V. Elected Emperor and Hereditary Ruler* (London, 1975) studies Charles V as a continental ruler but appreciates his Spanish base. The revolt of the *comuneros*, its economic and social setting, its character and its meaning, are explored by Joseph Pérez, *La revolución de las Comunidades de Castilla (1520–1521)* (Madrid, 1977), a basic interpretation first published in French in 1970. The anti-feudal inspiration of the revolt is underlined by Juan Ignacio

Gutiérrez Nieto, *Las Comunidades como movimiento antiseñorial* (Barcelona, 1973), while the contemporary though unrelated movement in Valencia is the subject of Ricardo García Cárcel, *Las Germanías de Valencia* (Barcelona, 1975).

Philip II has a modern biography worthy of the subject by Geoffrey Parker, *Philip II* (London, 1979), a work of research and of revision. The history of Spain's Mediterranean front was not exhausted even by Braudel. A further sector and new sources have been uncovered by Andrew C. Hess, *The Forgotten Frontier. A History of the Sixteenth-Century Ibero-African Frontier* (Chicago, 1978), while the same author in 'The Moriscos: An Ottoman Fifth Column in Sixteenth-Century Spain', *American Historical Review*, 74, 1 (1968), 1–25, demonstrates the relations between moriscos and the Ottoman government, using Turkish sources for the first time. To transfer troops from the Mediterranean to the Netherlands was a problem of logistics as well as of policy, and this aspect of Spain's war effort in northern Europe has been dealt with by Geoffrey Parker, *The Army of Flanders and the Spanish Road, 1567–1659* (Cambridge, 1972). The same author has written a new history of the revolt of the Netherlands, *The Dutch Revolt* (London, 1977). He has also placed the revolt in the context of Spain's wider problems in *Spain and the Netherlands, 1559–1659* (London, 1979); here he questions the correlation supposed by Chaunu between the rise and fall of American treasure receipts and the advance and retreat of the Spanish cause in the Netherlands, and he concludes that there was no discernible reduction in the provisions sent to the Low Countries before 1642–43, when it was the revolt of the Catalans rather than the exhaustion of Castile which caused resources to be diverted from the north.

Spain's policy in northern Europe and determination to establish her sea power between the peninsula and the Netherlands and beyond into the Baltic are studied in detail and in a sense made more credible by José Alcalá-Zamora y Queipo de Llano, *España, Flandes y el Mar del Norte (1618–1639)* (Barcelona, 1975). Peter Brightwell takes an expert look at the options open to Spain in the Netherlands in 'The Spanish System and the Twelve Years' Truce', *English Historical Review*, 89, 350 (1974), 270–92, and concludes that the decision to renew the war in 1621 was neither rash nor unreasoned. J. I. Israel, 'A Conflict of Empires: Spain and the Netherlands 1618–1648', *Past and Present*, 76 (1977), 34–74, places Spanish policy towards the Netherlands in a wider imperial context. Olivares and his Spain will be given their due history by J. H. Elliott, author of *Imperial Spain 1469–1716* (Pelican edition, London, 1970). Meanwhile the student of the period is well served by *Memoriales*

378   BIBLIOGRAPHY OF RECENT WORKS

y Cartas del Conde Duque de Olivares. Tomo 1. Política Interior: 1621 a 1627, ed. John H. Elliott and José F. de la Peña (Madrid, 1978).

The reign of Charles II is now immeasurably better known thanks to the pioneering work of Henry Kamen, *Spain in the Later Seventeenth Century 1665–1700* (London, 1980), which brings order out of confusion and fills the void between the Golden Age and the Enlightenment. The story which he tells is not one of decline but of recovery from the mid-century depression; population growth, industrial development in the periphery, agricultural expansion in Castile, and a return to better days in the American trade, these were the signs of a sure if slow revival. Some of these views were anticipated in the same author's study 'The Decline of Spain: A Historical Myth?', *Past and Present*, 81 (1978), 24–50, where he prefers to speak not of decline but of increased dependency and underdevelopment. The argument is part of a renewed interest in Spain's great depression, in which historians have sought to clarify the data and refine their analysis. Students and experts alike will profit from the following: J. H. Elliott, 'Self-Perception and Decline in Early Seventeenth-Century Spain', *Past and Present*, 74 (1977), 41–61; Charles Jago, 'The "Crisis of the Aristocracy" in Seventeenth-Century Castile', *Past and Present*, 84 (1979), 60–90, R. A. Stradling, 'Seventeenth Century Spain: Decline or Survival?', *European Studies Review*, 9, 2 (1979), 157–94, and items by Israel and TePaske mentioned below.

Economy and Society

Population figures, now firmly based, can be found in the appropriate chapters of Jordi Nadal, *La población española (siglos xvi a xx)* (3rd ed., Barcelona, 1973), the standard work. On the epidemic disaster of 1596–1602 more specific data and analysis than were hitherto available are to be found in Bartolomé Bennassar, *Recherches sur les grandes épidémies dans le Nord de l'Espagne à la fin du XVIᵉ siècle* (Paris, 1969). For a history of the moriscos, with a more precise estimate of their numbers, see Antonio Domínguez Ortiz and Bernard Vincent, *Historia de los moriscos* (Madrid, 1978), which sums up the results of research since the work of Halperin Donghi, Caro Baroja and Lapeyre in the 1950s and adds new data of its own.

The researches of Antonio Domínguez Ortiz on Spanish Society in the seventeenth century, *La sociedad española en el siglo XVII* (2 vols., Madrid, 1963–70) are basic to the subject, and students will find a useful concise version in *Las clases privilegiadas en la España del Antiguo Régimen* (Madrid, 1973). Charles Jago, 'The Influence of Debt on the Relations between Crown and Aristocracy in Seventeenth-Century Castile', *Economic History Review*, 26 (1973), 218–36, studies the aristocracy's service to and rewards from the crown. The subject of Richard L. Kagan, *Students and Society in Early Modern Spain* (Baltimore, 1974) is the university system of Habsburg Spain, its rôle in society, its response to the demands of the state; the author shows that in late sixteenth-century Castile there were 20,000 university students in a population of 6.9 million, and about 3.2 per cent of all males aged 15 to 24 attended university each year, a high level in contemporary Europe and a reserve of recruits for an imperial bureaucracy.

The trend towards regional studies has brought new areas of knowledge into economic and social history. Bartolomé Bennassar, *Valladolid au Siècle d'Or* (Paris, 1967) led the way with a total study of life and work in this important area of Old Castile in the sixteenth century. A rare study of an industrial centre has been undertaken by Angel García Sanz, *Desarrollo y crisis del Antiguo Régimen en Castilla la Vieja. Economía y sociedad en tierras de Segovia, 1500–1814* (Madrid, 1977), while the regional history of New Castile is well served by Carla Rahn Phillips, *Ciudad Real, 1500–1750: Growth, Crisis, and Readjustment in the Spanish Economy* (Cambridge, Mass., 1979). The society of Seville, centre of a regional economy and gateway to an empire, has been studied in two works by Ruth Pike, *Enterprise and Adventure. The Genoese in Seville and the Opening of the New World* (Ithaca, 1966), and *Aristocrats and Traders: Sevillian Society in the Sixteenth Century* (Ithaca, 1972). The *Historia de Sevilla* edited by Francisco Morales Padrón has two admirable volumes for the early modern period, *La Ciudad del Quinientos* (Seville, 1977) by the editor himself, and *El Barroco y la Ilustración* (Seville, 1976) by Antonio Domínguez Ortiz and Francisco Aguilar Piñal. Modern historiography has also been at work on eastern Spain. James Casey, *The Kingdom of Valencia in the Seventeenth Century* (Cambridge, 1979) shows in masterly fashion that the revival of Valencia after the expulsion of the moriscos and other adversities was slow and incomplete. Two works by Sebastian García Martínez deal with problems of law and order in their social context: *Bandolerismo, piratería y control de moriscos en Valencia durante el reinado de Felipe II* (Valencia, 1977), and *Valencia bajo Carlos II: Bandolerismo, revindicaciones agrarias y servicios a la monarquía* (Valencia, 1974). The neighbouring province of Murcia has been placed on the map of Spanish history by Francisco Chacón in his recent researches on the province; like James Casey he finds little evidence of any revival in the seventeenth century. Catalonia perhaps offers a different example, and Pere Molas, *Comerçi estructura social a Catalunya i Valencia als segles XVII i XVIII* (Barcelona, 1977), continues the search begun by Pierre Vilar for the origins of Catalan development.

Government and Administration

The institutions of Habsburg Spain were paradoxically neglected by traditional history, and we still await monographic studies of the cortes, the *corregidores*, and the municipalities, not to mention a number of the councils. Fortunately progress has recently been made in some areas of government. I. A. A. Thompson, *War and Government in Habsburg Spain* (London, 1976) detects, between 1560 and 1620, a steady retreat from the attempts of Philip II to nationalise military industries and their administration; under pressure of war, and its cost, his successors had to concede their private ownership. While the presence of the state was receding in one direction, in other respects absolute monarchy was increasing its effectiveness. The office of secretary is the subject of a large history by José Antonio Escudero, *Los Secretarios de Estado y del Despacho (1474–1724)* (4 vols., Madrid, 1969). A. W. Lovett, *Philip II and Mateo Vázquez de Leca: the Government of Spain (1572–1592)* (Geneva, 1977) not only increases our knowledge of the working of the bureaucracy, financial administration and the new juntas, but also shows the development of policy during the secretaryship of Mateo Vázquez. Spanish financial administration under Philip II is described in detail by Modesto Ulloa, *La Hacienda Real de Castilla en el reinado de Felipe II* (2nd ed., Madrid, 1977). Political and social ideas have a perceptive historian in José Antonio Maravall, *Estado moderno y mentalidad social (siglos XV a XVII)* (2 vols., Madrid, 1972).

Religion

The ecclesiastical history of Spain in the early modern period has not made fundamental advance in the last fifteen years, though particular aspects have been well studied. The religious policy of the Catholic Monarchs is a particular concern of Tarsicio de Azcona, *Isabel la Católica* (Madrid, 1964). Relations between church and state under Philip II have been described in more detail by J. I. Tellechea Idígoras, *El arzobispo Carranza y su tiempo* (Madrid, 1968) and José Luis Novalín, *El Inquisidor General Fernando de Valdés* (Oviedo, 1968). For a useful work of reference see *Diccionario de Historia Eclesiástica de España*, ed. Q. Aldea, T. Marín and J. Vives (4 vols., Madrid, 1972).

The study of the Spanish Inquisition has been transformed in recent years. The starting point is Henry Kamen, *The Spanish Inquisition* (London, 1965), which places the subject in a firmer structural and historical framework than hitherto. The two books of Ricardo García Cárcel, *Orígenes de la Inquisición española. El tribunal de Valencia, 1478–1530* (Barcelona, 1976) and *Herejía y sociedad en el siglo XVI. La Inquisición en Valencia 1530–1609* (Barcelona, 1980) are the fruit of basic new research into the religious, institutional, economic and social history of the Inquisition, and bring an element of measurement into the study of a particular tribunal. These are also the qualities, on a different scale, of the work of Bartolomé Bennassar, *L'Inquisition espagnole (xvᵉ–xixᵉ siècle)* (Paris, 1979).

Spanish America

Conquest and empire in the context of intellectual history is the subject of J. H. Elliott, *The Old World and the New 1492–1650* (Cambridge, 1970), which brings new understanding of the ideas involved in the European discovery of America and the American discovery of Europe. It is still difficult to measure precisely Spanish emigration to America in the early modern period, but the discussion of sources and methods is brought expertly up to date by Magnus Mörner, 'La emigración española al Nuevo Mundo antes de 1810. Un informe del estado de la investigación', *Anuario de Estudios Americanos*, 32 (1975), 43–131. The regional distribution of migration is established by Peter Boyd-Bowman, 'Patterns of Spanish Emigration to the Indies until 1600', *HAHR*, 56, 4 (1976), 580–604. Trade between Spain and America is known in great detail up to 1650, thanks to the work of Chaunu, and from 1717 (with a backward glance to 1680) in the more recent work of Antonio García-Baquero González, *Cádiz y el Atlántico (1717–1778)* (2 vols., Seville, 1976). The gap between these dates is now beginning to be filled, with positive results and suggestions even that collapse may have been followed by revival in the last decades of the seventeenth century. Firmer quantities were first suggested by Michel Morineau, 'D'Amsterdam à Séville: De quelle réalité l'histoire des prix est'elle le miroir?', *Annales*, 23, 1 (1968), 178–205, and 'Gazettes hollandaises et trésors americaines', *Anuario de Historia Económica y Social*, 2 (1969), 289–361, 3 (1970), 139–209. Further evidence was supplied by John Everaert, 'Le commerce colonial de la "Nation Flamande" à Cadix sous Charles II (Ca. 1670–1700)', *Anuario de Estudios Americanos*, 28 (1971), 139–51. These estimates are based mainly on foreign and non-official sources. Results from the Spanish sources for the period after 1650 are now available through the meticulous research of Lutgardo García

Fuentes, *El comercio español con América, 1650–1700* (Seville, 1980), a work which describes, measures and analyses the Indies trade, its shipping and tonnage, exports, imports and bullion returns. The author argues in favour of an upward turn from the 1670's, although the official sources and his own statistics appear to confirm the existence of a dominant downward trend throughout the period. For a further judgement see A. García-Baquero González, 'Andalucía y los problemas de la carrera de Indias en la crisis del siglo XVII', *Coloquio de Historia de Andalucía*, 1980.

Demographic history takes a major step forward in the work of Sherburne F. Cook and Woodrow Borah, *Essays in Population History* (3 vols., Berkeley and Los Angeles, 1974–79). The authors return to the problem of Indian population figures, on the basis of previous totals established for Central Mexico: 1518, 25·2 million; 1532, 16·8; 1568, 2·65; 1605, 1·075. They now take the discussion a stage further by considering various dates and estimates recently made by historians for the low point of Indian population in the seventeenth century, especially the date 1650 and the figure of under 1 million. From a revenue list of 1646 they compute a total of 702,929, and place the low point in 1620–25, when the Indian population of Central Mexico was approximately 3 per cent. of its size at the time the Europeans first landed. See *Essays*, iii, 1–102.

The colonial mining industry has emerged into the light of history in recent years. P. J. Bakewell, *Silver Mining and Society in Colonial Mexico: Zacatecas 1546–1700* (Cambridge, 1971) established new frontiers of knowledge and a new chronology of crisis in the seventeenth century. D. A. Brading and Harry E. Cross, 'Colonial Silver Mining: Mexico and Peru', *HAHR*, 52 4 (1972), 545–79, is an essay in comparative mining history and also suggests a new chronology of mining cycles. Knowledge of colonial Mexico has also been advanced by regional studies; see particularly William B. Taylor, *Landlord and Peasant in Colonial Oaxaca* (Stanford, 1972), and the same author's *Drinking, Homicide, and Rebellion in Colonial Mexican Villages* (Stanford, 1979). New research on the social structure of seventeenth-century Mexico and its significance for the imperial bureaucracy is contributed by J. I. Israel, *Race, Class and Politics in Colonial Mexico* (Oxford, 1975), and the same author participates in a more general debate with his 'Mexico and the General Crisis of the Seventeenth Century', *Past and Present*, 63 (1974), 33–57. He argues that there was a prolonged Mexican depression after 1620, in mining, inter-colonial trade, and industry, and that sustained tax returns were an index not of economic activity but of increased fiscal pressure from Spain, accompanied by a campaign against corruption; all this led to political conflict in seventeenth-century Mexico, and in particular to a rift between officials and colonists in 1620–64. Evidence for depression in another colony is provided by Murdo J. MacLeod, *Spanish Central America. A Socioeconomic History, 1520–1720* (Berkeley and Los Angeles, 1973), forgotten by Spain perhaps but, after this, not by historians.

Seventeenth-century Peru is also difficult to assess; there, as in Mexico, signs of promise and of prejudice existed side by side. The mining industry underwent slow rather than catastrophic recession. Peter J. Bakewell has again accomplished important work of measurement, 'Registered Silver Production in the Potosí District, 1550–1735', *Jahrbuch für Geschichte von Staat, Wirtschaft und Gesellschaft Lateinamerikas*, 12 (1975), 67–103; see also his *Antonio López de Quiroga (industrial minero del Potosí colonial)* (Potosí, 1973). The society of Upper Peru has been studied in a work of research and rare perception by Josep M. Barnadas, *Charcas. Orígenes históricos de una sociedad colonial* (La Paz, 1973). The agrarian history of colonial Peru is very much clarified by Robert G. Keith, *Conquest and Agrarian Change: the Emergence of the Hacienda System on the Peruvian Coast* (Cambridge, Mass., 1976). Peru, too, is part of the evidence for or against the existence of an absolute depression in Spanish America in the seventeenth century, and perhaps of a general crisis in the Hispanic world. Recent quantitative research appears to support the idea of change rather than depression, and to suggest a later date for this: John J. TePaske and Herbert S. Klein, 'The Seventeenth Century Depression in the Spanish Empire: Myth or Reality' (Paper presented to the American Historical Association, 1976). To cite only their evidence from Peru: total income recorded at the Lima treasury office, 1600–90, shows that income levels remained relatively stable until 1664, when serious recession began; annual revenues ranged between 2 and 4 million ducats, with cyclical fluctuations; from 1664 income began an uneven descent lasting into the eighteenth century. No doubt the discussion will continue. Meanwhile historians can now take account of yet another colony whose early modern history has been re-written from the archives: Germán Colmenares, *Historia económica y social de Colombia, 1537–1719* (2nd ed., Medellín, 1975).

BIBLIOGRAPHICAL INDEX

Guides to works used and to further reading are provided in the footnotes of each chapter, and in the Bibliography of Recent Works. The following index contains the names of authors. The number after a name refers to the page where, in a footnote, the author's work is first mentioned and given a full citation. Where the entry is followed by two or more numbers, these refer to other works by the same author. There are three indispensable bibliographies of Spanish history: B. Sánchez Alonso, *Fuentes de la historia española e hispano americana* (3rd edn., 3 vols., Madrid, 1952); *Indice histórico español*, Universidad de Barcelona, Centro de Estudios Históricos Internacionales (Barcelona, 1953–); and *Handbook of Latin American Studies* (Harvard University Press, 1936–50; University of Florida Press, 1951–).

GENERAL INDEX